Master Machine Learning

Master Scikit-learn algorithms and PyTorch deep learning architectures

Valencia Munoz Luis

www.bpbonline.com

First Edition 2026

ISBN: 978-93-78544-101

LIMITS OF LIABILITY AND DISCLAIMER OF WARRANTY

Distributors:

BPB PUBLICATIONS
20, Ansari Road, Darya Ganj
New Delhi-110002
Ph: 23254990/23254991

DECCAN AGENCIES
4-3-329, Bank Street,
Hyderabad-500195
Ph: 24756967/24756400

MICRO MEDIA
Shop No. 5, Mahendra Chambers,
150 DN Rd. Next to Capital Cinema,
V.T. (C.S.T.) Station, MUMBAI-400 001
Ph: 22078296/22078297

To View Complete
BPB Publications Catalogue
Scan the QR Code:

Published by Manish Jain for BPB Publications, 20 Ansari Road, Darya Ganj, New Delhi-110002 and Printed by him at Repro India Ltd., Rewari.

www.bpbonline.com

Dedicated to

My beloved wife, ***Margot Tudela***

and

My daughter, ***Victoria Charlotte***

About the Author

Valencia Munoz Luis is a senior AI/ML engineer and 10-time Microsoft **Most Valuable Professional (MVP)** in SharePoint and artificial intelligence, based in Brussels, Belgium. With a master's in computer science from University EAFIT and over 20 years of software architecture experience, including 5+ years of dedicated machine learning and deep learning engineering, he specializes in architecting scalable AI systems, multi-agent frameworks, and high-performance APIs.

Throughout his career, Luis has led AI engineering efforts at Element61 and PwC Belgium, where he has architected computer vision pipelines achieving 98.3% defect classification accuracy, built recommendation systems that improved user engagement by 22%, and established enterprise MLOps frameworks that cut deployment times by 40%. He has mentored over 100 professionals across AI bootcamp cohorts, achieving a 94% certification pass rate, and authored internal ML engineering playbooks.

Luis is an active author of technical articles on machine learning, deep learning, and cloud architecture. His decade-long recognition as a Microsoft MVP reflects his sustained commitment to technical excellence and community leadership. He is the founder of HarmoniqHub, where he builds native Apple applications for music organization and tagging using his expertise in AI.

About the Reviewers

- **Luiz Henrique** is a technology student with a strong interest in artificial intelligence, machine learning, and computer vision. His work focuses on developing intelligent systems and applying AI techniques to real-world problems, particularly in areas such as object tracking, healthcare applications, and data-driven solutions.

  He has experience working with computer vision systems, deep learning algorithms, and machine learning models for tasks such as object detection, tracking, and image analysis. Luiz has also worked with data processing and model development using tools and frameworks such as Python, XGBoost, and YOLO, exploring applications in video analysis and intelligent monitoring systems.

  His interests include developing efficient AI pipelines, experimenting with deep learning architectures, and applying machine learning techniques to analyze and interpret complex datasets. He is particularly motivated by projects that combine artificial intelligence with practical applications, especially those that can contribute to technological innovation and improvements in areas such as healthcare and intelligent systems.

- **Nseabasi Udondian** is a software engineer, AI researcher, and technical educator with a strong interest in intelligent systems, machine learning, and scalable software development. Her work spans full-stack engineering, cloud technologies, and applied artificial intelligence, with hands-on experience building generative AI applications, virtual assistants, and computer vision models. She has contributed to research in AI for agriculture, with conference presentations and published works. She is committed to using technology to create practical solutions that improve lives and expand access to innovation.

- **Ezekiel Diri** is a data scientist and analyst working across machine learning, data analytics, and security-focused data systems. He builds end-to-end solutions using Python, SQL, and Power BI, combining data quality, automation, and analytical insight to support business and operational decision-making. His experience includes designing reporting systems, developing validation frameworks, and creating data pipelines in environments where accuracy, governance, and reliability are essential.

  His work spans predictive modelling, fraud detection, and data-driven risk analysis, with a strong interest in the intersection of data science and cybersecurity. He focuses on developing practical solutions that translate complex ideas into tools that can be applied in real-world settings.

  Alongside his professional work, he has authored a beginner-friendly Python guide and contributed to academic research, with publications covering healthcare analytics, customer behaviour modelling, and applied machine learning. He is also engaged in technical writing and review, with a focus on making data science, programming, and security concepts clear, usable, and accessible to a wide audience.

Acknowledgement

I want to express my deepest gratitude to my family for their unwavering support and encouragement throughout the writing of this book. To my wife, Margot Tudela, who stood by me with patience and love during the countless hours of writing and revising, and to my daughter, Victoria Charlotte, who inspires me every day to build a better future, thank you for being my foundation.

I am deeply honored that Miguel González-Fierro, ex-principal data science manager at Microsoft and AI entrepreneur. His insights and perspective on machine learning have been invaluable, and his words capture the essence of what this book aspires to achieve.

I would also like to thank BPB Publications for their guidance, expertise, and patience in bringing this book to fruition. The collaboration with their editorial team, reviewers, and technical experts has been instrumental in shaping this book into its final form.

A special thank you goes to the Microsoft MVP community, whose passion for technology and knowledge sharing has inspired and motivated me for over a decade. Being recognized as a 10-time Microsoft MVP in SharePoint and artificial intelligence has been one of the most rewarding experiences of my career, and this community's spirit of collaboration is woven into every chapter of this book.

Finally, I want to thank every reader who picks up this book. Your curiosity and desire to learn are what make the effort worthwhile. I hope this book empowers you to build intelligent systems that make a real difference.

Preface

Machine learning is at the heart of a technological renaissance, transforming how we solve problems, from predicting climate patterns to crafting personalized experiences through generative AI.

Understanding the basics of AI is quickly becoming an essential skill for professionals in every field. The ability to engage with AI systems, ask the right questions, and critically evaluate their outputs will set you apart in nearly any industry or discipline. As a machine learning practitioner, gaining the confidence to navigate this new landscape with clarity and purpose is crucial.

Embracing this technology is one of the greatest challenges of our time. Rather than seeing AI as a replacement, it is better to view it as a powerful tool to enhance human cognitive and creative abilities in ways we are only beginning to explore. This book invites you to embrace that challenge: to learn, question, and actively shape a future where AI is developed responsibly for the benefit of all.

The book you have in your hands is a detailed hands-on guide to building smart systems with PyTorch and Scikit-learn, two powerful tools driving today's AI revolution. Whether you are new to machine learning or looking to sharpen your skills, this book will empower you to turn data into solutions that solve real-world problems, from automating tasks to generating creative content like art and text.

This book is for Python developers, data scientists, and machine learning engineers eager to master machine learning. You will begin with Python basics, using NumPy, Pandas, and Matplotlib, then set up a machine learning environment with Jupyter Notebook and Azure. With Scikit-learn, you will learn algorithms like linear regression and clustering. Using PyTorch, you will build neural networks for image classification, NLP, and generative AI, mastering tools like PyTorch Lightning, TorchRec, and Hugging Face Transformers through 50+ exercises and projects. You will also explore CNNs, GANs, reinforcement learning, and model deployment with TorchServe.

By the end of this journey, you will not only understand machine learning's core principles but also have the hands-on expertise to build and deploy advanced AI systems. You will be ready to tackle complex challenges, contribute to the fast-evolving field of artificial intelligence, and shape a future where technology amplifies human potential. This book is your roadmap to becoming a confident, creative, and responsible machine learning practitioner.

Chapter 1: Introduction to the Machine Learning World — This chapter defines machine learning and deep learning, distinguishing them from AI as a whole. It covers the three main categories (supervised, unsupervised, reinforcement learning), the ML project lifecycle, historical milestones, and real-world applications in healthcare, finance, retail, and transportation. It introduces Scikit-learn and PyTorch as the book's primary frameworks.

Chapter 2: Setting up Your Machine Learning Environment — This chapter walks through setting up a local and cloud-based ML development environment. It covers installing Python, choosing VS Code as a code editor, package management with pip and Anaconda, virtual environments, Jupyter Notebooks, cloud platforms (Google Colab, Azure ML Studio), and dependency management with Poetry.

Chapter 3: Python Fundamentals for Machine Learning — This chapter provides a comprehensive Python refresher covering data types, variables, control flow, functions, collections, error handling, code organization, and object-oriented programming. It concludes with a practical student gradebook project to apply the concepts.

Chapter 4: Essential Machine Learning Libraries in Python — This chapter introduces the three foundational Python libraries, such as NumPy for numerical computations, Pandas for data manipulation and analysis, and Matplotlib for data visualization. It demonstrates how these libraries integrate with ML workflows.

Chapter 5: Introduction to Machine Learning with Scikit-learn — This chapter covers Scikit-learn's core capabilities, including finding and using datasets, data preparation and preprocessing, evaluation metrics, and supervised learning algorithms such as linear regression, logistic regression, and SVM.

Chapter 6: Machine Learning with Scikit-learn Advanced Topics — This chapter explores advanced Scikit-learn techniques, such as unsupervised learning (K-means clustering, PCA), ensemble learning, gradient boosting machines, cross-validation, and hyperparameter tuning with practical examples like customer segmentation.

Chapter 7: Introduction to Deep Learning— This chapter introduces deep learning fundamentals, such as neural network architecture, activation functions, loss functions, optimization techniques, the training process, overfitting and underfitting, dropout, and transfer learning across computer vision, NLP, and healthcare applications.

Chapter 8: Introduction to PyTorch — This chapter covers PyTorch fundamentals, such as tensors, GPU acceleration with CUDA, automatic differentiation (Autograd), building neural networks, and performance benchmarks comparing CPU and GPU computation.

Chapter 9: Building Blocks of Neural Networks in PyTorch — This chapter focuses on PyTorch's nn.Module class for defining networks, covering linear, convolutional, pooling, and recurrent layers (RNN, LSTM, GRU), activation functions, loss functions, and optimizers with detailed code breakdowns.

Chapter 10: Training Neural Networks with PyTorch — This chapter covers the complete training pipeline, such as data loading, preprocessing and augmentation, training loops, validation monitoring, regularization techniques (dropout, batch normalization), and saving and loading models using the CIFAR-10 dataset.

Chapter 11: Convolutional Neural Networks with PyTorch — This chapter explores CNN architecture in depth, covering convolutional layers, pooling layers, the vanishing gradient problem, and architectural innovations including LeNet, VGGNet, Inception, and ResNet with practical implementation on CIFAR-10.

Chapter 12: Recurrent Neural Networks with PyTorch — This chapter covers sequential data processing with RNNs, LSTM networks, GRUs, and attention mechanisms. It uses sentiment analysis on the IMDB movie reviews dataset as a practical example with complete data pipelines.

Chapter 13: Generative Adversarial Networks with PyTorch — This chapter introduces GANs through the generator-discriminator adversarial framework, covering training dynamics, mode collapse, DCGANs, and practical applications in image synthesis, data augmentation, and style transfer.

Chapter 14: Reinforcement Learning with PyTorch — This chapter introduces RL fundamentals, such as agent-environment interactions, Q-learning, Deep Q-Networks, and policy gradient methods with a practical TreasureHunt grid-world example and applications in games, robotics, and autonomous vehicles.

Chapter 15: Advanced Deep Learning Topics — This chapter covers cutting-edge architectures, such as transformers and attention mechanisms, **graph neural networks** (**GNNs**), Bayesian neural networks, **neural architecture search** (**NAS**), self-supervised learning, and advanced optimization techniques.

Chapter 16: Building a Recommendation System — This chapter covers recommendation system fundamentals, such as collaborative filtering, content-based filtering, hybrid approaches, matrix factorization, and neural network-based recommenders in PyTorch with evaluation metrics.

Chapter 17: Natural Language Processing with PyTorch — This chapter walks you through the complete NLP pipeline: text preprocessing, tokenization, word embeddings (Word2Vec, GloVe), neural models from RNNs to Transformers, and practical projects using Hugging Face for sentiment analysis and text classification.

Chapter 18: Computer Vision with PyTorch — This chapter covers practical computer vision, such as image data handling, data augmentation, transfer learning with pre-trained models, object detection, image segmentation, and working with custom datasets using CIFAR-10 and ImageNet-pretrained architectures.

Chapter 19: Time Series Analysis with PyTorch — This chapter explores time series fundamentals, such as trends, seasonality, data preprocessing, building LSTM and GRU with attention models, multi-step forecasting, and anomaly detection across finance, healthcare, manufacturing, and energy domains.

Chapter 20: Deploying Machine Learning Models — This chapter brings the book full circle by deploying a trained PyTorch model to Azure Machine Learning as a real-time REST API endpoint. It covers model preparation, quantization, TorchScript and ONNX export, Docker environments, scoring scripts, and model versioning.

Code Bundle and Coloured Images

Please follow the link to download the
Code Bundle and the *Coloured Images* of the book:

https://rebrand.ly/f48e83

The code bundle for the book is also hosted on GitHub at
https://github.com/bpbpublications/Master-Machine-Learning.
In case there's an update to the code, it will be updated on the existing GitHub repository.

We have code bundles from our rich catalogue of books and videos available at **https://github.com/bpbpublications**. Check them out!

Errata

We take immense pride in our work at BPB Publications and follow best practices to ensure the accuracy of our content to provide an indulging reading experience to our subscribers. Our readers are our mirrors, and we use their inputs to reflect and improve upon human errors, if any, that may have occurred during the publishing processes involved. To let us maintain the quality and help us reach out to any readers who might be having difficulties due to any unforeseen errors, please write to us at: **errata@bpbonline.com**

Your support, suggestions and feedback are highly appreciated by the BPB Publications' Family.

Piracy

If you come across any illegal copies of our works in any form on the internet, we would be grateful if you would provide us with the location address or website name. Please contact us at **business@bpbonline.com** with a link to the material.

If you are interested in becoming an author

If there is a topic that you have expertise in, and you are interested in either writing or contributing to a book, please visit **www.bpbonline.com**. We have worked with thousands of developers and tech professionals, just like you, to help them share their insights with the global tech community. You can make a general application, apply for a specific hot topic that we are recruiting an author for, or submit your own idea.

Reviews

Please leave a review. Once you have read and used this book, why not leave a review on the site that you purchased it from? Potential readers can then see and use your unbiased opinion to make purchase decisions. We at BPB can understand what you think about our products, and our authors can see your feedback on their book. Thank you!

For more information about BPB, please visit **www.bpbonline.com**.

Join our Discord space

Join our Discord workspace for latest updates, offers, tech happenings around the world, new releases, and sessions with the authors:

https://discord.bpbonline.com

Table of Contents

CHAPTER 1
Introduction to the Machine Learning World

Introduction

Machine learning and deep learning are revolutionizing how we interact with technology and shaping our everyday lives. These technologies are not just powerful tools but sources of inspiration, enabling us to achieve what was once impossible and streamline daily tasks. This chapter serves as a comprehensive introduction to the world of machine learning and deep learning, providing a foundation for understanding their potential and how they work.

Structure

This chapter covers the following topics:

- Overview of machine learning and deep learning
- Understanding machine learning
- Historical context and evolution

Objectives

The objectives of this chapter are to provide a clear understanding of machine learning and deep learning. First, it will define machine learning and deep learning in simple terms and explain how they are different from **artificial intelligence** (**AI**) as a whole. The chapter will also describe how machine learning algorithms learn from data to make predictions or decisions. It will cover the three main categories of machine learning, which include supervised, unsupervised, and reinforcement learning, and give examples of how each is used. A historical overview will be included to show the key milestones and advancements in machine learning and deep learning. Finally, the chapter will show the importance of machine learning with practical examples of its use in healthcare, finance, retail, and other fields.

Overview of machine learning and deep learning

Nowadays, technology is used in almost every aspect of our lives, making interactions more and more common. Machine learning and deep learning have revolutionized the way we exchange and use technology, sparking a profound transformation in many aspects of our daily lives. From the personalized recommendations that we receive on websites, the help to manage an agenda, or the assistance to doctors in the surgeries or making diagnoses, these technologies are not just important but inspiring because they allow us to make things that were impossible before and reduce time in our daily tasks, either at work or at home.

Machine learning and deep learning are both behind AI, and together, they are building incredible advancements in multiple areas, industries, and aspects of life as we are witnessing, having the feeling of wanting to delve into their workings and capabilities to improve their skills more and more. Therefore, there is a desire and need to create this book to enlarge information that serves not only data scientists but everyone who wants to learn about it.

This comprehensive guide is meticulously structured to provide a solid foundation in machine learning and deep learning, covering everything from the basics to advanced topics. It is designed to equip you with the knowledge and skills to confidently apply these concepts in real-world scenarios, leaving no stone unturned in your learning journey.

Understanding machine learning

To get started in this AI world, it is fundamental to understand what machine learning is and how it works. There are several definitions of machine learning; in this book, we take a reference from the pioneer of AI, *Arthur Samuel, the field of study that gives computers the ability to learn without explicitly being programmed*[1]. In other words, machine learning is a subset of AI that focuses on developing systems capable of learning from data, finding patterns, and making decisions with minimal human intervention. Data is at the heart of this process, which involves the use of algorithms to parse data, learn from it, and then apply their knowledge to make informed decisions.

For example, if we consider teaching a child to recognize apples and oranges, a start could be showing the child many pictures of these fruits, and the child would learn to name them correctly over time. This is a similar process to how machine learning works; we use training algorithms and data to make correct predictions or decisions without being explicitly programmed for each task.

According to *Brown*, this process is not as easy for the machine as it is for humans due to its time-consuming nature. However, machine learning can help computers learn by analyzing data (such as photos, numbers, text, etc. and by gaining the experience to perform tasks through the development and refinement of algorithms.

Machine learning refers to a process that starts with a body of data and then tries to derive rules or procedures to explain the data or predict future data. The function of a machine learning system can be *descriptive*, meaning that the system uses the data to explain what happened; *predictive*, meaning the system uses the data to predict what will happen; or *prescriptive*, meaning the system will use the data to make suggestions about what action to take[2].

In other words, ML systems can have multiple purposes, but also need data in several spheres. More data in the system means a better model and more refined actions; in this sense, the quality of the output depends on the data. Also, it is essential to mention that the model is trained on historical data, and in that way, this can be used to make predictions on new data; ML finds patterns and insights in the datasets, also in vast quantities.

The following figure illustrates the lifecycle of a machine learning project, outlining the crucial stages from understanding the problem to monitoring and maintaining the deployed model. Each phase, depicted by a different arrow, emphasizes key activities like data collection, feature engineering, and hyperparameter tuning.

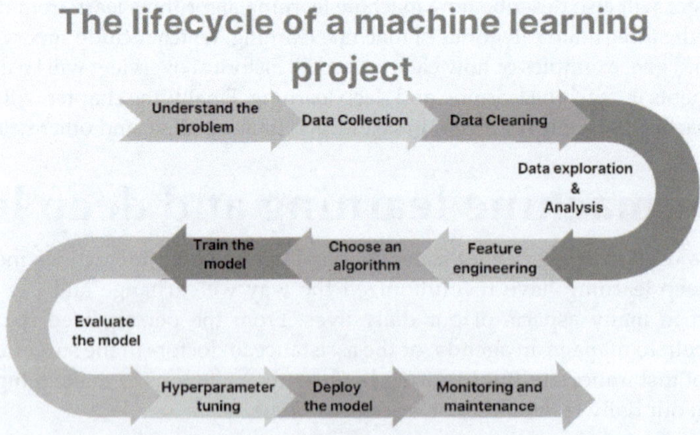

Figure 1.1: Lifecycle of a machine learning project

1(Brown, 2021)
2 (Malone et al., 2020)

In this book, we will study some of the phases in detail and briefly mention others. In this sense, the chapter briefly explain the process: Understand the problem; this part involves figuring out what you need the computer to learn to do, in other words, your objective, like recognizing pictures or predicting prices.

Then, you collect data. You gather data by collecting examples that the computer can learn from. Once you have your data, you clean it up. This means fixing any mistakes and filling in any missing information to make sure the computer learns the right things.

After cleaning the data, you explore and analyze it to see what patterns you can find. This helps you understand how different parts of the data relate to each other and to the problem you are solving.

Then comes **feature engineering**, which is where you decide which pieces of information from the data will be most helpful for the computer to learn from. You might create new features or adjust existing ones to make the computer's job easier. Once your data is ready, you choose a method (or algorithm) for the computer to learn from it. You teach the computer by showing it examples and helping it make predictions or decisions.

After teaching the computer, you check how well it learns by testing it with new examples. This is called evaluating the model. If it does not work well, you might make changes to how it learns to improve it. This is called **hyperparameter tuning**.

Finally, when your model works well, you deploy it. This means putting it to work in real-life situations where it can help make predictions or decisions automatically. You also monitor it to ensure it continues to work well over time.

Lastly, your model can learn from new data after the first training loop; you can retrain and get a new model version (v2). Model version is briefly explained in *Chapter 20, Deploying Machine Learning Models.*

Types of machine learning

Understanding the fundamental concepts in machine learning is crucial because they form the foundation of how intelligent systems are built, trained, and deployed. Machine learning systems can perform a variety of tasks, such as describing patterns, making predictions, and prescribing actions. By categorizing these tasks into supervised learning, unsupervised learning, and reinforcement learning, we can better understand their different mechanisms and applications. This foundational knowledge is essential for anyone looking to develop or utilize machine learning technologies effectively.

In **supervised learning**, algorithms are trained using labeled datasets, where each example pairs input data with corresponding output labels. This allows the algorithm to learn the relationship between inputs and outputs, enabling predictions or classifications on new, unseen data. Common algorithms in supervised learning include linear regression, logistic regression, and **support vector machines** (**SVM**). Linear regression models the relationship between variables by fitting a linear equation to observed data, which is helpful for tasks like predicting house prices based on features such as location and size. Logistic regression predicts binary outcomes, such as whether a customer will churn, based on behavior and demographics. SVMs excel in finding hyperplanes that best separate data points in high-dimensional spaces, which are used in applications like text categorization and image classification.

These concepts and algorithms will be explained in more detail in the later chapters to ensure understanding for readers who may find these terms unfamiliar at this point in the book. An example of supervised learning is a spam filter, which is trained on emails labeled as *spam* or *not spam* to predict the category of new emails. Another example would be the pictures labeled with an apple or an orange, and then once trained, the algorithm can predict if a picture is either an apple or an orange.

Unsupervised learning deals with unlabeled data; the algorithm tries to learn the underlying structure of the data without explicit instructions on what to predict. Clustering algorithms like k-means and hierarchical clustering are typical examples. An example is customer segmentation, where the goal is to group customers with similar behavior without pre-labeled categories.

Then, reinforcement learning involves an agent that interacts with an environment to achieve a goal. The agent receives rewards or penalties based on its actions and learns to maximize the cumulative reward. Examples include training a robot to navigate a maze or teaching an AI to play a game like chess.

Additional types of machine learning

While supervised, unsupervised, and reinforcement learning are the three main categories, the following list provides several other essential types of machine learning, which are worth mentioning:

- **Semi-supervised learning**: Combines labeled and unlabeled data, useful when labeling data is expensive (for example, medical image analysis with limited expert annotations).
- **Self-supervised learning**: The system creates its labels from the input data structure (for example, predicting the next word in a sentence).
- **Federated learning**: Training models across decentralized data sources without sharing raw data (for example, smartphone keyboard learning from user typing without sending personal data to servers).
- **Meta-learning**: Learning to learn is an algorithm that can quickly adapt to new tasks with minimal training data.
- **Active learning**: The algorithm selects which data points to learn from next, focusing on the most informative examples.

These specialized approaches address specific challenges in machine learning and are increasingly important in modern AI applications.

Historical context and evolution

AI, as we know it nowadays, has evolved through time, from the dreams we had in science fiction books to today's applications in real life; these changes have to do with how data is collected and classified, or how we understand the machine learning processes.

The journey of machine learning and deep learning started several decades ago, starting with *Alan Turing*, and the first object that could obtain and analyze data emerged in 1955; for the first time, the term artificial intelligence was introduced.[3] at MIT with an objective to find a way for machines to use languages or solve problems as humans do. At that time, the concept of neural networks was also introduced, and with that, the technological world was disrupted, but progress was slow due to limited computational resources and data.

The field saw a resurgence in the 1980s and 1990s with the development of more sophisticated algorithms and increased computing power. During this period, researchers and scientists made significant strides in understanding how computers could learn from data more effectively. This era marked a pivotal time when new algorithms were devised, allowing machines to process and interpret information with greater complexity than ever before. Additionally, advancements in computing power enabled these algorithms to be applied to more extensive and more diverse datasets, laying the groundwork for future breakthroughs in artificial intelligence.

The real breakthrough came in the 2010s with the advent of deep learning. Deep learning represents a significant advancement in AI. Researchers found that deep neural networks, which are models inspired by the human brain's structure, could be trained to learn directly from raw data such as images, text, and sound. Unlike earlier approaches, deep learning models became capable of automatically discovering intricate patterns and features in the data, leading to unprecedented levels of accuracy in tasks like image recognition, natural language processing, and autonomous driving.

Researchers discovered that deep neural networks could achieve remarkable results by leveraging large datasets and harnessing the computational power of powerful **graphics processing units (GPUs)**. GPUs, initially designed for rendering graphics in video games, were repurposed because they could perform numerous calculations simultaneously, making them ideal for training complex neural networks efficiently.

3 (Malone et al., 2020, p.6)

Importance of machine learning in modern applications

Machine learning is a transformative force that permeates nearly every industry and aspect of our lives, inspiring new possibilities and driving innovation. Here are a few examples of its real-world applications:

- **Healthcare**: Machine learning algorithms can analyze medical images, predict disease outbreaks, and help in diagnosing conditions, leading to better patient outcomes.
- **Finance**: Machine learning models detect fraudulent transactions, assess credit risk, and make investment predictions.
- **Retail**: Personalized recommendations, dynamic pricing, and inventory management are driven by machine learning.
- **Transportation**: Self-driving cars, route optimization, and predictive maintenance are all powered by machine learning.
- **Entertainment**: Streaming services use machine learning to suggest movies and shows tailored to your preferences.

By automating tasks and providing insights from data, machine learning helps improve efficiency, accuracy, and productivity across various sectors.

Scikit-learn and PyTorch

The two prominent frameworks in the realm of machine learning libraries are Scikit-learn and PyTorch. These libraries are included in this book due to their widespread popularity and powerful capabilities.

Scikit-learn is a versatile and user-friendly library that offers a wide array of tools for tasks like classification, regression, clustering, and dimensionality reduction. Its intuitive interface and comprehensive documentation make it an excellent choice for beginners and those seeking quick, reliable solutions for traditional machine learning problems. If some of these concepts seem complex, do not worry; they will be explained in detail in *Chapter 5, Introduction to Machine Learning with Scikit-learn*.

On the other hand, PyTorch, a dynamic and flexible deep learning framework, empowers researchers and practitioners to build and train complex neural networks with ease. Its dynamic computation graph and GPU acceleration capabilities make it ideal for cutting-edge research and large-scale deployments. While PyTorch might have a steeper learning curve for newcomers, its versatility and performance benefits make it a favorite among deep learning enthusiasts. In the upcoming chapters, we will understand Scikit-learn and PyTorch in great detail, exploring their features, functionalities, and real-world applications in detail. PyTorch will be explained in detail in *Chapter 8, Introduction to PyTorch*.

Conclusion

This chapter has laid the groundwork for understanding machine learning and deep learning, their types, historical development, and the profound impact they have on modern applications. In the following chapters, we will build a thorough understanding of the technical aspects of machine learning and deep learning, exploring algorithms, frameworks like Scikit-learn and PyTorch, and practical implementation strategies.

In the next chapter, you will learn how to set up your machine learning environment locally and in the cloud with providers like Google and Microsoft Azure. It will be exciting as you execute your first line of Python code and gain exponential knowledge to become the next master of machine learning and deep learning.

Exercises

Conceptual lifecycle design: To solidify your understanding of the machine learning lifecycle, as illustrated in *Figure 1.1*, select a real-world problem from the following list and map it to the stages of the machine learning lifecycle.

Scenarios:

- Predicting house prices in a specific city.
- Grouping customers of a supermarket based on purchasing habits.
- A chess-playing computer program.

Task: For your chosen scenario, write a short paragraph for each of the following stages describing what would happen:

1. **Understand the problem**: Is it supervised, unsupervised, or reinforcement learning? Is it predictive, descriptive, or prescriptive?
2. **Data collection**: What kind of data would you need? (for example, images, historical sales records, game logs).
3. **Feature engineering**: What specific features might be important? (e.g., square footage, time of day, winning moves).
4. **Evaluate the model**: How would you know if it is working?

Multiple choice questions

1. **Which of the following best describes machine learning?**
   a. A field distinct from AI
   b. A subset of AI that focuses on systems learning from data without explicit programming
   c. A system that only uses if-then rules created by humans
   d. The study of hardware for robots
2. **In the context of the machine learning lifecycle, what is the purpose of feature engineering?**
   a. To clean the data by removing mistakes
   b. To deploy the model to a server
   c. To decide which pieces of information from the data will be most helpful for the computer to learn
   d. To monitor the model after deployment
3. **Which type of machine learning is used when the data is labeled (e.g., input images paired with the correct fruit name)?**
   a. Unsupervised learning
   b. Reinforcement learning
   c. Supervised learning
   d. Clustering
4. **What is the primary goal of unsupervised learning?**
   a. To maximize a cumulative reward
   b. To predict a specific target label provided in the training data
   c. To find underlying structures or patterns in unlabeled data
   d. To play games like Chess or Go

5. **Which type of analysis is prescriptive?**
   a. Explaining what happened in the past
   b. Predicting what will happen in the future
   c. Suggesting what action to take based on data
   d. Visualizing raw data
6. **What triggered the real breakthrough in AI during the 2010s?**
   a. The invention of the first computer
   b. The advent of deep learning and the use of GPUs
   c. The creation of linear regression
   d. The decline of neural networks
7. **Which Python library is recommended in this book for traditional machine learning tasks like regression and clustering?**
   a. PyTorch
   b. Scikit-learn
   c. OpenGL
   d. React
8. **Reinforcement learning involves an agent that learns by:**
   a. Analyzing static historical records
   b. Interacting with an environment and receiving rewards or penalties
   c. Being explicitly programmed with all possible moves
   d. Grouping similar data points together
9. **According to the historical context, what role do GPUs play in modern deep learning?**
   a. They are used solely for video game graphics
   b. They perform numerous calculations simultaneously, speeding up the training of neural networks
   c. They replace the CPU entirely for all computer tasks
   d. They are used to store large databases
10. **What is federated learning?**
    a. Learning to learn from minimal data
    b. The system creates its own labels
    c. Training models across decentralized data sources without sharing raw data
    d. Selecting which data points to learn from next

Answers

1.	b.
2.	c.
3.	c.
4.	c.
5.	c.
6.	b.

7.	b.
8.	b.
9.	b.
10.	c.

Key terms

- **Machine learning**: A subset of AI that focuses on algorithms that learn from data.
- **Deep learning**: A subfield of ML that uses deep neural networks to learn from data.
- **Artificial intelligence**: The broader field of creating intelligent agents that can reason and act.
- **Supervised learning**: Learning from labeled data.
- **Unsupervised learning**: Learning from unlabeled data.
- **Reinforcement learning**: Learning through interaction with an environment.
- **Feature engineering**: The process of selecting and transforming raw data into features that better represent the underlying problem for the predictive models.
- **GPU**: Electronic circuits designed to manipulate memory to accelerate the creation of images, now heavily used to accelerate deep learning calculations.

References

1. *Brown, S. (2021, Avril 12). Machine learning explained | MIT Sloan.* **https://mitsloan.mit.edu/ideas-made-to-matter/machine-learning-explained**
2. *Malone, T. W., Rus, D., & Laubacher, R. (2020). Artificial intelligence and the future of work. A report prepared by the MIT Task Force on the work of the future, Research Brief, 17, 1-39.*

Join our Discord space

Join our Discord workspace for latest updates, offers, tech happenings around the world, new releases, and sessions with the authors:

https://discord.bpbonline.com

CHAPTER 2
Setting up Your Machine Learning Environment

Introduction

In the preceding chapter, you got to know a little about machine learning. However, let us be honest; the theory is great, but building stuff is where the real fun begins.

To get started, you need to set up your very own machine learning lab. Think of it like a workshop where you will build incredible **artificial intelligence** (**AI**) projects. Sometimes, your computer will be enough for your experiments, but for more significant projects or when you need a supercomputer's power, you will head to the cloud.

However, *what is the cloud?* Imagine the cloud as a giant network of super-powerful computers. You can access these computers over the internet to run your machine learning models, even if they need a ton of processing power. This is especially important for tasks like training large models or dealing with massive datasets. It is like having a superhero computer at your fingertips.

You have probably heard of **graphics processing units** (**GPUs**). They are chips initially designed for graphics in video games. They are also excellent at speeding up machine learning calculations. It is like having a team of math geniuses working together to solve problems lightning fast.

In this chapter, you will learn how to set up everything you need, both on your computer and in the cloud. You will even run your first line of Python code. No prior experience is needed; we will walk through it all step by step. Get ready to transform your computer into a machine learning powerhouse. All the book exercises and code are hosted in the GitHub repository of this book.

Structure

This chapter covers the following topics:

- Quick start, minimal setup
- Installing Python
- Choosing your code editor
- Package management Anaconda and Miniconda
- Creating isolated workspaces with conda and venv environments
- Jupyter Notebooks, your interactive coding playground
- Machine learning in cloud with Google Colab
- Managing project dependencies with pip and requirements.txt
- Introduction to Poetry
- Introduction to UV

Objectives

The aim of this chapter is to ensure you have a working Python installation on your computer and are familiar with **Visual Studio Code** (**VS Code**), along with the essential extensions for machine learning. You will gain an understanding of how to manage packages and environments using tools like *Anaconda* or *Miniconda*. Additionally, you will learn how to create and use *Jupyter Notebooks* for interactive coding and documentation. The chapter will also show you how to get access to free cloud resources such as *Google Colab* and *Azure Machine Learning Studio* for running machine learning models. You will develop the ability to manage project dependencies using pip and requirements.txt and acquire a basic understanding of Poetry as an alternative dependency manager.

Quick start, minimal setup

If you want to get started right away, follow these steps:

1. Download and install Python from python.org.
2. Open your terminal (Command Prompt or Terminal app).
3. Create a new folder for your projects.
4. Run `python -m venv venv to` create a virtual environment.
5. Activate the environment:
   - **On Windows**: `venv\Scripts\activate`
   - **On macOS/Linux**: `source venv/bin/activate`
6. **Install Jupyter Notebook**: `pip install notebook`
7. **Launch Jupyter**: `jupyter notebook`

For more details and advanced options, continue reading the following sections.

Installing Python

Before getting into machine learning, it is crucial to have Python installed on your computer. Python is the programming language of choice for most machine learning frameworks and libraries, and having it properly set up ensures that you can follow along with tutorials and implement machine learning algorithms efficiently.

Python as the primary language for machine learning

Imagine you want to build a robot, but you would not start by inventing a new language to communicate with it. You would probably use a language everyone understands, like English. In the world of machine learning, Python is the universal language.

The following are some reasons why Python is so popular for building AI:

- **Easy to read and learn**: Python's syntax (the way you write code) is super clear and straightforward, almost like reading everyday English. This makes it easier for you to understand what is happening in your code and even easier to get started.
- **Tons of tools for the job**: Imagine trying to build a house with just a hammer. That would not be very efficient. Similarly, Python has a whole toolbox of libraries specifically designed for machine learning. These libraries are like pre-made building blocks that help you create your AI projects faster and easier.
- **Everyone is using it**: Since it is so popular, there is a massive community of Python users. This means you can easily find help online, get inspired by other people's projects, and even collaborate with others to build amazing things.

So, think of Python as your trusty sidekick on your machine learning journey. It is the perfect language to help you bring your artificial intelligence ideas to life.

Downloading and installing Python

Refer to the following steps to install Python on your system:

1. **Go to the source**: Head over to the official Python website (**https://www.python.org/downloads/**) and download the latest version for your operating system (Windows, macOS, or Linux), as illustrated in the following figure:

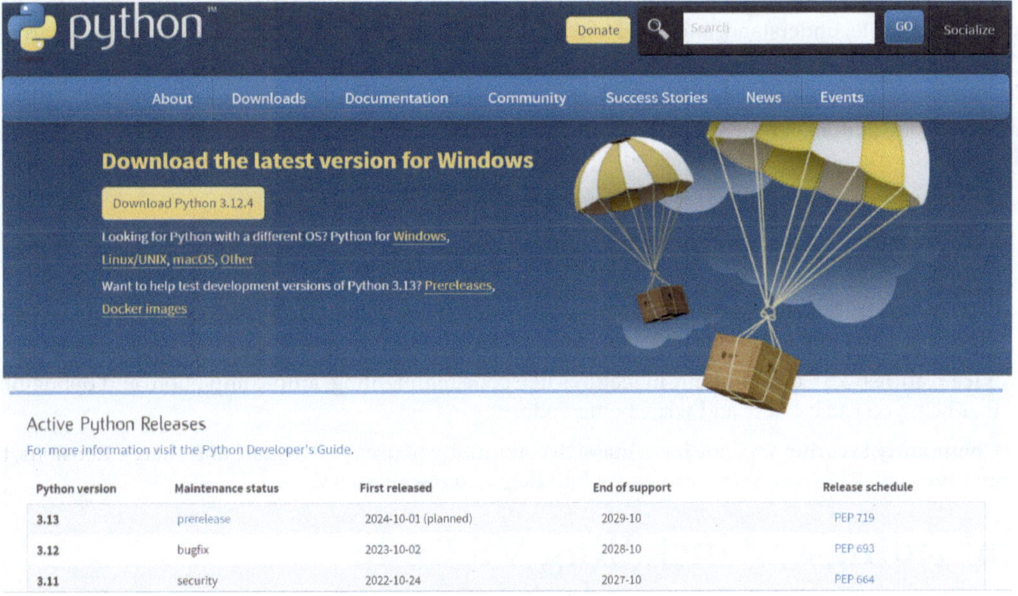

***Figure 2.1**: Python downloads page*

2. **Run the installer**: Double-click the downloaded file and follow the instructions. Make sure to check the box that says *Add Python to PATH* during the installation. This will make it easier for you to use Python from your command line.

You are done. Python is now installed on your computer.

Verifying the installation

Let us make sure Python is working correctly by running a simple script:

1. **Open your favorite text editor**: This could be Notepad on Windows, TextEdit on macOS, or something more advanced like VS Code.
2. **Type the following command**: `print("Hello, I am learning Python!")`
3. **Save the file**: Save it as `hello.py` (make sure it has the `.py` extension, which tells your computer it is a Python file).
4. **Run the script**: Open your command line (Terminal on macOS or Linux, Command Prompt on Windows) and navigate to the folder where you saved the file. Then, type `python hello.py` and press *Enter*.
5. **Check the output**: If you see `"Hello, I am learning Python!"` printed in your command line, congratulations. Python is up and running, and you are ready to start your machine learning adventure.

Choosing your code editor

When starting out with machine learning, selecting the right code editor is a key decision. A good code editor enhances your productivity by providing an environment that simplifies coding tasks, making it easier to write, test, and debug your machine learning models. The right editor should help you streamline your workflow, support your learning process, and integrate well with the tools and libraries you will be using.

Importance of a good code editor

Think of a code editor as your trusty friend in the coding world. It is not just a place to type code; it is a powerful tool that helps you write, understand, and debug your code more efficiently. It is like having a super-smart assistant who can autocomplete your sentences, check your grammar, and even give you suggestions on how to improve your writing.

There are many code editors out there, but VS Code is a popular choice for beginners and pros alike. It is free, easy to use, and packed with features that make coding a breeze.

VS Code is a great choice for machine learning due to the following reasons:

- **User-friendly**: VS Code has a clean and intuitive interface that is easy to navigate, even for newcomers to coding.
- **Customizable**: You can personalize VS Code to fit your preferences, from choosing your favorite color scheme to installing extensions that add new features.
- **Nice features**: VS Code has built-in features like code highlighting, auto-completion, and debugging tools that help you catch errors and write better code.
- **Community favorite**: VS Code has a massive community of users who create and share extensions, themes, and tutorials. This means you can easily find help and resources online.

Downloading and installing VS Code

The following are the steps to download and install VS Code:

1. **Visit the VS Code website**: Head over to the official VS Code website: **https://code.visualstudio.com/**.
2. **Download the installer**: Click the big blue download button and choose the version that matches your operating system (Windows, macOS, or Linux), as shown in the following figure:

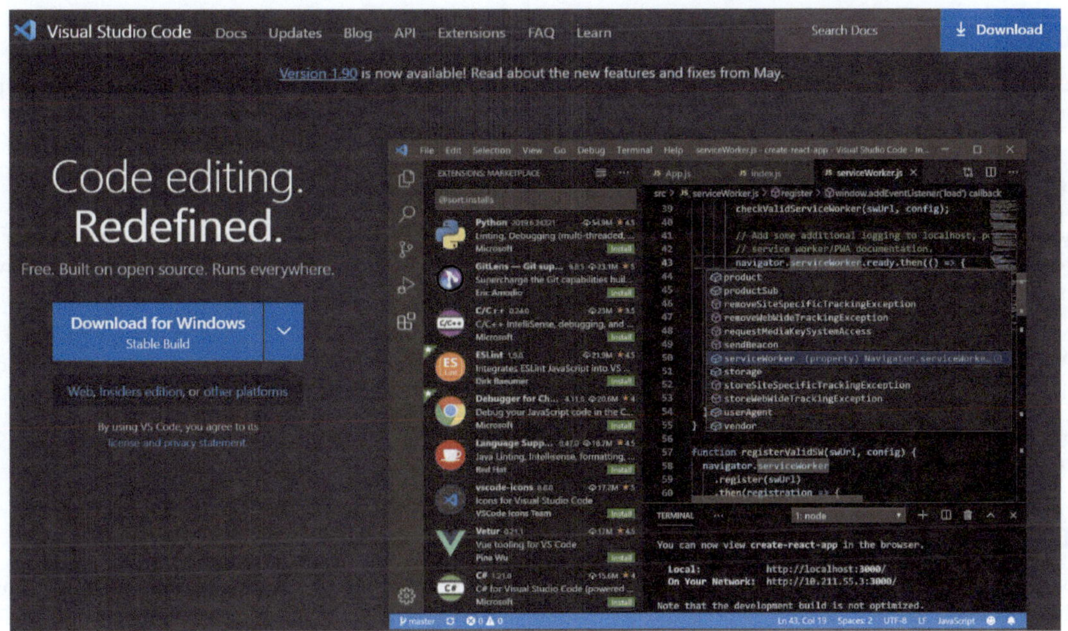

Figure 2.2: *VS Code download page*

3. **Run the installer**: Double-click the downloaded file and follow the on-screen instructions. It is straightforward, just like installing any other application.

Essential VS Code extensions

Once you have VS Code installed, it is time to supercharge it with some extensions. Here are a few must-haves for your machine learning journey:

- **Python**: This extension is a no-brainer. It provides everything you need for Python development, including code completion, linting (which helps you catch errors), debugging, and more.
- **Jupyter**: If you plan on working with Jupyter Notebooks (and you should), this extension is essential. It lets you create, edit, and run notebooks directly within VS Code.
- **Pylance**: This extension is like a super-smart language server for Python. It provides even more advanced code completion, type checking, and other features that will make your coding experience smoother.
- **Ruff**: This extension is a Python linter that helps you catch errors and enforce code style. It is like having a helpful friend who points out your mistakes before they become a problem.
- **Azure Machine Learning**: If you plan to use Azure Machine Learning, this extension will make your life easier. It provides tools for managing your Azure resources, deploying models, and more.

To install these extensions:

1. **Open the extensions' view**: Click the square icon on the left sidebar of VS Code or press *Ctrl+Shift+X* (or *Cmd+Shift+X* on macOS).
2. **Search for the extension**: Type the name of the extension (e.g., *Python*) in the search bar.
3. **Install the extension**: Click the *Install* button next to the extension you want to install.

Package management Anaconda or Miniconda

Imagine you are building a LEGO set. You would not want to create every single brick from scratch; that would take forever. Instead, you use pre-made bricks that come in different shapes and sizes. In the Python world.

Understanding Python packages and their importance

Packages are bundles of code that other people have already written and shared. They contain functions, classes, and other tools that you can use in your projects. This saves you a ton of time and effort because you do not have to reinvent the wheel every time you want to do something.

For example, instead of writing your code to calculate complex mathematical equations, you can use a package like NumPy, which is designed explicitly for numerical operations. Alternatively, if you want to create beautiful data visualizations, you can use a package like *Matplotlib* or *Seaborn*.

Packages are essential for machine learning because they provide the building blocks for everything from data preprocessing and model training to evaluation and deployment.

Comparison of Anaconda and Miniconda

Anaconda is like the deluxe all-inclusive package. It comes with a massive collection of pre-installed packages, including popular ones like *NumPy*, *Pandas*, *Matplotlib*, and *Scikit-learn*. It also includes tools like *Spyder* (an IDE) and *Navigator*, which is a graphical interface for managing environments and packages. This makes it an excellent choice for beginners who want everything in one place.

Miniconda, on the other hand, is the minimalist option. It comes with only the essentials: Python, conda, and a few other core packages. This makes it a lighter and faster option, especially if you have limited disk space or prefer to install only the packages you need.

Which one to choose:

- If you are new to Python and machine learning, **Anaconda** is a great starting point. It gives you everything you need to get started right away.
- If you are more experienced or want more control over your environment, **Miniconda** might be a better fit. You can customize it to your liking by installing only the packages you need.

Ultimately, the choice between Anaconda and Miniconda comes down to personal preference and your specific needs. Both are excellent tools that will help you on your machine learning journey.

Downloading and installing your chosen distribution

Once you have decided between Anaconda and Miniconda, follow these steps to download and install the distribution on your system:

1. **Head to the website**:
   - **For Anaconda**: Go to: **https://www.anaconda.com/download/**
   - **For Miniconda**: Go to: **https://docs.conda.io/en/latest/miniconda.html**
2. **Select your operating system**: Choose the installer that matches your computer (Windows, macOS, or Linux).
3. **Download the installer**: Click the download link for the Python version you want (the latest version is usually recommended).

4. **Run the installer**:
   - **Anaconda**: Double-click the downloaded file and follow the instructions. You can usually stick with the default settings.
   - **Miniconda**: Double-click the downloaded file and follow the instructions. You can usually stick with the default settings.

After the installation is complete, you will have access to the **`conda`** command, which you will use to manage your environments and packages. You will also have a base environment with some essential packages already installed.

Creating isolated workspaces with conda and venv environments

Imagine you are a scientist working in a lab. You would not want to mix chemicals from different experiments. That could lead to unexpected reactions and ruin your results. The same goes for your coding projects.

Reasons to use environments

In the Python world, environments are like separate lab spaces for your projects. Each environment is a self-contained space where you can install specific packages and their versions without affecting other projects. This is super important because different projects often require different versions of the same package.

For example, one project might need TensorFlow 2.5, while another might need TensorFlow 2.9. Using environments can avoid conflicts and ensure that each project has exactly what it needs to run smoothly.

Think of environments as clean rooms where you can experiment without worrying about messing things up. They keep your projects organized and prevent dependency conflicts, making your life as a developer much more accessible.

Creating environments with Anaconda Navigator

Anaconda Navigator provides a **graphical user interface** (**GUI**) to create environments. Observe *Figure 2.3* for a quick preview. The steps to follow to create an environment are as follows:

1. **Open Anaconda Navigator**: Launch Anaconda Navigator from your applications menu.
2. **Go to the Environments tab**: Click on the **Environments** tab on the left sidebar.
3. **Create a new environment**: Click the **Create** button.
4. **Name your environment**: Give your environment a descriptive name (e.g., **`mmlbook`**).
5. **Choose Python version**: Select the Python version you want to use.
6. **Click Create**: Anaconda will create the environment and install the necessary packages.

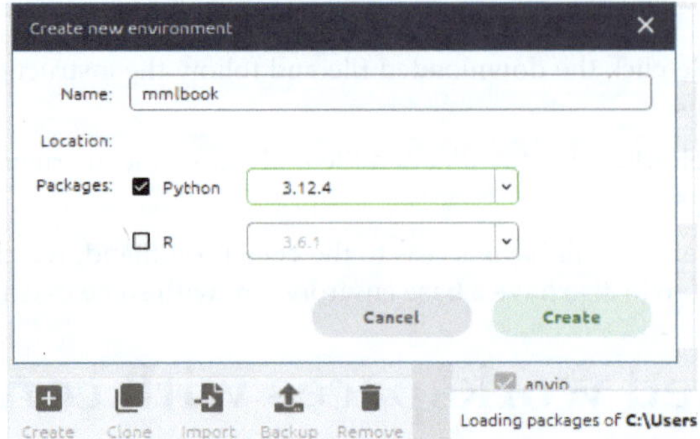

***Figure 2.3:** Creating an environment with Anaconda Navigator*

You can now manage your environments from the Navigator interface. You can install, update, and remove packages, as well as switch between different environments.

Creating environments with Conda

If you installed Anaconda or Miniconda, you already have a powerful tool called **conda** at your disposal. Conda is a package and environment manager that makes it super easy to create and manage environments.

At this point, you can download the repository as a **.zip** file from the GitHub repository, as shown in the following figure:

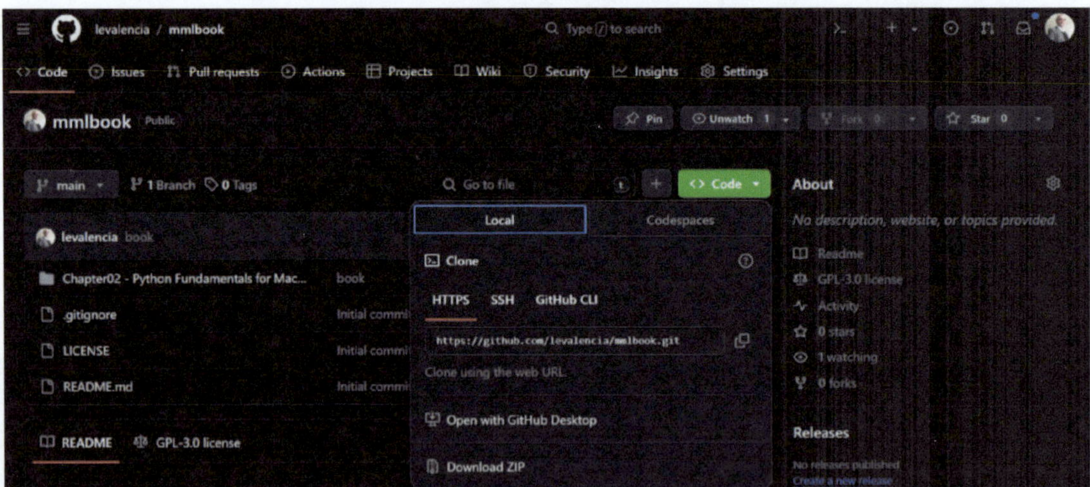

***Figure 2.4:** GitHub repository consisting of book exercises and lab files*

Once you have downloaded the repository, follow the given steps to set up your workspace:

1. Extract the contents of the **.zip** file to a location on your computer.
2. Open VS Code.
3. From the **File** menu, select **Open Folder**.
4. Navigate to the folder where you extracted the **.zip** file contents.
5. Select the folder and click **Open**.

To create a new environment with **conda**, open your terminal and type:

```
cd Chapter02
conda create -n Chapter02 python=3.12
```

It will prompt you to proceed with some standard packages, as shown in *Figure 2.5*:

```
The following NEW packages will be INSTALLED:

  bzip2              pkgs/main/win-64::bzip2-1.0.8-h2bbff1b_6
  ca-certificates    pkgs/main/win-64::ca-certificates-2024.3.11-haa95532_0
  expat              pkgs/main/win-64::expat-2.6.2-hd77b12b_0
  libffi             pkgs/main/win-64::libffi-3.4.4-hd77b12b_1
  openssl            pkgs/main/win-64::openssl-3.0.14-h827c3e9_0
  pip                pkgs/main/win-64::pip-24.0-py312haa95532_0
  python             pkgs/main/win-64::python-3.12.4-h14ffc60_1
  setuptools         pkgs/main/win-64::setuptools-69.5.1-py312haa95532_0
  sqlite             pkgs/main/win-64::sqlite-3.45.3-h2bbff1b_0
  tk                 pkgs/main/win-64::tk-8.6.14-h0416ee5_0
  tzdata             pkgs/main/noarch::tzdata-2024a-h04d1e81_0
  vc                 pkgs/main/win-64::vc-14.2-h2eaa2aa_1
  vs2015_runtime     pkgs/main/win-64::vs2015_runtime-14.29.30133-h43f2093_3
  wheel              pkgs/main/win-64::wheel-0.43.0-py312haa95532_0
  xz                 pkgs/main/win-64::xz-5.4.6-h8cc25b3_1
  zlib               pkgs/main/win-64::zlib-1.2.13-h8cc25b3_1


Proceed ([y]/n)?
```

***Figure 2.5**: Conda creates a new environment*

This will create a new environment named **Chapter02** with Python 3.12 installed. You can replace **Chapter02** with any name you like and specify a different Python version if you prefer.

To activate the environment, type:

```
(base) PS C:\mmlbook\Chapter02> conda activate Chapter02
```

You will know the environment is activated when you see its name in parentheses at the beginning of your command line prompt:

```
(Chapter02) PS C:\mmlbook\Chapter02>
```

Creating environments with venv

If you do not have Anaconda or Miniconda, you can still create environments using venv, a tool built into Python that is also available in VS Code.

To create a new environment with venv using VS Code, follow the given steps:

1. Press *Ctrl+P* (or *Cmd+P* on macOS) to open the command palette.
2. **Type** | **Python**: Create Environment in the command palette.
3. Select venv from the options presented, and you can also create conda environments from the VS Code command palette.
4. Select the Python installation you want to use (for example, Python 3.12.3).
5. Wait for VS Code to create the environment. A **.venv** folder will be created at the root of the directory structure, as shown in the following figure:

***Figure 2.6**: Command palette, create Python environment*

6. Then select venv; notice you can also create conda environments from the VS Code command palette:

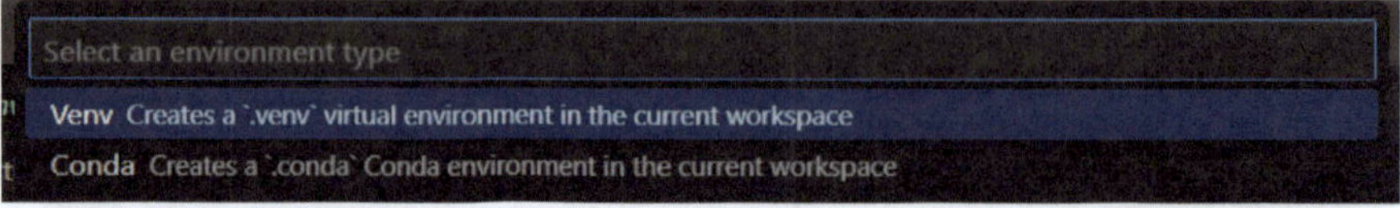

Figure 2.7: Selecting venv or conda

7. Then, select which Python installation you want to use. In our case, Python 3.12.3:

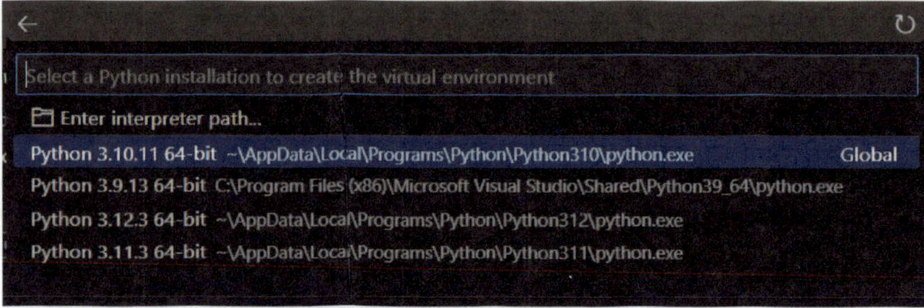

Figure 2.8: Selecting Python version

8. After the environment is created, a `.venv` folder is created at the root of the directory structure:

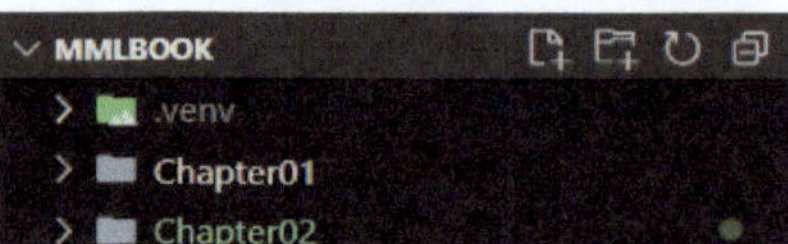

Figure 2.9: venv created

However, if you want to create a venv inside a specific folder (for example, `Chapter02`), you need to use commands instead of the Command Palette.

Open a terminal window in VS Code, on the menu Terminal, New Terminal, and type the following commands:

- **For Windows**:

```
(base) PS C:\mmlbook\Chapter02> python -m venv .venv
(base) PS C:\mmlbook\Chapter02> .venv\Scripts\activate
(.venv) PS C:\mmlbook\Chapter02>
```

- **For Mac/Linux**:

```
(base) PS C:\mmlbook\Chapter02> python -m venv .venv
(base) PS C:\mmlbook\Chapter02> source venv/bin/activate
(.venv) PS C:\mmlbook\Chapter02>
Jupyter Notebook
```

Again, you will see the environment's name in parentheses when it is activated.

Note: From now on, we will use this approach. This way, you can have a separate virtual environment for each chapter, which is very handy because the packages or libraries that we will use in each chapter could be different. If you use a general virtual environment for the entire book, you will finish with a giant virtual environment with lots of packages that are not needed in some chapters of the book.

Jupyter Notebooks, your interactive coding playground

Imagine a magical notebook where you can write code, see the results instantly, add explanations, and even include images or graphs. That is what Jupyter Notebooks are all about. They are like a playground for coding, where you can experiment, learn, and share your work with others.

Understanding Jupyter Notebooks for ML applications

Jupyter Notebooks are interactive documents that combine code, text, and visualizations. They are perfect for machine learning because they allow you to do the following:

- **Experiment and iterate quickly**: You can run small chunks of code and see the results immediately, making it easy to test different ideas and find what works best.
- **Document your work**: You can add explanations, notes, and even equations to your code, making it easier to understand and share with others.
- **Visualize your data**: You can create beautiful graphs and charts to explore your data and communicate your findings.
- **Share your work**: You can easily share your notebooks with others, allowing them to reproduce your results and build upon your work.

You can use Jupyter Notebooks directly within VS Code, thanks to the handy Jupyter extension mentioned earlier.

Launching and using Jupyter Notebook

The following steps will allow you to set up the Jupyter Notebook experience in your local Windows Machine:

1. First, you need to install Jupyter Notebooks:

   ```
   (.venv) PS C:\mmlbook\Chapter02>pip install notebook
   ```

2. Then you can run the notebook:

   ```
   (.venv) PS C:\mmlbook\Chapter02>jupyter notebook
   ```

3. You will get this result in the terminal:

   ```
   To access the server, open this file in a browser:
   file:///C:/Users/<Username>/AppData/Roaming/jupyter/runtime/jpserver-41200-open.html
   Alternatively, copy and paste one of these URLs:
   http://localhost:8888/tree?token=0013dfb62f907358134a9f8c394b6a6822eb3f3421f816b9
   http://127.0.0.1:8888/tree?token=0013dfb62f907358134a9f8c394b6a6822eb3f3421f816b9
   ```

   Note: The token would be different in your case.

4. After you open one of these links in the browser, you will be in the Jupyter Notebooks experience; first, you will see the folder contents from where you executed the last command, and then you can create your notebook using the file menu, as shown in the following figure:

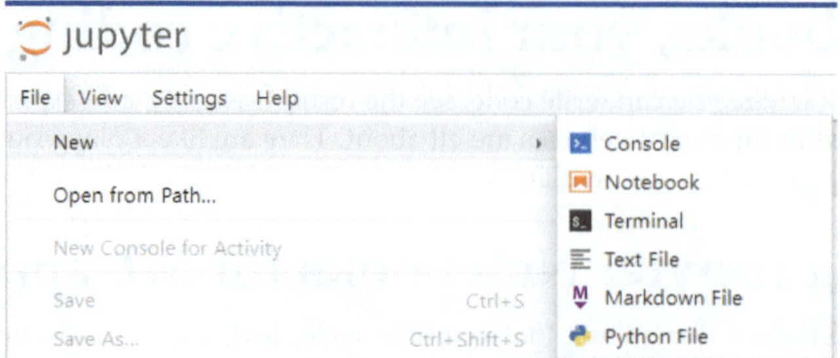

Figure 2.10: Create a new file

5. Alternatively, you can open an existing file (`FirstNotebook.ipynb`) and press the play button to execute your code, as shown in the following figure:

Figure 2.11: Open the existing file

Jupyter Notebooks inside VS Code

In the preceding section, you learned how to create or open existing notebooks using a browser; however, you can also create/run notebooks inside VS Code.

The only thing you need to do is open a file with the `.ipynb` extension. VS Code will automatically recognize it as a Jupyter Notebook and render it as such.

In VS Code, you will see the **Run All** button at the top of the screen, or you can execute cell by cell with the individual play button, as shown in the following figure:

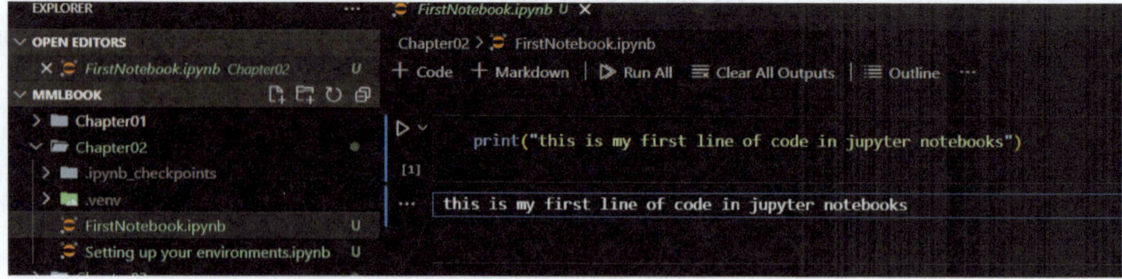

Figure 2.12: Opening and executing Jupyter Notebooks

Jupyter kernels and environments

Jupyter Notebooks do not just run Python code magically. They need something called a **kernel** to execute the code. Think of a kernel as the engine that powers your notebook. It is what understands your Python code and runs it.

The default kernel in Jupyter is called **ipykernel**. It is designed to work with Python and provides the interactive features you love in Jupyter Notebooks.

Understanding how kernels connect to environments

Remember those virtual environments we talked about earlier (conda or venv); each environment can have its own kernel. This means you can run different notebooks with different Python versions and packages, all within the same Jupyter instance.

For example, you could have one notebook running in an environment with Python 3.8 and TensorFlow 2.5 and another notebook running in an environment with Python 3.9 and PyTorch. This flexibility is super helpful when you are working on multiple projects with different requirements.

Choosing the right kernel

When you open a Jupyter Notebook, you can choose which kernel you want to use. This is usually done through a dropdown menu in the notebook interface. If you are using VS Code, the Jupyter extension will automatically detect the available kernels in your environments.

Installing kernels

If you create a new environment, you might need to install the **ipykernel** package in that environment to make it available as a kernel. You can do this using pip:

```
pip install ipykernel
```

Once you have installed **ipykernel**, you can make it available as a kernel by running:

```
python -m ipykernel install --user --name=my_env
```

Now, when you open a Jupyter Notebook, you should see your new environment listed as a kernel option.

Machine learning in cloud with Google Colab

In addition to local development, cloud-based platforms have revolutionized the way machine learning models are built and deployed. Google Colab, a free cloud service, allows you to run your machine learning experiments in the cloud without needing powerful hardware. It provides an easy-to-use interface for Python coding and integrates seamlessly with popular machine learning libraries, offering a great environment for beginners and advanced users alike.

Cloud is your machine learning superpower

Think of the cloud as a vast network of super-powerful computers connected through the internet. Instead of relying solely on your computer's resources, you can tap into this incredible computing power to run your machine learning models, no matter how demanding they are. It is like having a secret weapon that can handle even the most complex calculations and massive datasets with ease.

Google Collab, a free and easy way to get started

Now, you might be wondering how to access this cloud magic. That is where Google Collab comes in. It is a free platform that lets you harness the power of the cloud without any complicated setup. It is like a user-friendly gateway to the world of cloud computing, explicitly designed for machine learning enthusiasts like you.

Creating a Google account and using Colab

To start your Colab adventure, all you need is a Google account. If you do not have one already, head over to the Google homepage and create one. It is a quick and easy process. Once you have your account, you can dive right into Colab and start exploring its features.

To execute Python code in Colab:

1. Go to **https://colab.research.google.com/**
2. Create a **New notebook**, as shown in the following figure:

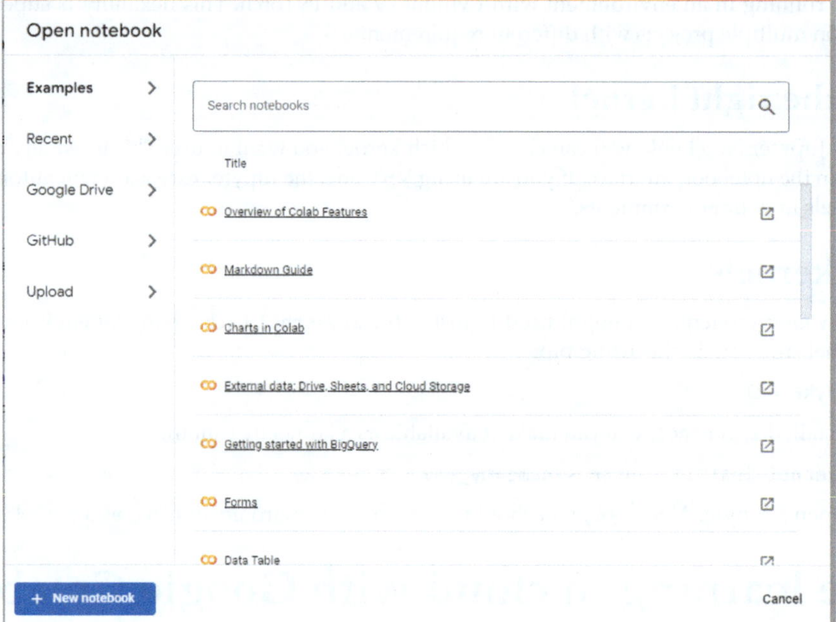

Figure 2.13: Google Colab welcome page

3. Type your code and press *Shift* + *Enter* to execute the current cell, as shown in the following figure:

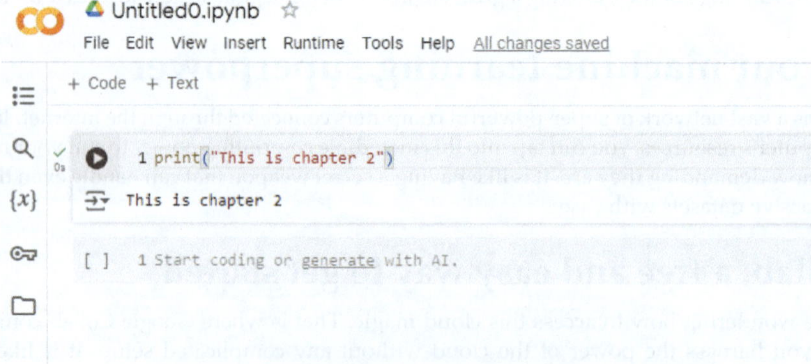

Figure 2.14: Google Colab: your first line of code in Colab

Another cloud option, Azure ML Studio

Google Colab is not the only player in the cloud game. Microsoft Azure is another powerful cloud platform that offers a wide range of machine learning tools and services. It is like a treasure trove of resources for building, deploying, and managing your AI projects.

Microsoft Azure, another powerful cloud platform

Azure provides a comprehensive suite of machine learning tools and services catering to beginners and experienced practitioners. It offers a flexible and scalable environment where you can experiment, train, and deploy your models with ease. It is like having a whole team of experts supporting your machine learning endeavors.

Azure ML Studio, a visual way to build models

One of Azure's standout features is its ML Studio. This visual interface allows you to build, test, and deploy machine learning models without writing a single line of code. It is like a drag-and-drop playground where you can connect different modules and create powerful workflows.

Creating an Azure account with free credits

The best part is that Azure offers free credits to get you started on your cloud journey. These credits are like a welcome gift that lets you explore the platform and its capabilities without any financial commitment. You can sign up for an Azure account and use it to experiment with different tools and services.

The procedure to get started is as follows:

1. Go to **https://azure.microsoft.com/en-us/free/** and create an Azure Account.
2. Search for Azure Machine Learning in the top search bar and select it, as shown in the following figure:

***Figure 2.15**: Search Azure Machine Learning*

3. Click on **Create new workspace**, as shown in the following figure:

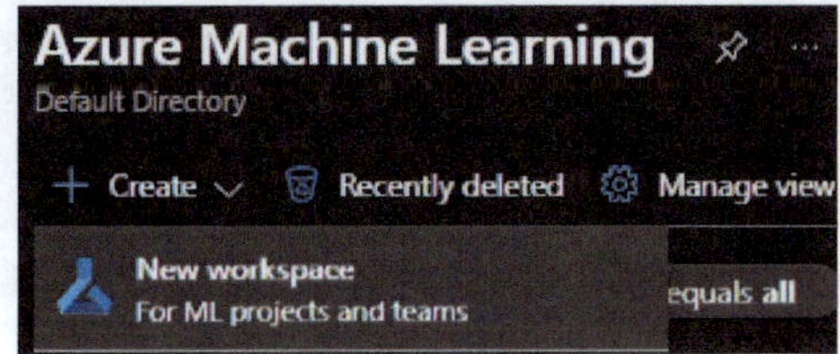

***Figure 2.16**: Create new workspace*

4. Then, fill the form with resource names, as shown in the following figure:

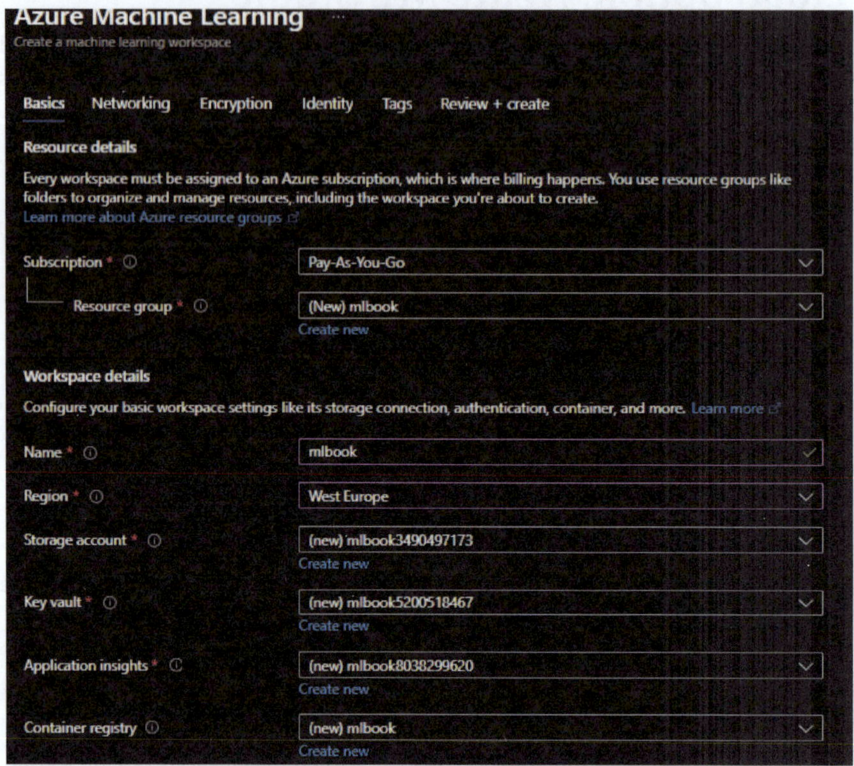

***Figure 2.17**: Filling the creation form*

5. Once the creation is finished, click on the blue button to go to your new Azure Machine Learning Studio resource, as shown in the following figure:

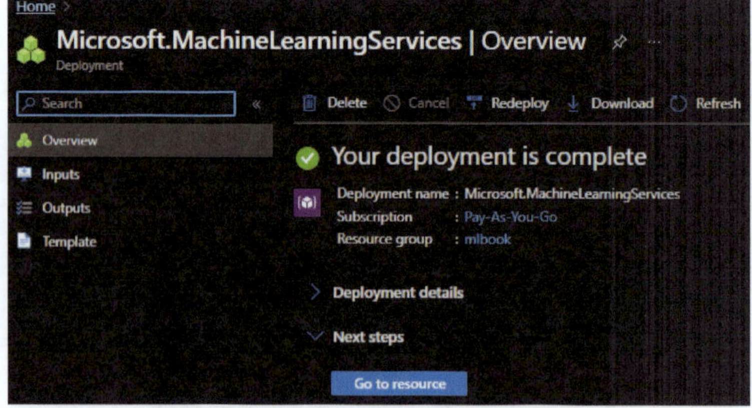

***Figure 2.18**: Resource created*

6. Click on **Launch Studio**, as shown in the following figure:

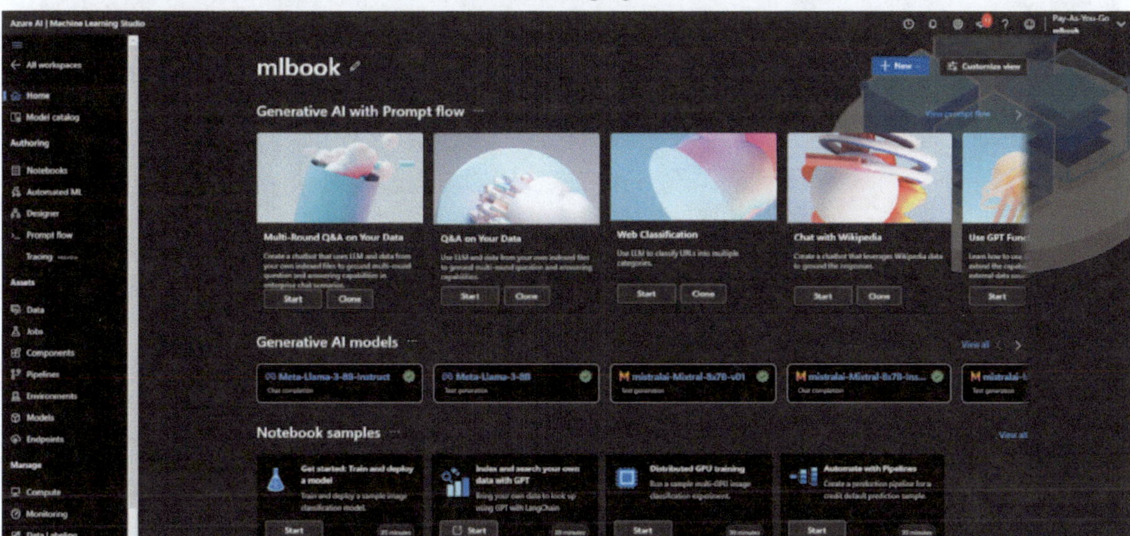

Figure 2.19: *Azure Machine Learning homepage*

To start developing in Azure Machine Learning Studio, you need to create a compute instance; a compute is your virtual server in the cloud, which will allow you to execute your Python code. It is essential to understand that these compute instances have different sizes (CPU Cores, RAM Size, and GPU). The bigger your **virtual machine (VM)**, the faster it is to execute or train machine learning models. VMs with GPUs are usually needed when training deep learning models with PyTorch; however, for the first chapters of the book, you can use a small VM without GPUs, or you can use Google Colab or VS Code with your local CPU.

Let us see how to create a compute in Azure Machine Learning Studio:

1. On the left menu, select **Compute**.
2. Then click on **New**.
3. Fill in the form with a compute instance name and select the size you require, as shown in the following figure:

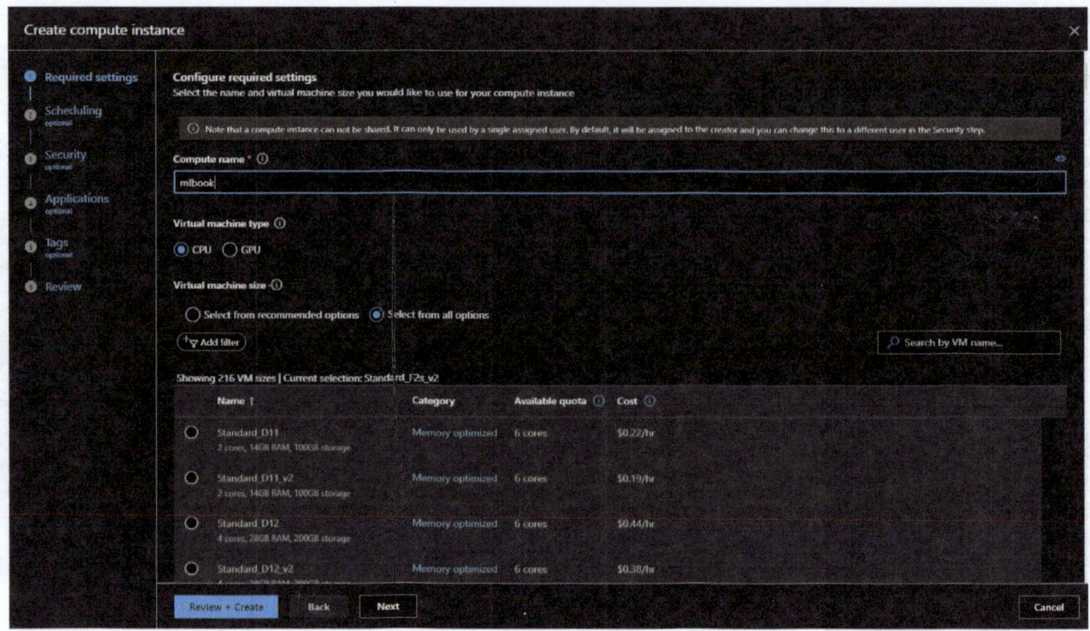

Figure 2.20: Creating a new compute

4. Set up **Auto shutdown** and other settings. Remember that these compute instances have a cost per hour, and if they are idle, you will still have to pay from your free credit, so it is better to shut them down automatically after some time, as shown here:

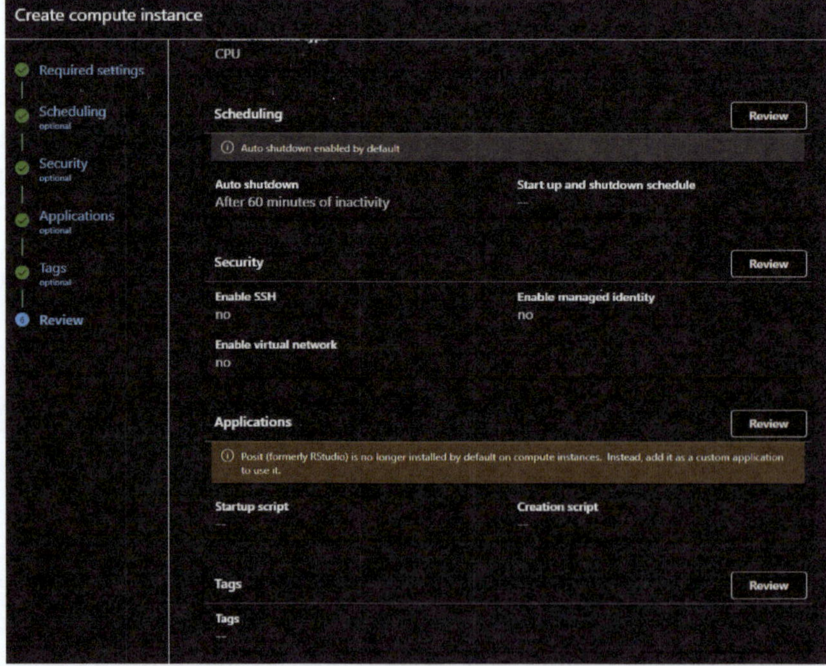

Figure 2.21: Azure ML Setting up Auto shutdown in compute

5. After the compute instance is created, select **Notebooks** on the left menu and then click on the blue button to select **Create a new file**, as shown in the following figure:

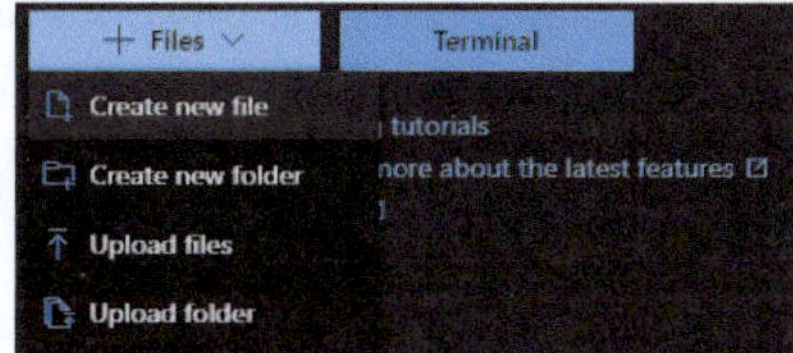

Figure 2.22: Create a new notebook

6. Then, type your code in a cell and press *Shift+Enter* to execute, as shown in the following figure:

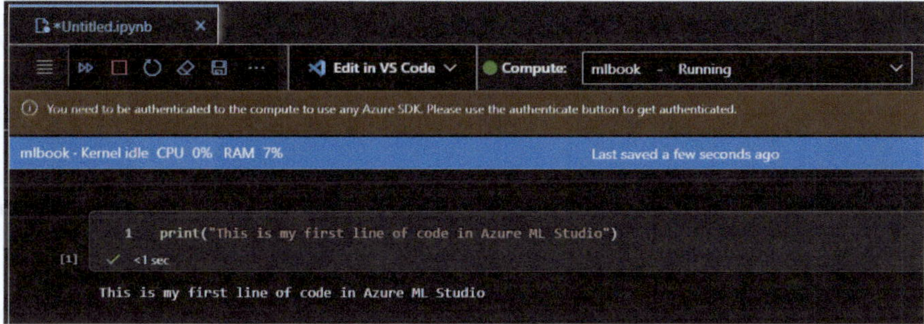

Figure 2.23: Azure ML running Python

From now on, unless stated otherwise, you will execute the code in VS Code on your local computer. In later chapters, when you learn to train deep learning models, you will need to compute instances with GPUs. That is where Azure ML becomes very useful.

Managing project dependencies with pip and requirements.txt

Imagine you are baking a cake. To make it delicious, you need flour, sugar, eggs, and other ingredients. In the coding world, these ingredients are called **dependencies**.

Project dependencies: In a nutshell, project dependencies are external pieces of code (like those handy Python packages we talked about) that your project relies on to function correctly. They are like the building blocks that help you create your masterpiece without starting from scratch.

Using pip to install and manage packages

Now, *how do you gather these ingredients for your coding cake?* That is where pip comes in. It is like your personal shopping assistant for Python packages. With pip, you can easily download and install the packages you need from the **Python Package Index** (**PyPI**), a vast online repository of Python goodies.

Example: `pip install pandas`

Creating and using requirements.txt

Imagine you want to share your delicious cake recipe with a friend. You would not just tell them to *get some ingredients*. You would give them a detailed list of everything they need and the exact amounts. That is where `requirements.txt` comes in handy.

This file lists all the Python packages your project needs and their specific versions. It is like a recipe card for your code, ensuring that anyone who wants to recreate your project has all the necessary ingredients. When you share your project, include the **requirements.txt** file, and others can easily install all the dependencies using pip.

Open a text editor and list the packages your project needs, one per line, like this:

```
numpy==1.23.5
scikit-learn==1.2.2
matplotlib==3.7.1
```

This file tells **pip** exactly which packages and versions to install. Your friends can then run the following command in their terminal:

```
pip install -r requirements.txt
```

Note: Make sure the preceding command is executed with your environment active, as explained in the preceding sections.

Introduction to Poetry

In the world of Python, there is an increasingly popular tool called **Poetry**. It simplifies creating, managing, and packaging Python projects. While **pip** and **requirements.txt** are excellent for essential dependency management, Poetry takes it a step further by offering a more streamlined and comprehensive solution.

Poetry handles everything from virtual environments and dependency resolution to building and publishing packages, all within a single tool. It uses a modern **pyproject.toml** file for configuration, making it easier to manage complex projects with many dependencies.

While Poetry offers many benefits, we will not get into its intricacies in this book. Our focus will primarily be on using **pip** and **requirements.txt** for dependency management. However, if you are interested in exploring more advanced dependency management options, it is recommended to check out the Poetry documentation and tutorials available online.

Introduction to UV

UV is a modern, Rust-based Python package and project manager that aims to replace tools like pip, pip-tools, virtualenv, poetry, and more, with a single, ultra-fast CLI. Its core features and commands.

The following list provides the key features:

- Lightning-fast package installation and dependency resolution (10–100x faster than pip)
- Built-in virtual environment management.
- Reliable dependency locking and reproducible environments.
- Python version management (install, list, pin, uninstall).
- Project scaffolding and management via pyproject.toml.
- Drop-in compatibility with pip and pip-tools commands.
- Tool management (install and run CLI tools globally or per project).

A workflow example is as follows:

1. Initialize a new project:

```
uv init myproject
cd myproject
```

2. Add dependencies:

```
uv add numpy pandas
```

3. Sync environment (installs/removes packages to match lockfile):

```
uv sync
```

4. Run your code:

```
uv run script.py
```

5. Export requirements for pip users:

```
uv export --format requirements-txt > requirements.txt
```

Command details are as follows:

- **uv init**: Sets up a new project directory with pyproject.toml, .venv, and optionally a README and gitignore.
- **uv add/remove**: Modifies dependencies in `pyproject.toml` and updates the lockfile. Removing a package also automatically cleans up unused dependencies.
- **uv sync**: Ensures your environment matches the lockfile precisely, removing any packages not specified, which is crucial for reproducibility.
- **uv run**: Runs scripts or commands in the project's environment, ensuring dependencies are up to date before execution.
- **uv python install**: Installs a specific Python version, similar to pyenv.
- **uv build/publish**: For packaging and distributing your project.

Conclusion

You have successfully set up your machine learning environment, both locally and in the cloud. You have learned how to install Python, choose a code editor, manage packages and environments, use Jupyter Notebooks, and even explore cloud platforms like Google Colab and Azure Machine Learning Studio. These are essential tools for your machine learning journey.

In the next chapter, we will look into Python fundamentals; in that chapter, you will need all the basic Python syntax in order to be able to create your next machine learning project.

Exercises

The Hello ML Environment Challenge: To verify that your local environment is set up correctly and that you understand dependency management, complete the following tasks:

1. **Create a Workspace**: Create a new folder on your computer named ML_Exercise_Ch2.
2. **Virtual environment**: Open VS Code in this folder and create a new virtual environment (using either venv or conda). Activate the environment in your terminal.
3. **Install dependencies**: Create a file named requirements.txt inside the folder. Add the following lines to it:
   - numpy
   - pandas
   - notebook
4. Run the command to install these requirements using pip.

5. **Verification script**: Create a new Jupyter Notebook file named verification.ipynb. Inside the first cell, write code to import numpy and print "Environment Setup Complete!".
6. **Run**: Execute the cell. If it prints the message without errors, you have successfully managed your environment and dependencies.

Multiple choice questions

1. **Why is Python considered the universal language for machine learning?**
   a. It is the fastest language available
   b. It is easy to read, has a massive community, and offers a vast toolbox of machine learning libraries
   c. It is the only language that supports GPUs
   d. It is pre-installed on every computer
2. **Which tool allows you to create isolated workspaces where you can install specific package versions without affecting other projects?**
   a. Visual Studio Code
   b. Virtual environments (venv or conda)
   c. Git
   d. The cloud
3. **What is the primary difference between Anaconda and Miniconda?**
   a. Anaconda is for Windows, Miniconda is for Mac
   b. Anaconda comes with many pre-installed packages; Miniconda is a minimalist installer with only essentials
   c. Miniconda cannot use Python
   d. Anaconda is free, but Miniconda is paid
4. **Which VS Code extension is described as essential for running interactive code cells directly within the editor**
   a. Docker
   b. C++
   c. Jupyter
   d. Azure Tools
5. **What is the function of the pip install -r requirements.txt command?**
   a. It installs Python on your computer
   b. It creates a new virtual environment
   c. It installs all dependencies listed in the text file in one go
   d. It updates VS Code to the latest version
6. **In the context of Jupyter Notebooks, what is a kernel?**
   a. The hardware processor (CPU)
   b. The file extension of the notebook
   c. The computational engine that executes the code contained in the notebook document
   d. A type of cloud storage

7. **Which file is used by the Poetry tool for configuration and dependency management?**
   a. requirements.txt
   b. setup.py
   c. pyproject.toml
   d. config.json
8. **What is a major advantage of using Google Colab?**
   a. It works offline without the internet
   b. It provides free access to powerful GPUs without requiring local hardware setup
   c. It is faster than any local computer
   d. It automatically writes the code for you
9. **When using Azure Machine Learning Studio, what must you create to execute Python code in the cloud?**
   a. A compute instance
   b. A SQL database
   c. A new email address
   d. A local virtual environment
10. **What is uv as described in the chapter?**
   a. A new programming language
   b. A virus protection software for machine learning
   c. An ultra-fast, Rust-based Python package and project manager
   d. A type of neural network

Answers

1.	b.
2.	b.
3.	b.
4.	c.
5.	c.
6.	c.
7.	c.
8.	b.
9.	a.
10.	c.

Key terms

- **Python**: A high-level programming language widely used for machine learning.
- **VS Code**: A popular code editor with extensive features and customization options.
- **Anaconda/Miniconda**: Python distributions that simplify package and environment management.
- **Virtual environment**: An isolated workspace where you can install specific Python packages and versions without affecting other projects.
- **Jupyter Notebook**: An interactive document that combines code, text, and visualizations, ideal for machine learning experimentation and documentation.
- **Google Colab**: A free cloud platform that provides access to powerful computing resources for running machine learning models.
- **Azure Machine Learning Studio**: A visual interface for building, testing, and deploying machine learning models on the Microsoft Azure cloud platform.
- **pip**: A package installer for Python.
- **requirements.txt**: A file that lists the Python packages required for a project.
- **Poetry**: A modern dependency manager for Python.
- **uv**: An extremely fast Python package and project manager, written in Rust.

Join our Discord space

Join our Discord workspace for latest updates, offers, tech happenings around the world, new releases, and sessions with the authors:

https://discord.bpbonline.com

CHAPTER 3
Python Fundamentals for Machine Learning

Introduction

Python has become the undisputed powerhouse of machine learning and deep learning. Its clean syntax, rich ecosystem of libraries, and emphasis on readability have propelled it to the forefront of cutting-edge research and practical applications. Whether you are developing algorithms to predict stock prices, building models to recognize patterns in medical images, or crafting intelligent chatbots, Python is the tool of choice for countless data scientists and machine learning engineers.

This chapter serves as your comprehensive guide to the Python fundamentals that underpin the vast and exciting field of machine learning. We will begin with a refresher on the basic building blocks, data types, variables, control flow, and functions, ensuring you have a solid grasp of the language's core syntax and structure.

The details of data structures, error handling, and coding best practices will be introduced in the subsequent sections.

Even the best software can have problems or mistakes, and machine learning code is no exception. Therefore, we will devote a section to understanding how to gracefully handle errors and exceptions, a crucial skill for creating robust and reliable machine learning and deep learning applications.

Writing clean, well-organized code is paramount in any programming endeavor, but it becomes even more critical in machine learning, where codebases can quickly grow in complexity. We will explore modules, packages, and the PEP 8 style guide, which provides the blueprint for creating code that is easy to read, maintain, and collaborate on.

Finally, for those looking to expand their skills further, we will discuss the basics of **object-oriented programming** (**OOP**) in Python. OOP offers a powerful way to structure your code, especially for larger projects, and it can help you create more modular, reusable, and maintainable machine learning and deep learning systems.

By the end of this chapter, you will have a strong foundation in Python fundamentals and be ready to apply them to machine learning tasks.

Structure

This chapter covers the following topics:

- Python basics review
- Data types
- Control flow
- Functions
- Working with lists, dictionaries, sets, and tuples
- Handling errors and exceptions
- Code organization and best practices
- Object-oriented programming in Python

Objectives

By the end of this chapter, you will have developed a comprehensive foundation in Python programming for machine learning applications. You will gain confidence in utilizing Python's core data types and control flow structures while mastering essential data structures for efficient data storage, manipulation, and analysis. The chapter will equip you with techniques for handling errors and exceptions gracefully, ensuring your machine learning projects remain robust under various conditions. You will also learn best practices for organizing and structuring your code to enhance readability, maintainability, and collaboration potential. Finally, you will discover how to leverage Python's extensive library ecosystem to streamline and optimize your machine learning workflows, setting you up for success in subsequent, more advanced topics. Apply object-oriented programming principles to design more modular and scalable machine learning code.

Python basics review

Python distinguishes itself from many other programming languages through its unique approach to code structure and syntax. Let us check some of the fundamental concepts that make Python so approachable and powerful for machine learning tasks.

Indentation

Unlike languages like C++, Java, or JavaScript, which use curly braces {} to define code blocks, Python relies on indentation to delineate the structure of your code. Consistent indentation (typically four spaces) is not just a stylistic choice; it is a requirement. This enforced indentation enhances code readability, making it easier to grasp the logical flow of your programs. The following is a small example of how Python code must be indented:

```
if temperature > 28:
    print("It's a hot day!")
else:
    print("The weather is pleasant.")
```

In this example, the indented lines under the if and else statements belong to their respective code blocks, *but what are code blocks?* They are pieces of code that belong together on the same level. What is inside the if statement is a code block, and what is in the else statement is another code block. Improper indentation will lead to errors, but proper indentation will ensure your code's structure remains unambiguous.

Variables

Variables are the first thing to learn in programming. They act as named containers for storing data. In Python, you create variables simply by assigning a value to a name.

Python is dynamically typed, meaning you do not need to declare a variable's type explicitly. The type is inferred from the assigned value.

The following demonstrates how you can define variables of different data types in Python:

```
age = 40
name = "Luis"
pi = 3.14159
```

The variable **age** is of the integer data type because its value, **30**, is a whole number, and the variable **name** is of the string data type because its value, **Alice**, is text enclosed in quotation marks

Later in this chapter, we will explain the data types you can use for variables.

Operator for calculation and comparison

Operators are symbols that perform specific operations on values. Python provides a rich set of operators for arithmetic, comparison, logical operations, and more. The details are as follows:

- **Arithmetic operators**: +, -, *, /, // (floor division), % (modulo), ** (exponentiation)
- **Comparison operators**: ==, !=, <, >, <=, >=
- **Logical operators**: and, or, not

This snippet demonstrates arithmetic, comparison, and logical operators in action:

```
result = 10 + 5 * 2 # Arithmetic calculation
is_equal = age == 30 # Comparison
is_valid = age > 18 and age < 65 # Logical operation
```

Data types

Python offers various data types, such as numbers, strings, lists, and dictionaries, each with specific methods and properties to manipulate and work with the data. For instance, if you are working with a dataset that includes age, you can use the 'int' data type to store a whole number (integer) representing a person's age. This is just one example of how data types classify data items and instruct the interpreter on managing the data. Python supports various data types, including integers, floats, strings, Booleans, lists, dictionaries, sets, and tuples, offering a wide range of options for representing and storing different kinds of data. Understanding the following data types is fundamental for working with data in Python:

- **Numbers**: Python supports various numeric types for mathematical operations and data representation. The primary numeric types include integers and floating-point numbers, each serving distinct purposes in machine learning applications.
- **Integers (int)**: Integers represent whole numbers (e.g., age, number of samples). In machine learning, integers are commonly used for:
    - Counting occurrences
    - Indexing data points within datasets
    - Defining model hyperparameters (e.g., number of layers in a neural network)
- **Floats (float)**: Floats represent decimal numbers (e.g., prices and weights in a neural network). In machine learning, floats are essential for:
    - Storing continuous data values (e.g., sensor readings, stock prices).
    - Representing model parameters and weights during training.
    - Calculating probabilities and confidence scores.

  This snippet shows how to declare numerical variables and assign values:

  ```
  age = 30          # Integer
  price = 29.99     # Float
  ```
- **Strings**: Strings store text data (e.g., labels, text documents). In machine learning, strings are used for:
    - Categorical features (e.g., *red, green, blue*).
    - Text preprocessing for **natural language processing** (NLP) tasks.
    - Storing file paths and URLs.
    - Both single quotes and double quotes are permitted.

The following snippet shows how to declare string variables and assign values:

```
name = "Luis"
message = 'Hello Luis'
```

- **Booleans**: Booleans represent logical values (True or False). In machine learning, Booleans are used for:
    - Decision-making in algorithms (e.g., *is a value above a threshold?*)
    - Filtering data based on conditions
    - Represent binary outcomes (e.g., *did a customer churn?*)

  This snippet shows how to declare Boolean variables and assign them True or False values:

```
is_student = True
is_raining = False
```

- **Lists**: Lists are ordered collections of items (e.g., a list of pixel values in an image). Lists are mutable (changeable). In machine learning, lists are used for:
    - Storing sequences of data (e.g., time-series data, text data).
    - Representing feature vectors (a collection of features for a data point).
    - Building and manipulating datasets

  The following snippet shows how to declare lists with some numbers or string values:

```
numbers = [1, 2, 3, 4]
fruits = ["apple", "banana", "orange"]
```

- **Dictionaries**: Dictionaries store data as key-value pairs (e.g., a dictionary of model hyperparameters). In machine learning, dictionaries are used for:
    - Organizing configuration settings.
    - Storing metadata about features.
    - Creating structured representations of data (e.g., JSON format).

  The following snippet shows how to create a dictionary with keys and values:

```
person = {"name": "Luis", "age": 45, "city": "Brussels"}
```

- **Sets**: Sets are unordered collections of unique elements. In machine learning, sets can be used for:
    - Removing duplicates from data.
    - Identifying unique categories or labels.
    - Performing set operations (e.g., finding common elements between sets).

  The following code shows how to create a Set:

```
unique_numbers = {5, 1, 3, 1, 7}
```

- **Tuples**: Tuples are like lists, but are immutable (unchangeable). In machine learning, tuples are used for:
    - Storing fixed combinations of values (e.g., coordinates).
    - Returning multiple values from a function.
    - Representing data where order is important but should not be modified.

  This snippet shows how to create coordinates:

```
coordinates = (10, 20)
```

Control flow

Control flow is important in machine learning because it enables the design of algorithms that can make decisions, adapt to different situations, and automate repetitive tasks. This is crucial for creating AI systems that can handle complex data and make accurate predictions or decisions based on that data.

Conditional statements

A conditional statement allows your program to make decisions. It checks whether a specific condition is true or false and then executes different blocks of code based on the outcome. This lets your program behave differently depending on the situation.

Conditional statements are crucial in machine learning and deep learning for tasks like:

- **Model selection**: Selecting the best model based on performance metrics.
- **Hyperparameter tuning**: Adjusting model settings based on validation results.
- **Data preprocessing**: Applying different transformations based on data characteristics.

The following code shows the syntax to create a complex conditional statement:

```
If-elif-else
```

Complex conditional statements can be constructed using if-elif-else syntax, as shown in the following example that evaluates model performance:

```
if accuracy > 0.9:
    print("Model is performing well")
elif accuracy > 0.8:
    print("Model needs improvement")
else:
    print("Model is underperforming")
```

Loops

A loop is a programming tool that lets you repeat a set of instructions multiple times. Loops are useful when you want to perform the same task repeatedly, such as going through all the items in a list or repeating an action until a specific condition is met.

Loops are essential in machine learning and deep learning for tasks like:

- **Training models**: Iterating over training data multiple times to update model parameters.
- **Data generation**: Creating synthetic data for training or testing.
- **Evaluation**: Calculating metrics over multiple batches of data.

The following example shows how to use a for loop to iterate over training epochs:

```
for epoch in range(10):  # Train for 10 epochs
    train_model(data)
```

This snippet shows how to code a while loop:

```
while loss > 0.1:  # Train until the loss is below 0.1.
    train_model(data)
```

Functions

Functions are essential in machine learning for organizing code, promoting reusability, and improving modularity. They encapsulate specific tasks, making complex ML workflows more manageable.

Defining functions involves creating reusable blocks of code using the **def** keyword. Function arguments and parameters allow for flexibility, while return values provide outputs. In machine learning, the following functions are used for:

- **Data preprocessing**: Cleaning and transforming data.
- **Feature engineering**: Creating new properties or metadata (also known as features) from existing ones.
- **Model training**: Implementing the learning algorithm.
- **Evaluation**: Assessing model performance.

Here is a simple function definition with input and return values:

```
def preprocess_data(data):
    # Data cleaning and transformation steps
    return processed_data

def calculate_accuracy(y_true, y_pred):
    # Accuracy calculation logic
    return accuracy
```

Lambda functions

Lambda functions offer a concrete way to define simple functions in a single line. They are often used in machine learning for:

- **Custom loss functions**: Defining specialized loss functions for optimization.
- **Activation functions**: Implementing non-linear transformations in neural networks.
- **Sorting**: Sorting data based on custom criteria.

Let us understand what Lambda functions are. Imagine you have a simple task, like doubling a number. Normally, you would write a function like the following:

```
def double(x):
    return x * 2
```

However, if you need this function only once or twice. *Do you need to name it and write a whole block of code?* Lambda functions offer a shortcut.

Lambda function syntax

Lambda functions have a unique syntax:

```
lambda arguments: expression
```

Where,

- **lambda**: This keyword signals you are creating a lambda function.
- **arguments**: These are your function's inputs (like x in our example).
- **expression**: This is a single expression that the function calculates and returns. No return statement is needed.

Here is the lambda version of our doubling function:

```
double = lambda x: x * 2
```

Both versions do the same thing, but the lambda version is more concise.

The following list outlines the reasons to use Lambda functions:

- **Brevity**: They are great for simple, one-off tasks where you do not want to write a full function definition.
- **Readability**: Sometimes, a lambda function can make your code more readable, mainly when used with higher-order functions.

The following list outlines the imitations:

- **One expression**: Lambda functions can only contain a single expression, which makes them unsuitable for complex tasks that require multiple steps.
- **No statements**: You cannot use statements like `if`, `for`, or `while` inside a lambda function.

Let us understand when to use them. Lambda functions shine with higher-order functions like `map`, `filter`, and `sort`. These functions take another function as an argument, and lambda functions are perfect for this role.

For example, sorting—let us say you have a list of points and want to sort them by their distance from the origin. You could use a lambda function like this:

```
points = [(1, 2), (3, 4), (-1, -1)]
sorted_points = sorted(points, key=lambda x: x[0]**2 + x[1]**2)
```

Here, the `lambda` function calculates the squared distance for each point and uses this to determine the order.

Some essential key points are as follows:

- Lambda functions are anonymous functions (no name).
- They are used for simple, single-expression tasks.
- They are often used with higher-order functions.
- They can make your code more readable.

Working with lists, dictionaries, sets, and tuples

Python offers a collection of data structures to organize and store data efficiently, including lists, dictionaries, sets, and tuples. Each structure has unique characteristics and applications in machine learning and deep learning.

Lists

Lists are versatile collections used to store sequences of data. In machine learning and deep learning, lists are commonly used for:

- **Storing training data**: Holding features and labels for model training.
- **Representing sequences**: Storing time-series data or text data for NLP tasks.
- **Building datasets**: Creating and manipulating collections of data points.

Refer to the following code snippet:

```
# Example: Storing training data
data = [
    [0.2, 0.5, 0.8, 1],  # Features, Label
    [0.1, 0.3, 0.6, 0],
```

```
    [0.3, 0.7, 0.9, 1]
]
```

Indexing and slicing

Indexing allows you to read individual elements in a list by their position, and slicing will enable you to extract a portion of a list. Refer to the following example:

```
first_data_point = data[0]          # Access the first data point
features = first_data_point[:-1]    # Slice to get features
label = first_data_point[-1]        # Get the last element (label)
```

List methods

Lists have built-in methods for modification:

- **append(item)**: Adds an item to the end of the list.
- **insert(index, item)**: Inserts an item at a specific index.
- **remove(item)**: Removes the first time an element appears.
- **pop(index)**: Removes and returns the item at the specified index.

Refer to the following built-in list methods:

```
# Example: Modifying a list of labels
labels = [1, 0, 1]
labels.append(2)          # Add a new label
labels.insert(1, 3)        # Insert a label at index 1
labels.remove(1)          # Remove the first occurrence of 1
removed_label = labels.pop()  # Remove the last label (2) and store it
```

List comprehensions provide a short way to create new lists based on existing ones:

```
# Example: Squaring each element in a list
numbers = [1, 2, 3, 4]
squared_numbers = [x**2 for x in numbers] # [1, 4, 9, 16]
```

The following list provides an explanation:

- A list is created using square brackets **[]**.
- An expression x**2 (x squared) is used to transform each element **x**.
- The for **x** in numbers part iterates over the numbers list.
- The result is a newly created list of **squared_numbers** containing the transformed values.

This is a brief overview of lists and their common uses in machine learning and deep learning. Lists are a fundamental building block for many algorithms, and their versatility makes them indispensable for working with data in Python.

Dictionaries

Dictionaries store data as key-value pairs, providing a flexible way to represent structured information. In machine learning and deep learning, dictionaries are used for:

- **Storing model hyperparameters**: Organizing learning rate, batch size, etc.
- **Representing feature metadata**: Associating names and types with features.
- **Creating JSON-like structures**: Storing and exchanging data in a structured format

Refer to the following code snippet:

```
# Example: Storing model hyperparameters
model_params = {"learning_rate": 0.01, "batch_size": 32, "epochs": 10}
```

- **Accessing values by keys**: You can read the values associated with keys using square brackets `[]`. Check the following snippet:

```
learning_rate = model_params["learning_rate"] # Access learning rate
```

- **Adding and modifying key-value pairs**: We can add new key-value pairs or modify existing ones using assignment, as shown in the next snippet:

```
model_params["optimizer"] = "adam"  # Add a new hyperparameter
model_params["epochs"] = 15         # Modify the number of epochs
```

- **Dictionary methods**: Dictionaries have built-in methods for working with keys and values:
  - **keys()**: Returns a view of all keys in the dictionary.
  - **values()**: Returns a view of all values in the dictionary.
  - **items()**: Returns a view of all key-value pairs as tuples.

  Refer to the following snippet to see how to iterate over all dictionary keys and values:

```
all_keys = model_params.keys()      # Get all keys
all_values = model_params.values() # Get all values
for key, value in model_params.items():  # Iterate over key-value pairs
    print(f"{key}: {value}")
```

This briefly overviews dictionaries and their common uses in ML and DL. Dictionaries are a powerful tool for organizing and managing data in a structured way, making them essential for many ML/DL workflows.

Sets

Sets are unordered collections of unique elements, valuable for tasks that require eliminating duplicates. In machine learning and deep learning, sets can be used for:

- **Finding unique labels**: Identifying distinct classes in a dataset.
- **Removing duplicate data**: Cleaning datasets by eliminating redundant entries.
- **Set operations**: Performing operations like finding common elements between sets of features.
- **Creating sets**: You can create sets using curly braces `{}` or the `set()` constructor, as shown:

```
# Example: Creating sets of features
features_set1 = {1, 2, 3}
features_set2 = set([2, 3, 4])
```

- **Set operations**: Sets support various operations:
  - **Union (|)**: Combines all unique elements from two sets.
  - **Intersection (&)**: Finds common elements between two sets.
  - **Difference (-)**: Returns elements in one set but not the other.

  Refer to the following set operations:

```
all_features = features_set1 | features_set2 #Union: {1, 2, 3, 4}
common_features = features_set1 & features_set2 #Intersection: {2, 3}
unique_to_set1 = features_set1 - features_set2 # Difference: {1}
```

Tuples

Tuples are ordered, immutable collections of elements, meaning their contents cannot be changed after creation. In machine learning and deep learning, tuples are used for:

- **Representing data points**: Storing fixed combinations of features and labels.
- **Returning multiple values**: Functions can return tuples to provide multiple results.
- **Data integrity**: Making sure that data remains unchanged throughout a process.

A tuple can be created as shown in the following snippet:

```
# Example: Representing a data point with features and a label
data_point = ([0.2, 0.5, 0.8], 1)  # Features: [0.2, 0.5, 0.8], Label: 1
```

In tuple packing and unpacking, tuple packing creates a tuple by enclosing values in parentheses, while tuple unpacking assigns the elements of a tuple to individual variables, as shown here:

```
# Tuple packing
point = (10, 20)  # Packing two values into a tuple

# Tuple unpacking
x, y = point      # Unpacking the values into x and y
```

Other uses of tuples in ML/DL

Other uses of tuples in machine learning and deep learning are as follows:

- **Fixed-length sequences**: Tuples are suitable for representing fixed-length sequences, such as image dimensions or color channels (RGB).
- **Dictionary keys**: Tuples can be used as keys in dictionaries when a composite key is needed (e.g., a combination of a user ID and timestamp).
- **Function arguments**: Tuples can be used to pass multiple arguments to a function concisely.

You can also use a tuple as a dictionary key, as shown in the following code:

```
# Example: Using a tuple as a dictionary key
image_data = {
    (1280, 720): "HD image",
    (1920, 1080): "Full HD image"
}
```

Tuples are valuable tools in machine learning and deep learning because they are immutable, ensuring data integrity and representing fixed combinations of values.

In the previous sections, you learned the basics of Python data types, control flow, functions, and advanced structures like dictionaries, lists, sets, and, finally, tuples. However, at any point when working with this knowledge, you can have errors in your code, or when calling functions from external libraries, you can get errors too. It is essential to handle errors and exceptions effectively to maintain robust and error-free code execution.

Handling errors and exceptions

Errors and exceptions are inevitable in programming, especially when working with complex machine learning and deep learning projects. Python provides a robust error-handling mechanism to manage these situations gracefully.

try-except blocks

The **try-except** block is the fundamental syntax for handling exceptions. It allows you to isolate code that might raise errors and define specific actions to take if an error occurs. The details are as follows:

- **Catching and handling exceptions**: The **try** block contains the code that you suspect might raise an exception. If an exception occurs, the execution jumps to the corresponding except block.
- **Exception types**: Python defines various exception types for different error conditions. Python includes many built-in exception types, each designed for specific error situations. Some common examples are **ZeroDivisionError**, **TypeError**, and **FileNotFoundError**, but there are many more. For a complete list of built-in exceptions, you can visit the official Python documentation on built-in exceptions.
- You can specify the types of exceptions you want to catch in the **except** block.

The following code demonstrates how to catch a **ZeroDivisionError** using a try-except block:

```
try:
    result = 10 / 0  # This will raise a ZeroDivisionError
except ZeroDivisionError:
    print("Error: Division by zero")
    result = float('inf')  # Handle the error by setting result to infinity
```

In this example, the code attempts to divide by zero, which would typically crash the program. The **try-except** block catches the **ZeroDivisionError** and handles it by printing a message and setting the **result** to infinity.

Let us understand raising exceptions. Sometimes, you may intentionally raise an exception to signal an error condition in your code. You can do this using the **raise** statement as shown here:

```
def validate_input(x):
    if x < 0:
        raise ValueError("Input must be a non-negative number")

    try:
      validate_input(-5)
    except ValueError as e:
      print(e)  # Print the error message
```

In this example, the **validate_input** function raises a **ValueError** if the input is negative. The **try-except** block in the main code catches this exception and prints the error message.

In machine learning and deep learning, error handling is crucial for:

- **Robustness**: Ensuring that your code can handle unexpected inputs or conditions.
- **Debugging**: Providing informative error messages to help you identify and fix issues.
- **Graceful degradation**: Allowing your models to continue operating even when some data is invalid.

By incorporating error handling into your machine learning and deep learning projects, you can create more reliable and resilient applications that can adapt to real-world scenarios.

Code organization and best practices

When writing code, it is crucial to ensure it is clean, well-organized, and properly documented. This is essential for long-term maintainability and effective collaboration among developers, especially in machine learning and deep learning projects where codebases can become complex.

Modules

A module is a Python file (with a **.py** extension) that contains definitions and statements. Modules are the building blocks of code organization. They allow you to:

- **Organize code**: Break down your code into smaller, manageable pieces, each with a specific purpose. This makes your code easier to read, maintain, and understand.
- **Promote reusability**: Define functions, classes, or variables in a module and reuse them in other parts of your project or even in different projects.
- **Avoid name clashes**: Modules create separate namespaces, preventing conflicts between names in different parts of your code.

Creating a module

Let us say you have a set of functions for data preprocessing. You can create a module named **data_preprocessing.py**, as shown here:

```
# data_preprocessing.py

def normalize_data(data):
    # ... (Normalization logic)

def clean_text(text):
    # ... (Text cleaning logic)
```

To use a module in another file, you can import and use the functions from your module as follows:

```
# main.py or .ipynb notebook

import data_preprocessing

data = ...  # Your raw data
normalized_data = data_preprocessing.normalize_data(data)
```

Packages

A package organizes related modules within a directory hierarchy. It is essentially a directory containing a particular file named **__init__.py** (which can be empty). Packages help you:

- **Structure large projects**: Group modules into logical categories, making your project's structure more transparent.
- **Create hierarchical namespaces**: Prevent name collisions in more significant projects by organizing modules into sub-packages.
- **Distribute code**: Easily share your code with others by packaging it up.

Creating a package

Let us extend our example. Create a directory named **my_ml_tools** and place **data_preprocessing.py** inside it. Also, create an empty **__init__.py** file in the same directory. Now you have the following package:

```
my_ml_tools/
    __init__.py
    data_preprocessing.py
```

Using a package

You can now import modules from your package, as shown here:

```
# main.py

from my_ml_tools import data_preprocessing

data = ...
normalized_data = data_preprocessing.normalize_data(data)
```

Reusable packages

We can create packages that can be installed and used in other projects. This is how we leverage the vast ecosystem of Python libraries for machine learning and deep learning:

- **Structure**: Organize your package with modules and subpackages.
- **Documentation**: Write clear docstrings and create a README file explaining how to use your package.
- **Distribution**: Use tools like **`setuptools`** and pip to package and distribute your code.

For example, to use a popular machine learning package, use the following code:

```
# main.py

from sklearn.model_selection import train_test_split
from sklearn.linear_model import LogisticRegression

# ... (Load your data)

X_train, X_test, y_train, y_test = train_test_split(X, y, test_size=0.2)
model = LogisticRegression()
model.fit(X_train, y_train)
```

In this example, we are using the **`scikit-learn`** package, a powerful library for machine learning. We import specific modules (**`train_test_split`** and **`LogisticRegression`**) to split our data and create a logistic regression model.

Accessing machine learning and deep learning tools by importing libraries

Python's strength in machine learning and deep learning lies in its rich library collection that provides pre-built implementations of algorithms, data structures, and utilities. Importing these libraries is essential to leverage their power and streamline your development process.

Standard libraries

Python's standard library offers modules that are useful for machine learning and deep learning tasks:

- **math**: Provides mathematical functions for operations like trigonometry, logarithms, and more.
- **random**: Generates random numbers, which are helpful in initializing model parameters or creating synthetic data.
- **os**: Interacts with the operating system, helpful for managing files and directories

For example, the following imports demonstrate how you can bring in some of Python's built-in standard libraries that are frequently useful in machine learning and deep learning projects:

```
import math
import random
import os
```

For a complete list and detailed documentation of all Python standard libraries, you can visit the official Python standard library documentation.

Third-party libraries

The real power of Python for machine learning and deep learning comes from its extensive collection of third-party libraries:

- **NumPy**: The fundamental library for numerical operations, providing support for arrays, matrices, and linear algebra.
- **Pandas**: A robust data analysis and manipulation tool, essential for working with structured data [e.g., **comma-separated values** (**CSV**) files, Dataframes].
- **Matplotlib**: A versatile plotting library for visualizing data and results.
- **Scikit-learn**: A comprehensive library for traditional machine learning algorithms (e.g., regression, classification, clustering).
- **TensorFlow and PyTorch**: Leading deep learning frameworks for building and training neural networks.

However, to import a third-party package, you first need to install it. For example, to import `numpy`, you need to execute the following command:

```
%pip install numpy
```

You can also install multiple third-party packages in one line, as shown here:

```
%pip install pandas matplotlib scikit-learn
```

Then, you can import the packages like this:

```
import numpy as np
import pandas as pd
import matplotlib.pyplot as plt
from sklearn.model_selection import train_test_split
import torch
```

Importing specific functions or classes

To avoid importing an entire library, you can import specific functions or classes using the `from ... import` syntax:

```
from sklearn.linear_model import LinearRegression
from torch import nn
```

Aliasing

An alias is an alternative, shorter name that you can give to a module (or a function, etc.) when you import it. This makes your code easier to read and type, especially if the original module name is long.

You can use the **as** keyword to create shorter aliases for long library names, as shown in the following code:

```
import numpy as np
import pandas as pd
```

Importance of importing libraries

The following are reasons why using libraries is important in any Python project:

- **Access to algorithms**: Libraries provide implementations of machine learning and deep learning algorithms, saving you from having to write them from scratch.
- **Data handling**: Libraries offer tools for loading, cleaning, transforming, and analyzing data.
- **Model building**: Frameworks like TensorFlow and PyTorch simplify the creation and training of complex neural networks.
- **Visualization**: Libraries like Matplotlib enable you to create informative plots and graphs to understand your data and results.

By mastering the art of importing libraries, you unlock a vast array of tools and resources that accelerate your machine learning and deep learning projects and empower you to build sophisticated models and applications.

Code formatting with PEP 8 standards

PEP 8, the official style guide for Python code, is a cornerstone of writing clean, readable, and maintainable code in the Python ecosystem. While adhering to PEP 8 might seem like a minor detail, it significantly impacts the long-term success of your machine learning and deep learning projects.

Importance of PEP 8 standards

PEP8 provides an extensive set of guidelines for Python code styling. The following are some reasons to use PEP8:

- **Readability**: PEP 8's guidelines ensure that your code is easy to read and understand, not just for you but also for others who might work on the project. This is particularly important in machine learning and deep learning, where code can quickly become complex due to intricate algorithms and data structures.
- **Consistency**: By following a typical style, you create a consistent codebase that is easier to navigate and debug. This consistency becomes invaluable when collaborating with other developers or revisiting your code after a long period.
- **Maintainability**: Clean and well-formatted code is more straightforward to maintain and modify. As your machine learning and deep learning projects evolve, PEP 8 helps ensure that changes can be made smoothly without introducing errors or inconsistencies.

Key PEP 8 recommendations

Some of the most important PEP8 recommendations are shown as follows:

- **Indentation**: Use four spaces for each level of indentation. Avoid tabs, as shown here:

```
# Good
for i in range(10):
    if i % 2 == 0:
        print(i)
```

- **Line length**: Limit lines to a maximum of 79 characters. This makes it easier to view code side-by-side in editors and prevents excessive horizontal scrolling:

```
# Good
result = some_function(argument1, argument2, argument3)
```

- **Blank lines**: Use blank lines to separate functions and classes and to group related code within functions:

```
def preprocess_data(data):
    # ... (Code for preprocessing)

def train_model(data):
    # ... (Code for training)
```

- **Naming conventions**: Use lowercase with underscores for variable and function names (`my_variable`, `calculate_loss`). Use CamelCase for class names (`MyClass`).
- **Comments**: Write clear and concise comments to explain the purpose and logic of your code. Use inline comments sparingly and focus on docstrings for functions, classes, and modules.

Observe the following code to understand the way to add comments and some naming conventions in action:

```
# Example of a docstring for a function
def calculate_accuracy(y_true, y_pred):
    """
    Calculates the accuracy of a model›s predictions.

    Args:
        y_true: True target values.
        y_pred: Predicted values.

    Returns:
        The accuracy score.
    «»»
    # ... (Code for calculating accuracy)
```

Tools for PEP 8 compliance

Many tools can help you check and automatically format your code to comply with PEP 8:

- **Linters**: Tools like ruff, flake8, and pylint analyze your code for style violations and potential errors.
- **Formatters**: Tools like black and autopep8 automatically reformat your code to adhere to PEP 8 standards.

Beyond PEP 8

While PEP 8 provides a solid foundation, there are other style guides and best practices you can explore to enhance your code quality further:

- **Google Python Style Guide**: A more comprehensive style guide with additional recommendations.
- **Clean code principles**: General principles for writing clean and maintainable code in any language.

By embracing PEP 8 and other best practices, you will create machine learning and deep learning code that is not only functional but also a pleasure to work with. Clean code leads to better collaboration, easier debugging, and, ultimately, more successful projects.

Comments and documentation

Comments and docstrings are essential for explaining your code.

- **Explaining your code for yourself and others**: Comments are brief notes within your code that clarify the purpose of specific lines or sections. Docstrings are more detailed explanations that describe functions, classes, or modules. In machine learning and deep learning, clear documentation is crucial for understanding complex algorithms and model architectures.

- You can also write comments on a single line, using the **#** character in front.

The following is an example of a function definition with a docstring that explains its purpose, inputs, and outputs:

```
def calculate_loss(y_true, y_pred):
    """
    Calculates the mean squared error loss between true - predicted values.

    Args:
        y_true: True target values.
        y_pred: Predicted values.

    Returns:
        The mean squared error loss.
    «»»
# This is a single line comment
return np.mean((y_true - y_pred) ** 2)
```

Object-oriented programming in Python

While optional for basic machine learning and deep learning tasks, OOP offers a powerful paradigm for structuring and organizing code, especially as projects grow in complexity. OOP principles like classes, inheritance, encapsulation, and polymorphism can be leveraged to create more modular, reusable, and maintainable machine learning and deep learning codebases. The details are as follows:

- **Classes and objects, blueprints and instances**: Think of a class as a blueprint for creating objects. The class defines the attributes (data) and methods (functions) that objects of that class will have. Objects are instances of a class, each with its unique set of attribute values.

  The following code shows a small example of how to create a class with an initializer and some methods:

```
class NeuralNetwork:
    def __init__(self, num_layers, num_neurons):
        self.num_layers = num_layers
        self.num_neurons = num_neurons
        # ... (Initialize weights and biases)

    def forward(self, inputs):
        # ... (Forward pass logic)

def backward(self, loss):
    # ... (Backpropagation logic)
```

  In this example, **NeuralNetwork** is a class that defines the structure of a neural network. The **__init__** method is a constructor method that initializes the object's attributes. The **forward** and **backward** methods implement the core functionality of the network.

- **Inheritance**: Inheritance enables the creation of new classes (child classes) that derive attributes and methods from existing classes (parent classes). This encourages code reuse and establishes a class hierarchy.

In machine learning and deep learning, you might have a base **`Model`** class and then create child classes for specific types of models like **`LinearRegression`**, **`DecisionTree`**, or **`NeuralNetwork`**.

The following code shows how to create a base class and then a class that inherits from the base class:

```
class Model:
    def __init__(self):
        # ... (Initialize common model attributes)

    def fit(self, X, y):
        # ... (Generic training logic)

    def predict(self, X):
        # ... (Generic prediction logic)

class LinearRegression(Model):
    def __init__(self):
        super().__init__()
        # ... (Initialize specific linear regression attributes)

    def fit(self, X, y):
        # ... (Specific linear regression training logic)
```

In the example aforementioned, **`super().__init__()`** is used inside the **`LinearRegression`** class's constructor. The **`super()`** function returns a temporary object of the parent class (Model), allowing you to call its methods. By calling **`super().In__init__()`**, you ensure that the initialization code in the parent class (**`Model`**) runs, so all the attributes and setup defined there are included in the child class (**`LinearRegression`**). This is crucial for proper inheritance and helps prevent code duplication.

- **Encapsulation, protecting data and behavior**: Encapsulation means bundling data and the methods that operate on that data within a class. This protects the data from being accidentally modified and provides a straightforward interface for interacting with objects. Refer to the following example:

```
class DataPreprocessor:
    def __init__(self, data):
        self._data = data  # Protected attribute

    def normalize(self):
        # ... (Normalization logic)

    def clean(self):
        # ... (Cleaning logic)
```

- **Polymorphism, flexibility with different objects**: Polymorphism allows you to use objects of different classes interchangeably if they share a standard interface. For instance, you could have other types of optimizers (e.g., **`SGD`**, **`Adam`**) that all implement a **`step()`** method to update model parameters. This lets you write code that works with any optimizer without needing to know its specific type. Do not worry if this seems complex at this time; we will learn PyTorch and optimizers in a later chapter.

```
def train_model(model, optimizer, data):
    # ...
    optimizer.step()  # Works with any optimizer that has a step() method
    # ...
```

In essence, OOP provides a structured way to think about and implement complex machine learning and deep learning systems. By leveraging its principles, you can create code that is easier to understand, maintain, and extend, ultimately leading to more successful and impactful projects.

Conclusion

In this chapter, we provided an overview of the foundations of Python on a solid groundwork covering essential concepts like data types, variables, control flow, functions, and object-oriented programming. With the knowledge from this chapter, you are well-equipped to tackle the exciting challenges and opportunities that machine learning presents. So, embrace Python, experiment, and keep learning–your machine learning adventure is just beginning.

In the next chapter, we will learn some of the most popular libraries in the world of machine learning in Python; these are considered the *go-to* tools for most projects.

Exercises

We will be building a simple student gradebook. This exercise brings together many of the concepts covered in this chapter, such as dictionaries, functions, classes, and error handling, into a small but practical project. By simulating a gradebook, you will see how Python data structures and programming techniques can be combined to solve a real-world problem.

The gradebook example mirrors how you might structure and manage data in actual machine learning or data science projects. While this project is simple, the same principles can later be applied to managing datasets, building modular code, and ensuring reliability through error handling.

Requirements

The exercise must comply with the following requirements:

- **Data structure**: Create a dictionary called gradebook to store student information. The keys should be student names (e.g., Luis), and the values should be lists containing their grades (e.g., [95, 88, 92]).
- **Function for average**: Write a function calculate_average(grades) that takes a list of grades as input and returns the average grade.
- **Class for gradebook**: Create a class Gradebook with the following methods:
  - **__init__**: Initializes an empty gradebook.
  - **add_student(name)**: Adds a new student to the gradebook with an empty list for grades.
  - **add_grade(name, grade)**: Adds a grade to the specified student's list of grades.
  - **get_average(name)**: Calculates and returns the average grade for the specified student using the calculate_average function.
- **Error handling**: Implement error handling in your add_grade and get_average methods using try-except blocks. For example, catch ValueError if the grade is not a number and KeyError if the student's name does not exist in the grade book.

Write a script as follows:

- Creates a Gradebook object.
- Add a few students to the gradebook.
- Prompts the user to enter grades for each student (or you can simulate this).
- Calculates and prints the average grade for each student.

Bonus challenges:

- Add a method to print the entire gradebook in a formatted way.
- Implement a feature to find the student with the highest average grade.
- Allow the user to remove a student or modify existing grades.

Note: Check the official GitHub repo for the solution.

Choose the odd one out from the following:

1. Which of the following are the primary data types used in Python for machine learning?
   a. char
   b. int
   c. float
   d. str
   e. bool
   f. list
   g. dict
   h. set
   i. tuple
2. Which of the following are popular third-party libraries used in machine learning with Python? (Select all that apply)
   a. NumPy
   b. Pandas
   c. Matplotlib
   d. Scikit-learn
   e. Requests
   f. TensorFlow
   g. PyTorch
3. Which of the following are the benefits of adhering to PEP 8 style guidelines in machine learning code? (Select all that apply)
   a. Improved code readability
   b. Easier collaboration with other developers
   c. Enhanced code maintainability
   d. Faster code execution

Answers: Char, request and faster code execution are the odd one out.

Multiple choice questions

1. **What is the crucial difference between a list and a tuple in Python?**
   a. Lists are mutable, while tuples are immutable.
   b. Lists can only contain numbers, while tuples can contain any data type.
   c. Lists are ordered, while tuples are unordered.
   d. Tuples can be used as dictionary keys, while lists cannot.

2. **How are dictionaries primarily used in machine learning?**
   a. Storing sequential data like time series.
   b. Organizing configuration settings and hyperparameters.
   c. Representing images and pixel data.
   d. Performing mathematical operations on arrays.
3. **What is the purpose of control flow in machine learning?**
   a. Defining the structure of neural networks.
   b. Making decisions and controlling the execution of code based on conditions.
   c. Storing large amounts of numerical data.
   d. Visualizing data and results.
4. **Which keyword is used to define a function in Python?**
   a. func
   b. define
   c. def
   d. function
5. **What are lambda functions in Python?**
   a. Functions that can only be used once.
   b. Functions that are imported from external libraries.
   c. Anonymous functions defined in a single line.
   d. Functions that always return a Boolean value.
6. **What is the primary purpose of the try-except block in Python?**
   a. Optimizing code for faster execution.
   b. Defining custom data types.
   c. Catching and handling exceptions (errors) during code execution.
   d. Creating loops for repetitive tasks.
7. **How do modules and packages contribute to the organization of machine learning projects?**
   a. They provide pre-built machine learning algorithms.
   b. They enable data visualization.
   c. They help structure code into reusable units and prevent naming conflicts.
   d. They automate the process of hyperparameter tuning.

Answers

1.	a.
2.	b.
3.	b.
4.	c.
5.	c.
6.	c.
7.	c.

Key terms

- **Data types**: The classifications of data items in Python, indicating how the data should be handled. Examples include **integers (int)**, **floats (float)**, **strings (str)**, **booleans (bool)**, **lists (list)**, **dictionaries (dict)**, **sets (set)**, and **tuples (tuple)**.
- **Variables**: Named containers used to store data values in Python. The type of data a variable holds can change dynamically.
- **Operators**: Symbols that perform specific operations on values. In Python, these include arithmetic operators (+, -, *, /, etc.), comparison operators (==, !=, <, >, etc.), and logical operators (and, or, not).
- **Control flow**: The order in which statements are executed in a program. Python uses conditional statements (if, elif, else) and loops (for, while) to control this flow.
- **Functions**: Reusable blocks of code designed to perform specific tasks. Functions in Python are defined using the def keyword.
- **Lambda functions**: Small, anonymous functions defined using the lambda keyword. They are typically used for short, one-time operations.
- **Lists**: Ordered collections of items that can be of any data type. Lists are mutable, meaning their contents can be changed.
- **Dictionaries**: Unordered collections of key-value pairs, where keys are unique, and values can be of any data type. Dictionaries are used for storing structured data.
- **Sets**: Unordered collections of unique items, useful for operations like finding unique elements or removing duplicates.
- **Tuples**: Ordered collections of items that are immutable (cannot be changed after creation). Tuples are often used to represent fixed combinations of values.
- **Error handling**: The process of anticipating, detecting, and resolving programming errors (exceptions). Python uses try-except blocks to handle exceptions.
- **Modules**: Python files (with a .py extension) that contain definitions and statements. Modules help organize code and promote reusability.
- **Packages**: Directories containing related modules and a special file named __init__.py. Packages allow for the hierarchical organization of larger projects.
- **PEP 8**: The official style guide for Python code. It provides recommendations for code formatting, naming conventions, and more, aiming to improve readability and consistency.
- **Object-oriented programming (OOP)**: A programming paradigm that uses objects (instances of classes) to represent and manipulate data. OOP concepts include classes, objects, inheritance, encapsulation, and polymorphism.
- **Docstrings**: String literals that occur as the first statement in a module, function, class, or method definition. They provide a convenient way of associating documentation with Python objects.

References

1. *Built-in Exceptions*, **https://docs.python.org/3/library/exceptions.html**
2. *The Python Standard Library*, **https://docs.python.org/3/library/**

CHAPTER 4

Essential Machine Learning Libraries in Python

Introduction

In the previous chapter, you learned the fundamentals of Python, equipping yourself with the essential building blocks for your machine learning journey. Now, it is time to level up your skills by exploring the powerful libraries that make Python the go-to language for AI enthusiasts and professionals alike.

Think of these libraries as your toolkit, filled with pre-built tools and gadgets that simplify complex tasks and accelerate your progress. They are like having a team of experts working behind the scenes, handling the tedious details so you can focus on the big picture—building intelligent models and applications.

In this chapter, you will be introduced to three indispensable libraries: NumPy, Pandas, and Matplotlib. These libraries are the backbone of many machine learning projects, providing the tools to handle, analyze, and visualize data efficiently.

Numerical Python (**NumPy**) is your numerical powerhouse, NumPy, enables you to perform lightning-fast calculations on arrays and matrices of data. It is like having a supercomputer at your disposal, crunching numbers with ease. Pandas is your data wrangler, Pandas, simplifies working with structured data, such as tables and spreadsheets. It is like having a personal assistant who organizes and cleans your data, making it ready for analysis. Matplotlib is your visualization wizard, and it empowers you to create stunning graphs and charts that bring your data to life. It is like having an artist who can paint a vivid picture of your findings.

Structure

This chapter contains the following topics:

- Introduction to NumPy for numerical computations
- Introduction to Pandas for data manipulation and analysis
- Introduction to Matplotlib for data visualization

Objectives

This chapter's objectives are to understand NumPy's core features and capabilities, learn advanced techniques for efficient data manipulation, and explore how NumPy integrates with machine learning workflows. Additionally, you will gain proficiency in using Pandas for data manipulation and analysis and master the basics of Matplotlib for data visualization. By the end of this chapter, you will have an understanding of these libraries and how to use them effectively in your machine learning projects. You will be able to manipulate data, perform calculations and create visualizations like a pro. Get ready to unlock the full potential of Python for machine learning.

Introduction to NumPy for numerical computations

Numpy is the backbone of all modern libraries for deep learning, including TensorFlow, PyTorch, and others, let us review why it is so important. Let us understand the reason to use NumPy. Imagine trying to build a skyscraper using only toothpicks and glue. It would be tedious and inefficient. Similarly, performing complex numerical computations in Python using only its built-in data types (like lists) would be slow and cumbersome. That is where NumPy comes to the rescue. NumPy is a powerful library designed explicitly for numerical operations, making it much faster and more efficient than using lists.

NumPy introduces the **n-dimensional array (ndarray)**, a flexible data type that can represent anything from simple vectors to complex matrices. This efficiency and flexibility make NumPy the foundation upon which many machine learning libraries are built. Its comprehensive set of mathematical functions makes it an indispensable tool for any aspiring data scientist or machine learning engineer.

Core features

The core features of NumPy provide a powerful foundation for numerical computing, with capabilities that include:

- **N-dimensional array (ndarray)**: The core data structure for efficient storage and manipulation of numerical data.
- **Broadcasting**: Seamless operations on arrays of different shapes.
- **Vectorization**: Apply operations to entire arrays at once, eliminating the need for slow Python loops.
- **Universal Functions (ufuncs)**: High-performance functions that operate elementwise on arrays.
- **Linear algebra**: Functions for matrix operations, including multiplication, inversion, and eigenvalue decomposition.
- **Random number generation**: Functions for generating random numbers from various distributions.
- **Fourier transforms**: Essential functions for signal processing and image analysis.

In the following sections, we will examine each of these topics in detail, using some code examples.

ndarray

ndarray is the core data structure of NumPy. With NumPy, you can create arrays of 1, 2, 3, or n dimensions; you will often use these ndarrays when using machine learning algorithms. A 2-dimensional (for example, 3x3) array is basically the same as a matrix.

Here is how you can create one-dimensional and two-dimensional arrays in NumPy:

```
import numpy as np

# 1D array from a list
arr1 = np.array([1, 2, 3])

# 2D array from a list of lists
arr2 = np.array([[1, 2], [3, 4]])

# 1D array from a tuple
arr3 = np.array((5, 6, 7))
```

Array creation, indexing, and slicing

NumPy provides powerful mechanisms for creating, accessing, and manipulating arrays, which form the foundation of numerical operations in machine learning applications.

Creating arrays

NumPy provides several ways to create ndarrays, including using built-in functions. As you can see, you can create arrays with zeros, ones, a fixed number, or even other handy functions to fill arrays based on your requirements. These functions offer versatility and convenience, allowing you to efficiently initialize arrays for various data manipulation and machine learning tasks.

Let us examine some common methods for creating arrays with NumPy:

```
# 2x3 array of zeros
arr4 = np.zeros((2, 3))
print(arr4)
# 3x2 array of ones
arr5 = np.ones((3, 2))
print(arr5)
# 2x2 array filled with 9
arr6 = np.full((2, 2), 9)
print(arr6)
# Array with elements from 10 to 19 (exclusive) with a step of 2
arr7 = np.arange(10, 20, 2)
print(arr7)
# Array with 5 evenly spaced numbers between 0 and 1 (inclusive)
arr8 = np.linspace(0, 1, 5)
print(arr8)
# 2x3 array of random numbers between 0 and 1
arr9 = np.random.rand(2, 3)
print(arr9)
```

Response:

```
[[0. 0. 0.]
 [0. 0. 0.]]
[[1. 1.]
 [1. 1.]
 [1. 1.]]
[[9 9]
 [9 9]]
[10 12 14 16 18]
[0.   0.25 0.5  0.75 1.  ]
[[0.96826702 0.09488261 0.38358317]
 [0.34148313 0.74309348 0.9412298 ]]
```

Indexing and slicing

Indexing and slicing in NumPy allow you to select and work with specific parts of an array. With indexing, you can access individual elements by their position; while slicing lets you extract entire sections or ranges of elements from an array. For example, you can retrieve a single value, a row, a column, or a subarray using simple, intuitive syntax. These features make it easy to manipulate and analyze data efficiently, which is especially useful in machine learning tasks where working with subsets of data is common.

The following example shows how to access and modify array elements in NumPy:

```
arr = np.array([10, 20, 30, 40, 50])

print(arr[0]) # Get first element. Output: 10
print(arr[2:4]) # Get elements in 3rd to 5th index. Output: [30 40]
print(arr[1:]) # Get elements starting at 2nd index. Output: [20 30 40 50]
print(arr[-1]) # Get last element. Output: 50

arr[1] = 25 # Modify an element, at index 2nd.
arr[3:] = [45, 55] # Modify multiple elements, starting at index 4th
```

Broadcasting

In NumPy, broadcasting facilitates operations on arrays with different shapes by automatically aligning their dimensions during arithmetic operations. This capability enables seamless computation across arrays of varying sizes and shapes, promoting efficient and concise code for data transformations and mathematical operations essential in machine learning applications.

Here is how NumPy automatically applies operations to arrays of different shapes using broadcasting:

```
arr1 = np.array([[1, 2, 3], [4, 5, 6]])
arr2 = np.array([10, 20, 30])
result = arr1 + arr2

print(result)
# Output:
# [[11 22 33]
#  [14 25 36]]
```

Vectorization

Vectorization in NumPy means performing operations on entire arrays without using explicit Python loops. Instead of processing each element one by one, NumPy applies operations to all elements at once using fast, optimized code written in lower-level languages like C. This approach makes calculations much faster and more efficient, especially when working with large datasets or complex mathematical tasks. Vectorization is a key technique in machine learning and scientific computing because it allows you to write simpler, more readable code that runs much faster.

This snippet demonstrates elementwise operations on arrays without explicit loops:

```
arr1 = np.array([1, 2, 3])
arr2 = np.array([4, 5, 6])

print(arr1 + arr2) # Output: [5 7 9]
print(arr1 - arr2) # Output: [-3 -3 -3]
print(arr1 * arr2) # Output: [4 10 18]
print(arr1 / arr2) # Output: [0.25 0.4 0.5]
```

Universal functions

NumPy's ufuncs are optimized functions that operate elementwise on arrays, providing high-performance computation of mathematical operations. These functions enable efficient processing of array data and support a wide range of mathematical transformations, such as trigonometric functions (**np.sin, np.cos**), exponential (**np.exp**), and logarithmic (**np.log**) operations. ufuncs are essential tools in numerical computing and machine learning because they can handle large datasets with speed and precision.

NumPy's ufuncs make it easy to apply mathematical functions elementwise:

```
arr = np.array([0, np.pi/2, np.pi])

print(np.sin(arr))  # Output: [0.0 1.0 0.0]
print(np.cos(arr))  # Output: [ 1.0 0.0 -1.0]
print(np.exp(arr))  # Output: [ 1.  2.71828183 23.14069263]
print(np.log(arr))  # Output: [-inf  0.45158271  1.14472989]
```

Linear algebra

In NumPy, linear algebra capabilities are robust, offering a comprehensive suite of functions tailored for essential operations like matrix multiplication, inversion, and eigenvalue decomposition. These functionalities are pivotal in scientific computing and machine learning, enabling tasks such as solving systems of linear equations (**np.linalg.solve**) with ease and efficiency. NumPy's optimized implementations ensure reliable and high-performance computations, making it a cornerstone for numerical methods in various domains.

The following example shows how to solve a system of linear equations with NumPy:

```
A = np.array([[1, 2], [3, 4]])
b = np.array([5, 6])

x = np.linalg.solve(A, b)
print(x) # Output: [-4.  4.5]
```

Random number generation

NumPy provides extensive capabilities for generating random numbers from different distributions, which is crucial for simulations and stochastic algorithms. Functions like **np.random.rand** allows creation of arrays filled with random numbers uniformly distributed between 0 and 1, facilitating tasks such as random sampling and statistical analysis in machine learning, statistical modeling, and computational simulations. These tools ensure reproducibility and control over randomness, which is essential for scientific research and experimentation.

You can generate arrays of random numbers for simulations and experiments:

```
random_array = np.random.rand(2, 3)  # 2x3 array of random numbers between 0 and 1
print(random_array)
```

Response:

```
[[0.73260584 0.52278857 0.44716718]
[0.71060512 0.26267776 0.99850241]]
```

Fourier transforms

NumPy includes powerful functions for performing Fourier transforms, which are fundamental tools in signal processing and image analysis. These transforms allow the decomposition of signals into frequency components, revealing patterns and structures that are otherwise hidden in the time or spatial domain. Functions like **np.fft.fft** efficiently compute the Fourier transform of arrays, enabling tasks such as spectral analysis, noise filtering, and compression in diverse fields, including telecommunications, medical imaging, and astronomy. NumPy's optimized implementations ensure rapid computation and accuracy, supporting advanced data analysis and processing workflows.

This snippet demonstrates how to compute a simple Fourier transform in NumPy:

```
# Simple example of a Fourier transform
signal = np.array([0, 1, 0, -1])
transformed_signal = np.fft.fft(signal)
print(transformed_signal)
```

Response:

```
[0.+0.j 0.-2.j 0.+0.j 0.+2.j]
```

Advanced indexing and slicing techniques

NumPy offers powerful indexing and slicing capabilities beyond basic operations, enabling efficient data manipulation.

NumPy offers powerful indexing and slicing capabilities beyond basic operations, enabling the following efficient data manipulation techniques:

- **Boolean indexing**: Use Boolean arrays to filter elements based on conditions.

  Here is an example of selecting elements based on conditions:

```
arr = np.array([1, 2, 3, 4, 5])
mask = arr > 2
print(arr[mask]) # Output: [3 4 5]
```

- **Fancy indexing**: Index arrays with arrays of indices or slices. The following example shows how to extract elements using an array of indices:

```
arr = np.array([10, 20, 30, 40, 50])
indices = np.array([1, 3])
print(arr[indices]) # Output: [20 40]
```

Performance optimization

Optimize NumPy operations for speed and memory efficiency. The details are as follows:

- **Avoiding copies**: NumPy provides techniques to avoid unnecessary array copies, such as using views and in-place operations, for example, using **arr.view()** creates a view of the original array **arr**, which shares the same underlying data but can have a different shape. This approach avoids memory duplication and improves performance by minimizing overhead associated with copying data.

  This code creates a view of an array without copying data:

```
arr = np.array([1, 2, 3])
arr_view = arr.view()
```

- **Memory management**: Effective memory management in NumPy involves strategies like resizing arrays and considering memory layout (C vs. Fortran order). Resizing arrays using **np.resize()** or **arr.resize()** allows efficient allocation and utilization of memory. Additionally, understanding and optimizing memory layout, whether arrays are stored in C-contiguous order (row-major) or Fortran-contiguous order (column-major), can impact performance, especially in operations involving large multidimensional arrays.

These optimization techniques are essential for maximizing computational efficiency, reducing runtime, and enhancing overall performance in data-intensive applications such as scientific computing, numerical simulations, and machine learning algorithms.

File I/O

NumPy provides methods to save and load arrays from disk efficiently.

Use **np.save** and **np.load** to save and load arrays in **.npy** format.

NumPy allows saving and loading arrays to disk:

```
arr = np.array([1, 2, 3])
np.save('array.npy', arr)

loaded_arr = np.load('array.npy')
print(loaded_arr)  # Output: [1 2 3]
```

Basic array operations

NumPy provides a comprehensive set of functions and operators to perform various operations on arrays, making complex calculations straightforward and efficient.

Arithmetic operations

NumPy allows you to perform element-wise arithmetic operations on arrays.

Refer to the following code to perform basic arithmetic operations on arrays:

```
arr1 = np.array([1, 2, 3])
arr2 = np.array([4, 5, 6])

print(arr1 + arr2)  # Output: [5 7 9]
print(arr1 - arr2)  # Output: [-3 -3 -3]
print(arr1 * arr2)  # Output: [4 10 18]
print(arr1 / arr2)  # Output: [0.25 0.4 0.5]
```

These operations apply arithmetic operations (+, -, *, /) elementwise between corresponding array elements. NumPy's optimized implementation ensures efficient computation, making it ideal for numerical computations in fields such as physics, engineering, and data science.

Mathematical functions

NumPy provides a wide range of mathematical functions that can be applied to arrays.

The following code applies trigonometric and exponential functions to arrays:

```
arr = np.array([0, np.pi/2, np.pi])

print(np.sin(arr))  # Output: [0.0 1.0 0.0]
print(np.cos(arr))  # Output: [ 1.0 0.0 -1.0]
print(np.exp(arr))  # Output: [ 1.          2.71828183 23.14069263]
print(np.log(arr))  # Output: [-inf  0.45158271  1.14472989]
```

These functions (**np.sin, np.cos, np.exp, np.log**, etc.) operate elementwise on arrays, allowing efficient computation of trigonometric, exponential, logarithmic, and other mathematical transformations. It is important to note that **np.log(arr)** returns **-inf** for elements where **arr** is 0, highlighting the need to handle edge cases in numerical computations. NumPy's optimized implementations ensure reliable and high-performance calculations, supporting advanced data analysis and scientific computing tasks.

NumPy in machine learning

NumPy plays a crucial role in machine learning workflows. The following sections provides a detailed explanation and examples of how NumPy integrates seamlessly with machine learning tasks.

Feature scaling

Feature scaling is a crucial preprocessing step in machine learning that standardizes the range of independent variables or features in the dataset. This process enhances the performance and stability of many machine learning algorithms, particularly those sensitive to the scale of input data.

In NumPy, feature scaling can be achieved using operations such as mean and standard deviation.

This snippet shows how to normalize data using mean and standard deviation:

```
data = np.array([[10, 2], [15, 5], [8, 3]])
scaled_data = (data - np.mean(data, axis=0)) / np.std(data, axis=0)
print(scaled_data)
```

Normalization is a data preprocessing technique that adjusts the values of features in a dataset so that they share a common scale. In the preceding example, normalization is performed by subtracting the mean and dividing by the standard deviation for each feature (column) in the data. This process ensures that each feature has a mean of 0 and a standard deviation of 1.

For instance:

- **np.mean(data, axis=0)** computes the mean along each column of **data**.
- **np.std(data, axis=0)** calculates the standard deviation along each column of **data**.
- **(data - np.mean(data, axis=0)) / np.std(data, axis=0)** performs the scaling operation, ensuring each feature in **scaled_data** has a mean of 0 and a standard deviation of 1.

Normalizing data in this way improves the convergence speed and performance of many machine learning algorithms, such as gradient-based methods (like linear regression and neural networks) and distance-based algorithms (like k-nearest neighbors). Properly scaled features prevent those with larger values from dominating the learning process, leading to more balanced and effective model training and evaluation.

Data transformation

NumPy is also useful for transforming data into the format required by machine learning algorithms. For example, you might need to reshape an array, transpose a matrix, or flatten a multi-dimensional array into a one-dimensional vector.

NumPy equips you with versatile tools to reshape and manipulate your data arrays effectively. Here is how you can perform common data transformations.

NumPy makes it easy to reshape, transpose, and flatten arrays:

```
import numpy as np

# Original data
```

```
data = np.array([[1, 2, 3],
                 [4, 5, 6]])

# Reshaping
reshaped_data = data.reshape(3, 2)  # Change to a 3x2 array
print("Reshaped Data:\n", reshaped_data)

# Transposing
transposed_data = data.T  # Swap rows and columns
print("\nTransposed Data:\n", transposed_data)

# Flattening
flattened_data = data.flatten()  # Convert to a 1D array
print("\nFlattened Data:\n", flattened_data)
```

Response:

```
Reshaped Data:
 [[1 2]
 [3 4]
 [5 6]]

Transposed Data:
 [[1 4]
 [2 5]
 [3 6]]

Flattened Data:
 [1 2 3 4 5 6]
```

The explanation is as follows:

- **Reshaping (data.reshape(3, 2))**: This operation rearranges the elements while maintaining their order. It transforms the original 2x3 array data into a new shape of 3 rows and 2 columns (`reshaped_data`).
- **Transposing (data.T)**: This transforms the original array data, effectively swapping its rows and columns. It produces `transposed_data`, where rows become columns and vice versa.
- **Flattening (data.flatten())**: Flattens the original multi-dimensional array data into a one-dimensional array (`flattened_data`). This transformation collapses all dimensions into a single sequence, which is helpful for operations requiring a linear sequence of data.

These transformations are crucial for preparing data before feeding it into machine learning algorithms. Reshaping ensures that data conforms to the expected input shape, transposing can be useful for manipulating data orientation, and flattening simplifies the handling of complex data structures. NumPy's efficient implementations ensure these operations are performed swiftly, even with large datasets, making it an invaluable tool in data preprocessing for machine learning tasks.

Introduction to Pandas for data manipulation and analysis

Pandas is a powerful and widely used Python library that provides flexible and intuitive data structures, most notably the DataFrame, which is like a spreadsheet or a **Structured Query Language** (**SQL**) table. It also offers a rich set of functions specifically designed for efficient data manipulation and analysis. With Pandas, you can easily load, clean, transform, and explore various types of datasets, making it an essential tool for the crucial steps of data preparation and **exploratory data analysis** (**EDA**) in any machine learning project. It simplifies everyday tasks such as handling missing data, filtering rows, selecting columns, merging datasets, and performing aggregations, all of which are fundamental for getting your data ready for modeling.

Reason to use Pandas

Imagine you have a massive spreadsheet filled with customer data, sales figures, or experimental results. Making sense of massive spreadsheets filled with customer data, sales figures, or experimental results requires efficient tools for cleaning, filtering, transforming, and extracting meaningful insights.

That is where Pandas comes in. Pandas, a master of data manipulation, is a powerful library designed to make working with structured data super easy. It provides intuitive data structures and functions that allow you to manipulate and analyze data effortlessly.

At the heart of Pandas are two primary data structures:

- **Series**: A one-dimensional labeled array capable of holding any data type. Think of it as a single column of data with an index (like row labels).
- **DataFrame**: A two-dimensional labeled data structure with columns of potentially different types. Think of it as a table where each column can hold a different kind of data (e.g., numbers, strings, Booleans).

These data structures, along with Pandas' extensive collection of functions, make it easy to perform a wide range of data manipulation and analysis tasks, such as:

- **Reading and writing data**: Load data from various formats (like CSV, Excel, SQL databases) and save it back in different formats.
- **Cleaning data**: Handle missing values, duplicates, and outliers.
- **Transforming data**: Add, delete, or modify columns, merge and reshape datasets, and apply functions to data.
- **Filtering and querying**: Select specific rows or columns based on conditions.
- **Aggregating and grouping**: Calculate summary statistics (like mean, median, sum) for groups of data.
- **Time series analysis**: Work with time-stamped data, resample it, and perform rolling calculations.

Pandas in machine learning

Pandas is indispensable in machine learning workflows, playing a crucial role in the following:

- **Data preparation**: Load, clean, and transform your data to make it suitable for training machine learning models.
- **Feature engineering**: Create new features from existing ones to improve model performance.
- **EDA**: Gain insights into your data by summarizing it, visualizing it, and identifying patterns.

Core features

Pandas offers a comprehensive set of features that make it the preferred tool for data manipulation in Python:

- **Data structures**: Series and DataFrames are the building blocks for working with structured data.
- **Input/Output**: Tools for reading and writing data in various formats.
- **Data cleaning**: Functions for handling missing data, duplicates, and outliers.
- **Data transformation**: Operations for merging, reshaping, and pivoting datasets.
- **Indexing and selection**: Flexible mechanisms for accessing and modifying data.
- **Aggregation and grouping**: These are functions for calculating summary statistics and performing group-by operations.
- **Time series**: Tools for working with time-stamped data.
- **Categorical data**: Support for categorical data types and operations.
- **Plotting**: Integration with Matplotlib for basic plotting.

Data loading, cleaning, and transformation

Effective machine learning requires high-quality data. Pandas excels at the critical tasks of loading data from various sources, cleaning it to address issues like missing values, and transforming it into formats suitable for analysis and modeling.

Reading data

Pandas provides functions to read and write data from various sources, which is crucial in machine learning and deep learning because data often comes in various formats. Efficiently loading this data is the first step in any data analysis or machine learning pipeline. The details are as follows:

- **CSV files**: `pd.read_csv()`
- **Excel files**: `pd.read_excel()`
- **SQL databases**: `pd.read_sql()`
- **JSON files**: `pd.read_json()`
- **HTML tables**: `pd.read_html()`

The `pd.read_html()` function allows you to extract tables from HTML pages.

Here is how to load a dataset from a CSV file into a Pandas DataFrame:

```
import pandas as pd

df = pd.read_csv("data.csv")  # Load data from a CSV file
print(df.head())  # Display the first few rows of the dataframe
```

Response:

```
   A  B   C
0  1  4   7
1  2 -5  -8
2 -3  6   9
3  4 -7  10
```

This snippet demonstrates how to load a dataset from a CSV file, which is a standard format for datasets. The **head()** function is used to verify that the data has been loaded correctly and quickly.

Cleaning data

In the context of machine learning, data cleaning is essential because models trained on clean data perform better and generalize well to new, unseen data. Data cleaning involves identifying and correcting errors or inconsistencies in your dataset. For example, missing data refers to instances where certain values are absent or undefined in your dataset, often represented as **not a number** (Nan). Pandas offers several functions to handle these missing values, as well as to remove duplicate entries and detect outliers, all of which contribute to preparing a high-quality dataset for model training. The details are as follows:

- Remove rows or columns with missing values: **df.dropna()**
- Fill missing values with a specified value (e.g., 0, mean, median): **df.fillna(value)**
- Fill missing values using interpolation methods: **df.interpolate()**

The following code shows how to remove rows, fill empty values with zeros, and drop duplicates. It also removes missing values, fills empty cells, and drops duplicates:

```
# Remove rows with missing values
df.dropna(inplace=True)

# Fill missing values with 0
df.fillna(0, inplace=True)

# Remove duplicate rows
df.drop_duplicates(inplace=True)

# Display the cleaned dataframe
print(df.head())
```

The **dropna()** function removes any rows with missing values, ensuring the dataset is complete. The **fillna(0)** function replaces missing values with 0, a common strategy to maintain dataset integrity. **drop_duplicates()** removes any duplicate rows, which is essential for preventing redundancy in the data.

Transforming data

Transforming data is critical for feature engineering, which directly impacts the performance of machine learning models. Pandas allows you to add, delete, or modify columns in a DataFrame.

This example demonstrates adding, deleting, and modifying columns:

```
df["new_column"] = df["A"] + df["B"]  # Add a new column
df.drop("C", axis=1, inplace=True)  # Delete a column
df["A"] = df["B"] * 2 # Modify a column
# Display the transformed dataframe
print(df.head())
```

Response:

```
    A  B  new_column
0   8  4           5
1 -10 -5          -3
2  12  6           3
3 -14 -7          -3
```

Creating new features (like **`new_column`**) can help models capture additional patterns in the data. Dropping irrelevant columns (**`column3`**) reduces noise, and modifying existing columns (**`column1`**) can help scale or normalize features for better model performance.

Advanced transformations

You can also merge and reshape datasets using functions like **`pd.merge()`**, **`pd.concat()`**, **`df.pivot()`**, and **`df.stack()`**. These are essential for combining datasets from different sources or reshaping data into a format suitable for analysis.

You can merge, concatenate, pivot, and stack DataFrames as shown here:

```
# Merging two dataframes on a common column
merged_df = pd.merge(df1, df2, on="common_column")

# Concatenating two dataframes
concatenated_df = pd.concat([df1, df2], axis=0)

# Reshaping a dataframe with pivot
pivot_df = df.pivot(index="date", columns="category", values="value")

# Stacking a dataframe
stacked_df = df.stack()

# Display the transformed dataframes
print(merged_df.head())
print(concatenated_df.head())
print(pivot_df.head())
print(stacked_df.head())
```

Response:

```
Merged DataFrame:
    common_column value1 value2
0               1      A      D
1               2      B      E

Concatenated DataFrame:
    common_column value1 value2
0               1      A    NaN
1               2      D    NaN
2               3      C    NaN
0               1    NaN      D
1               2    NaN      E


Pivoted DataFrame:
 category     X   Y
date
2021-01-01  10  30
2021-01-02  20  40
```

```
Stacked DataFrame:
 0  date          2021-01-01
    category               X
    value                 10
1  date          2021-01-02
    category               X
dtype: object
```

Refer to the following list to build an understanding:

- **Merged DataFrame**: The `pd.merge(df1, df2, on="common_column")` operation combines two DataFrames (`df1` and `df2`) by matching rows where the values in `common_column` are the same. The result is a new DataFrame that includes columns from both original `DataFrames`, but only for rows where the `"common_column"` values match. For example, if both `DataFrames` have rows with `common_column` values 1 and 2, those rows are merged, resulting in columns `common_column`, `value1`, and `value2`.
- **Concatenated DataFrame**: The `pd.concat([df1, df2], axis=0)` operation stacks the two DataFrames on top of each other, adding the rows of `df2` below the rows of `df1`. If the DataFrames have different columns, missing values are filled with `NaN`. In the example, the first three rows come from `df1` (with `value2` as `NaN`), and the next two rows come from `df2` (with `value1` as `NaN`).
- **Pivoted DataFrame**: The `df.pivot(index="date", columns="category", values="value")` operation reshapes the DataFrame so that each unique value in the `"category"` column becomes a new column, the `"date"` column becomes the index (row labels), and the `"value"` column fills the table. This is useful for turning long-form data into a wide format, making it easier to compare values across categories and dates.
- **Stacked DataFrame**: The `df.stack()` operation compresses the columns of the DataFrame into a single column, creating a Series with a multi-level index. This helps convert a wide DataFrame into a long format, which can be useful for certain types of analysis or plotting. The output shows each row's data as a sequence of key-value pairs, grouped by the original row index.

These advanced transformations allow for powerful data manipulation capabilities, making it possible to integrate and reshape datasets in ways that are necessary for complex data analysis tasks in machine learning projects.

Data types and conversion

Understanding and converting data types is essential because machine learning algorithms often require data to be in specific formats. Incorrect data types can lead to errors or suboptimal model performance.

Key data types in Pandas are as follows:

- **Numeric types**: `int`, `float`
- **String types**: In Pandas, text data is usually stored as the `object` data type. This can be confusing because when you check a DataFrame's data types, you will often see `object` instead of `str` or `string`. In most cases, `object` means the column contains strings, but it can also hold mixed types or even Python objects.
- **Datetime types**: `datetime64`
- **Categorical types**: `category`

The following are the details about converting data types:

- **Convert to numeric**: `pd.to_numeric()`
- **Convert to datetime**: `pd.to_datetime()`
- **Convert to categorical**: `df['column'] = df['column'].astype('category')`

As you can see in Python, it is easy to convert a value from one type to another, from string to number, from string to datetime, or even convert category values to Category type.

Here is how to convert DataFrame columns to numeric, datetime, or categorical types:

```
# Load dataset
df = pd.read_csv("data.csv")

# Convert a column to numeric
df["numeric_column"] = pd.to_numeric(df["numeric_column"])

# Convert a column to datetime
df["date_column"] = pd.to_datetime(df["date_column"])

# Convert a column to categorical
df["category_column"] = df["category_column"].astype('category')

# Display the dataframe with updated data types
print(df.dtypes)
```

Converting data types to the appropriate format ensures that machine learning algorithms process data correctly. For example, converting strings to numeric types allows for mathematical operations, and converting to datetime enables time series analysis.

Categorical data

Categorical data refers to data that represents categories or labels rather than numerical quantities. Think of it as data that can be divided into a limited number of distinct groups or classifications. Examples include:

- **Colors**: Red, Blue, Green
- **Sizes**: Small, Medium, Large
- **Genders**: Male, Female, Non-binary
- **Product types**: Electronics, Clothing, Books

Categorical data often needs special handling in machine learning because most algorithms are designed to work with numerical input. For instance, you cannot directly perform mathematical operations like addition or multiplication on *Red* or *Small*. Pandas provides efficient tools to work with this type of data, often by converting these categories into a numerical format that machine learning models can understand.

Handling categorical data

Convert to categorical type. This snippet demonstrates converting a column to categorical data:

```
import pandas as pd

# Load dataset
df = pd.read_csv("categorical_data.csv")

# Convert a column to categorical type
df["category_column"] = df["category_column"].astype('category')

# Display the dataframe with categorical data
print(df.head())
```

Converting a column to a categorical type helps reduce memory usage and can improve performance. It also allows Pandas to treat the data correctly in operations specific to categorical data.

Brief mention of encoding

In machine learning, categorical data often needs to be converted to a numerical format. Two standard methods are:

- **One-hot encoding**: This creates new columns for each category, with binary values indicating the presence of a category.

  Let us look at how label encoding works with Scikit-learn:

  ```
  # One-Hot Encode the categorical column
  df_one_hot_encoded = pd.get_dummies(df, columns=["category_column"])

  # Display the one-hot encoded dataframe
  print(df_one_hot_encoded.head())
  ```

  One-hot encoding transforms categorical variables into a format suitable for machine learning algorithms by creating binary columns for each category. This avoids the issue of misinterpreting ordinal relationships between categories.

- **Label encoding**: It is a technique used to convert categorical data (such as text labels) into numerical values, which are required by most machine learning algorithms. Each unique category is assigned a unique integer.

  For example, suppose you have a column of colors:

  Before encoding:

  ```
  Color
  Red
  Blue
  Green
  Blue
  Red
  ```

  After label encoding, each color is replaced by a unique integer:

  ```
  Color
  0 Red
  1 Blue
  2 Green
  3 Blue
  4 Red
  ```

  Here, **Red** is encoded as 0, **Blue** as 1, and **Green** as 2. This transformation allows machine learning models to work with the data, since they require numerical input.

  Let us look at how label encoding works with Scikit-learn:

  ```
  from sklearn.preprocessing import LabelEncoder

  # Initialize label encoder
  label_encoder = LabelEncoder()

  # Apply label encoding to a categorical column
  df["encoded_column"] = label_encoder.fit_transform(df["category_column"])
  ```

```

# Display the dataframe with encoded categorical data
print(df.head())
```

Label encoding assigns a unique integer to each category. This method is useful for algorithms that can work with ordinal relationships. However, it may not be suitable for all models due to the potential introduction of ordinal relationships where none exist.

For now, it is enough to understand that handling categorical data correctly is essential because many machine learning algorithms require numerical input. We will cover these concepts in more detail later in the book.

Data aggregation and grouping

Data aggregation and grouping are essential for summarizing data and extracting meaningful insights, crucial for feature engineering and EDA in machine learning.

GroupBy

The **`groupby()`** function allows you to split a DataFrame into groups based on one or more columns, apply a function to each group, and combine the results. This is especially useful in machine learning for understanding patterns and relationships within data.

This snippet shows how to group data by category and sum sales:

```
import pandas as pd

# Sample dataset
data = {
    'category': ['A', 'A', 'B', 'B', 'C', 'C'],
    'sales': [100, 150, 200, 130, 90, 120]
}
df = pd.DataFrame(data)

# Group by category and sum sales
grouped = df.groupby("category")["sales"].sum()

# Display the grouped data
print(grouped)
```

Response:

```
category
A    250
B    330
C    210
Name: sales, dtype: int64
```

This code groups the data by the category column and calculates the sum of `'sales'` for each category. Grouping data in this manner helps identify trends and patterns within specific groups, which can inform feature engineering and model selection.

Pivot tables

Pivot tables summarize and reorganize data in a DataFrame. They are helpful for exploring relationships between variables and can be used to create contingency tables, which are helpful in feature engineering and model evaluation.

Here is how to create a pivot table in Pandas:

```
# Sample dataset
data = {
    'category': ['A', 'A', 'B', 'B', 'C', 'C'],
    'year': [2020, 2021, 2020, 2021, 2020, 2021],
    'sales': [100, 150, 200, 130, 90, 120]
}
df = pd.DataFrame(data)

# Create a pivot table
pivot_table = df.pivot_table(values="sales", index="category", columns="year")

# Display the pivot table
print(pivot_table)
```

This code creates a pivot table that summarizes *sales* values, indexed by *category* and with columns representing the *year*. Pivot tables allow for quick data summarization and exploration of relationships between variables, which is helpful for generating insights and features for machine learning models.

Importance of machine learning

Aggregating and grouping data helps identify patterns and trends within subsets of data, leading to better feature engineering. For instance, understanding how sales vary by category can help create new features that capture these variations, improving a model's predictive power.

By leveraging functions like **groupby()** and pivot tables, you can efficiently explore and summarize your data, making it easier to derive actionable insights and prepare your data for machine learning algorithms.

Advanced data manipulation

Advanced data manipulation is essential for preparing datasets in machine learning. It allows for sophisticated data selection and transformation, which is crucial for feature engineering, data cleaning, and preprocessing.

Advanced indexing and selection

Pandas provide powerful indexing capabilities to select data in a variety of ways. Here are some advanced techniques:

- **.loc[]: Label-based indexing**: The **.loc[]** function allows for selecting data by label, making it intuitive to select rows and columns based on their names. The following example demonstrates row and column selection using labels:

```
import pandas as pd

# Sample dataset with datetime index
data = {
    'A': [1, 2, -3, 4],
    'B': [4, -5, 6, -7],
```

```
    'C': [7, -8, 9, 10]
}
df = pd.DataFrame(data, index=pd.date_range('2020-01-01', periods=4))

# Selecting rows by label
row = df.loc['2020-01-01']

# Selecting columns by label range
cols = df.loc[:, 'A':'C']

# Boolean indexing with labels
filtered = df.loc[df['A'] > 0]

print(row)
print(cols)
print(filtered)
```

This code demonstrates how to use **`.loc[]`** for selecting rows by label, columns by label range, and applying Boolean indexing with labels. These operations help in precisely selecting and filtering data, which is often needed in feature engineering and data preprocessing.

- **.iloc[]: Position-based indexing**: The **`.iloc[]`** function allows for selecting data by position, which is useful when you need to work with data based on its integer location.

  Here is how to select rows and columns by position:

```
# Selecting rows by position
row = df.iloc[0]

# Selecting columns by position range
cols = df.iloc[:, 1:3]

# Slicing rows and columns by position
slice = df.iloc[1:5, 0:2]

print(row)
print(cols)
print(slice)
```

  Position-based indexing is crucial when the data's structure is more important than the labels.

- **Boolean indexing**: Boolean indexing is a powerful way to filter data based on conditions, allowing for complex data queries. This snippet filters data using conditions:

```
# Filtering data based on conditions
filtered_A = df[df['A'] > 0]
filtered_AB = df[(df[‚A‘] > 0) & (df[‚B‘] < 0)]

print(filtered_A)
print(filtered_AB)
```

This code demonstrates how to filter data using Boolean conditions. Filtering data is essential for creating subsets that meet specific criteria, which can be used to train machine learning models on relevant data.

- **Multi-indexing**: Multi-indexing allows for handling more complex data structures with multiple levels of indexing, which is helpful for hierarchical data. Here is how to create a hierarchical DataFrame with multiple levels of indexing:

```
import numpy as np

# Creating and manipulating MultiIndex objects
arrays = [np.array(['bar', 'bar', 'baz', 'baz']),
          np.array(['one', 'two', 'one', 'two'])]
df_multi = pd.DataFrame(np.random.randn(4, 2), index=arrays, columns=['A', 'B'])
df_multi.index.names = ['first', 'second']

print(df_multi)
```

This code shows how to create and manipulate **MultiIndex** objects. **MultiIndexing** is particularly useful for working with hierarchical data, allowing for more sophisticated data manipulation and analysis.

Importance of Pandas in machine learning

Advanced data manipulation techniques are vital for preparing data for machine learning models. They allow for precise selection, filtering, and transformation of data, which is crucial for feature engineering, data cleaning, and ensuring the quality of the data fed into machine learning algorithms.

By mastering these techniques, you can handle complex datasets more efficiently, leading to better-prepared data and, ultimately, more accurate and reliable machine learning models.

Performance optimization

Pandas provide powerful tools for data manipulation, but handling large datasets or performing complex operations can sometimes lead to performance bottlenecks. Optimizing your Pandas code can significantly improve efficiency and reduce execution times. Here are some key strategies and techniques for performance optimization:

- **Use vectorized operations**: Pandas is built on top of NumPy, which enables vectorized operations. Vectorized operations apply functions and operations to entire arrays or columns at once instead of iterating through each element individually. This approach is typically faster and more efficient than using loops. Examples of vectorized operations include arithmetic operations (+, -, *, /) and NumPy functions applied to the Pandas Series. This example shows how to perform fast column-wise operations:

```
# Vectorized arithmetic operations
df['new_column'] = df['column1'] + df['column2']

# Applying NumPy functions
import numpy as np
df['log_values'] = np.log(df['numeric_column'])
```

- **Avoid iteration over rows**: Iterating over rows using traditional loops (e.g., **for index, row in df.iterrows():**) can be slow, especially for large datasets. Whenever possible, try to use vectorized operations or apply functions that operate on entire columns. An example (avoiding iteration) is as follows:

```
# Using vectorized operation instead of iteration
df['new_column'] = df['column1'] + df['column2']
```

- **Use .apply() judiciously**: While **.apply()** can be helpful in applying custom functions row-wise or column-wise, it can also be slower than vectorized operations. If performance is critical, consider whether the same operation can be achieved using vectorized methods:

```
# Using apply with a lambda function
df['processed_column'] = df['column'].apply(lambda x: custom_function(x))
# Instead, consider using vectorized operations:
df['processed_column'] = custom_function(df['column'])
```

- **Optimize memory usage**: Here is how to check and optimize memory usage in Pandas:

```
# Check memory usage of each column
print(df.memory_usage())

# Optimize memory usage by converting data types
df['numeric_column'] = pd.to_numeric(df['numeric_column'], downcast='integer')
```

  Use **downcast** parameter in methods like **pd.to_numeric()** or **astype()** to reduce memory usage, especially for integer and float types.

Introduction to Matplotlib for data visualization

Imagine trying to explain the intricate beauty of a neural network's decision boundary or the performance improvements over epochs using only numbers in a table. It would be like trying to describe a breathtaking landscape without ever showing a picture—challenging and far less impactful. This is where Matplotlib shines in the world of machine learning and deep learning.

Matplotlib is a powerful Python library specifically designed for creating static, animated, and interactive visualizations. Think of it as your artistic toolkit for transforming raw data into insightful charts and plots.

Importance of visualization in machine learning and deep learning

The importance of visualization in machine learning and deep learning is as follows:

- **Data exploration**: Visualizing your dataset before building a model helps you identify trends, spot outliers, and understand relationships between variables. This exploration is crucial for feature engineering and deciding which algorithms are best suited for your data.
- **Model evaluation and interpretation**: Visualizing model performance metrics (accuracy, loss, etc.) over time or epochs is critical to understanding how well your model is learning. Plots like confusion matrices provide insights into where your model makes mistakes, guiding you toward improvements.
- **Communication**: A clear visualization can communicate your findings far more effectively than tables of numbers. When presenting your machine learning and deep learning projects, well-crafted plots help your audience grasp complex concepts and insights quickly.

Core features and concepts

Core features and concepts are as follows:

- **Figure**: The entire plotting window or area where your visualization will be displayed. Think of it as the canvas for your art.
- **Axes**: A specific area within the figure where a single plot lives. A figure can contain multiple axes, allowing you to create subplots or visualizations side-by-side.

- **Artist**: Every element within axes, be it lines, points, text, labels, etc., is considered an 'artist'. Matplotlib provides fine-grained control over each artist, letting you customize colors, styles, and positions.
- **Pyplot**: A module within Matplotlib (**`matplotlib.pyplot`**) offering a simple, MATLAB-like interface for quick and easy plot creation. We will be using pyplot extensively.

Creating basic plots

Let us get into creating some essential plot types frequently used in machine learning and deep learning workflows.

- **Line plots, visualizing trends and progress**: Line plots are perfect for showing trends over time, epochs during training, or any situation where you want to see how a variable changes with respect to another. This example plots model accuracy over training epochs:

```
import matplotlib.pyplot as plt
import numpy as np

# Sample data: Simulating model accuracy over epochs
epochs = np.arange(1, 11)
accuracy = np.linspace(0.5, 0.95, 10)

plt.plot(epochs, accuracy)
plt.xlabel("Epochs")
plt.ylabel("Accuracy")
plt.title("Model Accuracy During Training")
plt.grid(True) # Add gridlines
plt.show()
```

The code produces the following chart:

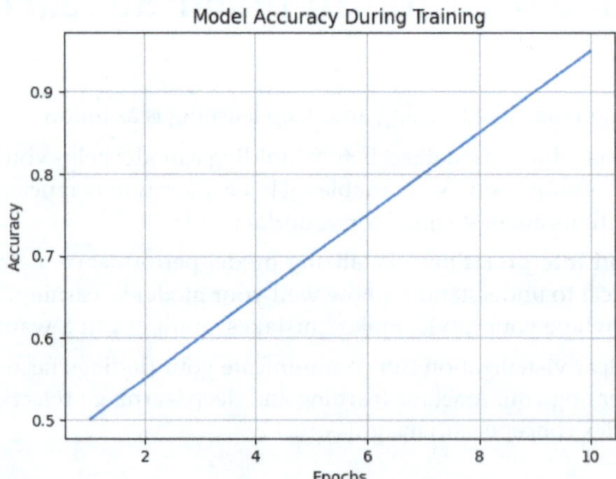

Figure 4.1: Linear plot

- **Explanation**:
  - We use **`np.arange()`** to create an array of epochs (1 to 10).
  - **`np.linspace()`** generates an array of accuracy values gradually increasing from 0.5 to 0.95, simulating improvement during training.

- **`plt.plot()`** creates the line plot.
- Labels, titles, and gridlines enhance readability.

- **Scatter plots: exploring relationships**: Scatter plots are excellent for visualizing the relationship between two variables. They are often used to identify patterns, clusters, or correlations within your data. The following code shows how to visualize relationships with scatter plots:

```
import matplotlib.pyplot as plt
import numpy as np

# Sample data: Simulating the relationship between learning rate and model loss
learning_rates = np.array([0.001, 0.01, 0.1, 1])
loss_values = np.array([0.8, 0.5, 0.2, 0.3])

plt.scatter(learning_rates, loss_values, marker='o', s=100)
plt.xlabel("Learning Rate")
plt.ylabel("Loss")
plt.title("Effect of Learning Rate on Model Loss")
plt.xscale('log') # Use logarithmic scale for learning rate
plt.show()
```

The code produces the following chart:

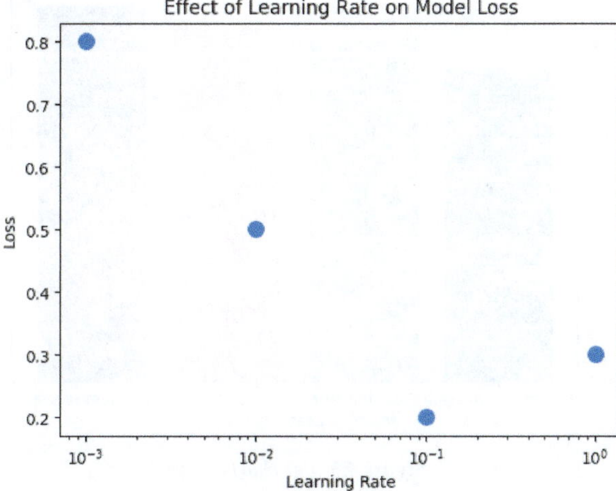

Figure 4.2: *Scatter plot*

- **Explanation**:
  - **`plt.scatter()`** creates the scatter plot.
  - We use **`marker='o'`** to represent data points as circles and **`s=100`** to adjust their size.
  - **`plt.xscale('log')`** applies a logarithmic scale to the x-axis, which is common when visualizing learning rates.

Bar charts for comparing categories

Bar charts are ideal for comparing values across different categories. In machine learning, you might use them to visualize:

- The performance of different algorithms on the same dataset.
- The importance of features in your model.
- The distribution of classes in a classification problem.

Here is how to compare model accuracies using bar charts:

```
import matplotlib.pyplot as plt

# Sample data: Comparing the accuracy of different ML models
models = ['Logistic Regression', 'Decision Tree', 'SVM', 'Random Forest']
accuracies = [0.75, 0.82, 0.85, 0.90]

plt.bar(models, accuracies, color=['blue', 'green', 'red', 'purple'])
plt.xlabel("Machine Learning Models")
plt.ylabel("Accuracy")
plt.title("Model Accuracy Comparison")
plt.ylim(0, 1) # Set y-axis limits for better visualization
plt.show()
```

The code produces the following chart:

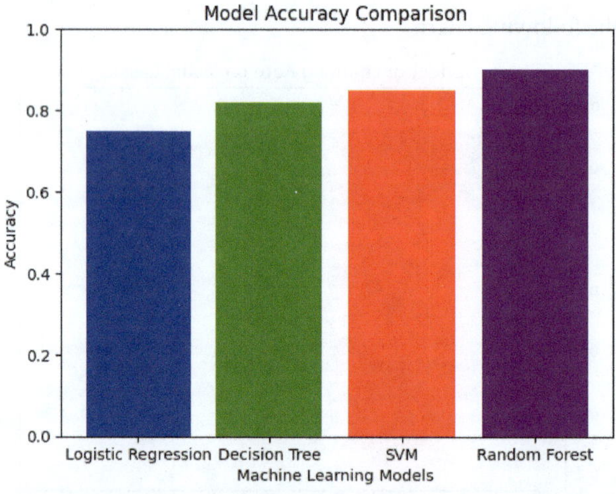

***Figure 4.3:** Bar charts*

- **Explanation**:
    - **`plt.bar()`** creates the bar chart.
    - We use different colors for each bar for visual clarity.
    - **`plt.ylim(0, 1)`** sets the y-axis range from 0 to 1, a standard practice when displaying accuracies.
- **Histograms, visualizing data distributions**: Histograms are essential for understanding the distribution of a single numerical variable. They divide the data into bins and show the frequency (or count) of data points falling within each bin. This code snippet generates a histogram of randomly distributed data:

```
import matplotlib.pyplot as plt
import numpy as np
```

```

# Sample data: Generating data with a normal distribution
data = np.random.randn(1000)

plt.hist(data, bins=30, edgecolor='black')
plt.xlabel("Values")
plt.ylabel("Frequency")
plt.title("Histogram of Randomly Generated Data")
plt.show()
```

The code produces the following chart:

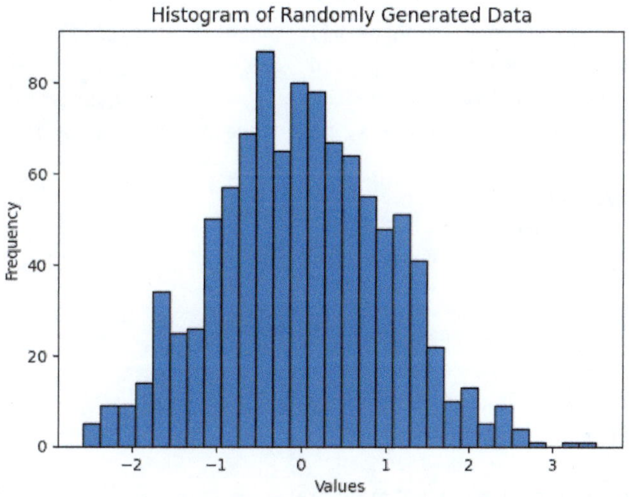

***Figure 4.4**: Histogram*

- **Explanation**:
  - **`plt.hist()`** creates the histogram.
  - **`bins=30`** divides the data into 30 bins.
  - **`edgecolor='black'`** adds black outlines to the bars for better visual separation.

Confusion matrix for visualizing classification performance

A confusion matrix is a powerful tool for evaluating the performance of a classification algorithm. It provides a detailed breakdown of correct and incorrect predictions, showing how often the model confuses one class for another.

The following code plots a confusion matrix for classification performance:

```
import matplotlib.pyplot as plt
import numpy as np
from itertools import product

# Sample confusion matrix (replace with your model's output)
confusion_matrix = np.array([[90, 10],
                             [5, 95]])
```

```python

# Function to plot the confusion matrix with labels
def plot_confusion_matrix(cm, classes, title='Confusion Matrix', cmap=plt.cm.Blues):
    plt.imshow(cm, interpolation='nearest', cmap=cmap)
    plt.title(title)
    plt.colorbar()
    tick_marks = np.arange(len(classes))
    plt.xticks(tick_marks, classes, rotation=45)
    plt.yticks(tick_marks, classes)

    thresh = cm.max() / 2.
    for i, j in product(range(cm.shape[0]), range(cm.shape[1])):
        plt.text(j, i, format(cm[i, j], 'd'),
                 horizontalalignment="center",
                 color="white" if cm[i, j] > thresh else "black")

    plt.tight_layout()
    plt.ylabel('True Label')
    plt.xlabel('Predicted Label')

# Example class labels
class_names = ['Class 0', 'Class 1']

# Plot the confusion matrix
plt.figure()
plot_confusion_matrix(confusion_matrix, classes=class_names)
plt.show()
```

The code produces the following chart:

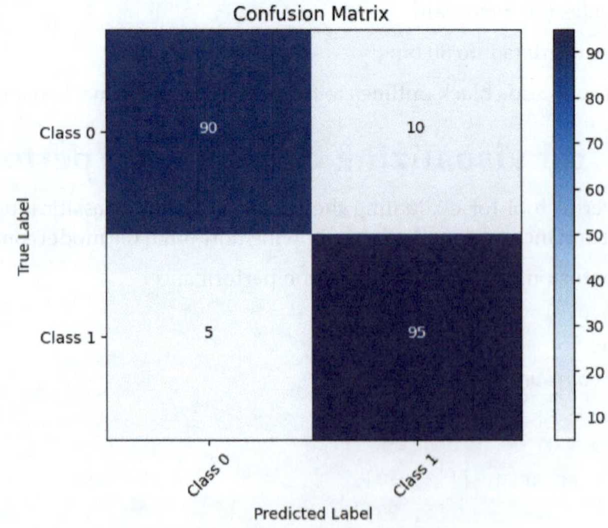

Figure 4.5: Confusion matrix

The explanation is as follows:

- **confusion_matrix**: This NumPy array represents a sample confusion matrix. Replace this with the actual confusion matrix generated by your classification model.
- **plot_confusion_matrix() function**: This function takes the confusion matrix, class names, and optional styling parameters to generate a visually appealing and informative heatmap-like plot.
- **Color coding**: The **cmap** parameter sets the colormap. Lighter colors usually represent higher values (more frequent predictions).
- **Text annotations**: The code within the nested loop adds text annotations to each cell of the confusion matrix, making it easier to read the exact number of predictions for each true/predicted class combination.

Visualizing image data and feature maps in CNN

In deep learning, particularly with **convolutional neural networks** (**CNNs**), visualizing image data and the intermediate feature maps learned by convolutional layers is crucial for understanding how the network processes images. You will know in future chapters what CNNs and feature maps are.

Here is how to visualize an image and feature maps from a CNN:

```
import matplotlib.pyplot as plt
import numpy as np

# Sample image data (replace with your  image)
image = np.random.rand(28, 28) # Simulating a 28x28 grayscale image

# Sample feature maps (replace with output from your CNN layer)
feature_maps = np.random.rand(8, 10, 10) # 8 filters, each producing a 10x10 feature map

# Plot the original image
plt.figure()
plt.imshow(image, cmap='gray')
plt.title("Original Image")
plt.axis('off')

# Plot the feature maps
plt.figure(figsize=(10, 5)) # Adjust figure size as needed
for i in range(feature_maps.shape[0]):
    plt.subplot(2, 4, i+1) # Create subplots (2 rows, 4 columns)
    plt.imshow(feature_maps[i], cmap='viridis')
    plt.title(f"Feature Map {i+1}")
    plt.axis('off')

plt.tight_layout()
plt.show()
```

The code produces the following visualizations:

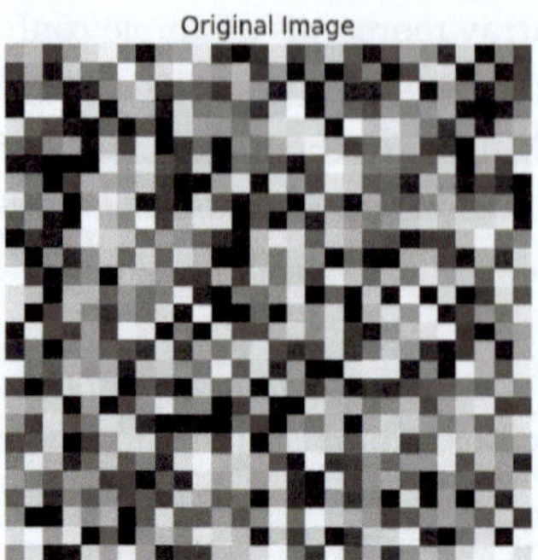

***Figure 4.6**: Original image*

The following image shows various kinds of feature maps:

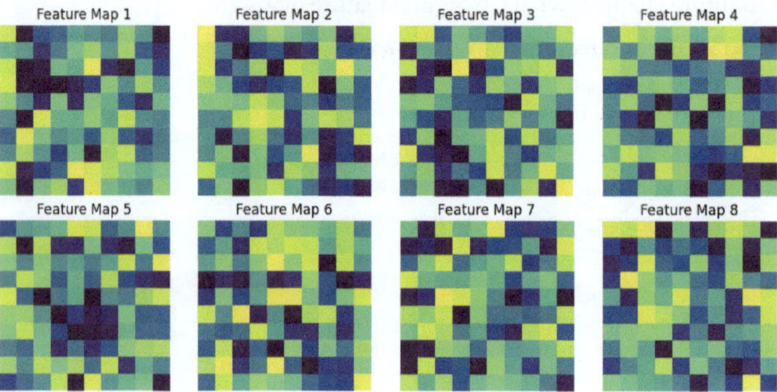

***Figure 4.7**: Feature maps*

The explanation is as follows:

- **Sample data**: We create a random image and `feature_maps` data. In a real CNN, you would use:
  - Your actual image data (e.g., loaded using libraries like PIL or OpenCV).
  - The output from a convolutional layer within your trained CNN model.
- **Image plotting**: We use `plt.imshow()` with the `cmap='gray'` colormap for grayscale images. For color images, use `cmap='viridis'` or others.
- **Feature map visualization**:
  - We loop through each feature map in the `feature_maps` array.
  - `plt.subplot()` creates a grid of subplots to display each feature map.
  - We use `cmap='viridis'` (or any other suitable colormap) to visualize the activations in each feature map.
  - This visualization provides insights into how different filters activate on different patterns in the input image, helping you understand what features the CNN is learning.

Conclusion

In this chapter, you explored the world of essential Python libraries for machine learning and deep learning. You explored the power of NumPy for numerical computations, Pandas for data manipulation and analysis, and Matplotlib for crafting insightful visualizations. Armed with these tools, you are well on your way to tackling real-world machine learning and deep learning problems. Remember that mastering these libraries takes time and practice. Experiment with the code examples, explore the documentation, and apply these skills to your projects.

In the next chapter, *Introduction to Machine Learning with Scikit-learn*, we will build upon these foundations; we will learn where to find datasets for our learning journey, how to prepare data, training, and cross-validation, and, of course, evaluation metrics.

Exercises

This exercise covers advanced data analysis and manipulation with NumPy and Pandas.

The following list outlines different tasks:

- **Data creation**: Create a NumPy array representing daily stock prices for a company over two years (730 days). Include the open, high, low, close prices, and volume traded for each day.
- **Data manipulation with Pandas**:
  - Convert the NumPy array into a Pandas DataFrame with appropriate column names: ['Open', 'High', 'Low', 'Close', 'Volume'].
  - Add a new column to calculate the daily price change percentage ((Close - Open) / Open * 100).
  - Resample the data to obtain the monthly average Open, High, Low, Close prices, and total Volume.
  - Calculate the rolling 30-day average of the Close prices.
- **Analysis and visualization**:
  - Identify and plot the top 5 days with the highest percentage gain.
  - Create a dual-axis plot showing both the monthly average Close prices and the total volume traded.

Step-by-step instructions are as follows:

1. **Create the NumPy Array**: Use np.random functions to generate the stock prices and volume data, ensuring that the prices make logical sense (e.g., Low <= Open <= Close <= High).
2. **Convert to Pandas DataFrame**:
   a. Create a DataFrame with appropriate columns and index (using pd.date_range for dates).
   b. Add calculated columns for analysis.
3. **Advanced manipulation**: Use resampling and rolling operations to aggregate and analyze the data.
4. **Data visualization**: Use plt functions to visualize key insights from the data.

Multiple choice questions

This quiz contains the topics of essential Machine Learning Libraries in Python.

1. **NumPy basics: Which of the following are core features of NumPy? (Select all that apply)**
   a. ndarray
   b. Broadcasting
   c. ufuncs
   d. DataFrame

2. **Pandas data structures: What are the primary data structures in Pandas? (Select all that apply)**
   a. Series
   b. DataFrame
   c. ndarray
   d. DataArray
3. **Creating arrays in NumPy: Which of the following code snippets correctly creates a 2x3 array filled with zeros in NumPy?**
   a. arr = np.array([[0, 0, 0], [0, 0, 0]])
   b. arr = np.zeros((2, 3))
   c. arr = np.zeros([2, 3])
   d. arr = np.empty((2, 3))
4. **Data cleaning with Pandas: Which Pandas function would you use to remove rows with missing values?**
   a. df.fillna()
   b. df.drop()
   c. df.dropna()
   d. df.remove_na()
5. **Indexing and slicing in NumPy: What will be the output of the following code?**

```
import numpy as np
arr = np.array([10, 20, 30, 40, 50])
print(arr[1:4])
```

   a. [10, 20, 30]
   b. [20, 30, 40, 50]
   c. [20, 30, 40]
   d. [30, 40, 50]
6. **Data loading in Pandas: Which Pandas function is used to load data from a CSV file?**
   a. pd.read_csv()
   b. pd.read_excel()
   c. pd.read_json()
   d. pd.read_sql()
7. **Broadcasting in NumPy: What is broadcasting in NumPy?**
   a. A method to visualize data.
   b. A function to handle missing data.
   c. A technique that allows operations on arrays of different shapes.
   d. A process to create arrays.
8. **EDA with Pandas: Which of the following tasks are part of EDA in Pandas? (Select all that apply)**
   a. Summarizing data
   b. Visualizing data
   c. Identifying patterns
   d. Training machine learning models

9. **Universal functions (ufuncs) in NumPy: Which of the following are examples of universal functions (ufuncs) in NumPy? (Select all that apply)**
   a. np.sin()
   b. np.exp()
   c. np.concat()
   d. np.log()
10. **Matplotlib usage: What is the primary purpose of Matplotlib in machine learning?**
   a. Data cleaning
   b. Numerical computations
   c. Data visualization
   d. Feature engineering

Answers

1.	a, b, c.
2.	a, b.
3.	b.
4.	c.
5.	c.
6.	a.
7.	c.
8.	a, b, c.
9.	a, b, d.
10.	c.

Key terms

- **NumPy**:
  - **ndarray**: NumPy's core data structure represents efficient multidimensional arrays.
  - **Vectorization**: Performing operations on entire arrays at once, leading to significant speed improvements over loops.
  - **Broadcasting**: How NumPy handles operations on arrays with different shapes (but compatible dimensions).
  - **Universal functions (ufuncs)**: Optimized functions that operate elementwise on arrays (e.g., np.sin(), np.exp()).
  - **Linear algebra**: NumPy provides functions for matrix operations (multiplication, inversion, etc.), essential in ML.
  - **Random number generation**: Functions for creating arrays of random numbers from various distributions.

- **Pandas**:
  - **Series**: A one-dimensional labeled array, like a column in a spreadsheet.
  - **DataFrame**: A two-dimensional labeled data structure, like a table, with rows and columns.
  - **Data cleaning**: The process of handling missing values, outliers, and inconsistencies in your data.
  - **Data transformation**: Modifying your data (adding columns, reshaping, merging, etc.) for analysis or modeling.
  - **Indexing**: Accessing specific rows and columns in a DataFrame using labels or positions.
  - **Grouping and aggregation**: Summarizing data by groups (e.g., calculating the average sales per category).
  - **Categorical data**: Data that represents categories (e.g., colors, types). Special handling is often needed in ML.
  - **One-hot encoding**: A method for converting categorical data into a numerical format suitable for ML models.
  - **Label encoding**: Assigning a unique integer to each category in a categorical variable.
- **Matplotlib**:
  - **Figure**: The entire plotting window or canvas in Matplotlib.
  - **Axes**: A specific area within a figure where a single plot is drawn.
  - **Artist**: Any individual element on a Matplotlib plot (lines, points, text, etc.).
  - **Pyplot**: A module in Matplotlib providing a simple interface for creating plots.
  - **Line plot**: Visualizes trends over a continuous variable, often used to show model performance over epochs.
  - **Scatter plot**: Shows the relationship between two variables, helpful for spotting correlations and clusters.
  - **Bar chart**: Compares values across different categories.
  - **Histogram**: Visualizes the distribution of a single numerical variable.
  - **Confusion matrix**: A visualization for evaluating the performance of a classification model.
  - **Feature map**: In CNNs, a visual representation of the activations learned by convolutional filters.

References

1. NumPy documentation: **https://numpy.org/doc/**
2. Pandas documentation: **https://pandas.pydata.org/docs/**
3. Matplotlib documentation: **https://matplotlib.org/stable/contents.html**

Chapter 5
Introduction to Machine Learning with Scikit-learn

Introduction

In the previous chapter, we explored the essential machine learning libraries in Python that form the backbone of many data science projects. Now, it is time to delve into Scikit-learn, a powerful and versatile library specifically designed for machine learning. Think of Scikit-learn as your sophisticated toolbox, filled with high-level functions that streamline the process of building and deploying machine learning models. By the end of this chapter, you will understand how to pre-process data, train models to predict numerical values (e.g., house prices) or classes (e.g., spam/not spam), and even evaluate model metrics to be aware of their performance. This chapter will walk you through the usual processing, training, and evaluation tasks that machine learning engineers usually do daily; this will give you the basic knowledge and tools required to build basic machine learning models to be embedded in your future applications.

Structure

This chapter covers the following topics:

- Introduction to Scikit-learn
- Finding and using datasets
- Data preparation and preprocessing
- Evaluation metrics
- Supervised learning with Scikit-learn
- Other algorithms

Objectives

By the end of this chapter, you will be able to understand the fundamental principles and applications of supervised and unsupervised learning algorithms, implement and evaluate various models using Scikit learn, recognize the importance of data preprocessing and feature engineering, apply different performance evaluation metrics to assess the accuracy and robustness of your models and explore other algorithms beyond the most used ones, gaining insights into when and how to use them.

Introduction to Scikit-learn

Scikit-learn is an open-source machine learning library built on top of NumPy, SciPy, and Matplotlib. It provides simple and efficient tools for data mining and data analysis, making it accessible to both beginners and experienced practitioners. Whether you are working on classification, regression, clustering, or dimensionality reduction, Scikit-learn offers a unified interface for implementing and comparing various machine learning algorithms.

The GitHub repo for the book contains all code examples; you can refer to it along with the provided code.

The key features and benefits are as follows:

- **Versatility**: Supports a wide range of supervised and unsupervised learning algorithms.
- **Ease of use**: User-friendly **application programming interface** (**API**) with consistent and comprehensive documentation.
- **Integration**: Seamlessly integrates with other Python libraries such as NumPy, Pandas, and Matplotlib.
- **Efficiency**: Optimized for performance, enabling fast computations on large datasets.
- **Community support**: Extensive community and active development, ensuring continuous improvements and updates.

Installation and setup

Before you can start using Scikit-learn, you need to install it on your system. This process makes the library's functions and tools available for your Python projects. Think of it like adding a new app to your phone—you need to install it before you can open and use it.

To install Scikit-learn, you can use `pip`, the Python package manager, `pip` is a tool that helps you easily install and manage software packages written in Python. When you run the following command, `pip` will automatically download Scikit-learn and its necessary dependencies (like NumPy and SciPy, if you do not already have them) and set them up for you.

```
pip install scikit-learn
```

Alternatively, you can install it as part of the Anaconda Distribution, which includes many other valuable packages for data science. Anaconda is a free, open-source distribution of Python (and R) that simplifies package management and deployment. It comes pre-installed with many popular libraries for data science, machine learning, and scientific computing, making it easier to set up your working environment. Anaconda also includes tools like Jupyter Notebook and Spyder, which are helpful for interactive coding and data analysis. Refer to the following command:

```
conda install scikit-learn
```

Once installed, you can verify the installation by importing Scikit-learn in your Python environment:

```
import sklearn
print(sklearn.__version__)
```

Finding and using datasets

A dataset is a structured collection of data, typically organized in a way that makes it easy to analyze and use for machine learning tasks. Datasets can come in many formats, such as **comma-separated values** (**CSV**), Excel spreadsheets, **JavaScript Object Notation** (**JSON**), **Structured Query Language** (**SQL**) databases, or even images and text files. For example, a CSV file might contain rows of information about houses, with columns for features like price, size, and location. In machine learning, datasets are used to train and evaluate models, helping algorithms learn patterns and make predictions. Choosing the right dataset and understanding its structure is a crucial first step in any data science project.

Accessing diverse datasets is a crucial part of machine learning development. Numerous repositories offer datasets spanning various domains, formats, and sizes. Here are some of the most popular repositories that you can leverage for your projects:

- **Kaggle**: Kaggle (**https://www.kaggle.com/**) is a platform for data science competitions and a comprehensive repository of datasets. It hosts thousands of datasets on various topics, from finance and economics to healthcare and image processing. Kaggle's community-driven approach ensures a steady stream of updated and well-maintained datasets.

- **UCI machine learning repository**: The UCI machine learning repository (**https://archive.ics.uci.edu/**) is one of the oldest and most popular sources for machine learning datasets. It provides datasets for a wide range of machine learning problems, including classification, regression, clustering, and more. The repository is widely used in academia and industry for benchmarking and educational purposes.
- **Data.gov**: **https://data.gov** is the home of the U.S. government's open data. It offers a vast collection of datasets from various government agencies, covering topics such as agriculture, climate, education, energy, and finance. This repository is an excellent resource for accessing high-quality, real-world data.
- **European Union Open Data Portal**: The European Union Open Data Portal (**https://data.europa.eu/en**) provides access to datasets from the European Union's institutions and other bodies. It includes data on economics, demographics, environment, and more, offering a wealth of information for various analytical needs.
- **World Bank Open Data**: The World Bank Open Data (**https://data.worldbank.org/**) repository offers global development data, including economic indicators, health statistics, education metrics, and environmental data. This repository is valuable for projects that require comprehensive international data.
- **United Nations Data**: The United Nations Data (**https://data.un.org/**) portal provides datasets from the United Nations on global issues such as population, energy, industry, and environment. It is a crucial resource for accessing international data to support global and regional analyses.
- **Statista**: Statista (**https://www.statista.com/**) offers statistics and datasets on various industries, economies, and consumer trends. While some data requires a subscription, it provides valuable insights and high-quality data across different sectors.

By exploring these repositories, you can find datasets suitable for various machine learning projects, from academic research to practical applications in the industry.

Downloading and using datasets

Accessing and using datasets effectively is fundamental for any machine learning project. This section will guide you through the process of obtaining datasets from popular sources like Kaggle, importing different file formats, and managing your datasets efficiently.

Accessing datasets from Kaggle

Kaggle is a rich resource for high-quality datasets, and accessing these datasets is straightforward. Follow these steps to download and use datasets from Kaggle:

1. **Create an account**: Sign up for a free account on Kaggle at **Kaggle.com**.
2. **Search for datasets**: Use the search bar or navigate to the Datasets section to find datasets relevant to your project.
3. **API setup**: Kaggle provides an API to facilitate dataset downloads programmatically.

An example of the Kaggle datasets website is as follows:

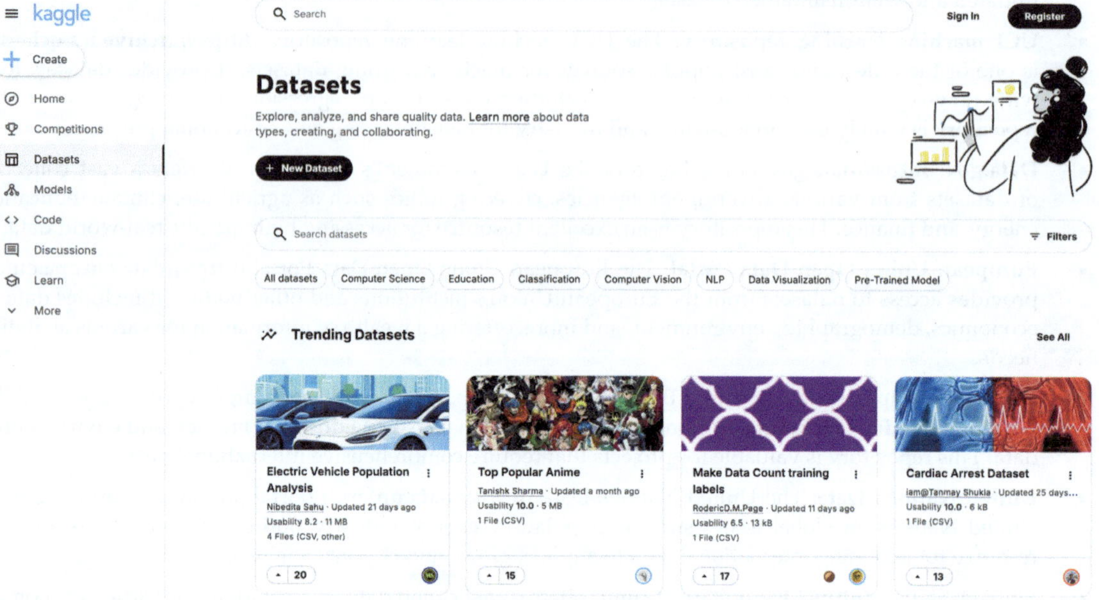

***Figure 5.1:** Kaggle Datasets screen*

To set up the API:

1. Install the Kaggle API client: `pip install kaggle`
2. Obtain your API credentials: Go to **My Account** on Kaggle, and under the API section, click **Create New API Token**. This will download a `kaggle.json` file containing your credentials.
3. Place the `kaggle.json` file in the `.kaggle` directory (usually in your home directory).
4. **Download datasets**: Use the Kaggle API to download datasets. For example:

```
from kaggle.api.kaggle_api_extended import KaggleApi

api = KaggleApi()
api.authenticate()
api.dataset_download_files('arindamsahoo/icc-mens-t20-world-cup-2024-stats', path='C:\\mmlbook\\Chapter05\\datasets', unzip=True)
```

Importing CSV, Excel, and other file formats

Once you have your dataset, importing it into your working environment is the next step. The following are examples of how to import CSV, Excel, and other common file formats using Python:

- **Importing CSV files**:

```
import pandas as pd
# Load a CSV file
df = pd.read_csv('datasets/bowling_stats_for_icc_mens_t20_world_cup_2024.csv')
```

- **Importing Excel files**:

```
import pandas as pd
```

```

# Load an Excel file
df = pd.read_excel('path/to/your/file.xlsx', sheet_name='Sheet1')
```

- **Importing other file formats**: For JSON, Parquet, and SQL databases, Pandas provides convenient methods:

```
# Load a JSON file
df = pd.read_json('path/to/your/file.json')

# Load a Parquet file
df = pd.read_parquet('path/to/your/file.parquet')

# Load data from a SQL database
import sqlite3

conn = sqlite3.connect('path/to/your/database.db')
df = pd.read_sql_query('SELECT * FROM table_name', conn)
```

Data preparation and preprocessing

Data preparation is the process of collecting, organizing, and formatting raw data so it can be used effectively in a machine learning project. This often involves gathering data from different sources, combining it, and ensuring it is in a consistent and usable format.

Data preprocessing refers to the specific techniques used to clean and transform the data before feeding it into a machine learning model. This can include handling missing values, encoding categorical variables, scaling numerical features, and splitting the data into training and testing sets.

Data preparation and preprocessing are critical steps in any machine learning pipeline. Properly prepared data can significantly improve the performance of your models. This section will cover the importance of data preparation, techniques for data cleaning, feature engineering, scaling, encoding, and splitting the dataset.

In this section, we will use the *building energy consumption dataset* to illustrate various data preparation and preprocessing techniques. This dataset includes information about energy consumption across different buildings, along with related features such as weather conditions, building types, and occupancy levels. The dataset is included in the book's GitHub repository.

Loading the dataset

First, we need to load the dataset from a local CSV file. Make sure the CSV file is in the same directory as your script or provide the correct path. The code is as follows:

```
import pandas as pd

# Load the dataset
df = pd.read_csv('building_energy_consumption.csv')
print("Initial dataset shape:", df.shape)
print(df.head())
```

Output is as follows:

```
Initial dataset shape: (48, 5)
         date building_type  temperature  occupancy  energy_consumption
0  2023-01-01   Residential        21.23      745.0             1091.46
1  2023-01-02    Commercial        16.78      625.0             1762.85
```

```
2  2023-01-03    Industrial         33.45      308.0                1735.28
3  2023-01-04    Industrial         25.37      178.0               10000.00
4  2023-01-05   Residential         22.50      210.0                3242.05
```

Importance of data preparation

The following list outlines the importance of data preparation:

- **Accuracy**: Well-prepared data can lead to more accurate models.
- **Efficiency**: Reduces the time required for data analysis and model training.
- **Robustness**: Helps in dealing with missing values, outliers, and noisy data, leading to more robust models.
- **Generalization**: Proper data splitting ensures that models generalize well to unseen data. It also refers to a model's ability to perform well on new, unseen data, not just the data it was trained on. In other words, a model that generalizes well can make accurate predictions on data it has not encountered before, which is the ultimate goal in most machine learning tasks.

Data cleaning

Data cleaning is a fundamental step in the preprocessing pipeline that involves removing or correcting inconsistencies, errors, and missing values in the dataset to ensure its quality and reliability.

Standard data cleaning techniques include:

- **Handling missing values**: Identifying and dealing with gaps in the data, either by filling them in or removing incomplete records.
- **Correcting errors**: Fixing typos, inconsistent formatting, or incorrect entries.
- **Removing duplicates**: Eliminating repeated rows or records.
- **Dealing with outliers**: Detecting and addressing data points that are unusually high or low compared to the rest of the data.
- **Standardizing formats**: Ensuring consistency in how data is represented, such as dates, units, or text capitalization.

Let us see some of these techniques in the following sections.

Handling missing values

Missing values can introduce bias or reduce the efficiency of your models. Here are common strategies to handle missing values:

- **Remove missing values**: If the proportion of missing data is small, you can remove these records using the **dropna** method. The code is as follows:

```python
initial_shape = df.shape
df.dropna(inplace=True)
print("Rows with missing values removed:", initial_shape[0] - df.shape[0])
print("Current dataset shape:", df.shape)
```

The output is as follows:

```
         date building_type  temperature  occupancy  energy_consumption
0  2023-01-01   Residential        21.23      745.0             1091.46
1  2023-01-02    Commercial        16.78      625.0             1762.85
2  2023-01-03    Industrial        33.45      308.0             1735.28
```

```
3  2023-01-04    Industrial     25.37    178.0       10000.00
4  2023-01-05   Residential     22.50    210.0        3242.05
Rows with missing values removed: 3
Current dataset shape: (45, 5)
```

- **Impute missing values**: Fill in missing values using statistical methods such as mean, median, or mode. The code is as follows:

```
from sklearn.impute import SimpleImputer

imputer = SimpleImputer(strategy='mean')
missing_before = df['energy_consumption'].isnull().sum()
df['energy_consumption'] = imputer.fit_transform(df[['energy_consumption']])
missing_after = df['energy_consumption'].isnull().sum()
print("Rows with missing values in 'energy_consumption' before imputation:", missing_before)
print("Rows with missing values in 'energy_consumption' after imputation:", missing_after)
```

The output is as follows:

```
Rows with missing values in 'energy_consumption' before imputation: 1
Rows with missing values in 'energy_consumption' after imputation: 0
```

Dealing with outliers

In any dataset, individual observations or measurements are referred to as data points. Each data point represents a specific piece of information collected, and collectively, these points form the complete dataset that we analyze. For instance, if you are tracking daily temperatures, each day's temperature reading would be a data point. When we discuss outliers, we are specifically referring to data points that stand out significantly from the general pattern or distribution of the other data points. Outliers can skew your model's performance. Common techniques to handle outliers include:

- **Identifying outliers**: Using the Z-score method to identify outliers. The code is as follows:

```
from scipy import stats
import numpy as np

z_scores = np.abs(stats.zscore(df['energy_consumption']))
outliers = df[z_scores > 3]
print("Identified outliers:\n", outliers)
```

  - **Identified outliers**:

```
          date building_type  temperature  occupancy  energy_consumption
30  2023-01-31    Industrial        18.67      390.0            20001.55
47  2023-02-17    Commercial        31.45      734.0            28247.33
```

- **Removing outliers**: Based on a threshold, such as Z-scores. The code is as follows:

```
df = df[z_scores < 3]
print("Rows after removing outliers:", df.shape[0])
```

  - **Output**: `Rows after removing outliers: 46`

- **Transforming outliers**: Using log transformation, capping, or flooring. The code is as follows:

```
upper_limit = df['energy_consumption'].quantile(0.95)
lower_limit = df['energy_consumption'].quantile(0.05)
df['energy_consumption'] = np.where(df['energy_consumption'] > upper_limit, upper_
limit, df['energy_consumption'])
df['energy_consumption'] = np.where(df['energy_consumption'] < lower_limit, lower_
limit, df['energy_consumption'])
print("Transformed outliers to within 5th and 95th percentiles.")
```

See the GitHub repo for a complete snippet of transforming outliers.

Feature engineering

Feature engineering is the process of creating new features or modifying existing ones to improve the performance of machine learning models. It requires domain knowledge and creativity to extract meaningful information from the data.

Creating new features

Creating new features from existing data can improve model performance by providing more relevant information. Here are some common techniques:

- **Date features**: Extracting year, month, day, or day of the week from a date column. The code is as follows:

```
df['date'] = pd.to_datetime(df['date'])
df['year'] = df['date'].dt.year
df['month'] = df['date'].dt.month
print("Created new date features: 'year' and 'month'.")
```

The output is as follows:

```
Created new date features: 'year' and 'month'.
        date  temperature  occupancy  energy_consumption  year  month  \
0 2023-01-01     0.333333      745.0            0.002773  2023      1
1 2023-01-02     0.090562      625.0            0.007992  2023      1
2 2023-01-03     1.000000      308.0            0.005802  2023      1
3 2023-01-04     0.559193      178.0            0.662370  2023      1
4 2023-01-05     0.402619      210.0            0.125503  2023      1
```

- **Interaction features**: Combining two or more features. The code is as follows:

```
df['temperature_energy'] = df['temperature'] * df['energy_consumption']
print("Created new interaction feature: 'temperature_energy'.")
```

Feature scaling and normalization

Feature scaling is a method for standardizing the range of independent variables or features of data. In other words, it helps bring all the features onto a similar scale, which is crucial for many machine learning algorithms that rely on the distance between data points [e.g., **K-nearest neighbors (KNNs)**, **support vector machines (SVMs)**].

The importance of feature scaling is explained in the following list:

- **Algorithm performance**: Algorithms that compute distances or gradients (like KNN or gradient descent-based methods) can be skewed if features are on different scales.
- **Convergence speed**: In gradient descent, scaled features can lead to faster convergence.

- **Interpretability**: Some algorithms benefit from having features on a similar scale for more interpretable results.

Standardization, the Z-score normalization

Standardization involves rescaling the features so that they have the properties of a standard normal distribution with a mean of 0 and a standard deviation of 1. The code is as follows:

```
from sklearn.preprocessing import StandardScaler

scaler = StandardScaler()
df[['temperature', 'energy_consumption']] = scaler.fit_
transform(df[['temperature', 'energy_consumption']])
print("Standardized 'temperature' and 'energy_consumption' features.")
```

The output is as follows:

```
Standardized 'temperature' and 'energy_consumption' features.
        date  temperature  occupancy  energy_consumption  year  month  \
0 2023-01-01    -0.550434      745.0           -0.592053  2023      1
1 2023-01-02    -1.459929      625.0           -0.567808  2023      1
2 2023-01-03     1.947098      308.0           -0.577983  2023      1
3 2023-01-04     0.295702      178.0            2.472195  2023      1
4 2023-01-05    -0.290871      210.0           -0.021895  2023      1
```

The explanation of the code is as follows:

- **StandardScaler**: This scaler removes the mean and scales each feature to unit variance.
- **Fit and transform**: The fit method computes the mean and standard deviation for scaling, while transform applies the scaling.

Normalization, the min-max scaling

Normalization scales the data to a fixed range, usually 0 to 1. It is useful when you know the boundaries of your data and want to bring all the feature values within this range. The code is as follows:

```
from sklearn.preprocessing import MinMaxScaler

normalizer = MinMaxScaler()
df[['temperature', 'energy_consumption']] = normalizer.fit_
transform(df[['temperature', 'energy_consumption']])
print("Normalized 'temperature' and 'energy_consumption' features.")
```

The output is as follows:

```
Normalized 'temperature' and 'energy_consumption' features.
        date  temperature  occupancy  energy_consumption  year  month  \
0 2023-01-01     0.333333      745.0            0.000000  2023      1
1 2023-01-02     0.090562      625.0            0.006244  2023      1
2 2023-01-03     1.000000      308.0            0.003623  2023      1
3 2023-01-04     0.559193      178.0            0.789141  2023      1
4 2023-01-05     0.402619      210.0            0.146834  2023      1
```

The explanation is as follows:

- **MinMaxScaler**: This scaler transforms features by scaling each feature to a given range (default is 0 to 1).
- **Fit and transform**: The fit method computes the minimum and maximum values for scaling, while transform applies the scaling.

Encoding categorical variables

This section will look at the different types of encoding.

One-hot encoding

One-hot encoding converts categorical variables into a series of binary variables. Each category is converted into a new column, and a 1 or 0 indicates the presence of each category. The code is as follows:

```
df = pd.get_dummies(df, columns=['building_type'])
print("Applied one-hot encoding to 'building_type' feature.")
```

See an example of how hot-encoded columns look:

```
Applied one-hot encoding to 'building_type' feature.
         date  temperature  occupancy  energy_consumption  year  month  \
0 2023-01-01     0.333333      745.0            0.000000  2023      1
1 2023-01-02     0.090562      625.0            0.007992  2023      1
2 2023-01-03     1.000000      308.0            0.005802  2023      1
3 2023-01-04     0.559193      178.0            0.662370  2023      1
4 2023-01-05     0.402619      210.0            0.125503  2023      1

   temperature_energy  building_type_Commercial  building_type_Industrial  \
0         35289.52504                     False                     False
1         29580.62300                      True                     False
2         58045.11600                     False                      True
3        253700.00000                     False                      True
4         72946.12500                     False                     False

   building_type_Residential
0                       True
1                      False
2                      False
3                      False
4                       True
```

Figure 5.2: One-hot encoding

Label encoding

Label encoding converts categorical variables into numerical labels. Based on alphabetical ordering, each category is assigned a unique integer:

```
from sklearn.preprocessing import LabelEncoder

le = LabelEncoder()
df['building_type'] = le.fit_transform(df['building_type'])
print("Applied label encoding to 'building_type' feature.")
```

The following figure is an example of how the **building_type** column is transformed with label encoding:

Applied label encoding to 'building_type' feature.

	date	building_type	temperature	occupancy	energy_consumption	year	month	tempe
0	2023-01-01	2	0.333333	745.0	0.000000	2023	1	
1	2023-01-02	0	0.090562	625.0	0.007992	2023	1	
2	2023-01-03	1	1.000000	308.0	0.005802	2023	1	

Figure 5.3: *Label encoding*

Splitting the dataset

This section looks at the different ways to split a dataset.

Train-test split

Splitting the dataset into training and testing sets ensures that the model can generalize well to unseen data. The code is as follows:

```
from sklearn.model_selection import train_test_split

X = df.drop(columns=['energy_consumption'])
y = df['energy_consumption']

X_train, X_test, y_train, y_test = train_test_split(X, y, test_size=0.2, random_state=42)
print("Performed train-test split with 80% training and 20% testing data.")
```

Cross-validation

Cross-validation is a robust method for assessing model performance. It involves splitting the data into k-folds and training the model k times, each time using a different fold as the validation set. The code is as follows:

```
from sklearn.model_selection import cross_val_score
from sklearn.linear_model import LinearRegression

model = LinearRegression()

# Remove the 'date' column for cross-validation
X_cv = X.drop(columns=['date'])

scores = cross_val_score(model, X_cv, y, cv=5)
print(f'Cross-validation scores: {scores}')
print(f'Mean cross-validation score: {scores.mean()}')
```

The output is as follows:

```
Cross-validation scores: [0.95684324 0.82168077 0.78305162 0.98597417 0.99412282]
Mean cross-validation score: 0.9083345235381396
```

Train-test-validation split

To further ensure the robustness of our model, we can also split the data into three sets: training, validation, and testing. This allows us to tune hyperparameters on the validation set and assess the final model performance on the test set. The code is as follows:

```
X_train, X_temp, y_train, y_temp = train_test_split(X, y, test_size=0.4, random_state=42)
X_val, X_test, y_val, y_test = train_test_split(X_temp, y_temp, test_size=0.5, random_
state=42)
print("Performed train-test-validation split with 60% training,
20% validation, and 20% testing data.")
print(f"Validation set: {X_val.shape[0]} samples")
print(f"Testing set: {X_test.shape[0]} samples")
```

The output is as follows:

```
Performed train-test-validation split with 60% training, 20% validation, and 20% testing data.
```

Figure 5.4 illustrates how each split (`X_train`, `X_Val`, `X_test`) has different sizes due to the defined split above (60, 20, 20):

```
X_train.shape, X_temp.shape, y_train.shape, y_temp.shape
✓ 0.0s                                                    Python
((26, 9), (18, 9), (26,), (18,))

X_val.shape, X_test.shape, y_val.shape, y_test.shape
✓ 0.0s                                                    Python
((9, 9), (9, 9), (9,), (9,))
```

***Figure 5.4**: Train-test split*

Evaluation metrics

Evaluation metrics are essential tools for assessing the performance of machine learning models. They help us understand how well a model is making predictions and where it might be falling short. Different types of machine learning tasks require different metrics. Here, we will cover the most common metrics used for linear regression and classification tasks. (These types of tasks will be explained in detail in later chapters.)

- **Linear regression**:
  - **Mean squared error (MSE)**:
    - **Definition**: MSE measures how close the predicted values are to the actual values by averaging the squared differences between them.
    - **Explanation**: Imagine you are trying to predict the price of a house. The MSE tells you, on average, how much your predictions are off from the actual prices. Lower MSE means your predictions are more accurate.
  - **R-squared (R^2)**:
    - **Definition**: R^2 indicates how well the independent variables explain the variability of the dependent variable.
    - **Explanation**: Think of R^2 as a measure of how well your model's predictions match the actual data. An R^2 of 1 means your model perfectly predicts the data, while an R^2 of 0 means it does no better than simply guessing the average value.

- **Classification**:
  - **Accuracy**:
    - **Definition**: Accuracy is the percentage of correct predictions out of all predictions made.
    - **Explanation**: If you have a model that predicts whether emails are spam or not, accuracy tells you how many of those predictions were correct. For instance, if your model made 100 predictions and 90 were accurate, your accuracy is 90%.
  - **Precision**:
    - **Definition**: Precision measures how many of the positive predictions were correct.
    - **Explanation**: In the context of spam detection, precision tells you how many of the emails your model flagged as spam were spam. High precision means that when your model predicts spam, it is usually correct.
  - **Recall (Sensitivity)**:
    - **Definition**: Recall measures how many actual positives were correctly predicted by the model.
    - **Explanation**: Using the spam detection example, recall tells you how many of the actual spam emails were correctly identified by your model. High recall means your model is good at finding most of the spam emails.
  - **F1-score**:
    - **Definition**: F1-score is the balance between precision and recall, providing a single metric that considers both false positives and false negatives.
    - **Explanation**: The F1-score is useful when you need a balance between precision and recall. If your model has high precision but low recall, or vice versa, the F1-score will reflect this imbalance. It is beneficial when you want to find an optimal balance between identifying positive cases and avoiding false alarms.
  - **Confusion matrix**:
    - **Definition**: A confusion matrix is a table that summarizes the performance of a classification model by comparing actual and predicted values.
    - **Explanation**: The confusion matrix shows four outcomes: true positives (correctly predicted positive cases), true negatives (correctly predicted negative cases), false positives (incorrectly predicted as positive), and false negatives (incorrectly predicted as negative). This matrix helps you see where your model is making mistakes and provides insights into specific areas for improvement.

Overfitting vs. underfitting

This section explores how to detect when models are too complex or too simple for your data. The details are as follows:

- **Overfitting**: Overfitting occurs when a model learns not only the underlying patterns in the training data but also the noise and outliers. This results in excellent performance on the training data but poor generalization to new, unseen data. To detect overfitting, we compare the model's performance on the training dataset with its performance on a validation or test dataset using various metrics:
  - **High training accuracy and low-test accuracy**: When a model performs significantly better on the training data compared to the test data, it is a strong indicator of overfitting. For example, if the accuracy of a classification model is 95% on the training data but only 70% on the test data, the model is likely overfitting.

- **Low cross-validation scores**: Using cross-validation, where the data is split into multiple folds and the model is trained and evaluated on each fold, can help detect overfitting. If the cross-validation scores vary widely or are generally lower compared to the training accuracy, overfitting may be occurring.

- **Underfitting**: Underfitting occurs when a model is too simple to capture the underlying patterns in the data. Poor performance on both the training and test datasets typically indicates that the model is not complex enough to learn from the data effectively. Here are key indicators of underfitting:
  - **Low training and test accuracy**: When both the training and test accuracies are low, it indicates that the model is underfitting. For instance, if a linear regression model consistently predicts poorly on both the training and test data, it might be underfitting because the true relationship between the variables is more complex.
  - **High bias in model predictions**: Underfitting models often have high bias, meaning they make strong assumptions about the data that are not valid. This can be detected through residual plots (for regression) or by analyzing error distributions.

Supervised learning with Scikit-learn

Supervised learning is a type of machine learning where the model is trained on a labeled dataset, meaning each training example is paired with an output label. The model learns to map input features to the output labels and can then make predictions on new, unseen data.

Supervised learning involves two main types of problems:

- **Regression**: Predicting a continuous output variable. For example, predicting energy consumption based on building characteristics and weather conditions.
- **Classification**: Predicting a discrete output variable. For example, classifying whether an email is spam or not based on its content.

This chapter focuses on two commonly used algorithms, namely, **linear regression** for regression tasks and **logistic regression** for classification tasks. However, many other algorithms are available for both types of problems, each with its strengths and weaknesses. For more information, check the Scikit-learn documentation.

(**https://scikit-learn.org/stable/supervised_learning.html**).

Linear regression

Linear regression is a simple yet robust algorithm used for predicting a continuous output variable based on one or more input features. It assumes a linear relationship between the input features and the output variable.

Predicting restaurant revenue, the problem statement

In this section, we will use linear regression to predict the monthly revenue of restaurants based on various features such as the number of customers, menu price, marketing spend, cuisine type, average customer spending, promotions, and reviews. We will use the **Restaurant Revenue Prediction Dataset** for this task, and this dataset is in the GitHub repository for the book with the filename: `Restaurant_revenue.csv`.

Loading the data

First, let us load the dataset from the local CSV file. The code is as follows:

```
import pandas as pd

# Load the dataset
```

```
url = 'dataset/restaurant_revenue.csv'
df = pd.read_csv(url)

# Display the first few rows of the dataset
df.head()
```

Let us examine the first few rows of our dataset to understand its structure and content:

	Number_of_Customers	Menu_Price	Marketing_Spend	Cuisine_Type	Average_Customer_Spending	Promotions	Reviews	Monthly_Revenue
0	61	43.117635	12.663793	Japanese	36.236133	0	45	350.912040
1	24	40.020077	4.577892	Italian	17.952562	0	36	221.319091
2	81	41.981485	4.652911	Japanese	22.600420	1	91	326.529763
3	70	43.005307	4.416053	Italian	18.984098	1	59	348.190573
4	30	17.456199	3.475052	Italian	12.766143	1	30	185.009121

***Figure 5.5:** Table rows preview*

Data preparation

Data preparation involves handling missing values, encoding categorical variables, and scaling numerical features. See the preceding sections of this chapter for a more detailed explanation of the steps involved. The following code shows some of the data preparation tasks that you will encounter in any real project:

```
# Check for missing values
print(df.isnull().sum())

# Delete missing values
df.dropna(inplace=True)

# Encode categorical variables
data = pd.get_dummies(df, columns=['Cuisine_Type'], drop_first=True)

# Feature scaling
from sklearn.preprocessing import StandardScaler

scaler = StandardScaler()
scaled_features = scaler.fit_transform(data.drop('Monthly_Revenue', axis=1))

# Split the data into features (X) and target (y)
X = pd.DataFrame(scaled_features, columns=data.columns[:-1])
y = data['Monthly_Revenue']

# Train-test-validation split
from sklearn.model_selection import train_test_split

X_temp, X_test, y_temp, y_test = train_test_split(X, y, test_size=0.2, random_state=42)
X_train, X_val, y_train, y_val = train_test_split(X_temp, y_temp, test_size=0.25, random_state=42)  # 0.25 * 0.8 = 0.2

print(f"Training set size: {X_train.shape[0]}")
```

```
print(f"Validation set size: {X_val.shape[0]}")
print(f"Test set size: {X_test.shape[0]}")
```

This script will perform the data processing steps explained in previous sections of the book. It will also split the data into 3 different datasets: train, test, and validation.

Training the model

We use the linear regression algorithm from Scikit-learn to train the model. The code is as follows:

```
from sklearn.linear_model import LinearRegression

# Initialize and train the model
model = LinearRegression()
model.fit(X_train, y_train)
```

Evaluating the model

Evaluation involves checking how well the model performs on the validation and test datasets using metrics such as MSE and R^2. The *validation dataset* is a subset of the data that is used during model development to tune parameters and make decisions about the model's structure. In contrast, the *test dataset* is a separate subset that is only used at the end to assess the model's final performance. This helps ensure that the evaluation reflects how the model will perform on new, unseen data. The code is as follows:

```
from sklearn.metrics import mean_squared_error, r2_score

# Predict on validation set
y_val_pred = model.predict(X_val)

# Calculate metrics
mse_val = mean_squared_error(y_val, y_val_pred)
r2_val = r2_score(y_val, y_val_pred)

print(f"Validation MSE: {mse_val}")
print(f"Validation R2: {r2_val}")

# Predict on test set
y_test_pred = model.predict(X_test)

# Calculate metrics
mse_test = mean_squared_error(y_test, y_test_pred)
r2_test = r2_score(y_test, y_test_pred)

print(f"Test MSE: {mse_test}")
print(f"Test R2: {r2_test}")
```

The output is as follows:

```
Validation MSE: 2802.9763800780643
Validation R2: 0.7141719467935193
Test MSE: 3596.3274835159245
Test R2: 0.6707772447786471
```

The following list provides an explanation of the metrics:

- **Validation MSE**: 2802.976380078064:
    - MSE measures the average squared difference between the actual and predicted values. A lower MSE indicates better performance. Here, the validation MSE is 2802.98, which suggests that, on average, the squared differences between the actual and predicted revenues are around 2802.98.
- **Validation R^2**: 0.7141719467935193:
    - R^2 indicates the proportion of the variance in the dependent variable that is predictable from the independent variables. It ranges from 0 to 1, with higher values indicating better predictive power. An R^2 value of 0.71 means that our model explains 71% of the variance in the validation set revenue.
- **Test MSE**: 3596.327483515923:
    - The test MSE is slightly higher than the validation MSE, which indicates that the model's performance on the unseen test data is worse than on the validation data. However, it is still within a reasonable range, suggesting that the model generalizes well.
- **Test R^2**: 0.6707772447786471:
    - The test R^2 is 0.67, which is slightly lower than the validation R^2, which indicates that our model explains 67% of the variance in the test set revenue. This slight drop compared to the validation R^2 is expected when dealing with real-world data.

Visualizing the results

To understand the model's performance visually, we can plot the actual versus predicted values. The following code uses Matplotlib to plot a chart of actual vs. predicted revenue. This kind of chart is very common when testing machine learning algorithm results:

```
import matplotlib.pyplot as plt

# Function to plot actual vs predicted values
def plot_actual_vs_predicted(y_actual, y_predicted, title):
    plt.figure(figsize=(10, 6))
    plt.scatter(y_actual, y_predicted, alpha=0.5, edgecolors='k', linewidth=0.5)
    plt.plot([y_actual.min(), y_actual.max()], [y_actual.min(), y_actual.max()], 'r--', lw=2)
    plt.xlabel('Actual Revenue')
    plt.ylabel('Predicted Revenue')
    plt.title(title)
    plt.grid(True)
    plt.show()

# Plotting the actual vs. predicted values for the validation set
plot_actual_vs_predicted(y_val, y_val_pred, 'Actual vs Predicted Revenue (Validation Set)')

# Plotting the actual vs. predicted values for the test set
plot_actual_vs_predicted(y_test, y_test_pred, 'Actual vs Predicted Revenue (Test Set)')
```

The following figure shows the actual vs predicted revenue according to the model trained in the previous code section; this chart uses the validation set:

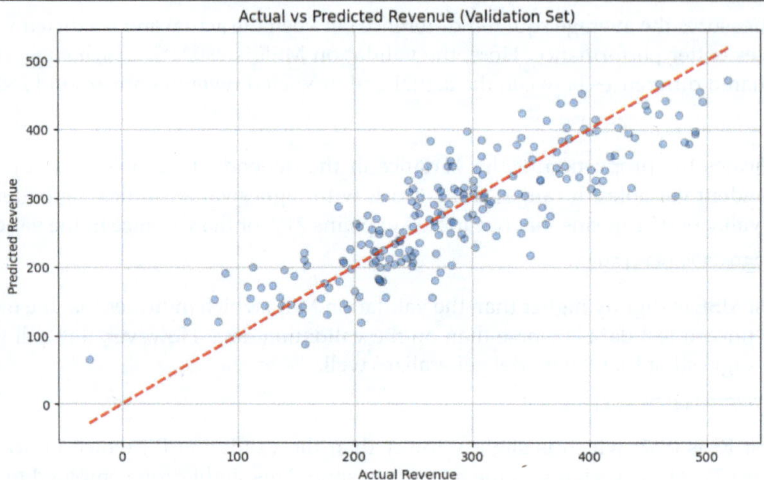

***Figure 5.6**: Actual vs. predicted revenue, validation set*

The following figure shows the actual vs. predicted revenue according to the model trained in the previous code section; this chart uses the test set:

***Figure 5.7**: Actual vs. predicted review, test set*

The visualizations show scatter plots of the actual versus predicted revenue for both the validation set (first chart) and the test set (second chart). Each point represents a data sample, with the actual revenue on the x-axis and the predicted revenue on the y-axis. The red dashed line is the ideal line where the actual revenue equals the expected revenue.

The explanation of the validation set is as follows:

- **Distribution**: The points are relatively close to the red dashed line, indicating that the model predictions are generally accurate. Most points are clustered along this line, showing a strong correlation between the actual and predicted values.

- **Errors**: Some points deviate from the red line, indicating prediction errors. However, the overall spread around the line is narrow, suggesting good performance.
- **Performance metrics**: The MSE for the validation set is 2802.976. This relatively low value indicates that the model's predictions are close to the actual values. The R^2 is 0.714, meaning that the model can explain approximately 71.4% of the variance in the actual revenue.

The explanation of the test set is as follows:

- **Distribution**: Like the validation set, the points on the test set plot are also close to the red dashed line. This suggests that the model generalizes well to unseen data.
- **Errors**: The spread of points around the red line is slightly more comprehensive compared to the validation set, indicating somewhat higher prediction errors. However, the deviations are not extreme.
- **Performance metrics**: The MSE for the test set is 3596.327, which is slightly higher than the validation set MSE, indicating more error in predictions on unseen data. The R^2 value is 0.671, showing that the model for the test set explains 67.1% of the variance in the actual revenue.

Saving and loading the model

To use the trained model for future predictions, we need to save it to disk. We can save the model using joblib or pickle. Here, we will use **`joblib`**:

```
import joblib

# Save the model to disk
joblib.dump(model, 'linear_regression_model.pkl')

# Load the model from disk
loaded_model = joblib.load('linear_regression_model.pkl')
```

Making predictions with new data

Finally, we make predictions on new, unseen data using the trained model.

When making predictions on new data, ensure that it undergoes the same preprocessing steps as the training data. This includes handling missing values, encoding categorical variables, and scaling numerical features. Additionally, make sure the new data has the same structure as the training data, including all required feature columns. The following code demonstrates how to prepare new data and make predictions using our trained model:

```
new_data = pd.DataFrame({
    'Number_of_Customers': [50, 70, 60],
    'Menu_Price': [40, 45, 55],
    'Marketing_Spend': [10, 15, 12],
    'Cuisine_Type': ['Italian', 'Japanese', 'Mexican'],
    'Average_Customer_Spending': [20, 30, 25],
    'Promotions': [1, 0,1],
    'Reviews': [30, 60, 20]
})

# Preprocessing the new data
#new_data.fillna(method='ffill', inplace=True)
new_data = pd.get_dummies(new_data, columns=['Cuisine_Type'], drop_first=False)
```

```

# Ensure new_data has the same columns as the training data
missing_cols = set(X.columns) - set(new_data.columns)
for col in missing_cols:
    new_data[col] = 0
new_data = new_data[X.columns]

# Scale the new data
new_data_scaled = loaded_scaler.fit_transform(new_data)

# Making predictions
new_predictions = loaded_model.predict(new_data_scaled)
print("Predicted Monthly Revenue:", new_predictions)
```

The following is the result or the output of the preceding code, which is the predicted monthly revenue for each of the three customers in the code:

```
Predicted Monthly Revenue: [120.48211747 394.02316696 287.4656673 ]
```

As you can see, the results return an array with 3 values; this is due to our new dataset with unseen information, which also contains 3 records.

Logistic regression

Logistic regression is a supervised learning algorithm used for classification tasks. Unlike linear regression, which predicts continuous values, logistic regression predicts the probability of an instance belonging to a particular class. It is especially useful for binary classification problems where the outcome has only two possible values (e.g., yes/no, true/false, 0/1). In this section, we will apply logistic regression to predict employee attrition.

Predicting employee attrition, the problem statement

Employee attrition, or employee turnover, refers to the process of employees leaving the company. By using logistic regression, we can predict whether an employee is likely to leave the company based on various features such as age, job satisfaction, and years at the company.

Dataset

The dataset we will be using is the HR analytics employee attrition dataset.

Loading the data

First, let us load our dataset, which is in a CSV file format:

```
import pandas as pd

# Load the dataset
url = 'datasets/Human_Resources.csv'
df = pd.read_csv(url)

# Display the first few rows of the dataset
df.head()
```

The preceding code allows us to preview the first rows of the dataset in the CSV file, as shown in the following figure:

	Age	Attrition	BusinessTravel	DailyRate	Department	DistanceFromHome	Education	EducationField	EmployeeCount	EmployeeNumber
0	41	Yes	Travel_Rarely	1102	Sales	1	2	Life Sciences	1	1
1	49	No	Travel_Frequently	279	Research & Development	8	1	Life Sciences	1	2
2	37	Yes	Travel_Rarely	1373	Research & Development	2	2	Other	1	4
3	33	No	Travel_Frequently	1392	Research & Development	3	4	Life Sciences	1	5
4	27	No	Travel_Rarely	591	Research & Development	2	1	Medical	1	7

5 rows × 35 columns

***Figure 5.8:** Human resources table preview*

Data preparation

Data preparation involves several steps to make the data suitable for training a model. We need to handle missing values, convert categorical variables into numerical format, and split the dataset into training, validation, and testing sets. The following code implements these preprocessing steps for our employee attrition dataset:

```
# Check for missing values
print(df.isnull().sum())

# Drop missing values (if any)
df.dropna(inplace=True)

# Encode categorical variables into numerical format
df = pd.get_dummies(df, drop_first=True)

# Split the data into features (X) and target (y)
X = df.drop('Attrition_Yes', axis=1)  # Features (all columns except Attrition)
y = df['Attrition_Yes']  # Target (Attrition column)

# Split the data into training, validation, and testing sets
from sklearn.model_selection import train_test_split
X_train, X_temp, y_train, y_temp = train_test_split(X, y, test_size=0.3, random_state=42)
X_val, X_test, y_val, y_test = train_test_split(X_temp, y_temp, test_size=0.5, random_state=42)

print(f"X Train: {X_train.shape}, X Val: {X_val.shape}, X Test:{X_test.shape}")
print(f"y Train: {y_train.shape}, y_val: {y_val.shape}, y_test:{y_test.shape}")
```

The preceding script splits the data into training, test, and validation sets, and then we print the shape of each dataset, which is shown in the following output. Basically, this is the number of rows and columns in each set:

```
X Train: (1029, 47), X Val: (220, 47), X Test:(221, 47)
y Train: (1029,), y_val: (220,), y_test:(221,)
```

This gives a clear overview of the size of the training, validation, and test datasets.

Training the model

Now, we will train the logistic regression model using the training data. The code is as follows:

```
from sklearn.linear_model import LogisticRegression

# Initialize the model
model = LogisticRegression(max_iter=1000)

# Train the model with the training data
model.fit(X_train, y_train)
```

Evaluating the model

After training, we need to evaluate the model to see how well it performs on the validation data. We will use accuracy, a confusion matrix, and a classification report for evaluation. If satisfied with the validation performance, we can then evaluate the test set.

```
from sklearn.metrics import classification_report, confusion_matrix, accuracy_score

# Predict on validation data
y_val_pred = model.predict(X_val)

# Evaluation metrics on validation set
print("Validation Accuracy:", accuracy_score(y_val, y_val_pred))
print(«Validation Confusion Matrix:\n», confusion_matrix(y_val, y_val_pred))
print(«Validation Classification Report:\n», classification_report(y_val, y_val_pred))

# If satisfied with validation performance, evaluate on test set
y_test_pred = model.predict(X_test)

# Evaluation metrics on test set
print("Test Accuracy:", accuracy_score(y_test, y_test_pred))
print("Test Confusion Matrix:\n", confusion_matrix(y_test, y_test_pred))
print("Test Classification Report:\n", classification_report(y_test, y_test_pred))
```

Explanation of results

Let us examine the evaluation metrics for both the validation and test sets.

- **Validation set results:**
  - **Validation accuracy:** 0.8727272727272727
  - **Validation confusion matrix:**

```
[[186 2]
 [ 26 6]]
```

- **Validation classification report**:

```
              precision    recall  f1-score   support

       False       0.88      0.99      0.93       188
        True       0.75      0.19      0.30        32

    accuracy                           0.87       220
   macro avg       0.81      0.59      0.61       220
weighted avg       0.86      0.87      0.84       220
```

- **Test set results**:
  - **Test accuracy**: 0.8552036199095022
  - **Test confusion matrix**:

```
[[185   7]
 [ 25   4]]
```

- **Test classification report**:

```
              precision    recall  f1-score   support

       False       0.88      0.96      0.92       192
        True       0.36      0.14      0.20        29

    accuracy                           0.86       221
   macro avg       0.62      0.55      0.56       221
weighted avg       0.81      0.86      0.83       221
```

The interpretation of metrics is explained as follows:

- **Accuracy**: This is the percentage of correct predictions made by the model. For the validation set, the accuracy is 87.27%, meaning the model correctly predicted 87.27% of the cases. For the test set, the accuracy is 85.52%.
- **Confusion matrix**: This matrix shows the number of correct and incorrect predictions.
  - **True Positives (TP)**: Employees who left and were correctly predicted to leave.
  - **True Negatives (TN)**: Employees who stayed and were correctly predicted to stay.
  - **False Positives (FP)**: Employees who stayed but were incorrectly predicted to leave.
  - **False Negatives (FN)**: Employees who left but were incorrectly predicted to stay
- **Precision**: This metric indicates the proportion of positive identifications that were correct. For the class `"True"` (employees who left), the precision is 0.75 in the validation set and 0.36 in the test set.
- **Recall**: This metric indicates the proportion of actual positives that were identified correctly. For the class `"True"` (employees who left), the recall is 0.19 in the validation set and 0.14 in the test set.
- **F1-score**: This is the harmonic mean of precision and recall. For the class `"True"` (employees who left), the F1-score is 0.30 in the validation set and 0.20 in the test set.

Visualizing the results

To better understand the model's performance, we can visualize the confusion matrix for both validation and test sets. This is the same confusion matrix printed out in the previous step, just in a graphical manner. See the confusion matrix in the following figure for the validation set:

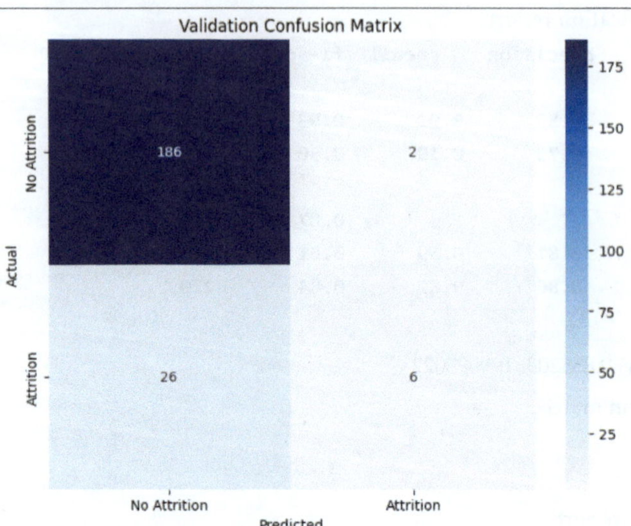

Figure 5.9: Confusion matrix for validation set

See the confusion matrix in the following figure for the test set:

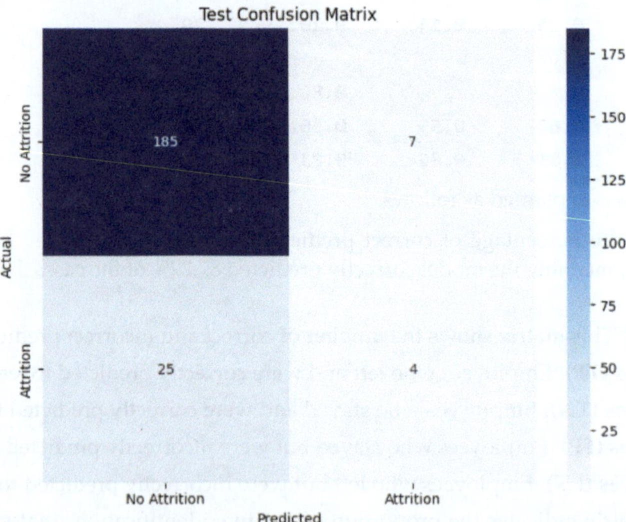

Figure 5.10: Confusion matrix for test set

Other algorithms

In addition to the well-known algorithms like linear regression and logistic regression, several other important supervised learning algorithms are essential for different types of tasks:

- **SVMs:**
  - **When to use**: Effective for tasks involving many features and useful for both classification and regression problems.

  - **Explanation**: SVMs work by finding a boundary that best separates different classes in the data. They are particularly good when the classes are well-separated.
- **KNN**:
  - **When to use**: Useful for classification and regression problems, especially when the data is not too large, and the relationship between features and output is complex.
  - **Explanation**: k-NN is a simple algorithm that classifies new data points based on **the** majority class among its nearest neighbors.
- **Naive Bayes**:
  - **When to use**: Effective for large datasets and real-time predictions, particularly useful for text classification tasks like spam detection.
  - **Explanation**: Naive Bayes classifiers assume that the presence of a particular feature in a class is unrelated to the presence of any other feature. They are based on Bayes' theorem.
- **Random Forests**:
  - **When to use**: Preferred for handling large datasets with many features and effective for both classification and regression.
  - **Explanation**: Random Forests create a collection of decision trees from random subsets of the training set and average their predictions to improve accuracy and reduce overfitting.
- **Gradient Boosting Machines (GBM)**:
  - **When to use**: Suitable for both classification and regression problems when high predictive accuracy is required, often used in competitive machine learning.
  - **Explanation**: GBMs build models sequentially, where each new model corrects errors made by the previous ones, leading to better overall performance.

Conclusion

In this chapter, we looked into the fundamental concepts and applications of supervised learning algorithms using Scikit-learn. We explored the importance of data preprocessing, feature engineering, and various performance evaluation metrics for linear regression and classification problems. Additionally, we introduced several other algorithms that are essential for different machine learning tasks and discussed when to use them. By understanding and applying these techniques, you are now equipped to tackle a wide range of machine learning problems with confidence.

In the next chapter, we will review some advanced topics using Scikit-learn, including ensemble learning, gradient boosting machines, and, of course, hyperparameter tuning, which is a topic that any machine learning engineer needs to master.

Exercises

The following are various exercises to build a comprehensive understanding.

1. **Data preparation and feature engineering**:
   - **Objective**: Prepare a dataset for modeling by handling missing values, engineering features, and splitting the data.
   - **Task**:
     - Load and inspect the dataset:
       - Load the building_energy_consumption.csv dataset.

        - Inspect the dataset for missing values and outliers.
  - **Handle missing values**:
    - Remove rows with missing values and inspect the effect on the dataset.
    - Alternatively, impute missing values using the mean for numerical columns.
  - **Feature engineering**:
    - Create an interaction feature between temperature and energy_consumption.
    - Extract the month from a date column (if available) and create a new Month feature.
  - **Feature scaling**: Scale the numerical features using standardization.
  - **Data splitting**: Split the dataset into training (80%) and testing (20%) sets.
2. **Linear regression model development and evaluation:**
  - **Objective**: Develop, train, and evaluate a linear regression model for predicting a target variable.
  - **Task**:
    - Load the restaurant_revenue.csv dataset.
    - Perform data cleaning: handle missing values and encode categorical variables.
  - **Split the data**:
    - Split the dataset into features (X) and target (y).
    - Perform a train-test split (80%-20%).
  - **Train a linear regression model**: Train a linear regression model on the training set.
  - **Evaluate the model**:
    - Use MSE and R^2 to evaluate the model's performance on the test set.
    - Visualize the results by plotting actual vs. predicted values.
3. **Classification with logistic regression**:
  - **Objective**: Build and evaluate a logistic regression model to predict a binary outcome.
  - **Task**:
    - Load the dataset:
      - Load the Human_Resources.csv dataset.
    - Perform data preparation steps, including handling missing values and encoding categorical variables.
  - **Split the data**:
    - Split the dataset into features (X) and target (y).
    - Perform a train-test split (80%-20%).
  - **Train a logistic regression model**: Train a logistic regression model to predict employee attrition.
  - **Evaluate the model**: Evaluate the model using accuracy, confusion matrix, and classification report on the test set.
  - **Cross-validation**: Use 5-fold cross-validation to evaluate the model's performance.

Multiple choice questions

1. **What is Scikit-learn primarily used for in the context of Python?**
   a. Web development
   b. Machine learning
   c. Data visualization
   d. Network security
2. **Which of the following is not a key feature of Scikit-learn?**
   a. Versatility
   b. Ease of use
   c. Limited integration with other Python libraries
   d. Community support
3. **Which command is used to install Scikit-learn via pip?**
   a. pip install scikit-learn
   b. install scikit-learn
   c. conda install scikit-learn
   d. python install scikit-learn
4. **What is the primary purpose of data preprocessing in machine learning?**
   a. To generate more data
   b. To transform raw data into a suitable format for analysis
   c. To remove all missing data
   d. To ensure data privacy
5. **Which method is used to handle missing values by replacing them with the mean value?**
   a. Dropna
   b. SimpleImputer
   c. Remove
   d. Normalization
6. **What does the Z-score method help identify in a dataset?**
   a. Missing values
   b. Outliers
   c. Categorical variables
   d. Correlated features
7. **Which of the following is a common evaluation metric for linear regression models?**
   a. Precision
   b. Recall
   c. MSE
   d. F1-score

8. **What problem occurs when a model performs well on training data but poorly on new, unseen data?**
   a. Underfitting
   b. Cross-validation
   c. Overfitting
   d. Normalization
9. **Which of the following is not an unsupervised learning algorithm provided by Scikit-learn?**
   a. K-means clustering
   b. **Principal component analysis (PCA)**
   c. Linear regression
   d. Hierarchical clustering
10. **What does the train_test_split function do in Scikit-learn?**
    a. Trains a model
    b. Splits data into training and testing sets
    c. Tests the performance of a model
    d. Scales the data

Answers

1.	b.
2.	c.
3.	a.
4.	b.
5.	b.
6.	b.
7.	c.
8.	c.
9.	c.
10.	b.

Key terms

- **Scikit-learn**: An open-source Python library that provides simple and efficient tools for data mining, data analysis, and machine learning.
- **Supervised learning**: A type of machine learning where the model is trained on a labeled dataset, meaning each input has an associated output label.
- **Regression**: A supervised learning task that involves predicting a continuous output variable based on one or more input features.
- **Classification**: A supervised learning task that involves predicting a discrete output label from a set of input features.

- **Evaluation metrics**: Statistical measures used to assess the performance of a machine learning model, including metrics like accuracy, precision, recall, F1-score, and MSE.
- **Overfitting**: A modeling error that occurs when a machine learning model learns not only the underlying patterns in the training data but also the noise, resulting in poor performance on new, unseen data.
- **Underfitting**: A modeling error that occurs when a machine learning model is too simple to capture the underlying patterns in the data, leading to poor performance on both training and test datasets.
- **Cross-validation**: A technique used to assess the performance of a model by splitting the data into multiple folds and training the model multiple times, each time using a different fold as the validation set.
- **Linear regression**: A supervised learning algorithm used for predicting a continuous output variable, assuming a linear relationship between the input features and the output variable.
- **Logistic regression**: A supervised learning algorithm used for classification tasks, predicting the probability that a given input belongs to a certain class.
- **SVMs**: A supervised learning algorithm used for both classification and regression tasks, which works by finding the optimal boundary that separates different classes in the data.
- **KNN**: A simple, instance-based learning algorithm used for classification and regression, which classifies a data point based on the majority class among its nearest neighbors.

Reference

1. **https://scikit-learn.org/stable/supervised_learning.html**

Chapter 6
Machine Learning with Scikit-learn Advanced Topics

Introduction

In the previous chapter, we explored various essential machine learning algorithms and how to implement them using Scikit-learn. Now, we will delve into more advanced topics that will help you tackle complex problems and enhance the performance of your models. Even if some of these concepts sound new or challenging, we will break them down into simple, easy-to-understandable steps.

Structure

This chapter covers the following topics:

- Unsupervised learning algorithms
- Ensemble learning
- Gradient boosting machines
- Cross-validation techniques
- Hyperparameter tuning

Objectives

By the end of this chapter, you will be able to understand and apply some of the more advanced techniques in machine learning. You will learn how to group data that has no labels, find patterns, and reduce the number of features in a dataset to make it easier to work with. Additionally, you will discover how to use powerful algorithms to improve the accuracy of your models, evaluate their performance more effectively, and fine-tune them to achieve the best results.

Unsupervised learning algorithms

Unsupervised learning is a type of machine learning where we do not have labeled data. Instead, the algorithm attempts to identify patterns and structures within the data on its own. This is crucial in scenarios where labeling data is expensive or time-consuming. Two essential techniques in unsupervised learning are clustering and dimensionality reduction.

K-means clustering

K-means clustering is a method for grouping data points into clusters. Imagine you have a collection of marbles of different colors, mixed together, and you want to sort them into groups based on their colors. K-means helps you find the natural groupings in your data.

The importance of k-means clustering lies in its ability to identify patterns or groups within datasets without requiring prior knowledge of the data. It is widely used in market segmentation, image compression, and anomaly detection.

The working of k-means clustering is explained as follows:

1. **Choosing the number of clusters**: First, you decide how many groups (clusters) you want to divide your data into.
2. **Assigning data points**: The algorithm randomly assigns each data point to one of the clusters.
3. **Updating clusters**: It then calculates the center of each cluster and reassigns the data points to the cluster center that is nearest to them.
4. **Repeating**: This process is repeated until the clusters do not change significantly, indicating that the algorithm has found the optimal groupings.

Use case

Imagine you are a marketing analyst for an e-commerce website. You want to group customers into different segments based on their purchasing behavior to create targeted marketing campaigns. K-means clustering can help you find these customer segments.

Here is how you can use k-means in Scikit-learn:

```
import pandas as pd
from sklearn.cluster import KMeans
import matplotlib.pyplot as plt

# Load the dataset
url = "https://raw.githubusercontent.com/tirthajyoti/Machine-Learning-with-Python/master/Datasets/Mall_Customers.csv"
data = pd.read_csv(url)

# Select features for clustering
X = data[['Annual Income (k$)', 'Spending Score (1-100)']]

# Fit the K-Means model
kmeans = KMeans(n_clusters=5, random_state=42)
data['Cluster'] = kmeans.fit_predict(X)

# Visualize the clusters
plt.scatter(X['Annual Income (k$)'], X['Spending Score (1-100)'], c=data['Cluster'], cmap='viridis')
plt.xlabel('Annual Income (k$)')
plt.ylabel('Spending Score (1-100)')
plt.title('Customer Segments')
plt.show()
```

The output is as follows:

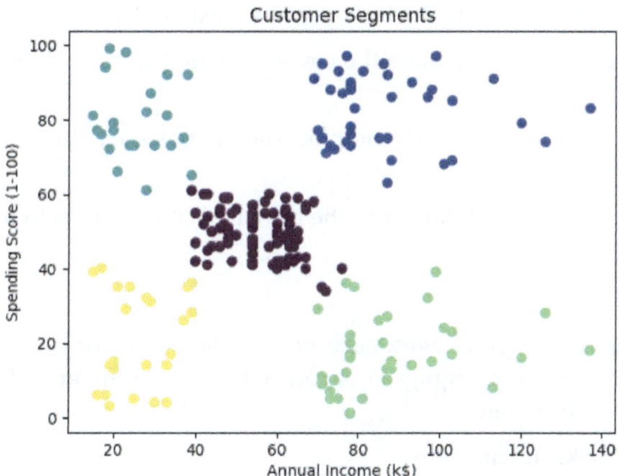

Figure 6.1: Customer segmentation using k-means clustering based on annual income and spending score

Visual explanation

The provided visual is a scatter plot showing customer segments based on their annual income and spending score. The k-means algorithm has clustered the data into five distinct segments. Here is a breakdown of the visual:

- **Axes**: The x-axis represents annual income in thousands of dollars (k$), and the y-axis represents the spending score (1-100), which measures customer spending behavior.
- **Data points**: Each dot represents a customer. The color of the dot indicates the cluster to which the customer has been assigned.
- **Clusters**: Different colors represent different clusters, with each cluster grouping customers with similar income and spending patterns.

For instance:

- The **teal cluster** (top left) represents customers with lower annual income but higher spending scores.
- The **purple cluster** (center) represents customers with average annual income and spending scores.
- The **yellow cluster** (bottom left) represents customers with lower annual income and spending scores.
- The **blue cluster** (top right) represents customers with higher annual income and higher spending scores.
- The **green cluster** (bottom right) represents customers with higher annual income but lower spending scores.

Principal component analysis

Principal component analysis (PCA) is a technique used to simplify a dataset. Sometimes, we have too many features (columns), making it difficult to analyze the data. PCA helps by reducing the number of features while keeping the vital information. Think of it as summarizing a long story into a short paragraph without losing the main points.

The importance of PCA is that it is essential for visualizing high-dimensional data, reducing computational costs, and removing noise. It helps identify the most significant features and simplify the dataset while retaining most of the original variance.

The working of PCA is explained as follows:

1. **Standardize the data**: Standardize the dataset to have a mean of zero and a standard deviation of one.
2. **Compute the covariance matrix**: Calculate the covariance matrix to understand how the variables in the dataset relate to each other.
3. **Eigen decomposition**: Perform eigen decomposition on the covariance matrix to find the principal components.
4. **Project the data**: Project the original data onto the principal components to reduce the dimensionality.

Use case

Suppose you are working with a dataset of images, each having thousands of pixels as features. Analyzing such high-dimensional data directly can be challenging. PCA can reduce the number of features to a manageable size while retaining most of the vital information.

Here is how you can use PCA in Scikit-learn:

```
import pandas as pd
import matplotlib.pyplot as plt
from sklearn.decomposition import PCA
from sklearn.preprocessing import StandardScaler
from sklearn.datasets import load_wine

# Load the dataset
wine = load_wine()
X = wine.data
y = wine.target

# Standardize the data
scaler = StandardScaler()
X_scaled = scaler.fit_transform(X)

# Fit PCA
pca = PCA(n_components=2)
X_pca = pca.fit_transform(X_scaled)

# Plot the PCA results
plt.figure(figsize=(8, 6))
colors = ['purple', 'yellow', 'teal']
for i in range(len(colors)):
    px = X_pca[:, 0][y == i]
    py = X_pca[:, 1][y == i]
    plt.scatter(px, py, c=colors[i], label=wine.target_names[i])

plt.title('PCA of Wine Dataset')
plt.xlabel('Principal Component 1')
plt.ylabel('Principal Component 2')
```

```
plt.legend()
plt.show()
```

The following figure shows a PCA visualization:

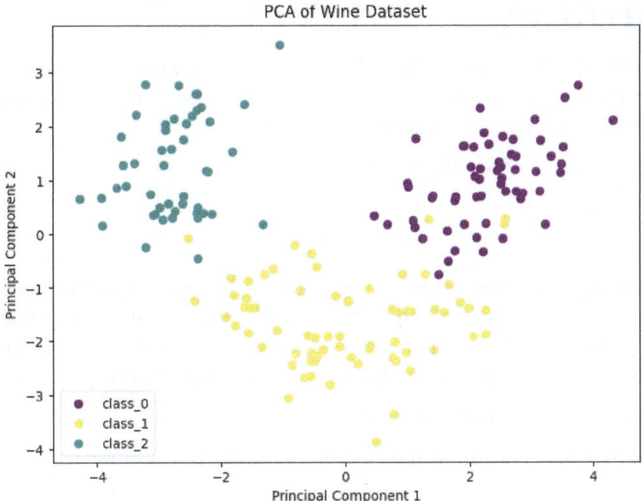

Figure 6.2*: PCA visualization of the wine dataset showing separation between the three classes*

Figure 6.2 is a scatter plot illustrating the result of applying PCA to a wine dataset. The wine dataset contains measurements of various chemical properties of wines, which belong to three different classes, listed as follows:

- **Axes**:
    - The x-axis represents the first principal component (PC1).
    - The y-axis represents the second principal component (PC2).
    - These principal components are linear combinations of the original features, capturing the directions of maximum variance in the data.
- **Data points**:
    - Each point on the plot represents a wine sample.
    - The color of the points indicates the class of the wine sample.
    - **Class 0**: Represented by purple points.
    - **Class 1**: Represented by yellow points.
    - **Class 2**: Represented by teal points.
- **Clusters**:
    - The clusters of points show how the data samples are distributed in the reduced two-dimensional space.
    - Points that are close to each other in this plot are similar in the context of the original feature space, whereas points that are far apart are dissimilar.

The PCA plot helps in visualizing the separation between the three classes of wine based on their chemical properties. It is evident from the plot that:

- **Class 0 (Purple)**: Mostly occupies the right side of the plot.
- **Class 1 (Yellow)**: Predominantly found in the bottom center of the plot.
- **Class 2 (Teal)**: Mainly located on the left side of the plot.

This separation indicates that PCA has effectively captured the variance in the data and has helped distinguish between the different classes of wine.

Ensemble learning

Ensemble learning is a highly effective approach in machine learning that involves combining diverse models to enhance the overall predictive performance and robustness. It can be likened to seeking advice from multiple experts and amalgamating their responses to attain the most accurate result.

This section discusses various types of ensemble methods.

Bagging

Bootstrap aggregating (**Bagging**) involves training multiple models on different subsets of the training data. These subsets are created by random sampling with replacements from the original dataset, a technique known as **bootstrapping**. Each of these models is then trained independently, and their predictions are combined, typically by averaging in the case of regression or majority voting in the case of classification.

Here is a step-by-step breakdown of how bagging works:

1. **Bootstrap sampling**: Create multiple datasets by randomly sampling from the original dataset with replacement.
2. **Model training**: Train a model (e.g., a decision tree) on each of the bootstrapped datasets.
3. **Aggregation**: Combine the predictions from each model to form the final prediction. For classification tasks, this usually means taking the majority vote, and for regression, it involves averaging the predictions.

Why use bagging? Bagging is beneficial when dealing with high-variance models, such as decision trees. Decision trees are prone to overfitting, meaning they might perform well on the training data but poorly on unseen data. By averaging multiple decision trees, bagging reduces the likelihood of overfitting and results in a more generalizable model.

Implementing bagging with decision trees in Scikit-learn

The following is an example of how to implement bagging using **`BaggingClassifier`** with a **`DecisionTreeClassifier`** as the base estimator. This example uses the Indian Liver Patient Dataset to classify whether a patient has a liver disease:

```
from sklearn.ensemble import BaggingClassifier
from sklearn.tree import DecisionTreeClassifier
from sklearn.metrics import accuracy_score
from sklearn.preprocessing import LabelEncoder

# Load the dataset
url = "https://raw.githubusercontent.com/mikeizbicki/datasets/master/csv/uci/Indian%20
Liver%20Patient%20Dataset%20(ILPD).csv"
data = pd.read_csv(url, header=None)

# Assign columns based on the dataset description
data.columns = ["Age", "Gender", "Total_Bilirubin", "Direct_Bilirubin", "Alkaline_Phosphotase",
                «Alamine_Aminotransferase», «Aspartate_Aminotransferase», «Total_Proteins»,
                "Albumin", "Albumin_and_Globulin_Ratio", "Selector"]
```

```

# Preprocess the data
# Convert gender to numerical
data['Gender'] = LabelEncoder().fit_transform(data['Gender'])

# Separate features and target
X = data.drop('Selector', axis=1)
y = data['Selector']

# Split the data into train, validation, and test sets
X_train, X_temp, y_train, y_temp = train_test_split(X, y, test_size=0.4, random_state=42)
X_val, X_test, y_val, y_test = train_test_split(X_temp, y_temp, test_size=0.5, random_
state=42)

# Initialize the base estimator with some complexity
base_estimator = DecisionTreeClassifier(max_depth=4, random_state=42)

# Initialize the bagging classifier
bagging_model = BaggingClassifier(estimator=base_estimator, n_estimators=10, random_
state=42, n_jobs=-1)

# Train the bagging classifier on the training set
bagging_model.fit(X_train, y_train)

# Validate the model on the validation set
y_val_pred = bagging_model.predict(X_val)
val_accuracy = accuracy_score(y_val, y_val_pred)
print(f'Validation Accuracy: {val_accuracy}')

# After tuning, evaluate the final model on the test set
y_test_pred = bagging_model.predict(X_test)
test_accuracy = accuracy_score(y_test, y_test_pred)
print(f'Test Accuracy: {test_accuracy}')
```

Visualizing a decision tree from the bagging model

To provide a visual understanding, we can extract one of the decision trees from the bagging ensemble and plot it. This visualization helps you visualize how the decision tree makes predictions based on the features. The code is as follows:

```
import matplotlib.pyplot as plt
from sklearn.tree import plot_tree

# Extract the first tree from the ensemble
estimator = bagging_model.estimators_[0]

# Plot the tree
```

```
plt.figure(figsize=(20, 10))
plot_tree(estimator, feature_names=X.columns, filled=True, rounded=True)
plt.show()
```

This code snippet utilizes the **`plot_tree`** function from Scikit-learn to visualize the decision tree. It shows the tree's structure, including the features used for splitting, the Gini index at each node, and the class distribution. This visualization helps understand how the model makes its predictions and helps interpret the importance of different features.

The following figure shows a visualization of one decision tree from our bagging ensemble model; this visualization is meant to illustrate the structure and complexity of the decision tree rather than specific decision criteria:

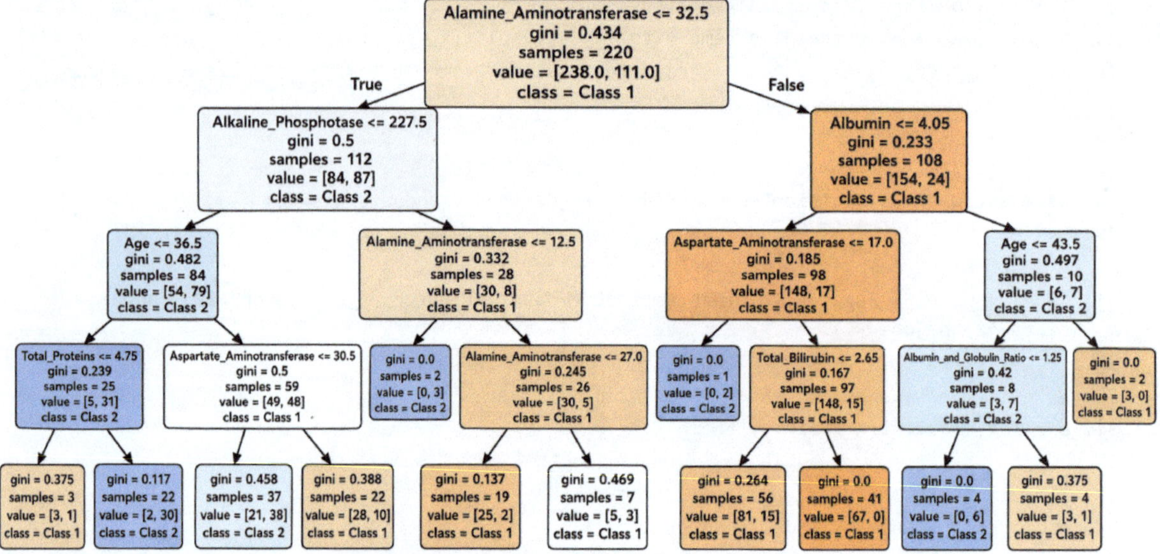

Figure 6.3: *Decision tree visualization from a bagging ensemble model for liver disease prediction*

Understanding the decision tree visualization

The decision tree visualization represents the decision-making process of one of the decision trees in the bagging model. Each node in the tree corresponds to a feature, and the tree splits the data based on the values of these features:

- **Nodes**: Each internal node represents a feature used to make a decision, with the decision criteria (e.g., **`Alamine_Aminotransferase <= 32.5`**) displayed on the node. The Gini index, which measures the impurity of the node, is also shown, along with the number of samples and the class distribution.
- **Leaves**: The terminal nodes (leaves) of the tree represent the final class prediction. These are colored based on the majority class in that node, with the class label shown at the bottom.
- **Feature importance**: The tree visually demonstrates how different features contribute to the classification decision. The higher up a feature appears in the tree, the more critical it is in making decisions.
- **Interpretation**: By following the branches from the root to the leaves, you can trace the decision-making process for a particular prediction. For example, if a patient's **`Alamine_Aminotransferase`** value is less than or equal to 32.5, the tree follows the left branch; otherwise, it follows the right branch.

This visual representation of a decision tree facilitates understanding of the reasoning behind the model's predictions, making it easier to interpret and explain the results.

Boosting

Boosting is an ensemble learning technique that enhances the performance of predictive models by combining several weak learners into a single, stronger learner. The primary goal of boosting is to reduce model bias and improve accuracy, making it a valuable tool for many machine learning tasks. Basic details of boosting are as follows:

- Boosting involves training models sequentially, where each new model attempts to correct the errors made by its predecessors. By focusing on the mistakes of earlier models, boosting methods aim to create a highly accurate and robust predictive model.
- **Importance of boosting**: Boosting enhances model accuracy by mitigating bias in predictive models. It is beneficial for complex datasets where simple models might not capture intricate patterns. Due to their high performance, boosting techniques are widely used in practical applications and competitions.

The working of boosting is explained as follows:

- **Initialization**: Start with a base model (weak learner) and train it on the dataset.
- **Error calculation**: Compute the errors (residuals) of the model's predictions.
- **Model training**: Train a new model, focusing on the residuals to correct the errors of the previous model.
- **Update weights**: Adjust the weights of instances to emphasize misclassified examples.
- **Combine models**: Add the new model to the ensemble and combine predictions from all models to make the final prediction.

Types of boosting algorithms

While **gradient boosting machines (GBM)** are a popular form of boosting, there are other noteworthy boosting techniques, such as AdaBoost and XGBoost. Since AdaBoost is included in Scikit-learn, we will focus on it. The details of AdaBoost are as follows:

- **Adaptive boosting (AdaBoost)**: AdaBoost focuses on enhancing the performance of weak learners by adjusting the weights of incorrectly classified instances, thereby causing subsequent models to pay more attention to these instances.
- **Why use AdaBoost**: AdaBoost effectively reduces bias and is relatively simple to implement. It is helpful for binary classification tasks and can significantly improve model accuracy with relatively few iterations.
- The working of AdaBoost is listed as follows:
    - **Initialization**: Assign equal weights to all training instances.
    - **Model training**: Train a weak learner on the weighted dataset.
    - **Error calculation**: Compute the error rate of the weak learner.
    - **Update weights**: Increase the weights of misclassified instances and decrease the weights of correctly classified ones.
    - **Combine models**: Aggregate the predictions of all weak learners using a weighted voting approach.

Let us implement an AdaBoost classifier using Scikit-learn:

```
from sklearn.ensemble import AdaBoostClassifier
from sklearn.tree import DecisionTreeClassifier
from sklearn.metrics import accuracy_score
from sklearn.model_selection import train_test_split
import pandas as pd

```

```
# Load the dataset
url = "https://www.openml.org/data/get_csv/31/dataset_31_adult.csv"
data = pd.read_csv(url)

# Assign columns based on the dataset description
data.columns = ["checking_status","duration","credit_history","purpose","credit_amount","savings_status", "employment", "installment_commitment",
                "personal_status","other_parties","residence_since","property_magnitude","age","other_payment_plans","housing","existing_credits",
                "job","num_dependents","own_telephone","foreign_worker","class"]
# # Separate features and target
X = data.drop("class", axis=1)
y = data['class']

# # Convert categorical columns to numerical
X = pd.get_dummies(X, drop_first=True)

# # Split the data into train and test sets
X_train, X_test, y_train, y_test = train_test_split(X, y, test_size=0.3, random_state=42)

# # Initialize the AdaBoost Classifier
ada = AdaBoostClassifier(estimator=DecisionTreeClassifier(max_depth=1), n_estimators=50, random_state=42)

# # Train the AdaBoost model
ada.fit(X_train, y_train)

# # Make predictions and evaluate the model
y_pred = ada.predict(X_test)
accuracy = accuracy_score(y_test, y_pred)
print(f'Test Accuracy: {accuracy}')
```

Visualizing weak learners in AdaBoost

In AdaBoost, the ensemble consists of multiple weak learners, typically decision trees. Visualizing these weak learners is like what we did with bagging, as both methods often use decision trees as base estimators.

Visualizing decision trees is used to visualize individual decision trees; you can use Matplotlib to plot them. This is especially useful to understand how each tree contributes to the final prediction in the ensemble.

The following code visualizes a decision tree from our AdaBoost ensemble:

```
from sklearn.tree import DecisionTreeClassifier, plot_tree
import matplotlib.pyplot as plt

# Initialize and train a single decision tree
tree = DecisionTreeClassifier(max_depth=1)
tree.fit(X_train, y_train)

```

```
# Plot the decision tree
plt.figure(figsize=(12, 8))
plot_tree(tree, feature_names=X.columns, class_names=y.unique(), filled=True, rounded=True)
plt.title('Decision Tree Visualization')
plt.show()
```

Let us visualize a simple decision tree to understand how it makes classification decisions:

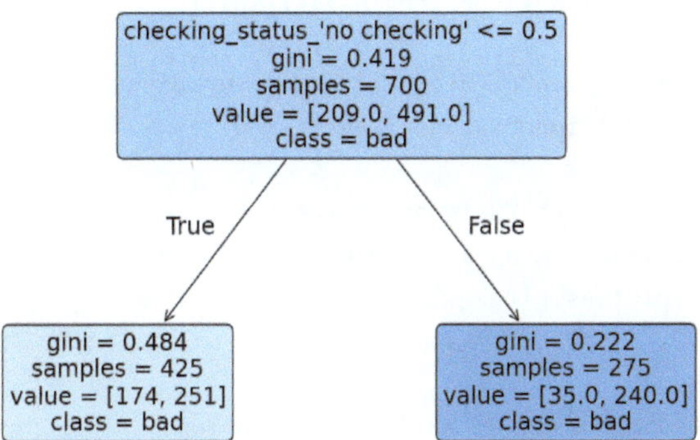

***Figure 6.4**: Decision tree visualization of a weak learner used in the AdaBoost ensemble model for classification*

Stacking

Stacking, also known as **stacked generalization**, is an advanced ensemble learning technique that aims to improve the accuracy and robustness of predictive models. Unlike other ensemble methods, such as bagging and boosting, which typically combine models of the same type, stacking leverages the power of diverse models by integrating their predictions through a meta-model.

Importance of stacking

Stacking is powerful because it combines the strengths of multiple different algorithms, allowing them to complement each other's weaknesses. By learning how to effectively incorporate the predictions of these base models, the meta-model can often achieve superior performance compared to any single model on its own. This technique is beneficial when different models have varied predictive power across different parts of the data.

The working of stacking is explained as follows:

- **Base models (Level-0 models)**: Multiple base models are trained on the training data. Each model generates its predictions, which serve as the input features for the next layer.
- **Meta-model (Level-1 model)**: A meta-model is trained on the outputs (predictions) of the base models. The meta-model learns how to combine these predictions best to make the final prediction. Depending on the problem, this model can be a simple linear model or a more complex one.
- **Cross-validation in stacking**: To avoid overfitting, stacking often uses cross-validation to generate predictions for the meta-model training. For each fold in cross-validation, the base models are trained on the training folds and make predictions on the validation fold. These predictions are then used as inputs to train the meta-model.

- **Use case**: Imagine you are building a predictive model for house prices. You want to predict house values based on features such as surface area, number of rooms, and location. Different models, such as linear regression, SVM, and KNN, might perform well on different subsets of data. By stacking these models, you can leverage their strengths and improve the overall prediction accuracy.

Here is how you can implement stacking using Scikit-learn:

```
import pandas as pd
import numpy as np
from sklearn.datasets import fetch_california_housing
from sklearn.model_selection import train_test_split
from sklearn.ensemble
import StackingRegressor, RandomForestRegressor, GradientBoostingRegressor
from sklearn.linear_model import LinearRegression
from sklearn.svm import SVR
from sklearn.neighbors import KNeighborsRegressor
from sklearn.metrics import mean_squared_error, r2_score
import matplotlib.pyplot as plt

# Load the dataset
data = fetch_california_housing()
X = pd.DataFrame(data.data, columns=data.feature_names)
y = pd.Series(data.target)

# Split the data into train and temporary sets (70% train,
30% temporary)
X_train, X_temp, y_train, y_temp = train_test_split(X, y, test_size=0.3, random_state=42)

# Split the temporary set into validation and test sets (50%
validation, 50% test)
X_val, X_test, y_val, y_test = train_test_split(X_temp, y_temp, test_size=0.5, random_
state=42)

# Define the base models
base_models = [
    ('rf', RandomForestRegressor(n_estimators=100, random_state=42)),
    ('gb', GradientBoostingRegressor(n_estimators=100, random_state=42)),
    ('svr', SVR()),
    ('knn', KNeighborsRegressor()),
]

# Define the meta-model
meta_model = LinearRegression()

# Create the stacking regressor
stacking_model = StackingRegressor(estimators=base_models, final_estimator=meta_
model, cv=5)
```

```

# Train the stacking model
stacking_model.fit(X_train, y_train)

# Evaluate the model on the validation set
y_val_pred = stacking_model.predict(X_val)
val_mse = mean_squared_error(y_val, y_val_pred)
val_r2 = r2_score(y_val, y_val_pred)
print(f'Validation MSE: {val_mse}')
print(f'Validation R^2: {val_r2}')

# Evaluate the model on the test set
y_test_pred = stacking_model.predict(X_test)
test_mse = mean_squared_error(y_test, y_test_pred)
test_r2 = r2_score(y_test, y_test_pred)
print(f'Test MSE: {test_mse}')
print(f'Test R^2: {test_r2}')

# Plotting predicted vs true values
plt.scatter(y_test, y_test_pred)
plt.plot([min(y_test), max(y_test)], [min(y_test), max(y_
test)], color='red', linestyle='--')
plt.xlabel('True Values')
plt.ylabel('Predictions')
plt.title('True vs Predicted Values')
plt.show()
```

The output is as follows:

```
Validation MSE: 0.27063119426915266
Validation R^2: 0.7922644386215157
Test MSE: 0.23686529696482603
Test R^2: 0.820870127646605
```

The output indicates that the stacking regressor performs well, with a validation MSE of 0.2706 and an R^2 of 0.7923, suggesting that it explains approximately 79% of the variance in the validation data. On the test set, the model performs even better, with a lower MSE of 0.2369 and a higher R^2 of 0.8209, meaning it explains over 82% of the variance. These results suggest that the model generalizes effectively, making accurate predictions on unseen data without overfitting.

The following scatter plot visualizes how well our stacking model's predictions match the actual values:

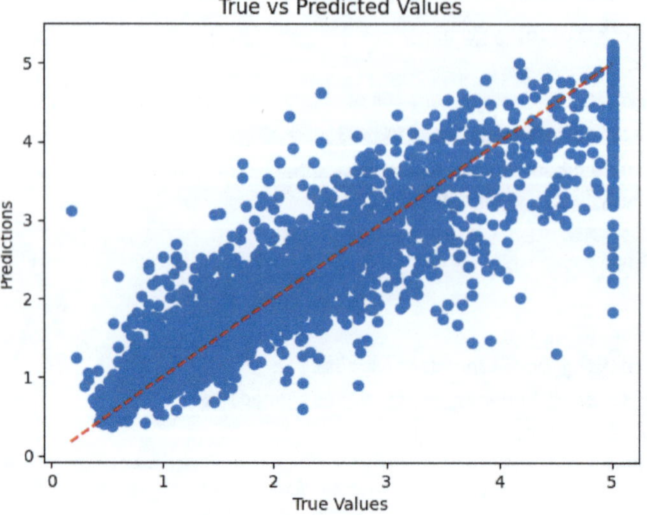

***Figure 6.5**: Scatter plot showing predicted vs. actual values from the stacking regressor model*

The scatter plot shows the relationship between the actual values (x-axis) and the predicted values (y-axis) from your stacking regressor. Most points are close to the red dashed line, which represents perfect predictions, indicating that the model generally makes accurate predictions. However, some dispersion and outliers, especially at higher actual values, suggest the model is less precise in those cases but still performs well overall.

The explanation is as follows:

- **Base models**: Base learners include **random forest (RF) regressor**, **gradient boosting** (**GB**), **support vector regression** (**SVR**), and KNN.

  Each base learner captures different aspects of the data and contributes to the overall performance of the stacking model. You can change each model's hyperparameters.
- **Meta-model**: The meta-model is a linear regression model that takes the predictions from the base models as input and produces the final prediction.

A representation of stacking architecture is shown in the following figure:

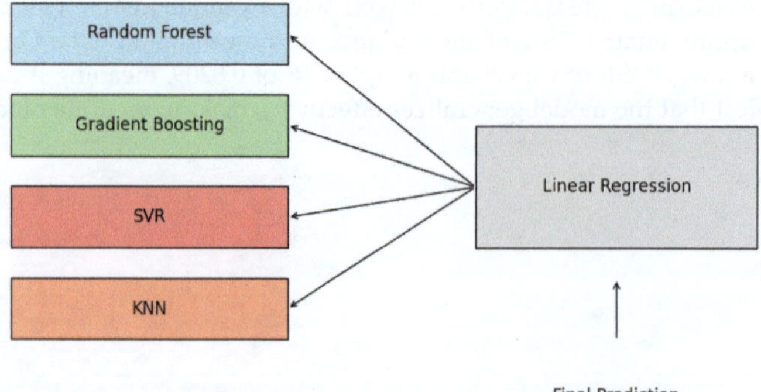

***Figure 6.6**: Stacking architecture diagram showing multiple base models feeding into a meta-model*

The following list outlines when to use stacking:

- **Complex datasets**: Stacking is particularly useful when dealing with complex datasets where different models may capture different patterns in the data.
- **Model diversity:** It is most effective when the base models are diverse, meaning they differ in their algorithmic approaches and decision boundaries.
- **When other ensemble methods fail**: If bagging or boosting methods do not improve performance, stacking might offer a significant boost by leveraging multiple models.

Stacking can be slightly more computationally intensive and complex to implement than straightforward ensemble techniques, but the potential gains in accuracy and robustness often make it worthwhile.

Gradient boosting machines

Gradient boosting is a powerful machine learning technique used for regression and classification problems. It builds models sequentially, where each new model attempts to correct the errors made by the previous models. This iterative process yields a robust model that minimizes both bias and variance, resulting in enhanced predictive performance.

Importance of gradient boosting machines

GBM is widely regarded for its ability to produce high-accuracy models. It excels in various tasks, such as structured data prediction, and its flexibility allows it to be applied to a wide range of problems. Unlike simple models, GBM can capture complex patterns in data by combining multiple weak learners into a robust model.

Working of gradient boosting machines

Imagine you are trying to guess a number, and you are not sure what it is at first. You make a guess, but it is not quite right. Instead of giving up, you use the information from your first guess to make a better guess the next time. You keep repeating this process, learning from your mistakes each time, until your guess is very close to the actual number. This is similar to how gradient boosting works, but instead of guessing a number, it attempts to predict something like the price of a house or whether an email is spam.

Here is how it works step-by-step:

1. **Start with a simple model**: GBM begins by creating a simple model to make predictions. This first model might not be very accurate, just like your first guess in the number game.
2. **Look at the mistakes**: After making predictions with the simple model, GBM checks how far off these predictions are from the actual answers. These differences are referred to as *errors* or *residuals.*
3. **Try to correct the mistakes**: GBM then creates a new model that focuses on predicting these errors. It is like asking, *Where did I go wrong?* and then using that information to make a better guess.
4. **Combine the models**: GBM adds the new model to the original model to improve its predictions. This new, combined model should be more accurate than the first one.
5. **Repeat the process**: This process of examining mistakes, building a new model to fix them, and combining it with the previous models is repeated several times. With each new model, the overall prediction improves.
6. **Final prediction**: After performing this process multiple times, the final prediction is made by combining all the models. This final model is much more accurate than any of the individual models because it has learned from its mistakes repeatedly.

In simple terms, gradient boosting is akin to a team effort in which each team member (model) learns from the mistakes of the previous one, and together, they make a strong prediction.

Use case

Breast cancer is one of the most common cancers affecting women worldwide, and early detection is crucial for effective treatment. The code example further down this section demonstrates how machine learning, specifically gradient boosting, can be used to predict whether a breast tumor is malignant (cancerous) or benign (non-cancerous) based on data from medical examinations.

About the dataset

The dataset used in this example is the Breast Cancer Wisconsin dataset, which contains information from digitized images of breast tissue samples obtained through a procedure called **fine needle aspiration (FNA)**. This procedure collects cells from a breast mass for examination under a microscope.

The dataset includes 30 features that describe various characteristics of the cell nuclei in the tissue samples. Some key features include:

- **Radius (mean radius)**: The average size of the cell nuclei in the image.
- **Texture (mean texture)**: A measure of the variation in grayscale intensity, which can indicate irregularities in the cell structure.
- **Perimeter (mean perimeter)**: The average distance around the cell nuclei.
- **Area (mean area)**: The size of the area occupied by the cell nuclei.
- **Smoothness (mean smoothness)**: Describes how smooth the cell nuclei are, with smoother cells typically being more regular in shape.

These features help to quantify the characteristics of the cells in a way that a computer model can analyze. The goal is to use these measurements to predict whether the tumor is malignant (coded as 1) or benign (coded as 0).

Here is the implementation of a GBM classifier for breast cancer prediction:

```
import pandas as pd
from sklearn.datasets import load_breast_cancer
from sklearn.model_selection import train_test_split, GridSearchCV
from sklearn.ensemble import GradientBoostingClassifier
from sklearn.metrics import classification_report, confusion_matrix, roc_auc_score, roc_curve
import matplotlib.pyplot as plt
import seaborn as sns

# Load the Breast Cancer dataset
data = load_breast_cancer()
df = pd.DataFrame(data.data, columns=data.feature_names)
df['target'] = data.target

# Display basic statistics and class distribution
print(df.describe())
print(df['target'].value_counts())

# Prepare features (X) and target (y)
```

```
X = df.drop('target', axis=1)
y = df['target']

# Split the data into training and testing sets
X_train, X_test, y_train, y_test = train_test_split(X, y, test_size=0.3, random_
state=42, stratify=y)

# Initialize and train the Gradient Boosting model with
hyperparameter tuning using GridSearchCV
param_grid = {
    'n_estimators': [100, 200, 300],
    'learning_rate': [0.01, 0.1, 0.2],
    'max_depth': [3, 4, 5],
    'min_samples_split': [2, 5, 10]
}

gbm = GradientBoostingClassifier(random_state=42)
grid_search = GridSearchCV(estimator=gbm, param_grid=param_grid, cv=5, n_jobs=-
1, verbose=1)
grid_search.fit(X_train, y_train)

# Best parameters found by GridSearchCV
print(f"Best Parameters: {grid_search.best_params_}")

# Make predictions on the test set
y_pred = grid_search.best_estimator_.predict(X_test)
y_pred_proba = grid_search.best_estimator_.predict_proba(X_test)[:, 1]

# Evaluate the model
print("Classification Report:\n", classification_report(y_test, y_pred))
print(«Confusion Matrix:\n», confusion_matrix(y_test, y_pred))

# Calculate ROC AUC score
roc_auc = roc_auc_score(y_test, y_pred_proba)
print(f»ROC AUC Score: {roc_auc:.3f}»)

# Plot ROC curve
fpr, tpr, _ = roc_curve(y_test, y_pred_proba)
plt.figure(figsize=(10, 8))
plt.plot(fpr, tpr, label=f'ROC Curve (AUC = {roc_auc:.3f})')
plt.plot([0, 1], [0, 1], 'k--')
plt.xlabel('False Positive Rate')
plt.ylabel('True Positive Rate')
plt.title('ROC Curve')
plt.legend(loc='lower right')
```

```
plt.show()

# Visualize the confusion matrix
sns.heatmap(confusion_matrix(y_test, y_pred), annot=True, fmt='d', cmap='Blues')
plt.xlabel('Predicted')
plt.ylabel('Actual')
plt.title('Confusion Matrix for Breast Cancer Prediction')
plt.show()

# Feature importance
feature_importances = grid_search.best_estimator_.feature_importances_
sorted_idx = feature_importances.argsort()
plt.figure(figsize=(10, 8))
plt.barh(range(len(sorted_idx)), feature_importances[sorted_idx], align='center')
plt.yticks(range(len(sorted_idx)), X.columns[sorted_idx])
plt.xlabel("Feature Importance")
plt.title("Feature Importance in GBM Model")
plt.show()
```

The output is as follows:

```
Confusion Matrix:
 [[ 57   7]
 [  2 105]]
ROC AUC Score: 0.992
```

The following figures show the model evaluation results for our GBM classifier; the first one is the ROC curve:

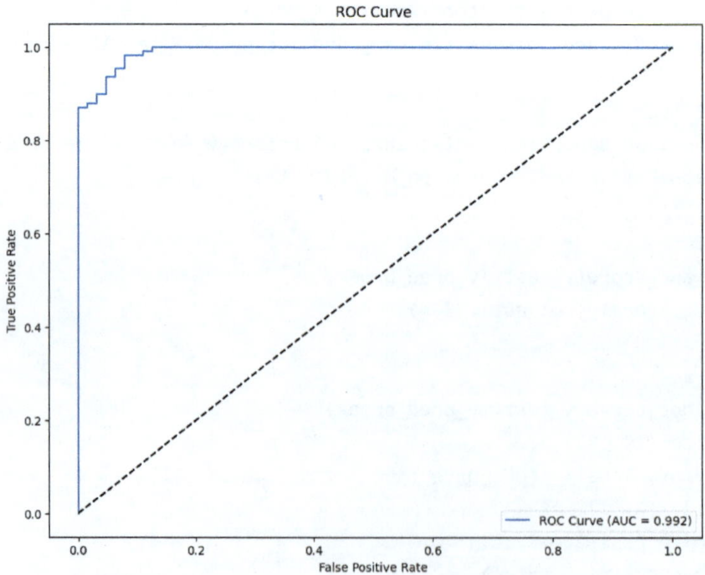

***Figure 6.7**: ROC curve for the GBM breast cancer classification model*

The second one is the confusion matrix for the breast cancer prediction:

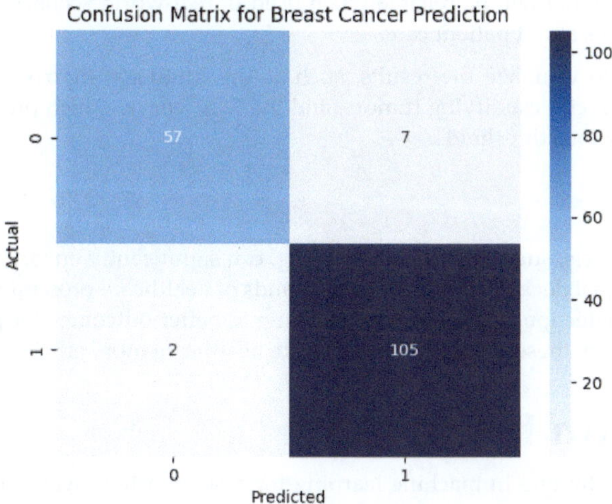

***Figure 6.8:** Confusion matrix for breast cancer prediction*

Then it is the feature importance, which clearly shows which features are weighted higher when doing a prediction:

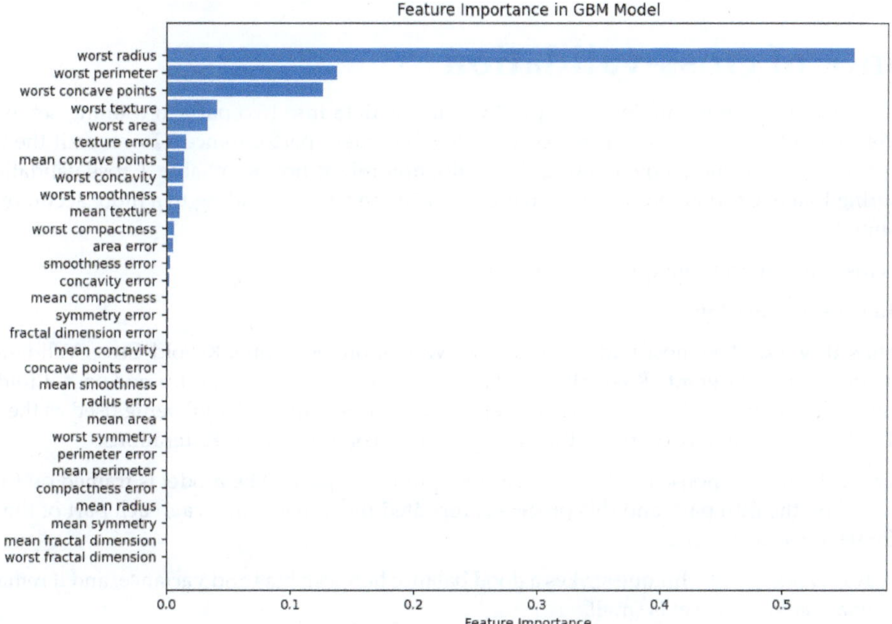

***Figure 6.9:** Feature importance plot*

How the model works

In the code example, a GBM is trained on the dataset to learn how these features relate to the type of tumor. By examining patterns in the data, the model learns to differentiate between malignant and benign tumors with a high degree of accuracy.

After training, the model is tested on new data (which it has not previously seen) to evaluate its performance. This process helps ensure that the model will be reliable when used in real-world scenarios, such as aiding doctors in making more informed decisions about patient care.

The code also includes steps to visualize the results, such as the confusion matrix, which displays the model's accuracy in correctly and incorrectly classifying tumors, and the ROC curve, which provides a detailed view of the model's performance across various thresholds.

Why this matters

Utilizing machine learning models, such as gradient boosting, can significantly enhance the speed and accuracy of medical diagnoses. While the final decision is always in the hands of healthcare professionals, such models can serve as valuable tools in the early detection of breast cancer, leading to better outcomes for patients. By automating the analysis of complex medical data, these models can help make healthcare more efficient and accessible.

Cross-validation techniques

Cross-validation is a crucial technique in machine learning for assessing how well a model will generalize to an independent dataset. Instead of relying on a single train-test split, cross-validation provides a more robust evaluation by repeatedly splitting the dataset into different training and testing sets. This process helps in better estimating the model's performance and ensures that it does not just memorize the training data (overfitting) but learns to generalize.

Importance of cross-validation

When building a machine learning model, we typically split the data into two parts: a training set, which is used to train the model, and a test set, which is used to evaluate the model's performance. However, if the test set is too small or not representative of the whole dataset, the evaluation might not be reliable. Cross-validation mitigates this risk by ensuring that every data point gets a chance to be in the test set, leading to a more accurate and reliable performance estimate.

Some standard cross-validation techniques are as follows:

- **K-Fold Cross-Validation**:
  - **How it works**: The most widely used cross-validation technique, K-Fold Cross-Validation, involves splitting the dataset into K equally sized folds or subsets. The model is trained on K-1 folds and tested on the remaining folds. This process is repeated K times, with each fold being used as the test set once. The final performance metric is the average of the scores across all K iterations.
  - **Example**: If you choose K = 5, the dataset is split into 5 parts. The model is trained on four parts and tested on the fifth part, and this process is repeated five times. This way, each part of the data is used for testing exactly once.
  - **Advantages**: This technique strikes a good balance between bias and variance, and it remains effective even when the dataset is small.
- **Stratified K-Fold Cross-Validation**:
  - **How it works**: Like K-Fold Cross-Validation, but with an added step to ensure that the distribution of classes (for classification tasks) is the same in each fold as it is in the whole dataset. This is particularly important when dealing with imbalanced datasets where some classes are underrepresented.
  - **Example**: In a breast cancer classification task, if 70% of the data points are benign and 30% are malignant, Stratified K-Fold ensures that each fold has the same 70-30 split.

  - **Advantages**: This technique is particularly useful in classification problems with imbalanced classes, as it provides a more accurate estimate of model performance across different folds.

- **Leave-One-Out Cross-Validation (LOOCV)**:
  - **How it works**: LOOCV is a particular case of K-Fold Cross-Validation, where K equals the number of data points in the dataset. This means that for each iteration, the model is trained on all data points except one, and it is tested on that single data point. This is repeated for every data point in the dataset.
  - **Advantages**: LOOCV uses the maximum possible data for training, which can provide a comprehensive evaluation. However, it can be computationally expensive for large datasets since it requires as many models as there are data points.

- **Time Series Cross-Validation**:
  - **How it works**: This technique is specifically designed for time series data, where the order of data points is important. Instead of random splitting, the data is split based on time, ensuring that future points are not used to predict past points. Typically, the model is trained on past data and validated on a future segment.
  - **Example**: To predict stock prices, you might train the model on data from January to March, test it on data from April, and then shift the window forward to include data from May.
  - **Advantages**: This method respects the temporal structure of the data, preventing data leakage, which could lead to overly optimistic performance estimates.

- **Nested Cross-Validation**:
  - **How it works**: Nested Cross-Validation is used when hyperparameter tuning is involved. It includes two loops, namely, the inner loop is used for hyperparameter tuning, and the outer loop is used for model evaluation. This technique ensures that the hyperparameters are tuned without biasing the model evaluation.
  - **Advantages**: Nested Cross-Validation provides an unbiased estimate of model performance when model selection and hyperparameter tuning are involved, avoiding overfitting on the validation data.

The following is an example code:

```
# test classification dataset
from sklearn.datasets import make_classification
from numpy import mean
from numpy import std
from sklearn.model_selection import KFold
from sklearn.model_selection import cross_val_score
from sklearn.linear_model import LogisticRegression


# define dataset
X, y = make_classification(n_samples=100, n_features=20, n_informative=15, n_redundant=5, random_state=1)

# Evaluate a logistic regression model using k-fold cross-validation
# Create dataset
X, y = make_classification(n_samples=100, n_features=20, n_informative=15, n_redundant=5, random_state=1)
# Prepare the cross-validation procedure
```

```
cv = KFold(n_splits=10, random_state=1, shuffle=True)
# Create model
model = LogisticRegression()
# Evaluate model
scores = cross_val_score(model, X, y, scoring='accuracy', cv=cv, n_jobs=-1)
# report performance
print('Accuracy: %.3f (%.3f)' % (mean(scores), std(scores)))
```

In the preceding example, we create a synthetic dataset with `make_classification`, then train a classification model with `LogisticRegression` using `cross_val_score` to train it with different splits (10). We then calculate the average score for each split and report it to the user.

The following list tells us when to use each technique:

- **K-Fold and Stratified K-Fold**: These are generally the go-to methods for most classification and regression tasks, especially when you want a balance between computational efficiency and reliable performance estimation.
- **LOOCV**: It is best used when the dataset is minimal, and you want to use as much data as possible for training. However, it is computationally intensive and may not be practical for larger datasets.
- **Time Series Cross-Validation**: The obvious choice for time series data, where temporal order is crucial.
- **Nested Cross-Validation**: This is ideal when hyperparameter tuning is part of the modeling process, and you need to avoid overfitting the validation set.

Hyperparameter tuning

Hyperparameters are the configuration choices of a learning algorithm that are not learned from data. They are set before training and govern how the model learns and how complex it can become—for example, the learning rate, depth of a decision tree, number of trees in a forest, dropout rate, and batch size, among others. By contrast, parameters (such as the weights of a neural network) are estimated from the training data.

Hyperparameter tuning is the process of selecting the values of these hyperparameters to optimize model performance on a validation criterion. This typically involves systematic search strategies, such as grid or random search, Bayesian optimization, or multi-fidelity methods, often combined with cross-validation to choose settings that generalize well rather than overfit.

Importance of hyperparameter tuning

Choosing the correct hyperparameters can mean the difference between a model that performs well and one that does not. Poorly chosen hyperparameters can lead to underfitting or overfitting, resulting in a model that either fails to capture essential patterns in the data or performs well on the training data but poorly on unseen data. Therefore, hyperparameter tuning is necessary to achieve the best possible model performance.

Standard techniques for hyperparameter tuning

Several techniques are available for hyperparameter tuning, the most common of which are covered in this section.

Grid Search

Grid Search is an exhaustive search method where you specify a list of possible values for each hyperparameter, and the algorithm tests every possible combination of these values. This method is straightforward but can be computationally expensive, especially when dealing with a large number of hyperparameters or an extensive range of values. The code is as follows:

```
# Import necessary libraries
import numpy as np
import pandas as pd
from sklearn.datasets import make_classification
from sklearn.model_selection import GridSearchCV, train_test_split
from sklearn.ensemble import RandomForestClassifier
from sklearn.metrics import classification_report

# Step 1: Generate a synthetic dataset
X, y = make_classification(n_samples=1000, n_features=20, n_classes=2, random_state=42)

# Split the data into training and testing sets
X_train, X_test, y_train, y_test = train_test_split(X, y, test_size=0.3, random_state=42)

# Step 2: Create a model
model = RandomForestClassifier(random_state=42)

# Step 3: Set up the hyperparameter grid
param_grid = {
    'n_estimators': [50, 100, 200],
    'max_depth': [None, 10, 20, 30]
}

# Initialize GridSearchCV
grid_search = GridSearchCV(estimator=model, param_grid=param_
grid, cv=5, scoring='accuracy', verbose=1)

# Step 4: Fit GridSearchCV
grid_search.fit(X_train, y_train)

# Print the best parameters and best score
print("Best Parameters:", grid_search.best_params_)
print("Best Score:", grid_search.best_score_)

# Evuluate the best model on the test set
best_model = grid_search.best_estimator_
y_pred = best_model.predict(X_test)

# Print classification report
print(classification_report(y_test, y_pred))
```

The output is as follows:

```
Fitting 5 folds for each of 12 candidates, totalling 60 fits
Best Parameters: {'max_depth': None, 'n_estimators': 50}
Best Score: 0.9
              precision    recall  f1-score   support
```

```
           0       0.82      0.89      0.85       145
           1       0.89      0.81      0.85       155

    accuracy                           0.85       300
   macro avg       0.85      0.85      0.85       300
weighted avg       0.85      0.85      0.85       300
```

The explanation is as follows:

- **Generating the dataset**: We use the **`scikit-learn`** function **`make_classification`** to create a synthetic dataset with 1,000 samples, 20 features, and 2 classes.
- **Model creation**: We utilize the **`RandomForestClassifier`**, a commonly used ensemble method for classification tasks.
- **Hyperparameter grid**: We define a grid of hyperparameters to search through. In this case, we are testing different numbers of trees (**`n_estimators`**) and different maximum depths of the trees (**`max_depth`**).
- **Grid Search and evaluation**: We utilize **`GridSearchCV`** to optimize the hyperparameters using cross-validation. After fitting, we evaluate the best model on the test set and print the classification report to assess its performance.

The Grid Search process involved evaluating 12 different combinations of hyperparameters across five cross-validation folds, resulting in 60 model fits. The best-performing model had no limit on tree depth (**`max_depth=None`**) and used 50 trees (**`n_estimators=50`**), achieving an average cross-validation accuracy of 0.9. When tested on the holdout set, the model demonstrated an accuracy of 0.85, with both classes having balanced precision and recall, resulting in an overall robust performance, as reflected in the F1-scores of 0.85 for each class.

Random Search

Unlike Grid Search, Random Search does not try every combination of hyperparameters. Instead, it selects random combinations, which reduces the computational cost and can be more efficient in finding optimal hyperparameters, especially when only a subset of them significantly impacts model performance. The code is as follows:

```
# Import necessary libraries
import numpy as np
import pandas as pd
from sklearn.datasets import make_classification
from sklearn.model_selection import RandomizedSearchCV, train_test_split
from sklearn.ensemble import RandomForestClassifier
from sklearn.metrics import classification_report

# Step 1: Generate a synthetic dataset
X, y = make_classification(n_samples=1000, n_features=20, n_classes=2, random_state=42)

# Split the data into training and testing sets
X_train, X_test, y_train, y_test = train_test_split(X, y, test_size=0.3, random_state=42)

# Step 2: Create a model
model = RandomForestClassifier(random_state=42)

# Step 3: Set up the hyperparameter distribution
```

```
param_dist = {
    'n_estimators': [50, 100, 200, 300, 400],
    'max_depth': [None, 10, 20, 30, 40],
    'min_samples_split': [2, 5, 10],
    'min_samples_leaf': [1, 2, 4]
}

# Initialize RandomizedSearchCV
random_search = RandomizedSearchCV(estimator=model, param_distributions=param_dist,
                                   n_iter=10, cv=5, scoring='accuracy',
                                   verbose=1, random_state=42)

# Step 4: Fit RandomizedSearchCV
random_search.fit(X_train, y_train)

# Print the best parameters and best score
print("Best Parameters:", random_search.best_params_)
print("Best Score:", random_search.best_score_)

# Evaluate the best model on the test set
best_model = random_search.best_estimator_
y_pred = best_model.predict(X_test)

# Print classification report
print(classification_report(y_test, y_pred))
```

The output is as follows:

```
Fitting 5 folds for each of 10 candidates, totalling 50 fits
Best Parameters: {'n_estimators': 400, 'min_samples_split': 2, 'min_samples_leaf': 1, 'max_depth': 40}
Best Score: 0.9
              precision    recall  f1-score   support

           0       0.83      0.89      0.86       145
           1       0.89      0.83      0.86       155

    accuracy                           0.86       300
   macro avg       0.86      0.86      0.86       300
weighted avg       0.86      0.86      0.86       300
```

The explanation is as follows:

- **Generating the dataset**: We use the **`scikit-learn`** function **`make_classification`** to create a synthetic dataset with 1,000 samples, 20 features, and 2 classes.
- **Model creation**: We use **`RandomForestClassifier`** for classification.
- **Hyperparameter distribution**: Instead of a fixed grid, we define a distribution of hyperparameters from which to sample. Here, we specify ranges and lists for various hyperparameters, including **`n_estimators`**, **`max_depth`**, **`min_samples_split`**, and **`min_samples_leaf`**.

- **Random Search and evaluation**: We use `RandomizedSearchCV` to sample from the specified distributions. We specify `n_iter` (number of parameter settings sampled) and perform cross-validation. After fitting, we evaluate the best model on the test set and print the classification report.

The Randomized Search process evaluated 10 different hyperparameter combinations across 5 cross-validation folds, resulting in 50 model fits. The best model was found with 400 trees (`n_estimators=400`), a maximum tree depth of 40 (`max_depth=40`), a minimum of 2 samples required to split a node (`min_samples_split=2`), and a minimum of 1 sample needed for a leaf node (`min_samples_leaf=1`). This model achieved an average cross-validation accuracy of 0.9. When tested on the holdout set, the model achieved an accuracy of 0.86, with balanced precision and recall across both classes, resulting in F1-scores of 0.86 for each class. This indicates that the model is both precise and consistent in its predictions, performing well across the different classes in the dataset.

Conclusion

In this chapter, we explored advanced topics in machine learning that are crucial for improving model performance and handling more complex datasets. We explored unsupervised learning techniques, such as k-means clustering and PCA, which aid in identifying patterns and reducing dimensionality in data. We also examined ensemble learning methods, such as bagging and boosting, which combine multiple models to enhance accuracy and robustness.

Furthermore, we covered essential concepts like cross-validation and hyperparameter tuning, which are vital for optimizing models and preventing overfitting. These advanced techniques equip you with the tools necessary to tackle real-world machine learning challenges more effectively.

In the next chapter, we will shift our focus from traditional machine learning techniques to the fascinating world of deep learning. We will explore neural networks, which are computational models inspired by the structure and function of the human brain. You will learn about the architecture of neural networks, including input, hidden, and output layers, and understand how activation functions enable these networks to learn complex patterns from data. We will also cover essential concepts, including loss functions, gradient descent optimization, and practical training techniques to prevent overfitting. Additionally, we will examine advanced techniques such as dropout and transfer learning and highlight how neural networks are transforming real-world applications in image recognition, natural language processing, healthcare, and autonomous vehicles.

Exercises

The following exercises will allow the reader to practice the concepts we learned in this chapter:

1. **K-means clustering on the Iris dataset**:
   - **Problem**: The Iris dataset contains measurements of different iris flowers (sepal length, sepal width, petal length, and petal width) for three species of iris (setosa, versicolor, virginica). Your task is to implement k-means clustering to group the data into three clusters and compare the resulting clusters with the actual species labels.
   - **Hint**:
     - o Load the Iris dataset from Scikit-learn.
     - o Use the KMeans class to perform clustering.
     - o Visualize the clusters using a scatter plot of the first two principal components.
2. **Ensemble learning with the Titanic dataset**:
   - **Problem**: Using the Titanic dataset, build a model to predict survival. Implement a bagging classifier using decision trees as the base estimator and evaluate the model's performance.
   - **Hint**:
     - o Load the Titanic dataset using Pandas.

- Preprocess the data (e.g., handle missing values, encode categorical variables).
- Use BaggingClassifier with DecisionTreeClassifier as the base estimator.
- Evaluate using cross-validation.

3. **PCA on the Wine Quality dataset**:
   - **Problem**: Apply PCA to the Wine Quality dataset to reduce its dimensionality. Visualize the first two principal components and analyze how well they represent the original data.
   - **Hint**:
     - Load the Wine Quality dataset from a URL.
     - Standardize the features before applying PCA.
     - Visualize the first two principal components with a scatter plot.

Multiple choice questions

1. **What is the primary goal of cross-validation?**
   a. To increase the dataset size.
   b. To prevent overfitting, evaluate model performance on different data splits.
   c. To reduce the number of features in a dataset.
   d. To enhance model interpretability.
2. **Which of the following are types of ensemble learning?**
   a. K-means clustering
   b. Bagging
   c. Boosting
   d. PCA
3. **In the context of boosting, what is a weak learner?**
   a. A model that performs poorly on the training data.
   b. A simple model that is slightly better than random guessing.
   c. A model that uses very few features.
   d. A model that overfits the training data.
4. **Which of the following are the benefits of using PCA?**
   a. Reduces dimensionality.
   b. Increases dataset size.
   c. Retains most of the original variance.
   d. Improves model interpretability.
5. **Which metric is commonly used in bagging to combine predictions from multiple models?**
   a. Mean squared error
   b. Majority voting
   c. Principal components
   d. Gini Index

6. **Hyperparameter tuning aims to:**
   a. Adjust model parameters during training.
   b. Optimize the training dataset.
   c. Find the best settings for model training.
   d. Reduce the number of features.
7. **What are the primary steps in k-means clustering?**
   a. Assigning data points to clusters.
   b. Training the model on labeled data.
   c. Calculating cluster centers.
   d. Repeating the process until clusters stabilize.
8. **What does the term ensemble refer to in machine learning?**
   a. A large dataset.
   b. A collection of models working together.
   c. A deep learning network.
   d. A method of dimensionality reduction.
9. **In the context of AdaBoost, what happens to the weights of misclassified instances?**
   a. They are decreased.
   b. They are increased.
   c. They remain unchanged.
   d. They are removed from the dataset.
10. **Why is cross-validation considered a robust method for model evaluation?**
   a. It uses the entire dataset for training.
   b. It provides a single accuracy metric.
   c. It tests the model on different subsets of the data.
   d. It reduces the training time.

Answers

1.	b.
2.	b, c
3.	b.
4.	a, c
5.	b.
6.	c.
7.	a, c, d
8.	b.
9.	b.
10.	c.

Key terms

- **Cross-validation:** It is a technique used to evaluate machine learning models. It involves splitting the data into multiple subsets, training the model on some subsets, and validating it on others. This reduces overfitting and provides a better estimate of model performance.
- **Hyperparameter tuning:** It is the process of finding the best hyperparameters for a machine learning model. Hyperparameters are the settings that control the behavior of the training process and are not learned from the data.
- **K-means clustering**: This is an unsupervised learning algorithm that groups data into k clusters based on feature similarity.
- **Principal component analysis (PCA)**: A dimensionality reduction technique used to reduce the number of features in a dataset while retaining most of the variance.
- **Ensemble learning**: A machine learning technique that combines multiple models to produce a more robust and accurate predictive model.
- **Bagging (Bootstrap aggregating)** is an ensemble method that involves training multiple models on different subsets of the data and combining their predictions to form a single, more accurate prediction.
- **Boosting**: An ensemble technique that sequentially builds models by correcting the errors of previous models, thus improving the overall performance.
- **AdaBoost (Adaptive boosting)** is a specific type of boosting that adjusts the weights of incorrectly classified instances, allowing the model to focus on more challenging cases.

References

1. **https://scikit-learn.org/stable/supervised_learning.html**

Join our Discord space

Join our Discord workspace for latest updates, offers, tech happenings around the world, new releases, and sessions with the authors:

https://discord.bpbonline.com

CHAPTER 7

Introduction to Deep Learning

Introduction

In machine learning, deep learning has become one of the most powerful tools for addressing complex problems. It has transformed industries by driving progress in image recognition, language processing, and autonomous vehicles. Its effectiveness lies in learning complex patterns directly from data, thereby eliminating the need for explicit feature engineering.

At its core, deep learning relies on neural network models inspired by how the human brain processes information. Just like how your brain recognizes faces, understands speech, and remembers patterns, neural networks help computers do the same by learning from data.

In this chapter, we will get into the basics of deep learning, starting with neural networks. While we will show you some formulas, we will focus on understanding the concepts in simple, everyday terms. By the end of this chapter, you will clearly understand what neural networks are, how they work, and why they are essential for deep learning.

Structure

This chapter contains the following topics:

- Understanding deep learning
- Overview of deep learning applications
- Basics of neural networks
- Loss functions and how networks learn
- Optimization techniques
- Training neural networks
- Hyperparameter tuning and advanced techniques
- Real-world application of neural networks

Objectives

This chapter offers a comprehensive overview of neural networks and deep learning. By examining the architecture and elements of neural networks, including input, hidden, and output layers, you will gain insight into how these systems operate, much like the human brain. Furthermore, the chapter will clarify the function of neurons and activation functions in data processing and prediction-making.

You will learn how loss functions evaluate the network's performance and how optimization methods, such as gradient descent, improve its accuracy. Additionally, this chapter explores the training process of a neural network, guiding you on how to strike a balance between learning and preventing overfitting or underfitting.

Additionally, this chapter presents hyperparameter tuning to refine the learning process and explores advanced methods, such as dropout and transfer learning, to enhance neural network efficiency. Ultimately, you will see how neural networks are utilized in practical applications, including image recognition, **natural language processing (NLP)**, recommendation systems, and advancements in healthcare.

Understanding deep learning

Deep learning, which constitutes a subset of machine learning, employs neural networks characterized by multiple layers (thus the designation *deep*). These networks possess the capacity to acquire data representations across various levels of abstraction, thereby facilitating the identification of intricate patterns within complex datasets. In contrast to conventional machine learning techniques that depend on manual feature engineering, deep learning algorithms automatically detect the necessary features for classification or prediction.

Deep learning has a fantastic ability to turn raw data into deeper insights through its many processing layers. Each layer of a deep neural network plays a unique role in this transformation: earlier layers focus on simple patterns, such as edges in images, while the deeper layers get into the more intricate details, identifying complex concepts like objects and even faces. It is fascinating how these layers work together to enhance our understanding.

Deep learning has gained tremendous popularity in recent years due to three key factors:

- The availability of massive datasets for training.
- Advances in computing power, especially **graphics processing units** (**GPUs**).
- Improvements in algorithms and network architectures.

Due to these factors, deep learning has made significant progress, achieving remarkable performance in various areas. It is exciting to see it outperform traditional methods and sometimes reach incredible human-level accuracy.

Overview of deep learning applications

Deep learning has significantly transformed various industries through its robust pattern recognition capabilities. Notable application areas include:

- **Computer vision**: Image classification, object detection, facial recognition, and medical image analysis.

  Example: Image classification is used in photo apps to group pictures by people or places automatically; object detection helps self-driving cars recognize pedestrians and traffic signs; facial recognition is used to unlock smartphones; medical image analysis assists doctors in detecting tumors in X-rays or MRIs.

- **NLP**: Language translation, sentiment analysis, chatbots, and text generation.

  Example: Language translation tools, such as Google Translate, convert text between languages; sentiment analysis helps companies gauge customer opinions from reviews; chatbots provide automated customer support; and text generation powers tools that write emails or articles.

- **Speech recognition**: Voice assistants, transcription services, and voice-controlled systems.

  Example: Voice assistants like Siri or Alexa transcribe and respond to spoken requests; transcription services convert meeting recordings into written notes; voice-controlled systems enable users to operate devices hands-free.

- **Autonomous systems**: Self-driving vehicles, drones, and robotics.

  Example: Self-driving vehicles utilize deep learning to detect obstacles and navigate roads; drones employ it to avoid collisions and track objects; robotics applications include warehouse robots sorting packages and home robots vacuuming floors.

- **Healthcare**: Disease diagnosis, drug discovery, personalized medicine, and genomics.

Example: Disease diagnosis models can identify signs of pneumonia in chest X-rays; drug discovery uses deep learning to predict which molecules might become effective medicines; personalized medicine tailors treatments to individual patients; genomics analyzes DNA sequences to find disease risks

- **Financial services**: Fraud detection, risk assessment, algorithmic trading, and customer service automation.

  Example: Fraud detection systems flag unusual credit card transactions; risk assessment models help banks determine loan approvals; algorithmic trading utilizes deep learning to predict market trends; customer service automation addresses routine banking queries.

- **Entertainment**: Content recommendation, game AI, music generation, and video analysis.

  Example: Content recommendation systems suggest movies or songs on streaming platforms; game AI adapts to player behavior; music generation tools compose new melodies; video analysis helps platforms automatically tag or moderate content.

Deep learning's versatility continues to expand as researchers develop more sophisticated architectures and training methods, enabling solutions to increasingly complex problems across disciplines.

Basics of neural networks

Neural networks are the heart of deep learning, and they function in a manner similar to how our brains process information. Imagine your brain as an extensive network of interconnected cells, known as **neurons**. When you see something, like a dog, specific neurons in your brain activate and help you recognize it. Neural networks in computers function similarly, utilizing layers of artificial *neurons* to learn from data and make informed decisions.

Structure of neural networks

The following figure shows the structure of a neural network, including the input layer (left), two hidden layers (middle), and the output layer (right). Each neuron connects to every neuron in the next layer, creating a fully connected network that processes information through multiple transformations.

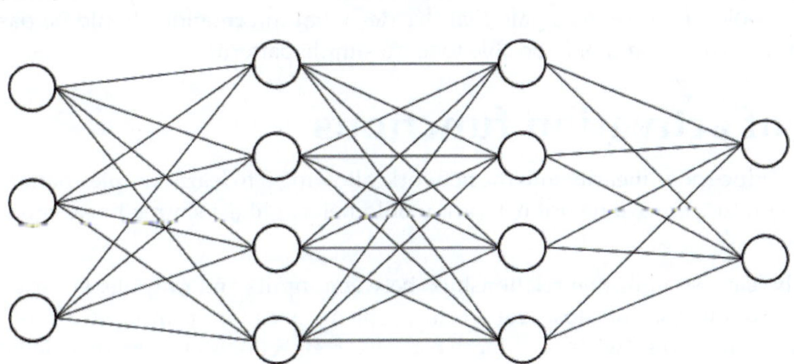

***Figure 7.1**: Illustrates the typical structure of a neural network with multiple layers*

A neural network is made up of different layers, each with its own job:

- **Input layer**: This is the first layer of a neural network, where data is introduced into the system. It simply receives the raw information you want the network to learn from. For example, if you are using a picture of a dog, each pixel value from the image becomes an input to this layer. The input layer does not process or modify the data; it simply passes it along to the next layer in the network.

- **Hidden layers**: These are the *thinking* layers. The hidden layers take the input data and process it to understand patterns. They are called **hidden** because you do not directly see what they are doing—it is all behind the scenes. A network's depth increases with the number of hidden layers it contains, and the more complex it becomes, which is why we call this deep learning.
- **Output layer**: Finally, this is where the network makes its decision or prediction. If you were training the network to recognize animals, the output layer might say, *I think this is a dog* or *This is a cat*. The output depends on the network's knowledge of the input and hidden layers.

Working of neurons

Each neuron in a neural network is like a tiny decision-maker. It takes in information, adds up the inputs (often multiplying each by a weight), applies a simple mathematical function (called an activation function), and then passes the result to the next layer. Here is an easy way to think about it:

Imagine you have a list of ingredients and want to determine whether they would make a cake or a salad. Each neuron examines one or more ingredients (such as flour, sugar, or lettuce) and asks, *Is this more like a cake or a salad ingredient?*

Each neuron adds up its information, makes a simple calculation, and then sends its *opinion* to the next neuron in the network.

If a neuron thinks an ingredient strongly points to a cake, it might pass along a higher value. If it is unsure, it might pass along a lower value.

All the neurons work together, layer by layer, until the network can make a final decision -whether it is cake or salad.

Activation functions

An activation function is a mathematical function applied to the output of each neuron in a neural network. It determines whether a neuron should be activated or not by transforming the input signal into an output signal for the next layer.

You can think of the activation function as a gate that decides what information should be passed forward in the network. Without it, the network would only be able to learn simple patterns.

Importance of activation functions

Activation functions introduce non-linearity into the network, allowing it to learn complex patterns and relationships in data. Without activation functions, a neural network would behave like a simple linear model, regardless of the number of layers it has.

A linear model can only learn straight-line relationships between inputs and outputs. For example, if you double the input, the output also doubles. But most real-world problems are more complicated than that. Non-linearity means the network can learn curves, twists, and more complex connections—like recognizing objects in images or understanding language, because the relationship between input and output does not have to be a straight line.

The following figure shows the three standard activation functions, which are discussed further:

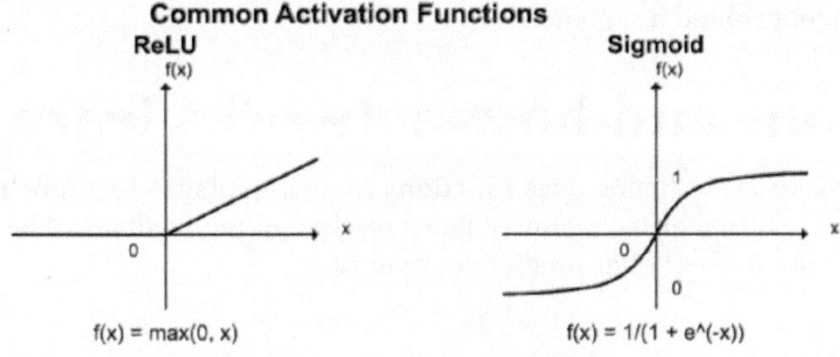

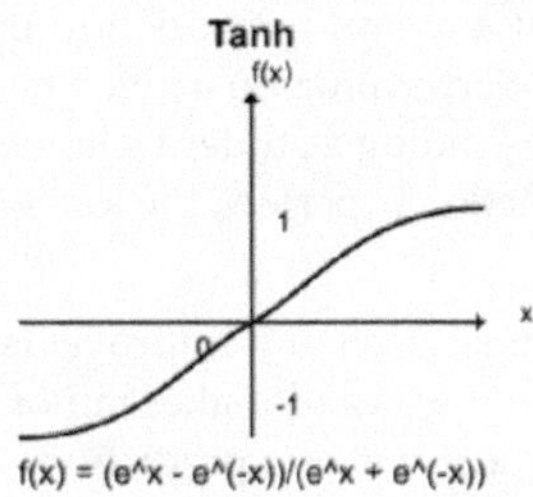

Figure 7.2: Common activation functions used in neural networks

Let us understand each one in detail:

- **Rectified Linear Unit (ReLU)**:

$$ReLU(z)=max(0,z)$$

  This is one of the most popular activation functions. Imagine you have a switch that turns on when the light is bright enough. ReLU works like that switch—it only *activates* when the input exceeds a certain level (much like turning on when the light is bright). If the input is too low, it simply stays off (much like a light switch staying off in dim light). This helps the network focus on the critical information and ignore the noise.

- **Sigmoid function**:

$$\sigma(z) = \frac{1}{1 + e^{-z}}$$

  Think of this like a dimmer switch that gradually turns on the light, from completely off to fully on, depending on how vital two things are, like yes or no.

- **Tanh (Hyperbolic tangent)**:

$$tanh(z) = \frac{e^{z} - e^{-z}}{e^{z} + e^{-z}}$$

  This one is similar to the sigmoid function but offers a bit more flexibility. It is akin to a dimmer switch, which can make the light both brighter (positive) and darker (negative), giving the network more options in how it reacts to the input.

Each function helps the network learn by adjusting how the neurons respond to the information they receive. They enable the network to understand and model complex patterns, such as recognizing a face in a photo or understanding the sentiment behind a sentence.

Loss functions and how networks learn

Once a neural network makes a prediction, **loss functions** come into play. A loss function tells the network how far off its prediction is from the actual answer, almost like a teacher giving feedback. The goal is to minimize this loss (or error) so that the network makes better predictions over time.

Loss function

A loss function (also called a **cost function** or **objective function**) is a mathematical formula that measures the difference between the predicted output of a neural network and the actual, correct output (the target or label). It quantifies how well or poorly the model is performing on a given task. Think of a loss function as a measure of how wrong the network's prediction is. It is like grading a student's homework- the closer they are to the correct answer, the better their score. If the network's prediction is perfect, the loss will be shallow (close to zero). If it is way off, the loss will be high.

The network uses this loss as a signal to adjust itself and improve its performance. Here is the basic idea; after each prediction, the network looks at how wrong it was and makes minor changes to its thinking (adjusts its weights and biases). It will be more accurate the next time it makes a prediction.

Types of loss functions

There are various types of loss functions, depending on the specific task at hand. Here are a few common ones:

- **Mean squared error (MSE)**: This is commonly used for tasks where the goal is to predict a numerical value, such as predicting house prices. The formula looks like this:

$$MSE = \frac{1}{n}\sum_{i=1}^{n}(y_i - \hat{y}_i)^2$$

  What does this mean?

  - y_i Is the actual value (what you want the network to predict).
  - $\hat{y}$ is the network's prediction.
  - The formula calculates the difference between the actual and predicted values, squares it (so negatives do not cancel out), and averages its overall predictions. The smaller this number, the better the predictions will be.

  Imagine you are trying to predict the price of a house. If your network predicts $500,000 but the actual cost is $550,000, the loss will reflect the difference between these two amounts. The goal is to shrink this gap over time.

- **Cross-entropy loss**: This loss function is often used for classification tasks, where the network predicts categories (e.g., whether an image is a cat, dog, or bird). The formula for cross-entropy is:

$$Cross - Entropy = -\sum_{i=1}^{n} y_i \log(\hat{y}_i)$$

- This loss measures the discrepancy between the network's predicted probabilities and the actual label (typically 1 for the correct class and 0 for the incorrect classes).
- The smaller the cross-entropy value, the closer the network's prediction is to accuracy.

This loss function works well because it heavily penalizes wrong predictions, making the network more cautious in future guesses.

Optimization techniques

Once the network recognizes its error (thanks to the loss function), it must determine how to improve. Optimization involves finding the network's best *settings* (or weights) that minimize the loss.

Gradient descent

Gradient descent is an algorithm used to minimize the loss function of a neural network. It works by gradually adjusting the network's parameters (weights and biases) to reduce the difference between the predicted and actual outputs.

The following figure illustrates how gradient descent works to find the minimum of the loss function:

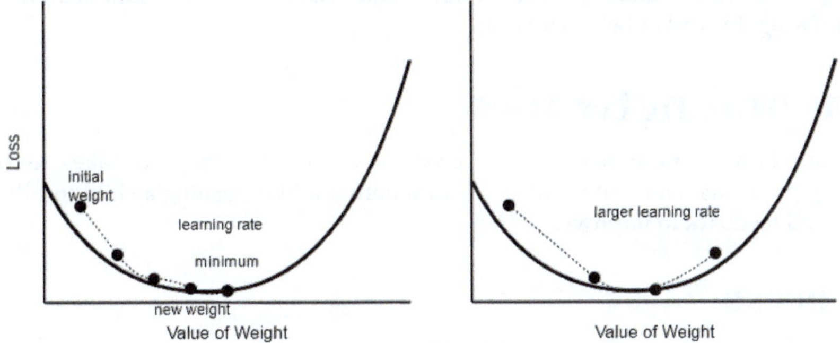

Figure 7.3: Gradient descent optimization

The most common optimization method is gradient descent. Think of this like hiking down a mountain: your goal is to get to the lowest point (where the loss is minimized). Every time the network makes a prediction, it moves down the mountain toward the lowest loss.

Here is how it works:

1. The network calculates the loss's slope (or gradient) with respect to its weights.
2. Then, it takes a small step in the opposite direction of the slope (downhill) to reduce the loss.
3. This process repeats over and over, and with each step, the network gets closer to the best solution.

The formula for updating the weights using gradient descent is:

$$w_{new} = w_{old} - \eta . \frac{\partial L}{\partial w}$$

Where:

- w_{old} : The current weight.
- η: It is the learning rate, which controls how big a step the network takes.

- $\frac{\partial L}{\partial w}$: It is the gradient (or slope) of the loss function with respect to the weight.

If the learning rate is too large, the network might take too many steps and miss the optimal solution. If it is too small, the network might take tiny steps and take an extremely long time to reach the solution. Finding the correct learning rate is vital to successful training.

Stochastic gradient descent

Stochastic gradient descent (**SGD**) is a variation of the standard gradient descent algorithm.

How is it different from gradient descent?

- In **standard (or batch) gradient descent**, the algorithm calculates the gradient of the loss function using the entire training dataset before updating the model's parameters. This can be slow and requires a lot of memory, especially with large datasets.
- In **SGD**, the algorithm updates the model's parameters using only a single training example (or a small random batch) at each step. This enables the updates to occur much faster, allowing the model to start learning immediately, even with very large datasets.

In summary, gradient descent uses all the data at once for each update, while SGD uses just one (or a few) data points at a time. This makes SGD faster and more suitable for large datasets, but it also introduces more randomness (the path to the minimum *zig-zags* instead of being smooth).

Training neural networks

Now that we understand how neural networks make predictions and learn from mistakes, let us examine how they improve at solving problems. Think of training a neural network like teaching a child to ride a bike—it takes practice, adjustments, and feedback to improve.

Training process

Training a neural network involves a loop that repeats until the network improves. Here is how it works:

- **Forward pass (making a guess)**: First, the network gets input data (like a picture of an animal). It then goes through the network's layers, and each layer makes some decisions based on what it has learned so far. In the end, the network gives its best guess - like saying, *I think this is a cat*.
- **Calculate the mistake (how wrong was it?)**: After the guess, the network compares its prediction (cat) to the actual answer (dog). This is like a teacher grading a test - *how close was the guess to the correct answer?* The difference is referred to as the *loss* or *error*. The bigger the mistake, the higher the loss.
- **Backward pass (learning from the mistake)**: After the network knows how wrong it was, it needs to learn from that mistake. This is where a process called **backpropagation** occurs. It simply means the network examines every decision it makes and determines how much each part of the network is responsible for the mistake.
- **Update (making adjustments)**: Finally, the network makes minor changes to improve. It tweaks its internal settings (called **weights**) to be slightly more accurate the next time it makes a guess. It is like adjusting your balance while learning to ride a bike—you get better with each try.

This entire process is repeated multiple times, with the network learning a little more each time. Each time the network processes all the data and makes adjustments, we refer to it as an *epoch*. The more epochs, the more practice the network receives, and the better it becomes.

Batch size and epochs

Let us break this down more with two essential ideas: **batch size** and **epochs**.

- **Batch size**: Imagine you are teaching a class. You could prepare one student at a time (small batch) or a whole group of students simultaneously (large batch). Similarly, a neural network is capable of learning from both small and large batches of data. Smaller batches result in more frequent network updates (although noisier), while larger batches are slower but more stable.
- **Epochs**: An epoch is one that entirely passes through all the data, like going through all the flashcards once when studying. If you only do one epoch, the network will not learn much. However, if you review the flashcards (or data) multiple times, the network will begin to recognize patterns more effectively.

Overfitting and underfitting

The following figure compares the three common scenarios encountered when training models:

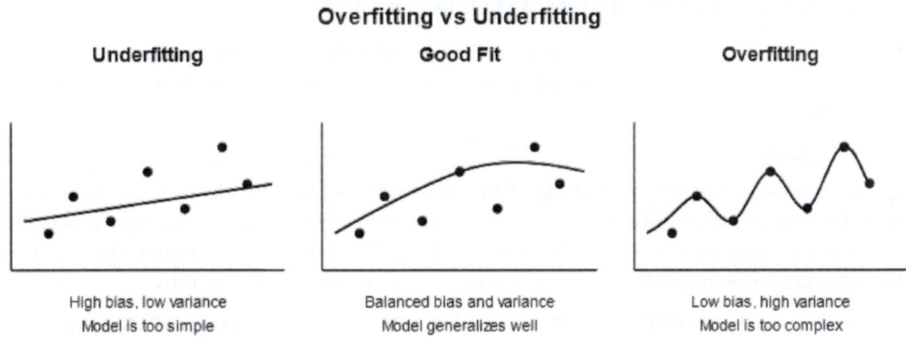

Figure 7.4: *Compares the three common scenarios encountered when training models*

When training a neural network, you want to teach it just the right amount - enough to make good predictions but not so much that it memorizes everything. Let us think of this like studying for an exam:

- **Underfitting**: If the network does not learn enough from the data, it will do poorly on the training and new data. It is like a student who did not study enough and failed the test.
- **Overfitting**: On the other hand, if the network learns too much from the training data, it becomes too specific and will not do well on new data. This is like a student who memorizes every answer in the practice test but struggles when faced with different questions on the actual exam.

To avoid overfitting, we can use a few tricks; let us briefly see these concepts; we will explain them in detail in the next section:

- **Early stopping**: Stop training the network once it memorizes the training data.
- **Dropout**: Randomly *turn off* some parts of the network during training so that it does not rely too much on any one part.
- **Regularization**: Add a minor penalty to prevent the network from becoming too complex, ensuring it remains simple and general.

How to know when the network is good

Once the network is trained, *how do we know if it is good at making predictions?* This is where we use a **validation set**. Think of it like a practice test—the network makes predictions on a new set of data (that it has not seen before), and we see how well it does.

If the network performs well on both the training and validation data, that is a good sign. However, it is overfitting if it only performs well on the training data and struggles with the validation data. In that case, we should stop the training earlier or use one of the abovementioned tricks.

Hyperparameter tuning and advanced techniques

When training a neural network, you can adjust several settings to make the network learn better or faster. These settings are called **hyperparameters**. Think of hyperparameters as the rules of a game; changing them can significantly affect how well the network plays the game (or, in this case, how well it learns from the data).

Understand what hyperparameters are

Hyperparameters are like the settings or knobs that can be tweaked before training a neural network. They differ from the weights inside the network because hyperparameters are set *before* training starts, while the network adjusts the weights *during* training.

Here are some common hyperparameters:

- **Learning rate**: This controls the magnitude of the network's adjustments to its weights. A small learning rate means the network takes tiny steps and learns slowly. A significant learning rate means the network takes big steps but risks jumping over the best solution. Think of it like walking, tiny steps might take longer but are safe, while big jumps might get you there faster or cause you to trip.
- **Batch size**: This parameter controls the number of examples the network sees before updating. Smaller batch sizes update more frequently but can be noisy, while larger batch sizes smooth out the learning process but take longer.
- **Number of epochs**: This refers to the number of times the network traverses the entire dataset. More epochs mean more practice, but too many can lead to overfitting, like studying the same material repeatedly.

How to tune hyperparameters

Hyperparameter tuning involves finding the optimal settings for these parameters to enable the network to learn as effectively as possible. It is like adjusting the heat when cooking—too low, and the food will not cook properly, and too high, and it might burn.

Here are some common ways to tune hyperparameters:

1. **Manual tuning**: You try different values for each hyperparameter and see what works best. It is like experimenting with varying amounts of sugar in a recipe until it tastes right. While simple, it can be time-consuming.
2. **Grid search** is a more systematic approach to exploring different combinations of hyperparameters. Imagine you make a grid of all possible values for each hyperparameter and then try each combination individually. It can be effective, but it is like trying every possible setting on a video game until you find the perfect one - it takes a lot of time.
3. **Random search**: Instead of trying every combination, a random search picks random values for each hyperparameter. This can sometimes be faster than grid search, but it is akin to throwing darts at a dartboard and hoping to hit the bullseye.

Advanced techniques

Now that we have covered hyperparameter tuning, let us explore some advanced techniques to enhance your neural network's performance and mitigate issues such as overfitting.

- **Dropout**: Dropout is like playing a game of musical chairs with neurons in the network. During training, some neurons are randomly *turned off* or ignored in each batch. This forces the network to learn more general patterns, rather than relying too heavily on specific neurons. It is a clever trick to prevent overfitting because the network must learn to be flexible and adapt to various combinations of neurons.

  Example: If you are training a network to recognize objects in images, a dropout might randomly *turn off* some of the neurons responsible for recognizing shapes or colors. This forces the network to improve its understanding of the overall picture rather than relying on just one feature.

- **Regularization**: Regularization is another way to help the network stay balanced and not overfit the training data. It adds a minor penalty to the loss function for making the network too complex. This encourages the network to keep things simple and avoid memorizing the training data.

  Regularization is like reminding the network not to *overthink* things. By keeping the model more straightforward, regularization helps it better generalize new data.

Transfer learning

Transfer learning is an advanced technique that allows you to use a neural network that has undergone training on a substantial dataset for a new task. It is like learning a new skill based on something you already know. If you already know how to ride a bike, learning to ride a motorcycle will be much easier.

Here is how it works:

- You take a pre-trained network, such as one trained to recognize objects in images (e.g., cats, dogs, cars), and use its knowledge as a starting point.
- Instead of training the network from scratch, you only need to train the last few layers to fit your specific task.

This saves time and effort, especially if you do not have a large dataset to train on from the beginning. Transfer learning is widely utilized in domains such as image recognition and NLP, where training a network from scratch can take a long time.

Suppose you want to build a model that can identify different types of flowers, but you only have a small set of flower images. Instead of training a neural network from scratch, you can start with a model that has already been trained to recognize general objects in images (like the ImageNet dataset, which includes millions of images of everyday objects). You then *fine-tune* this pre-trained model on your flower images, because the model has already learned to detect basic shapes, colors, and textures, it can quickly adapt to recognizing flowers with much less data and training time.

Real-world applications of neural networks

Now that we know how neural networks work and how to train them, we can see how they are applied in the real world. You have already interacted with neural networks daily, even if you did not realize it. From voice assistants like *Siri* and *Alexa* to recommendations on *Netflix* and *YouTube*, neural networks are behind many of the technologies we use today.

Image recognition

One of the most famous applications of neural networks is **image recognition**. Neural networks can be trained to recognize objects in pictures or videos, such as faces, animals, or handwritten text.

For instance, when one uploads a photograph to Facebook and the platform proposes tagging friends, it employs a neural network to identify faces within the image. These networks are trained using millions of photographs, thereby acquiring knowledge of distinct facial features through the discernment of subtle pixel patterns. In the realm of healthcare, neural networks are utilized to analyze medical images, including X-rays and **magnetic resonance imaging** (**MRIs**). These advanced technologies aid medical professionals in identifying diseases, including cancer, and detecting fractures that may be difficult for the human eye to perceive. Such capabilities are particularly beneficial for facilitating early diagnosis and enhancing patient outcomes.

Natural language processing

Neural networks also power NLP, which refers to computers' capability to comprehend and generate human language. If you have ever used a virtual assistant like *Siri*, *Alexa*, or *Google Assistant*, you have benefited from NLP.

Here are some examples of how NLP is used:

- **Voice assistants**: When you ask Siri or Alexa to set a reminder or play a song, the system processes your speech, understands the words, and acts accordingly. Neural networks help convert spoken language into text and determine the meaning behind the words.
- **Language translation**: If you have ever used *Google Translate* to convert text from one language to another, neural networks are behind the scenes. These systems are trained on vast amounts of text in different languages, learning how words and phrases in one language map to those in another.
- **Chatbots**: Many companies use chatbots on their websites to answer customer questions. These chatbots use neural networks to understand your questions and give relevant responses, often mimicking a human conversation.

Recommendation systems

A typical application of neural networks is found within recommendation systems. For instance, Netflix proposes films that may appeal to your preferences, while Amazon suggests products based on your historical purchases. These recommendations are facilitated by neural networks that analyze both your behavior and the behaviors of other users.

Here is how it works:

- The network looks at what you have watched or bought in the past and compares it to other users with similar tastes.
- It finds patterns and suggests new content or products that match your preferences.

The more you use these services, the better the recommendations get because the network continues to learn from your interactions.

Autonomous vehicles

One of the most exciting applications of neural networks is in self-driving cars. Companies like *Tesla* and *Google's Waymo* are using neural networks to help cars drive themselves. These cars are packed with sensors that feed data to the network, such as information about nearby vehicles, pedestrians, traffic signs, and the road itself.

Here is what the network does:

- It processes this massive amount of data in real-time, helping the car decide when to stop, turn, or change lanes.
- The network learns from past experiences, both from the car's driving and other vehicles in the fleet, to handle new situations more safely.

While we are still a few years away from fully autonomous vehicles, neural networks are already helping cars assist drivers with parking, lane-keeping, and avoiding collisions.

Healthcare

Neural networks are transforming the healthcare sector by assisting medical professionals in making more accurate diagnoses and informed treatment decisions. The following are several applications of their utilization:

- **Disease prediction**: Neural networks possess the capability to analyze patient data and forecast the probability of diseases such as heart attacks, diabetes, and various genetic conditions. This facilitates healthcare professionals' taking preventative measures prior to the progression of the disease into a severe state.
- **Drug discovery**: In pharmaceutical research, neural networks are helping scientists discover new drugs faster. By analyzing data from millions of chemical compounds, networks can predict which treatments will most likely be effective.
- **Personalized medicine**: Neural networks can also help create customized treatment plans for patients based on their unique genetic makeup and medical history. This means treatments can be tailored to the individual, leading to better outcomes.

Gaming and entertainment

In gaming and entertainment, neural networks create more realistic and interactive experiences. Some of the most fantastic applications include:

- **Game AI**: Neural networks create more intelligent, adaptive, **non-player characters** (**NPCs**) in video games. These NPCs can learn from the player's actions and adapt their strategies in real-time, making the game more challenging and engaging.
- **Content creation**: Neural networks are also used to generate new content, such as artwork, music, and even short stories. For example, some games use AI to create vast, detailed worlds that are different every time you play, providing endless variety.

Conclusion

In this chapter, we explored the world of deep learning and neural networks, breaking down complex ideas into simple terms. We began with the basics of neural networks, learning how they function like the brain's decision-making process through layers of neurons. We also discussed loss functions, which indicate to the network how well it is performing, and optimization techniques, which help it improve.

From there, we looked at the training process - how networks learn by making predictions, adjusting based on mistakes, and repeating the process to improve. We also covered critical concepts like overfitting and underfitting, and how to balance learning just the right amount. Hyperparameter tuning and advanced techniques like dropout and transfer learning were introduced to enhance network performance further.

Ultimately, we observed how neural networks are applied in the real world, enabling technologies such as image recognition, voice assistants, self-driving cars, and healthcare diagnostics. Neural networks are revolutionizing numerous industries, and understanding their inner workings is crucial to harnessing their full potential.

In the next chapter, we will transition from these theoretical foundations to practical implementation using PyTorch, one of the most popular deep learning frameworks. You will learn about tensors (PyTorch's fundamental data structure), GPU acceleration with CUDA, automatic differentiation for computing gradients, and how to build neural networks using PyTorch's intuitive tools. Understanding PyTorch will enable you to transform the concepts learned in this chapter into working models that can solve real-world problems.

Exercises

Simulate a Dummy Training Process Using NumPy

Aim: Your task is to simulate a basic training loop for a neural network with one input, one hidden layer, and one output. This will give you hands-on experience with the mechanics of how a neural network learns through multiple epochs. By the end of this exercise, you will understand the key steps of training a neural network using pure NumPy.

Step-by-step instructions

The step-by-step instructions are as follows:

1. **Define the neural network**: The network architecture for this exercise is straightforward:
   a. **Input layer**: 1 neuron (to handle a single input feature).
   b. **Hidden layer**: 2 neurons (for intermediate processing).
   c. **Output layer**: 1 neuron (for binary classification or a simple prediction task).

   You will start by initializing **random weights** for the connections between:
   a. The input and the hidden layer.
   b. The hidden and the output layer.
2. **Activation functions**: You will need two activation functions:
   a. **ReLU** for the hidden layer. This function outputs the input if it is positive and zero otherwise.
   b. **Sigmoid** for the output layer. This function squashes the output to a value between 0 and 1, making it suitable for binary classification.
3. **Forward pass**: During the forward pass, the neural network calculates its **predicted output** based on the current weights:
   a. The input data will be multiplied by the weights for the input-to-hidden layer.
   b. The result will be passed through the ReLU activation function to get the hidden layer's output.
   c. The hidden layer's output will then be multiplied by the weights for the hidden-to-output layer.
   d. Finally, the result will be passed through the Sigmoid activation function to get the network's final prediction.
4. **Loss calculation**: Once the network makes a prediction, you will calculate how far off this prediction is from the actual output using the **mean squared error** (**MSE**) loss function. This function measures the average squared difference between the predicted and actual values. The goal of the training process is to **minimize this loss.**
5. **Backward pass (gradient descent)**: After calculating the loss, the network will adjust its weights through **backpropagation**. In this step:
   a. You will compute how much the loss changes with respect to the weights (these are called gradients).

b. Using **gradient descent**, you will update the weights by subtracting a small fraction (called the **learning rate**) of the gradient from the current weights. This helps reduce the loss over time.

The backward pass involves calculating gradients for both the hidden-to-output weights and the input-to-hidden weights:

a. For the hidden-to-output weights, you will need the **Sigmoid derivative**.

b. For the input-to-hidden weights, you will use the **ReLU derivative**.

6. **Training loop**: Finally, you will put everything together into a loop that:

a. Performs the forward pass to calculate predictions.

b. Computes the loss based on how far the predictions are from the actual output.

c. Executes the backward pass to adjust the weights.

d. Repeats this process for a specified number of iterations (**epochs**).

After several epochs, you should observe that the network's **loss decreases**, meaning that its predictions improve over time.

Multiple choice questions

1. **Which of the following is true about neural networks?**

a. Neural networks work exactly like the human brain.

b. Neural networks are inspired by how the human brain works.

c. Neural networks are only used for image recognition.

d. Neural networks cannot make decisions.

2. **What is the function of the input layer in a neural network?**

a. It processes data and makes decisions.

b. It receives the initial data from the outside world.

c. It compares predictions with actual results.

d. It adjusts the weights of the network.

3. **Which of the following best describes the ReLU activation function?**

a. It always outputs a value between 0 and 1.

b. It turns off negative inputs and passes positive inputs unchanged.

c. It outputs values between -1 and 1.

d. It is only used in the output layer.

4. **What is a loss function used in a neural network?**

a. To initialize the network's weights.

b. To calculate how well the network is predicting.

c. To adjust the learning rate.

d. To process input data.

5. **In which scenario would you use cross-entropy loss?**

a. When predicting a number.

b. When categorizing data into classes.

   c. When tuning hyperparameters.
   d. When adjusting weights using backpropagation.

6. **Which optimization technique is like "hiking down a mountain" to minimize loss?**
   a. Regularization
   b. Grid Search
   c. Gradient descent
   d. Dropout

7. **What is overfitting in neural networks?**
   a. When the network performs poorly on both training and new data.
   b. When the network learns patterns that are too specific to the training data, it does not generalize well to new data.
   c. When the network underperforms on the training data but excels on new data.
   d. When the network adjusts weights incorrectly.

8. **How does dropout help prevent overfitting?**
   a. It adjusts the weights based on the loss.
   b. It reduces the learning rate.
   c. It randomly turns off neurons during training.
   d. It increases the batch size.

9. **Which of the following is an example of transfer learning?**
   a. Training a neural network from scratch on a new dataset.
   b. Using a pre-trained network and retraining only the last layers for a new task.
   c. Adjusting hyperparameters during the training process.
   d. Reducing the complexity of the model to prevent overfitting.

10. **What is the main role of a validation set?**
   a. To train the model more efficiently.
   b. To test the model's performance on new, unseen data during training.
   c. To adjust the learning rate.
   d. To generate predictions after training

Answers

1.	b.
2.	b.
3.	b.
4.	b.
5.	b.
6.	c.

7.	b.
8.	c.
9.	b.
10.	b.

Key terms

- **Neural network**: A model inspired by the human brain, comprised of layers of interconnected neurons that process data to make decisions or predictions.
- **Input layer**: The first layer in a neural network that receives the input data.
- **Hidden layers**: Layers in a neural network where data is processed, and patterns are learned.
- **Output layer**: The final layer in a neural network that produces the prediction or decision.
- **Activation function**: A function applied to a neuron's output that introduces non-linearity into the network. Typical examples are ReLU, Sigmoid, and Tanh.
- **The loss function:** It measures the distance between the network's prediction and the actual value. Common types are MSE and cross-entropy loss.
- **Gradient descent**: An optimization technique that helps the network adjust its weights to minimize the loss.
- **Overfitting**: When the network performs well on training data but struggles on new, unseen data due to learning overly specific patterns.
- **Dropout**: A technique that randomly turns off neurons during training to prevent overfitting.
- **Transfer learning**: Using a pre-trained network and fine-tuning it for a new task to save time and resources.

References

1. *Michael Nielsen, Neural Networks and Deep Learning:* **http://neuralnetworksanddeeplearning.com/**
2. *Andrew Ng's Deep Learning Specialization:* **https://www.coursera.org/specializations/deep-learning**
3. *3Blue1Brown's Neural Networks Series:* **https://www.youtube.com/playlist?list=PLZHQObOWTQDNU6R1_67000Dx_ZCJB-3pi**
4. *Deep Learning by Ian Goodfellow, Yoshua Bengio, and Aaron Courville:* **https://www.deeplearningbook.org/**

CHAPTER 8
Introduction to PyTorch

Introduction

In the rapidly evolving domain of deep learning, PyTorch stands out as one of the most popular frameworks, attributable to its exceptional flexibility, dynamic computation graphs, and seamless integration with Python. Whether undertaking a minor project or tackling a significant research challenge, the array of tools provided by PyTorch makes it a preferred choice among machine learning enthusiasts. This chapter will explore the fundamental concepts of PyTorch, including tensors, automatic differentiation, **graphics processing unit** (**GPU**) acceleration (CUDA), and key components of neural networks. Grasping these concepts is crucial for establishing a solid foundation and training efficient machine learning models.

Structure

This chapter contains the following topics:

- Understanding tensors
- GPU acceleration with CUDA
- Automatic differentiation and gradients
- Building neural networks in PyTorch
- Activation functions and the forward pass
- Model weights and optimizers

Objectives

The main goal of this chapter is to introduce you to the core functionalities of PyTorch. By the end, you should understand tensors and how they compare to NumPy arrays, which are commonly used for numerical computations in Python. You will grasp the importance of GPU acceleration through CUDA and learn how to leverage it for faster computations. The chapter will explain how automatic differentiation works and why it is essential for training neural networks. You will become familiar with neural network structure in PyTorch, learn about activation functions that add non-linearity to models, and understand the role of model weights and optimizers in the training process.

Understanding tensors

Tensors are the backbone of PyTorch. They are multidimensional arrays, similar to NumPy arrays. However, there is an important distinction: PyTorch tensors have the advantage of being utilized on GPUs, allowing for quicker computations. They also support automatic differentiation, which is essential for training neural networks.

Comparing tensors with NumPy arrays

While NumPy arrays are a standard tool for numerical computations in Python, PyTorch tensors have additional capabilities:

- **GPU support**: Tensors can seamlessly transfer between the **central processing unit** (**CPU**) and GPU, enabling significant speedups when performing large-scale computations.
- **Autograd**: They can automatically compute gradients, which helps simplify backpropagation during the training of neural networks.

In addition to basic tensor creation and conversion from NumPy arrays, PyTorch tensors support complex operations, including broadcasting, reshaping, slicing, and reduction.

Let us look at basic tensor creation and conversion between NumPy arrays and PyTorch tensors:

```
import torch
import numpy as np

# NumPy array
np_array = np.array([[1, 2], [3, 4]])

# PyTorch Tensor
tensor = torch.tensor([[1, 2], [3, 4]])

# Converting between NumPy arrays and PyTorch tensors
tensor_from_numpy = torch.from_numpy(np_array)
numpy_from_tensor = tensor.numpy()
```

Output:

```
tensor([[1, 2],
        [3, 4]])
[[1 2]
 [3 4]]
```

Tensors also support broadcasting, a powerful feature that allows operations on tensors of different shapes by automatically expanding the smaller tensor to match the larger one.

Here is an example demonstrating broadcasting in PyTorch:

```
import torch

# Broadcasting example
tensor_a = torch.tensor([[1, 2], [3, 4]])
tensor_b = torch.tensor([10, 20])
result = tensor_a + tensor_b
print(result)
```

Output:

```
tensor([[11, 22],
        [13, 24]])
```

Another essential operation is tensor slicing and indexing. PyTorch enables you to access and modify parts of a tensor easily.

The following code demonstrates tensor slicing and indexing:

```
tensor = torch.tensor([[1, 2, 3], [4, 5, 6], [7, 8, 9]])
# Slicing the first row
print(tensor[0, :])
```

```
# Modifying the first element
tensor[0, 0] = 99
print(tensor)
```

Output:

```
tensor([1, 2, 3])
tensor([[99,  2,  3],
        [ 4,  5,  6],
        [ 7,  8,  9]])
```

GPU acceleration with CUDA

Compute Unified Device Architecture (**CUDA**) is a parallel computing platform that enables computations on the GPU, significantly accelerating tasks. Deep learning models with large datasets can take hours or even days to train on a CPU. PyTorch makes it easy to leverage the GPU for faster training.

Importance of GPU acceleration

GPUs are optimized for parallel processing, making them significantly faster for matrix operations, which are vital in neural networks. A GPU can perform many calculations concurrently, a feature essential for models with millions of parameters during the training process.

Example: Tensor Operations on CPU vs. GPU

Let us compare the performance of matrix multiplication on the CPU and GPU:

```
import torch
import time

# Perform matrix multiplication on CPU
tensor_cpu = torch.randn(10000, 10000)
start_time = time.time()
tensor_cpu.matmul(tensor_cpu)
print(f"CPU Time: {time.time() - start_time} seconds»)

# Perform matrix multiplication on GPU (if available)
if torch.cuda.is_available():
    tensor_gpu = tensor_cpu.cuda()
    start_time = time.time()
    tensor_gpu.matmul(tensor_gpu)
    print(f"GPU Time: {time.time() - start_time} seconds»)
```

Output:

```
CPU Time: 28.686336040496826 seconds
GPU Time: 0.14478135108947754 seconds
```

Using a GPU usually results in a dramatic speed improvement. The code was tested on Google Colab with a T4 GPU.

Beyond basic GPU operations, PyTorch supports multi-GPU setups for even faster training. You can distribute computations across multiple GPUs using DataParallel or torch.

Here is an example of how to implement multi-GPU support in PyTorch:

```
import torch
import torch.nn as nn

# Define a simple neural network model
class SimpleNet(nn.Module):
    def __init__(self):
        super(SimpleNet, self).__init__()
        self.fc1 = nn.Linear(10, 50)
        self.fc2 = nn.Linear(50, 2)

    def forward(self, x):
        x = torch.relu(self.fc1(x))
        x = self.fc2(x)
        return x

# Instantiate the model
model = SimpleNet()

# Check if multiple GPUs are available and apply DataParallel
device = torch.device("cuda" if torch.cuda.is_available() else "cpu")
if torch.cuda.device_count() > 1:
    model = nn.DataParallel(model)

# Move the model to the GPU(s)
model.to(device)

# Create dummy input for testing
input_data = torch.randn(64, 10).to(device)  # Batch of 64, input size 10

# Forward pass (distributed across GPUs if available)
output = model(input_data)
print(output)
```

Automatic differentiation and gradients

In deep learning, models are trained by modifying their weights to minimize error. To do this, we need to compute gradients, the rate at which the model's output varies in relation to its inputs. The PyTorch framework offers a convenient method for calculating gradients through its **autograd** package.

Importance of differentiation in deep learning

When a neural network generates a prediction, an assessment is conducted to determine the extent of its inaccuracy by calculating a loss function. Differentiation allows us to adjust the network's parameters (weights) to minimize this loss, making the model more accurate over time.

Using Autograd to compute gradients

Here is a simple example of how PyTorch computes gradients:

```
x = torch.tensor([2.0], requires_grad=True)
y = x ** 2
y.backward()  # Compute the gradient
print(x.grad)
```

In this case, the gradient is 2x2x2, and PyTorch automatically tracks all operations on x to compute this gradient.

When working with multi-dimensional tensors, PyTorch efficiently tracks all operations. You can even supply custom gradients for backpropagation.

The following code shows how to apply custom gradients to multi-dimensional tensors:

```
x = torch.tensor([1.0, 2.0, 3.0], requires_grad=True)
y = x ** 3  # Some arbitrary operation
y.backward(torch.tensor([1.0, 0.5, 0.25]))  # Custom gradient
print(x.grad)
```

Building neural networks in PyTorch

A neural network comprises layers that transform input data into valuable predictions. These layers are organized into three types:

- **Input layer**: Receives the raw data (e.g., pixels from an image).
- **Hidden layers**: Process the data through multiple transformations. These layers help the network learn complex patterns.
- **Output layer**: This layer produces the final prediction (e.g., the probability of an image being a dog).

Creating a simple neural network

Here is an example of defining a basic neural network using PyTorch's **`nn.Module`**:

```
import torch.nn as nn

class SimpleNet(nn.Module):
    def __init__(self):
        super(SimpleNet, self).__init__()
        self.fc1 = nn.Linear(4, 16)  # Input layer (4 features) to hidden layer (16 neurons)
        self.fc2 = nn.Linear(16, 3)  # Hidden layer to output layer (3 classes)

    def forward(self, x):
        x = torch.relu(self.fc1(x))  # Activation function
        x = self.fc2(x)
        return x
```

In this network, we transform the input and hidden layers using a fully connected (linear) layer.

In more advanced neural networks, you may encounter convolutional layers or recurrent layers. The following is an example of a simple **convolutional neural network** (CNN):

```
class SimpleCNN(nn.Module):
    def __init__(self):
        super(SimpleCNN, self).__init__()
        self.conv1 = nn.Conv2d(1, 32, kernel_size=3)
        self.pool = nn.MaxPool2d(2, 2)
        self.fc1 = nn.Linear(32 * 13 * 13, 10)  # Adjusted for input size

    def forward(self, x):
        x = self.pool(F.relu(self.conv1(x)))
        x = x.view(-1, 32 * 13 * 13)  # Flatten
        x = self.fc1(x)
        return x
```

Activation functions and the forward pass

The **forward pass** refers to passing the input data through the network to generate an output. During this process, each neuron applies an **activation function** to its input, introducing non-linearity (a concept explained in previous chapters), which enables the network to model complex patterns.

Common activation functions

Let us explore the most common activation functions used in neural networks:

- **Rectified Linear Unit (ReLU)**: If the input is positive, it is output directly; otherwise, it is zero. It is the most used activation function in deep learning:

  ```
  x = torch.relu(tensor)
  ```

- **Sigmoid**: Maps values to a range between 0 and 1, often used for binary classification (Classification with only 2 classes):

  ```
  x = torch.sigmoid(tensor)
  ```

- **Tanh**: This function maps values to a range between -1 and 1, which is useful when you want positive and negative outputs:

  ```
  x = torch.tanh(tensor)
  ```

Model weights and the role of optimizers

Each layer in a neural network has weights learned during training. These weights are numerical parameters that determine the strength of the connection between neurons, essentially acting as the network's memory of what it has learned from the data. An optimizer adjusts these weights based on the gradients calculated during the backpropagation process.

Model weights

Weights are the model parameters that change during training to improve the accuracy of predictions. The model learns by updating these weights to minimize the difference between its predictions and target values.

Need for optimizers

An **optimizer** helps update the weights based on the computed gradients. The most common optimizers in PyTorch are:

- **Stochastic gradient descent (SGD)**: Updates the weights based on the gradients:

```
optimizer = torch.optim.SGD(model.parameters(), lr=0.01)
```

- **Adam**: An optimizer that dynamically adjusts the learning rate:

```
optimizer = torch.optim.Adam(model.parameters(), lr=0.001)
```

Conclusion

In this chapter, we introduced the foundational concepts of PyTorch, one of the most popular frameworks for deep learning. You learned how PyTorch tensors differ from NumPy arrays and how their GPU support and integration with automatic differentiation make them essential tools for machine learning practitioners. We explored how CUDA acceleration can significantly improve training times by leveraging GPUs. Moreover, you have acquired an understanding of the structure of neural networks, the significance of activation functions, and how PyTorch's Autograd feature facilitates gradient calculations. In conclusion, we covered model weights and optimizers, essential elements in the training process. They enable the adjustment of model parameters to reduce errors and improve accuracy. Armed with this understanding, you are now well-equipped to start building, training, and optimizing neural networks using PyTorch.

In the next chapter, *Building Blocks of Neural Networks in PyTorch*, we will expand on the fundamental concepts covered here by delving deeper into the practical components required to build sophisticated neural network architectures. You will learn to implement various layer types, construct complex model architectures, and work with different data types in PyTorch. We will explore techniques for efficiently loading and preprocessing data, implementing custom loss functions, and managing the training process. By the end of the next chapter, you will have the skills to build and train your custom neural networks for various machine learning tasks.

Exercises

Build and train a simple neural network

Using the concepts covered in this chapter, develop and train a simple neural network to classify images from the MNIST dataset (handwritten digits). Follow the given steps:

1. **Data loading**: Use PyTorch's torchvision.datasets to load the MNIST dataset.
2. **Define a neural network**: Create a basic neural network model using the nn.Module class. Use at least one hidden layer and experiment with different activation functions, such as ReLU and Sigmoid.
3. **Training loop**: Implement a training loop that:
    a. Uses cross-entropy loss as the loss function.
    b. Utilizes the Adam optimizer.
    c. Trains the model for at least 5 epochs and prints the loss for each epoch.
4. **Evaluation**: After training, evaluate the model on the test dataset and calculate its accuracy.

Hints:

- Start using a simple, fully connected (linear) network with layers like nn.Linear().
- You can use torch.optim.Adam as the optimizer and torch.nn.CrossEntropyLoss as the loss function.

Multiple choice questions

1. **What is the main difference between PyTorch tensors and NumPy arrays?**
   a. PyTorch tensors support GPU acceleration and automatic differentiation.
   b. PyTorch tensors can be used only for integer operations.
   c. NumPy arrays are faster than PyTorch tensors.
   d. PyTorch tensors do not support multi-dimensional data.
2. **What is the purpose of the Autograd feature in PyTorch?**
   a. To accelerate computations on the CPU.
   b. To automatically compute gradients for backpropagation.
   c. To help manage memory usage in deep learning models.
   d. To simplify data loading operations.
3. **Which activation function outputs values between 0 and 1, making it suitable for binary classification?**
   a. ReLU
   b. Tanh
   c. Sigmoid
   d. Softmax
4. **How is a nn module class represented in PyTorch?**
   a. A function for computing matrix multiplication.
   b. The base class for all neural network models in PyTorch.
   c. A class that handles GPU memory management.
   d. A module that optimizes models.
5. **Which optimizer dynamically adjusts the learning rate during training?**
   a. SGD
   b. Adagrad
   c. Adam
   d. RMSprop

Answers

1.	a.
2.	b.
3.	c.
4.	b.
5.	c.

Key terms

- **Tensor**: A multi-dimensional array used as the basic building block in PyTorch to represent data.
- **CUDA**: A parallel computing platform that enables computations on NVIDIA GPUs, allowing for faster large-scale data processing.
- **Autograd**: PyTorch's automatic differentiation system tracks operations and computes gradients during backpropagation.
- **nn.Module**: This is the base class for all neural network models in PyTorch, used to define layers and forward passes.
- **Activation function**: A mathematical function applied to neurons in a neural network to introduce non-linearity, helping the model learn complex patterns. Common examples include the ReLU, Sigmoid, and Tanh functions.
- **Optimizer**: An algorithm that adjusts model weights based on the gradients computed during backpropagation. Examples include SGD and Adam.
- **Loss function**: A function that calculates the difference between what the model predicts and the actual target, guiding the learning process.
- **Backpropagation**: The process by which gradients are computed and used to update model weights during training.

References

1. **https://pytorch.org/**

Join our Discord space

Join our Discord workspace for latest updates, offers, tech happenings around the world, new releases, and sessions with the authors:

https://discord.bpbonline.com

CHAPTER 9
Building Blocks of Neural Networks in PyTorch

Introduction

In this chapter, we will explore the fundamental building blocks of neural networks using PyTorch. You will learn how to create and manipulate layers, apply activation functions, define loss functions, and optimize your models. Understanding these concepts is essential for constructing more sophisticated models in the future.

By the end of this chapter, you will have a clearer picture of how different components interact within a neural network and how they contribute to the learning process. We will also explore convolutional and recurrent layers, key building blocks for tasks such as image and sequence-based data. Additionally, this chapter will introduce practical concepts related to loss functions and optimizers.

Structure

This chapter contains the following topics:

- Overview of PyTorch's nn.Module
- Creating different neural network layers
- Activation functions in PyTorch
- Loss functions
- Optimizers in PyTorch
- Building and training a basic neural network

Objectives

By the end of this chapter, you should have a solid understanding of how to define neural networks using PyTorch's nn.Module class. You will be able to differentiate between various layer types, including linear, convolutional, and recurrent layers, and explain the mechanics of convolution operations, along with the significance of spatial relationships in image processing. Furthermore, you will learn how to select the appropriate activation functions, loss functions, and optimizers tailored to the specific problems you are solving. Ultimately, you will gain the skills to build and train basic neural networks in PyTorch, which apply to image- and sequence-based data tasks.

Overview of PyTorch's nn.Module

In PyTorch, the `nn.Module` class is the base class for building neural networks. This class allows you to define layers and a forward pass, the sequence of operations that transforms input data into predictions.

Here is a simple example of defining a neural network:

```
1.  import torch
2.  import torch.nn as nn
3.
4.  class SimpleNet(nn.Module):
5.      def __init__(self):
6.          super(SimpleNet, self).__init__()
7.          self.fc1 = nn.Linear(10, 50)  # Fully connected layer: 10 inputs to 50 outputs
8.          self.fc2 = nn.Linear(50, 2)   # Fully connected layer: 50 inputs to 2 outputs
9.
10.     def forward(self, x):
11.         x = torch.relu(self.fc1(x))   # ReLU activation after the first layer
12.         x = self.fc2(x)               # Output layer (no activation function here)
13.         return x
```

The following list outlines the code breakdown:

- **Line 2 (import torch.nn as nn)**: This imports the neural network module from PyTorch, which contains the building blocks for creating layers (like `Linear`), activation functions, and loss functions.
- **Line 4 (class SimpleNet(nn.Module):)**: We define our class `SimpleNet` by inheriting from `nn.Module`. This inheritance is crucial because it allows the object to automatically track the parameters (weights and biases) of the layers we define inside it.
- **Line 6 (super(SimpleNet, self).__init__())**: This line calls the constructor of the parent `nn.Module` class. It is a mandatory step to ensure that the internal structures of the PyTorch model are initialized correctly before we add our own layers.
- **Line 7 (self.fc1 = nn.Linear(10, 50))**: We define the first layer using `nn.Linear`. This is a fully connected layer where every input is connected to every output. The arguments indicate that the layer accepts 10 input features and transforms them into 50 output features (hidden units).
- **Line 8 (self.fc2 = nn.Linear(50, 2))**: We define the second layer. Note that its input size (50) matches the output size of the previous layer. It maps these 50 features to 2 outputs, representing the final class scores.
- **Line 11 (x = torch.relu(self.fc1(x)))**: In the `forward` method, we define the flow of data. Here, the input `x` is passed through the first layer (`fc1`), and the result is immediately passed through the **Rectified Linear Unit** (**ReLU**) activation function. This introduces non-linearity, allowing the network to learn patterns more complex than simple straight lines.
- **Line 12 (x = self.fc2(x))**: The data is then passed through the final layer (`fc2`). We generally do not apply an activation function like ReLU to the final output layer if we intend to use a loss function (like `CrossEntropy`) that expects raw scores (logits).

Creating different neural network layers

Neural networks are composed of different layers, each responsible for a different kind of data transformation. Let us explore some key types.

Linear layers

A linear layer is fully connected, meaning every neuron in the previous layer is connected to every neuron in the next. These are simple matrix multiplications followed by a bias addition.

```
nn.Linear(in_features, out_features)
```

Example:

```
self.fc = nn.Linear(128, 10)  #Maps 128 input features to 10 output classes
```

Convolutional layers

Convolutional layers are vital components in image processing tasks. They apply filters (small matrices) to extract features like edges, textures, and shapes while maintaining spatial relationships in the data.

Convolution

Convolution is like sliding a magnifying glass (filter) over an image to detect important features. The filter captures local patterns in small regions, and by sliding it across the image, the network learns various features like edges, corners, and textures.

Filter

A filter (or kernel) is a small matrix of weights, such as 3x3 or 5x5, that slides over the input image, computing a dot product at each location. The weights in the filter are learned during training, allowing the network to focus on important visual patterns.

Stride and padding

The following parameters control how convolution operations process input data:

- **Stride** controls how much the filter moves across the image. A stride of 1 means the filter moves by one pixel at a time, whereas a stride of 2 moves it by two pixels, reducing the output size.
- **Padding**: This method adds extra pixels (usually zeros) around the edges of the input, preserving its size after applying the filter. It ensures that edge information is not lost.

Example of a convolutional layer:

```
nn.Conv2d(in_channels, out_channels, kernel_size, stride=1, padding=0)
```

The code breakdown is as follows:

- **in_channels**: Number of input channels (e.g., 1 for grayscale, 3 for RGB images).
- **out_channels**: Number of filters (the number of learned feature maps).
- **kernel_size**: Size of the filter (e.g., 3x3).

Example:

```
self.conv1 = nn.Conv2d(1, 16, 3)  # Applies 16 filters to a grayscale image (1 channel), with 3x3 filters
```

Pooling layers

After convolutional layers, pooling layers (like **max pooling**) reduce the input's spatial dimensions. Max pooling selects the maximum value from a region, reducing its size while keeping important features:

```
nn.MaxPool2d(kernel_size, stride=None)
```

Example:

```
self.pool = nn.MaxPool2d(2, 2)  # Reduces the size by
taking the max from 2x2 regions
```

Understanding recurrent layer architecture

Recurrent layers are used for sequence-based data, like time series or text. They retain information from previous inputs in the sequence, allowing the network to make better predictions based on context. The details are as follows:

- **RNN**: A simple recurrent layer that passes information from one time step to the next. However, it struggles with long sequences.
- **Long short-term memory (LSTM)**: This solves the RNN's limitation by controlling information flow with gates, making it capable of remembering information over longer sequences.
- **Gated Recurrent Unit (GRU)**: A simpler version of LSTM that is faster to train but handles long sequences effectively.

Use recurrent layers for tasks like:

- Text generation (predicting the next word in a sentence)
- Time series forecasting
- Speech recognition

Example:

```
nn.LSTM(input_size, hidden_size, num_layers)
```

Activation functions in PyTorch

Activation functions are essential for introducing non-linearity into neural networks. They allow the model to capture complex patterns beyond linear transformations. Let us briefly recap and expand on the activation functions:

- **ReLU**: This unit outputs the input directly if it is positive; otherwise, it returns zero. Its popularity stems from its straightforwardness and efficiency.

  ```
  x = torch.relu(tensor)
  ```

- **Leaky ReLU**: Like ReLU, but allows a small, non-zero output for negative inputs to avoid dying neurons.

  ```
  nn.LeakyReLU(negative_slope=0.01)
  ```

- **Sigmoid**: Maps inputs to a range between 0 and 1, making it ideal for binary classification tasks.

  ```
  torch.sigmoid(tensor)
  ```

- **Tanh**: Maps inputs between -1 and 1, valid for tasks requiring positive and negative outputs.

  ```
  torch.tanh(tensor)
  ```

- **Softmax**: Often used in the output layer of multi-class classification tasks, softmax converts raw outputs into probabilities that sum to 1.

  ```
  nn.Softmax(dim=1)
  ```

Loss functions

Loss functions quantify a neural network's performance by measuring the difference between predictions and actual values. Selecting the proper loss function depends on the type of problem you are solving.

- **MSE**: Used for **regression** problems where the goal is to predict a continuous value (e.g., house prices):

```
nn.MSELoss()
```

- **Cross-entropy loss**: Commonly used for classification tasks. It compares the predicted probabilities to the actual class labels:

```
nn.CrossEntropyLoss()
```

- **Binary cross-entropy (BCE)**: Used for binary classification tasks (e.g., detecting spam vs. non-spam):

```
nn.BCELoss()
```

Loss functions for LLMs

You might be curious about **large language models (LLMs)**. *Are they considered regression or classification, and which loss function should we use for them?*

Cross-entropy loss is used in LLMs, such as GPT. Even though the model generates text, it can be considered a classification problem in which the model tries to predict the next word from a large vocabulary (each word is a class).

Loss functions for image detection

Cross-entropy loss is used in supervised learning, where you have labeled images for image classification tasks, such as detecting whether an image contains a cat or a dog. For object detection tasks, models might combine classification loss with localization loss (to locate objects in an image).

Optimizers in PyTorch

Optimizers update the model's weights based on the gradients calculated during backpropagation. Different optimizers perform this weight adjustment in different ways:

- **Stochastic gradient descent (SGD)**: A basic optimizer that updates weights by following the gradient direction. It can be slow, but it works well for large datasets:

```
torch.optim.SGD(model.parameters(), lr=0.01)
```

- **Adam**: Combines the benefits of both SGD and momentum-based optimizers. It adapts the learning rate for each parameter, making it widely used for most tasks:

```
torch.optim.Adam(model.parameters(), lr=0.001)
```

- **RMSprop**: Often used in recurrent networks. It helps stabilize training by adjusting the learning rate based on recent gradients:

```
torch.optim.RMSprop(model.parameters(), lr=0.001)
```

- **AdamW**: Similar to Adam but includes weight decay to prevent overfitting, making it useful in large models:

```
torch.optim.AdamW(model.parameters(), lr=0.001)
```

Building and training a basic neural network

Now that we have covered layers, activation functions, loss functions, and optimizers, let us build a simple neural network and train it. We will use a combination of convolutional and fully connected layers:

```
import torch
import torch.nn as nn
```

```
3. import torch.optim as optim
4.
5. class SimpleCNN(nn.Module):
6.     def __init__(self):
7.         super(SimpleCNN, self).__init__()
8.         self.conv1 = nn.Conv2d(1, 16, 3)  # Convolutional layer
9.         self.pool = nn.MaxPool2d(2, 2)  # Pooling layer
10.        self.fc1 = nn.Linear(16 * 13 * 13, 128)  # Fully connected layer
11.        self.fc2 = nn.Linear(128, 10)     # Output layer for 10 classes
12.
13.    def forward(self, x):
14.        x = torch.relu(self.conv1(x))
15.        x = self.pool(x)
16.        x = x.view(-1, 16 * 13 * 13)  # Flatten
17.        x = torch.relu(self.fc1(x))
18.        x = self.fc2(x)
19.        return x
20.
21. # Instantiate the model, define the loss and optimizer
22. model = SimpleCNN()
23. loss_fn = nn.CrossEntropyLoss()
24. optimizer = optim.Adam(model.parameters(), lr=0.001)
```

The following list outlines the code breakdown:

- **Line 8 (self.conv1 = nn.Conv2d(1, 16, 3))**: This defines a 2D convolutional layer, essential for image tasks.
    - **1**: The number of input channels (e.g., 1 for a grayscale image).
    - **16**: The number of filters (feature maps) the layer will learn to detect.
    - **3**: The kernel size, meaning each filter is a 3x3 matrix.
- **Line 9 (self.pool = nn.MaxPool2d(2, 2))**: This defines a Max Pooling layer. It reduces the spatial size of the image to lower computation and control overfitting. The arguments `(2, 2)` specify a 2x2 window and a stride of 2, effectively cutting the image height and width in half.
- **Line 10 (self.fc1 = nn.Linear(16 * 13 * 13, 128))**: This is the first fully connected layer.
    - The input size **`16 * 13 * 13`** is calculated based on the output of the previous layers: 16 channels times the remaining spatial dimensions (13x13).
    - It transforms this flattened data into 128 features.
- **Line 16 (x = x.view(-1, 16 * 13 * 13))**: Before passing data from a convolutional layer (which outputs 3D data: channels, height, width) to a linear layer (which expects a 1D vector), we must *flatten* it. The `view` method reshapes the tensor; **`-1`** tells PyTorch to automatically infer the batch size, while the rest matches the input size required by **`fc1`**.
- **Line 23 (loss_fn = nn.CrossEntropyLoss())**: We define the loss function. Cross-entropy is the standard choice for classification tasks (like recognizing digits 0-9), as it measures the difference between the predicted class probabilities and the actual class labels.
- **Line 24 (optimizer = optim.Adam(...))**: We initialize the optimizer, which is responsible for updating the model's weights.

- **model.parameters()**: This passes all the trainable weights of our `SimpleCNN` to the optimizer.
- **lr=0.001**: This sets the learning rate, controlling how large the adjustments to the weights are at each step. Adam is chosen here because it adapts the learning rate efficiently for most tasks.

With the model defined, you can train it using a training loop, optimize the weights using Adam, and evaluate the performance.

Conclusion

In this chapter, we explored the building blocks of neural networks in PyTorch, focusing on layers, activation functions, loss functions, and optimizers. You now have a solid foundation for building and training neural networks.

In the next chapter, we will explore the process of training neural networks using PyTorch. You will learn how to load and preprocess data using the dataset and DataLoader classes, implement data augmentation techniques, write effective training loops, and apply regularization methods such as dropout and batch normalization to improve model performance.

Exercises

In this exercise, you will train a simple feed-forward neural network on the MNIST dataset using different optimizers and compare the performance of SGD and Adam optimizers.

The following are the steps to complete the exercise:

1. **Prepare the environment**: Confirm that PyTorch and torchvision are installed.
2. **Retrieve the MNIST dataset**: Utilize torchvision to download and load the dataset.
3. **Design a basic neural network**: Construct a network featuring a single hidden layer.
4. **Train the model**: Train the network using SGD and Adam optimizers and log the training loss.
5. **Assess performance**: Evaluate the model on the test dataset and display the accuracy for both optimizers.

Multiple choice questions

1. **What does a convolutional filter do in an image?**
   a. Adds color
   b. Captures features like edges
   c. Changes the size of the image
   d. Adds noise to the image
2. **Which activation function is often used for binary classification?**
   a. ReLU
   b. Sigmoid
   c. Softmax
   d. Tanh
3. **What does padding do in convolutional layers?**
   a. Reduces the output size
   b. Increases the input size by adding zeros

c. Changes the stride
d. Normalizes the input

4. **Which optimizer is suitable for noisy gradients?**
   a. SGD
   b. Adam
   c. Adagrad
   d. RMSprop
5. **What type of layer is typically used for time series data?**
   a. Convolutional
   b. Linear
   c. Recurrent
   d. Pooling
6. **What is the purpose of the activation function in a neural network?**
   a. To linearize the output
   b. To introduce non-linearity
   c. To compute gradients
   d. To initialize weights
7. **Which loss function would you use for a regression task?**
   a. Cross-entropy loss
   b. Mean squared error
   c. Binary cross-entropy
   d. Hinge loss
8. **What does the stride parameter control in a convolutional layer?**
   a. The size of the filter
   b. The amount the filter moves across the input
   c. The number of filters
   d. The padding around the input
9. **What type of layer is a MaxPooling layer?**
   a. Convolutional
   b. Fully connected
   c. Recurrent
   d. Dimensionality reduction
10. **When should you use Adam optimizer instead of SGD?**
    a. For all models
    b. When you have large datasets and noisy gradients
    c. When you want to avoid overfitting
    d. For models that require high interpretability

Answers

1.	b.
2.	b.
3.	b.
4.	b.
5.	c.
6.	b.
7.	b.
8.	b.
9.	d.
10.	b.

Key terms

- **Activation function**: A mathematical function applied to the output of each neuron, introducing non-linearity to the model.
- **Convolution**: An operation that filters input data, extracting features while preserving spatial relationships.
- **Filter (Kernel)**: A small matrix of weights used in convolutional layers to detect patterns in the input data.
- **Stride**: The step size with which the filter moves across the input image during convolution.
- **Padding**: Additional pixels are added around the edges of an input image, allowing the filter to cover the edges without shrinking the output.
- **Loss function**: A function that measures how well a model's predictions match the actual target values.
- **Optimizer**: An algorithm that adjusts the model weights based on the loss and computed gradients.
- **Stochastic gradient descent (SGD)**: A basic optimizer that updates weights by following the gradient direction for each batch of data.
- **Adam**: An adaptive optimizer that adjusts learning rates based on the moving averages of gradients.
- **Recurrent neural networks (RNN)**: Networks that process sequential data by retaining information over time steps.

References

1. *Build the Neural Network – PyTorch Documentation.* **https://pytorch.org/tutorials/beginner/basics/buildmodel_tutorial.html**
2. *Defining a Neural Network in PyTorch – Official Recipe.* **https://pytorch.org/tutorials/recipes/recipes/defining_a_neural_network.html**
3. *PyTorch for Deep Learning - Dataquest.* **https://www.dataquest.io/blog/pytorch-for-deep-learning/**
4. *PyTorch Tutorial GitHub Repository.* **https://github.com/yunjey/pytorch-tutorial**
5. *How to Implement Neural Networks in PyTorch - GeeksforGeeks.* **https://www.geeksforgeeks.org/how-to-implement-neural-networks-in-pytorch/**
6. *Zero to Mastery: Learn PyTorch for Deep Learning.* **https://www.learnpytorch.io**

CHAPTER 10
Training Neural Networks with PyTorch

Introduction

In this chapter, we will address a fundamental element of deep learning: training neural networks. Up to this point, we have reviewed the essentials of neural networks, activation functions, loss functions, and the creation of basic models using PyTorch. Now, we will investigate efficient training methods for these models. Training a neural network involves inputting data, optimizing parameters, and monitoring performance throughout the process.

In this chapter, we will outline the training process in PyTorch, covering key concepts like data loading, preprocessing, augmentation, and how to set up the training loops. We will also focus on regularization methods such as dropout and batch normalization that help improve model generalization and reduce overfitting. Finally, we will explain the steps for saving and loading models using the .pth format. By the end of this chapter, you will understand how to train neural networks in PyTorch, monitor their performance, and save trained models for future use.

Structure

This chapter contains the following topics:

- Data loading with dataset and DataLoader
- Data preprocessing and augmentation
- Training loops
- Defining validation dataset and DataLoader
- Monitoring training and validation performance
- Regularization techniques
- Understanding and improving low accuracy
- Saving and loading models

Objectives

This chapter aims to help readers develop a comprehensive understanding of the training process in PyTorch. We will begin by explaining how to load and preprocess data, using PyTorch's dataset and DataLoader classes. We will also explore data augmentation techniques to enhance the diversity of the training data and improve model generalization. The chapter will then cover how to write effective training loops for neural networks and monitor model performance during training and validation. Furthermore, we will discuss the importance of regularization, focusing on dropout and batch normalization techniques, which prevent overfitting and help models generalize better. Additionally, readers will learn how to save and load models in PyTorch, mainly using the .pth format.

Data loading with dataset and DataLoader

Before we train a neural network, we need to load and prepare our dataset. PyTorch provides two key classes for this purpose:

- **Dataset**: This class represents a collection of data. It provides methods to load and access individual samples of the data.
- **DataLoader**: This utility allows us to load data in batches, shuffle it, and apply parallel loading to improve efficiency.

This chapter will use the CIFAR-10 dataset, a widely used deep learning dataset. CIFAR-10 consists of 60,000 color images in ten different classes, such as airplanes, cars, birds, and cats. Each image is 32x32 pixels. We will use this dataset to demonstrate the process of training a neural network.

Let us start by loading CIFAR-10 using PyTorch's built-in dataset utilities:

```
from torchvision import datasets, transforms
from torch.utils.data import DataLoader

# Define transformations for data preprocessing
transform = transforms.Compose([
    transforms.ToTensor(),
    transforms.Normalize((0.4914, 0.4822, 0.4465), (0.2470, 0.2435, 0.2616)) # Normalize pixel values
])

# Download and load the CIFAR-10 training data
trainset = datasets.CIFAR10(root='./data', download=True, train=True, transform=transform)
trainloader = DataLoader(trainset, batch_size=64, shuffle=True)
```

Here, we apply a transformation that converts the images to tensors and normalizes the pixel values. It is because each image in CIFAR-10 has three color channels (red, green, and blue), we normalize each channel separately.

Data preprocessing and augmentation

Preparing data is a crucial part of the machine learning process. If done right, preprocessing and augmentation can really boost the performance of your model. These methods help convert raw data into a format that works well with neural networks, while also increasing the variety of your training examples.

Data preprocessing

Data preprocessing is essential in preparing your dataset for training. Raw data is often not immediately suitable for training a model. Preprocessing techniques can include:

- **Normalization**: Adjusting pixel values to a consistent scale (e.g., between -1 and 1).
- **Resizing**: Adjusting the dimensions of images to fit the input size expected by the model.
- **Conversion to Tensor**: PyTorch requires data to be in the form of tensors.

We normalized the pixel values in the previous code to center them around zero. This helps neural networks converge faster during training.

Data augmentation

Data augmentation involves creating new training samples from the original data by applying random transformations. These transformations can introduce variations in the dataset that help the model generalize better to unseen data.

Standard data augmentation techniques include:

- **Random flipping**: Flipping images horizontally or vertically.
- **Random cropping**: Cropping out a portion of the image randomly.
- **Random rotation**: Rotating images by a random degree.
- **Color jittering**: Randomly changing an image's brightness, contrast, and saturation.

Here is an example of data augmentation applied to CIFAR-10:

```
transform = transforms.Compose([
    transforms.RandomHorizontalFlip(),   # Randomly flip images horizontally
    transforms.RandomCrop(32, padding=4),# Randomly crop with padding
    transforms.ToTensor(),
    transforms.Normalize((0.5, 0.5, 0.5), (0.5, 0.5, 0.5)) # Normalize
])
```

In this example, we have incorporated techniques like random horizontal flipping and random cropping to introduce more variations in our data. Regarding the cropping, you will notice we used **`padding=4`**. Since the CIFAR-10 images are already 32x32, cropping them to size 32 without padding would simply return the original image every time. By adding a 4-pixel border (padding) first, we temporarily increase the image size to 40x40. The transformer then randomly selects a 32x32 window from this larger area. This effectively shifts the subject within the frame, teaching the network to recognize objects regardless of their exact position.

Training loops

Training a neural network involves multiple iterations, known as **epochs**, where the model processes the entire dataset numerous times. During each epoch, the model undergoes a forward pass to make predictions, a backward pass to compute gradients, and an optimization step to update its parameters.

Let us break down a basic training loop in PyTorch. The following code shows how to implement a complete training cycle.

Note on model architecture is that in the following example, we define a simple fully connected network (**`SimpleNN`**) to clearly demonstrate how a training loop is structured. Please note that this architecture is intentionally basic. For complex image datasets like CIFAR-10, this specific model will likely yield lower accuracy because it lacks the ability to capture spatial features effectively. We will address this limitation and discuss how to switch to more powerful architectures, such as **convolutional neural networks** (**CNNs**), in the *low accuracy* section later in this chapter.

```
import torch
import torch.nn as nn
import torch.optim as optim

# Define a simple neural network
class SimpleNN(nn.Module):
    def __init__(self):
        super(SimpleNN, self).__init__()
        self.fc1 = nn.Linear(32*32*3, 256)
```

```
        self.fc2 = nn.Linear(256, 10)

    def forward(self, x):
        x = x.view(x.size(0), -1) # Flatten the image
        x = torch.relu(self.fc1(x))
        return self.fc2(x)

# Initialize the model, loss function, and optimizer
model = SimpleNN()
criterion = nn.CrossEntropyLoss()
optimizer = optim.SGD(model.parameters(), lr=0.01)

# Training loop
for epoch in range(10): # 10 epochs
    running_loss = 0.0
    for images, labels in trainloader:
        optimizer.zero_grad()       # Zero the gradients

        outputs = model(images)     # Forward pass
        loss = criterion(outputs, labels) # Compute loss
        loss.backward()             # Backward pass
        optimizer.step()            # Update weights

        running_loss += loss.item()
    print(f"Epoch {epoch+1}, Loss: {running_loss/len(trainloader)}")
```

In this training loop:

- **Forward pass**: The input data is passed through the model to generate predictions.
- **Loss calculation**: The predictions are compared with the true labels using the cross-entropy loss.
- **Backward pass**: Gradients are calculated by backpropagating the error through the network.
- **Optimizer step**: The optimizer updates the model parameters based on the computed gradients.

Defining validation dataset and the DataLoader

Before monitoring validation performance, we need to set up a validation dataset and a corresponding DataLoader. This is similar to how we defined the training dataset and DataLoader, but we will use a separate data split for validation.

Here is how to define a validation dataset and loader using CIFAR-10:

```
# Validation data transformations (only normalization, no augmentation)
val_transform = transforms.Compose([
    transforms.ToTensor(),
    transforms.Normalize((0.5, 0.5, 0.5), (0.5, 0.5, 0.5)) # Normalize pixel values
])

# Download and load the CIFAR-10 validation data
```

```
valset = datasets.CIFAR10(root='./data', download=True, train=False, transform=val_transform)
valloader = DataLoader(valset, batch_size=64, shuffle=False)
```

Monitoring training and validation performance

We monitor training and validation loss to ensure the model is learning correctly. Training loss gives us an idea of how well the model performs on the training data, while validation loss measures performance on unseen data, helping to detect **overfitting**.

You can also track **accuracy** to measure the percentage of correct predictions during training and validation. Here is a simple validation loop:

```
# Validation loop
val_loss = 0.0
correct = 0
total = 0

# Switch the model to evaluation mode
model.eval()

with torch.no_grad():  # No need to track gradients during validation
    for images, labels in valloader:
        outputs = model(images)
        loss = criterion(outputs, labels)  # Compute the loss on the validation set
        val_loss += loss.item()

        # Calculate accuracy
        _, predicted = torch.max(outputs, 1)  # Get the predicted class with the highest score
        total += labels.size(0)
        correct += (predicted == labels).sum().item()

# Calculate average loss and accuracy
avg_val_loss = val_loss / len(valloader)
accuracy = 100 * correct / total

print(f"Validation Loss: {avg_val_loss}, Validation Accuracy: {accuracy}%")
```

Why `model.eval()` is critical: You will notice the loop begins with **`model.eval()`**. This step is essential because certain layers, such as **dropout** and **batch normalization**, behave differently during training versus testing:

- **During training**: Dropout randomly deactivates neurons to force learning, and batch normalization calculates statistics based on the current batch of data.
- **During validation/testing**: We need the model to be deterministic and stable. **`model.eval()`** signals these layers to switch modes: Dropout stops deactivating neurons (using all of them), and batch normalization uses the running statistics learned during training rather than the current batch's statistics.

Failing to switch to evaluation mode can lead to inconsistent predictions and inaccurate validation metrics. We will explore these specific layers in detail in the next section, *regularization techniques*.

Regularization techniques

Regularization is crucial for preventing overfitting, a situation where a model performs well on training data but poorly on unseen data. The two most common regularization techniques are **dropout** and **batch normalization**.

Dropout

Dropout helps prevent overfitting by randomly *dropping out* a percentage of neurons during training. This makes the network more robust, as it cannot rely on any specific neuron for making predictions. The following code snippet shows how to apply dropout:

```
import torch.nn.functional as F

class SimpleNNWithDropout(nn.Module):
    def __init__(self):
        super(SimpleNNWithDropout, self).__init__()
        self.fc1 = nn.Linear(32*32*3, 256)
        self.dropout = nn.Dropout(0.5)  # Randomly Zero Out 50% of neurons
        self.fc2 = nn.Linear(256, 10)

    def forward(self, x):
        x = x.view(x.size(0), -1)
        x = F.relu(self.fc1(x))
        x = self.dropout(x) # Apply dropout
        return self.fc2(x)
```

Batch normalization

Batch normalization is a methodological approach designed to stabilize the training process in neural networks by normalizing the inputs to each layer. This methodology results in more consistent performance and enables the utilization of larger learning rates. Furthermore, it serves as a regularization technique, thereby reducing the necessity of relying on alternative methods such as dropout to mitigate overfitting. The following is a straightforward code snippet illustrating the implementation of batch normalization:

```
class SimpleNNWithBatchNorm(nn.Module):
    def __init__(self):
        super(SimpleNNWithBatchNorm, self).__init__()
        self.fc1 = nn.Linear(32*32*3, 256)
        self.batch_norm = nn.BatchNorm1d(256)
        self.fc2 = nn.Linear(256, 10)

    def forward(self, x):
        x = x.view(x.size(0), -1)
        x = F.relu(self.batch_norm(self.fc1(x)))  # Apply batch normalization
        return self.fc2(x)
```

After applying regularization techniques like dropout and batch normalization, it is common to still see lower-than-expected accuracy, especially on challenging datasets like CIFAR-10. This is where we can explore techniques to enhance accuracy and generalization and understand why the model's performance is suboptimal. Let us discuss what may be causing low accuracy and how we can improve the performance of our neural networks.

Understanding and improving low accuracy

Training deep learning models can often result in low accuracy, especially when addressing more complex datasets, such as CIFAR-10, which exhibits significant variability across its ten classes. It is important to consider the performance metrics of your model. If your model attains approximately 50% accuracy, it may not seem encouraging. To put this in perspective, random guessing on a 10-class dataset like CIFAR-10 yields only 10% accuracy. While 50% is a significant improvement over random chance—indicating the model is learning—it is widely considered a low-performance metric typical for fundamental networks that lack extensive optimization. Several factors contribute to low accuracy, and understanding these can help guide us toward practical solutions.

Reasons why accuracy might be low

The following are the reasons why accuracy might be low:

- **Model simplicity**: A basic neural network often struggles to learn complex patterns, particularly when handling high-dimensional datasets such as CIFAR-10. Simple architectures may find it challenging to distinguish between different classes without the incorporation of additional layers or more advanced structures.
- **Hyperparameters**: The choice of hyperparameters, such as the learning rate, batch size, and number of epochs, is vital for the model's performance. A high learning rate can cause the model to overshoot optimal weights, whereas a low learning rate may lead to slow convergence.
- **Overfitting**: The model may exhibit strong performance on the training data; however, it may not generalize effectively to previously unseen validation data. This is often due to overfitting, where the model becomes overly specialized in the training data, picking up noise instead of valuable insight patterns.
- **Underfitting**: Conversely, the model may be exhibiting underfitting with respect to the data, indicating that it is excessively simplistic in its representation of the underlying patterns.
- **Insufficient regularization**: While dropout and batch normalization can help, they may not address all overfitting issues, especially in complex datasets.

How to improve performance

Improving the performance of a neural network typically requires **hyperparameter tuning**, more advanced model architectures, and fine-tuning the training process. The following are some common strategies:

- **Model architecture enhancements**: Consider using CNNs for image datasets like CIFAR-10. CNNs are specifically designed to manage spatial data and significantly improve performance over fully connected layers for image classification tasks.
- **Hyperparameter tuning**: Hyperparameters are values that define the network's training process. Adjusting them can often lead to significant performance improvements.
    - **Learning rate**: The learning rate controls how quickly or slowly the model updates its weights. You should reduce the learning rate if the validation loss fluctuates too much.

    ```
    optimizer = torch.optim.Adam(model.parameters(), lr=0.001)  # Experiment with different learning rates
    ```

    - **Batch size**: Smaller batch sizes can introduce noise in the gradient updates, but they allow the model to generalize better. Conversely, larger batch sizes stabilize training but might overfit the data.

    ```
    trainloader = DataLoader(trainset, batch_size=32, shuffle=True)  # Try 32, 64, or 128
    ```

    - **Number of epochs**: Training for more epochs allows the model to refine its weights over time.

However, validation performance must be monitored carefully to avoid overfitting.

- **Optimizer choice**: While **SGD** is simple, optimizers like **Adam** or **RMSprop** can offer faster convergence and more stable updates.

```
optimizer = torch.optim.Adam(model.parameters(), lr=0.0001)  # Switch to Adam
optimizer
```

- **Regularization techniques**:
  - **Dropout rate**: Adjusting the dropout rate can improve generalization by preventing the network from relying too much on specific neurons.

```
self.dropout = nn.Dropout(p=0.5)  # Experiment with dropout rates
```

  - **Weight decay (L2 regularization)**: Adding L2 regularization to your optimizer can help prevent the model's weights from growing too large, a common cause of overfitting.

```
optimizer = torch.optim.SGD(model.parameters(), lr=0.01, weight_decay=0.0005)  # L2
regularization+
```

- **Data augmentation**:
  - Implementing supplementary data augmentation techniques, including random cropping, rotation, color jittering, and cutout, can enhance the diversity of training examples and boost generalization.

```
transform = transforms.Compose([
    transforms.RandomHorizontalFlip(),
    transforms.RandomRotation(10),  # Rotate up to 10 degrees
    transforms.ColorJitter(brightness=0.2, contrast=0.2),
    transforms.ToTensor(),
    transforms.Normalize((0.5, 0.5, 0.5), (0.5, 0.5, 0.5))
])
```

Understanding the reasons behind low accuracy and applying the strategies outlined here can significantly improve your neural network's performance. When used correctly, model tuning, regularization, and augmentation are potent tools that can help bridge the gap between low initial accuracy and optimal model performance. These techniques are essential to deep learning and will continue to be useful as models grow in complexity.

Saving and loading models

Once a model has been trained, we often want to save it for later use. In PyTorch, models are typically saved in **`.pth` files**, which store the model's state dictionary (i.e., its learned parameters).

- **Saving a model:**

```
torch.save(model.state_dict(), 'model.pth')
```

- **Loading a model:**

```
model = SimpleNN()
model.load_state_dict(torch.load('model.pth'))
```

Best practices and saving checkpoints to resume training

The preceding method is perfect if you only need the model for making predictions. However, if you plan to pause and resume training later (e.g., if the training process is interrupted or takes days), saving only the model parameters is not enough. You also need to preserve the state of the optimizer (which holds momentum and learning rate info) and the current epoch.

To do this, you should save a dictionary containing all relevant components:

```
# Save a general checkpoint
torch.save({
            'epoch': epoch,
            'model_state_dict': model.state_dict(),
            'optimizer_state_dict': optimizer.state_dict(),
            'loss': loss,
            }, 'checkpoint.pth')
```

Loading a checkpoint to resume training:

```
checkpoint = torch.load('checkpoint.pth')
model.load_state_dict(checkpoint['model_state_dict'])
optimizer.load_state_dict(checkpoint['optimizer_state_dict'])
epoch = checkpoint['epoch']
loss = checkpoint['loss']

model.train() # Set the model back to training mode
```

This approach ensures that when you restart, the optimizer continues exactly where it left off, rather than resetting its internal statistics.

Conclusion

This chapter explored the essential aspects of training neural networks in PyTorch, including data loading, preprocessing, and augmentation. We also learned how to set up training loops, monitor performance, and implement regularization techniques. Additionally, we discussed common pitfalls leading to low accuracy and strategies for improving model performance.

Understanding how to train models effectively is a foundational skill in deep learning. Mastering it will empower you to tackle various real-world problems using neural networks.

In the next chapter, we will learn about the transformative CNNs.

Exercises

Build a complete training and validation pipeline for a neural network using the CIFAR-10 dataset in PyTorch. Your solution should incorporate the following features:

- **Data loading and preprocessing**:
  - Use the dataset and DataLoader classes to load and preprocess CIFAR-10 images.
  - Implement data augmentation techniques (e.g., random horizontal flip, random crop).
- **Model definition**:
  - Define a neural network that includes:
    - At least two hidden layers.
    - Dropout layers for regularization.
    - Batch normalization layers for stabilization.
- **Training and validation loops**:
  - Create a training loop that:

        - Tracks training and validation loss and accuracy.
        - Implements early stopping based on validation loss.
        - Saves the best model parameters to a file.
- **Visualization**:
    - After training, visualize:
        - Training and validation loss over epochs.
        - Training and validation accuracy over epochs.
- **Hyperparameter tuning**:
    - Allow for hyperparameter tuning options such as learning rate, batch size, and number of epochs.
    - **Bonus**: Implement a confusion matrix to analyze model predictions across different classes after validation.

Multiple choice questions

1. **What is the primary purpose of normalization in data preprocessing?**
    a. Increase the size of the dataset
    b. Reduce computational cost
    c. Center and scale the data to improve training convergence
    d. Eliminate the need for data augmentation
2. **What does dropout do in a neural network?**
    a. Prevents overfitting by randomly setting some neurons to zero
    b. Increases the number of parameters
    c. Speeds up the training process
    d. Reduces the size of the model
3. **Which of the following is a benefit of using batch normalization?**
    a. It eliminates the need for activation functions
    b. It reduces internal covariate shift
    c. It increases model complexity
    d. It replaces the need for data augmentation
4. **What is the function of the DataLoader class in PyTorch?**
    a. To define the model architecture
    b. To load data in batches and shuffle it
    c. To compute gradients during backpropagation
    d. To visualize model performance
5. **How can data augmentation help improve model performance?**
    a. It reduces the number of epochs needed for training
    b. It increases the size of the model parameters
    c. It creates variations of the training data to help prevent overfitting
    d. It automatically selects the optimal learning rate

6. **What is the primary goal of a training loop in PyTorch?**
   a. To define the model architecture
   b. To save the model to a file
   c. To optimize the model's parameters based on training data
   d. To create visualization charts of model performance
7. **What might indicate that your model is overfitting?**
   a. High training accuracy and low validation accuracy
   b. High validation accuracy and low training accuracy
   c. Consistent performance across training and validation datasets
   d. Rapid convergence of both training and validation loss
8. **When should you consider using a pre-trained model?**
   a. When you want to create a model from scratch
   b. When you have a small dataset and limited computational resources
   c. When you have ample data and want to optimize training time
   d. Only when working with image classification tasks
9. **In the context of training a neural network, what is early stopping?**
   a. A method to increase the batch size during training
   b. A way to accelerate the training process by skipping epochs
   c. A technique to halt training when validation loss starts to degrade
   d. A method to initialize model weights optimally
10. **What are standard techniques to handle an unbalanced dataset?**
   a. Ignore it since neural networks can handle imbalances automatically
   b. Oversampling, under-sampling, or using class weights
   c. Increase the learning rate proportionally to class imbalance
   d. Only use data from the majority class for more reliable training

Answers

1.	c.
2.	a.
3.	b.
4.	b.
5.	c.
6	c.
7.	a.
8.	b.
9.	c.
10.	b.

Key terms

- **Dataset**: A class representing a collection of data samples.
- **DataLoader**: A utility for loading data in batches.
- **Data augmentation**: Techniques for generating new training samples through transformations.
- **Dropout**: A regularization technique that randomly sets a fraction of input units to zero.
- **Batch normalization**: A technique to normalize layer inputs to improve training stability.
- **Early stopping**: A technique to halt training when validation performance degrades.

Join our Discord space

Join our Discord workspace for latest updates, offers, tech happenings around the world, new releases, and sessions with the authors:

https://discord.bpbonline.com

CHAPTER 11
Convolutional Neural Networks with PyTorch

Introduction

Convolutional neural networks (**CNNs**) represent one of the most transformative advancements in artificial intelligence, particularly for image processing and computer vision. Unlike fully connected neural networks, which struggle with complex spatial patterns, CNNs excel at identifying and learning hierarchical spatial features within images. This is accomplished using convolutional layers, which reduce the need for manual feature engineering by automatically detecting patterns such as edges, textures, and, eventually, entire objects. This chapter introduces CNNs, introduces their innovative architecture, and provides a practical guide to building and optimizing CNNs in PyTorch. By the end, you will be equipped to implement CNNs for image classification tasks, fully leveraging their unique structure and capabilities for enhanced accuracy and efficiency. In the previous chapter, we trained a simple neural network for image classification using the CIFAR-10 dataset. While this provided a good introduction, we encountered limitations in accuracy due to the challenges faced by fully connected networks. CNNs address these limitations and are designed explicitly for image-related tasks. CNNs have revolutionized image processing by automatically learning spatial hierarchies of features.

This chapter will introduce CNNs, explore their architecture, and guide you through building, training, and fine-tuning a CNN using PyTorch. By the end of this chapter, you will have developed a CNN that significantly enhances performance on image classification tasks compared to a basic, fully connected network.

Structure

This chapter contains the following topics:

- Understanding convolutional neural networks
- Architectural innovations in CNNs
- Basic CNN implementation
- LeNet CNN implementation

Objectives

The objectives of this chapter are to provide a comprehensive understanding of CNNs and explore their architecture and functional advantages over traditional neural networks for image-related tasks. We will examine each layer within a CNN, including convolutional, pooling, and fully connected layers, as well as activation functions. Special attention is given to the architectural innovations that have propelled CNNs to new levels of performance, such as spatial exploration, depth and width expansion, and multipath structures that mitigate issues like the vanishing gradient problem. Practical sections guide you through implementing CNNs in PyTorch, from basic setup to training on the CIFAR-10 dataset. By the end of this chapter, you will be able to create, train, and refine CNN models, understand the benefits of data augmentation and regularization techniques, and harness pre-trained models via transfer learning to optimize for different applications.

Understanding convolutional neural networks

The following figure shows the basic architecture of a CNN:

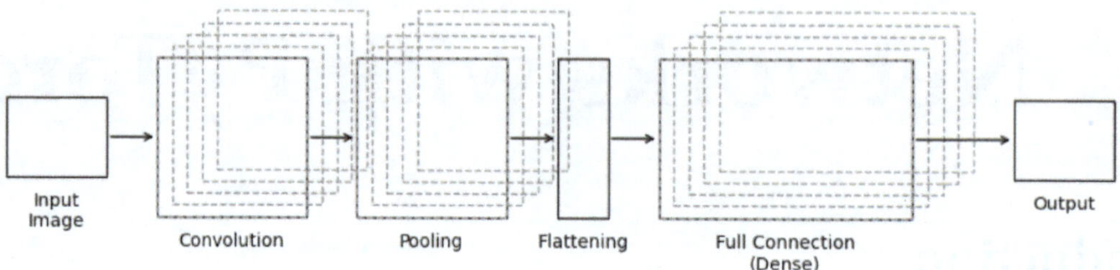

***Figure 11.1**: Basic architecture of a CNN*

CNNs are designed to process structured grid-like data, as shown in *Figure 11.1*, such as images. CNNs use layers that apply filters to learn patterns (like edges or textures) from small portions of the input data. As we go deeper into the network, CNNs learn more complex patterns.

Key components of CNNs are:

- **Convolutional layers**: They apply filters to the input, creating feature maps. Each filter detects specific features (e.g., edges, textures) in the image.
- **Pooling layers**: These layers reduce the spatial dimensions of the feature maps, making the network more efficient and reducing overfitting.
- **Fully connected layers**: After several convolutional and pooling layers, the data is flattened and passed through fully connected layers for classification.
- **Activation functions**: Activation functions, such as ReLU, are applied after convolutional layers to introduce non-linearity, helping the network learn more complex patterns.

Activation functions like ReLU are essential in CNNs, as they introduce sparsity to help the network learn complex patterns more efficiently. Additionally, modern optimization techniques (like Adam) and regularization methods (dropout and batch normalization) have significantly improved CNNs' ability to generalize to new data, addressing challenges like overfitting.

Vanishing gradient problem

The vanishing gradient problem, where gradients diminish during backpropagation, hindering learning in deep networks challenged early neural networks. The ReLU activation function mitigates this issue by allowing gradients to flow more effectively, making deeper networks feasible.

Architectural innovations in CNNs

As CNNs evolved, researchers discovered architectural innovations that made these networks more powerful and effective for complex tasks. Here, we will explore four main architectural types with advanced CNN capabilities: spatial exploration-based, depth-based, width-based, and multipath-based architectures.

Spatial exploration-based CNNs

Spatial exploration-based CNNs focus on extracting spatial features from images. By adjusting filter sizes and using specialized convolutional and pooling layers, these architectures capture a broad range of spatial details from local patterns (such as edges and textures) to more global structures. This approach is particularly beneficial for tasks where capturing fine information and spatial relationships within the image is crucial.

Example: Early CNNs like LeNet, as shown in *Figure 11.2*, used smaller filters, which limited their spatial exploration. Modern CNNs have larger filters in initial layers to capture broader spatial features and smaller filters in deeper layers for detailed feature extraction.

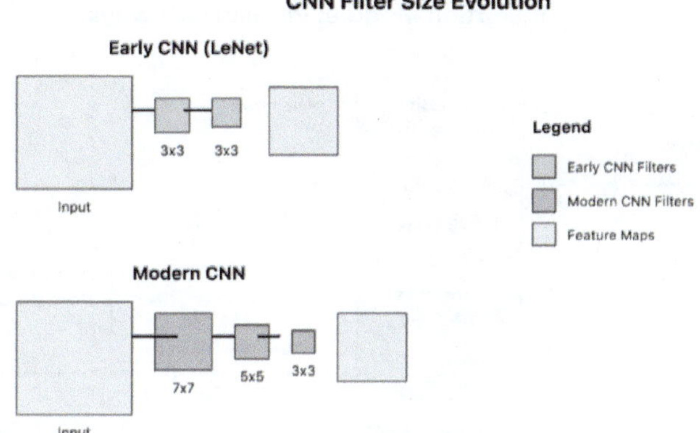

Figure 11.2: *Early CNNs*

Depth-based CNNs

Depth-based CNNs focus on increasing the number of layers in the network to capture hierarchical features at different levels. Adding layers allows these models to learn complex patterns and representations, making them highly effective for tasks with intricate features like object recognition and classification.

Example: **VGGNet** (2014) introduced the idea of deep CNNs, as illustrated in *Figure 11.3*, by stacking many convolutional layers, resulting in a network that is 16-19 layers deep. This approach enabled VGGNet to learn more detailed image patterns, improving classification accuracy. However, increasing depth requires significant computational resources and introduces challenges like the vanishing gradient problem.

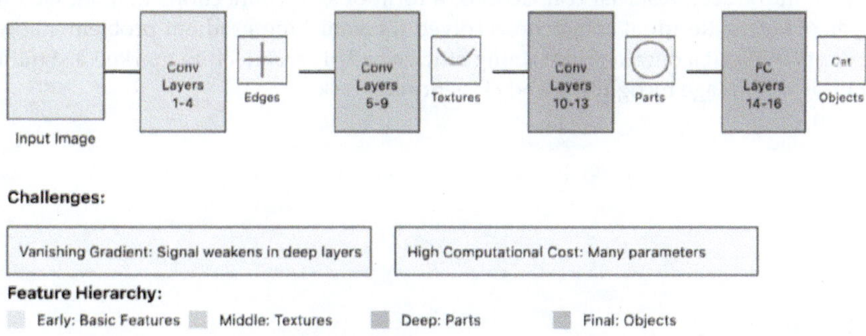

Figure 11.3: *VGGNet: Deep architecture*

Width-based CNNs

Width-based CNNs focus on widening the network architecture rather than solely deepening it. By introducing multiple parallel convolutional paths with varying filter sizes, these architectures can capture multi-scale features within an image, improving the model's ability to handle diverse and complex image features.

Example: Inception networks (2014) introduced the concept of wider networks, as shown in *Figure 11.4* with parallel convolutional layers of different filter sizes. The Inception module allowed the network to learn features simultaneously at multiple scales, resulting in an efficient and effective model that captures fine and broad image details.

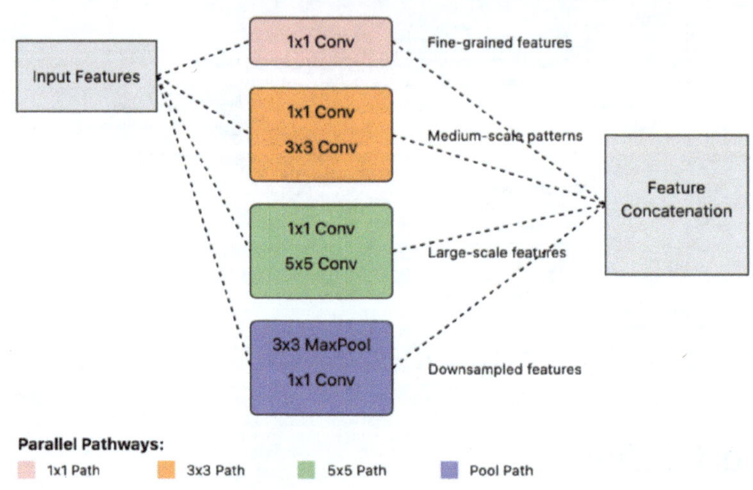

Figure 11.4: *Inception module*

Multipath-based CNNs

Multipath-based CNNs leverage the concept of multiple paths through the network, which allows information to flow more freely across layers. This approach helps alleviate the vanishing gradient problem by adding *skip* or *residual* connections that bypass one or more layers. These connections enable gradients to reach earlier layers more effectively, facilitating the training of deep networks.

Example: ResNet (2015) introduced residual connections, a form of skip connections that allowed networks to be trained with hundreds of layers. Residual connections solved the vanishing gradient problem, allowing ResNet to achieve remarkable depth without a decrease in training efficiency. This architecture marked a significant milestone in CNN design and improved image recognition and classification tasks.

The following figure shows the architecture of ResNet:

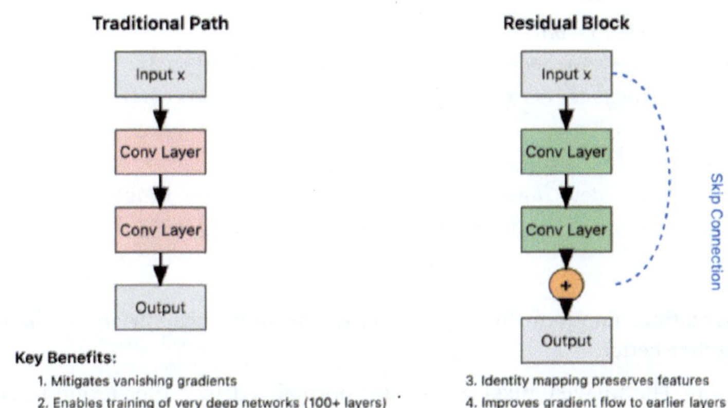

***Figure 11.5**: Residual connections*

Basic CNN implementation

The following sections will check the steps necessary to implement CNN with PyTorch and torchvision:

1. **Loading and preprocessing the CIFAR-10 dataset**: We will use the **CIFAR-10** dataset, which consists of 60,000 32x32 color images in ten classes. We will also apply data augmentation techniques like random cropping and flipping to improve model generalization, as you can see in the following code.

   This code sets up our tools. It defines a *recipe* to prepare the images (flipping and cropping them to help the AI learn better), downloads the dataset, and packages the data into small batches so the model can process them one by one.

```
import torch
import torchvision
import torchvision.transforms as transforms
from torch.utils.data import DataLoader

# Data augmentation and normalization for the training set
transform_train = transforms.Compose([
    transforms.RandomHorizontalFlip(),  # Randomly flip images
    transforms.RandomCrop(32, padding=4),  # Randomly crop images
    transforms.ToTensor(),  # Convert images to PyTorch tensors
    transforms.Normalize((0.5, 0.5, 0.5), (0.5, 0.5, 0.5))  # Normalize pixel values
])

# Only normalization for the validation/test set
transform_test = transforms.Compose([
    transforms.ToTensor(),
```

```
    transforms.Normalize((0.5, 0.5, 0.5), (0.5, 0.5, 0.5))
])

# Load CIFAR-10 dataset
trainset = torchvision.datasets.CIFAR10(root='./data', train=True, download=True, transform=transform_train)
trainloader = DataLoader(trainset, batch_size=64, shuffle=True)

testset = torchvision.datasets.CIFAR10(root='./data', train=False, download=True, transform=transform_test)
testloader = DataLoader(testset, batch_size=64, shuffle=False)
```

Explanation:

- **Data augmentation**: Random flipping and cropping introduce variety to the dataset, helping the model generalize better.
- **Normalization**: The images' pixel values are normalized to center around zero, which helps the network converge faster during training.

2. **Building a simple CNN in PyTorch**: Now that we have the data ready, let us define a simple CNN. The CNN will have two convolutional layers, followed by max-pooling layers and fully connected layers, as you can see in the following code.

   Here, we build the structure of our AI. We create a class that lists the layers we need: **convolutional layers** to spot patterns and **fully connected layers** to make decisions. The **`forward`** section connects these layers, creating a path for the image data to flow through and be transformed into a prediction.

```
import torch.nn as nn
import torch.nn.functional as F

# Define a simple CNN
class SimpleCNN(nn.Module):
    def __init__(self):
        super(SimpleCNN, self).__init__()
        self.conv1 = nn.Conv2d(3, 32, 3, padding=1)  # Convolutional Layer 1
        self.conv2 = nn.Conv2d(32, 64, 3, padding=1)  # Convolutional Layer 2
        self.pool = nn.MaxPool2d(2, 2)  # Max pooling layer
        self.fc1 = nn.Linear(64 * 8 * 8, 512)  # Fully connected layer 1
        self.fc2 = nn.Linear(512, 10)  # Output layer for 10 classes (CIFAR-10)

    def forward(self, x):
        x = self.pool(F.relu(self.conv1(x)))  # Apply conv1, ReLU, and pooling
        x = self.pool(F.relu(self.conv2(x)))  # Apply conv2, ReLU, and pooling
        x = x.view(-1, 64 * 8 * 8)  # Flatten the feature maps
        x = F.relu(self.fc1(x))  # Apply fully connected layer
        x = self.fc2(x)  # Output layer
        return x

# Instantiate the model, loss function, and optimizer
model = SimpleCNN()
```

```
criterion = nn.CrossEntropyLoss()
optimizer = torch.optim.Adam(model.parameters(), lr=0.001)
```

Explanation:

- **Convolutional layers**: We use two convolutional layers, each followed by a ReLU activation and max pooling. The first convolutional layer has 32 filters, and the second has 64 filters.
- **Max pooling**: Pooling reduces the spatial dimensions of the feature maps, improving computational efficiency.
- **Fully connected layers**: After flattening the output from the pooling layers, we pass it through two fully connected layers. The final layer produces ten outputs (one for each class in CIFAR-10).

3. **Training the CNN**: Now, we will train the CNN. We will loop through the dataset for several epochs, calculate the loss, and update the model parameters using backpropagation, as you can see in the following code.

   This is the learning loop. The code cycles through the data 10 times (epochs). In each cycle, it makes a guess, checks how wrong it was (loss), and then mathematically updates the model's internal numbers (optimizer) to make it smarter for the next round.

```
# Training Loop
for epoch in range(10):  # Train for 10 epochs
    running_loss = 0.0
    model.train()  # Set the model to training mode
    for images, labels in trainloader:
        optimizer.zero_grad()  # Zero the gradients
        outputs = model(images)  # Forward pass
        loss = criterion(outputs, labels)  # Compute the loss
        loss.backward()  # Backpropagation
        optimizer.step()  # Update model parameters

        running_loss += loss.item()

    print(f"Epoch {epoch+1}, Loss: {running_loss/len(trainloader)}")
```

   Explanation:

   - **Training mode**: The model is set to training mode using **`model.train()`**. This ensures that any layers, such as dropout or batch normalization, behave correctly during training.
   - **Zeroing gradients**: The optimizer's gradients are reset to zero before computing the new ones.
   - **Backpropagation**: The gradients are computed using **`loss.backward()`**, and the optimizer updates the model's parameters based on these gradients.

4. **Evaluating the CNN on the validation/test set**: Once training is done, we evaluate the model on the test set to see how well it performs on unseen data, as you can see in the following code.

   Now we test the model on images it has not seen before. We switch the model to *evaluation mode* to prevent it from learning or changing its settings, then feed it the test images and count how many times it correctly guesses the category.

```
correct = 0
total = 0
model.eval()  # Set the model to evaluation mode (no backpropagation)
with torch.no_grad():  # Disable gradient calculation during evaluation
```

```
    for images, labels in testloader:
        outputs = model(images)
        _, predicted = torch.max(outputs, 1)  # Get the predicted class
        total += labels.size(0)
        correct += (predicted == labels).sum().item()

print(f'Accuracy on the test set: {100 * correct / total}%')
```

```
Accuracy on the test set: 77.05%
```

As you can see, this result is already better than the one we got in our previous chapter using standard neural networks for image classification.

Explanation:

- **Evaluation mode**: The model is set to evaluation mode using **`model.eval()`**. This ensures that specific layers, like dropout, behave differently during testing than during training.
- **Disabling gradients**: We use **`torch.no_grad()`** to turn off gradient computation, which reduces memory usage and speeds up evaluation.

5. **Adding regularization techniques**: We can randomly apply dropout to drop neurons to prevent overfitting during training. Let us add a dropout layer to the fully connected layer, as you can see in the following code.

   This code is almost identical to our previous model, but we have added a **`Dropout`** layer. This layer randomly turns off different neurons during training, which forces the remaining ones to work harder. This prevents the model from lazily memorizing the images and helps it learn more robust features.

```
# CNN with Dropout
class CNNWithDropout(nn.Module):
    def __init__(self):
        super(CNNWithDropout, self).__init__()
        self.conv1 = nn.Conv2d(3, 32, 3, padding=1)
        self.conv2 = nn.Conv2d(32, 64, 3, padding=1)
        self.pool = nn.MaxPool2d(2, 2)
        self.fc1 = nn.Linear(64 * 8 * 8, 512)
        self.dropout = nn.Dropout(0.5)  # Dropout layer with 50% dropout rate
        self.fc2 = nn.Linear(512, 10)

    def forward(self, x):
        x = self.pool(F.relu(self.conv1(x)))
        x = self.pool(F.relu(self.conv2(x)))
        x = x.view(-1, 64 * 8 * 8)
        x = F.relu(self.fc1(x))
        x = self.dropout(x)  # Apply dropout
        x = self.fc2(x)
        return x

# Instantiate the model with dropout, loss function, and optimizer
model = CNNWithDropout()
```

```
criterion = nn.CrossEntropyLoss()
optimizer = torch.optim.Adam(model.parameters(), lr=0.001)
```

Explanation:

- **Dropout layer**: Adding a dropout layer with a 50% dropout rate prevents the model from overfitting by randomly turning off half the neurons in the fully connected layers during each training iteration.
- **Transfer learning**: Instead of training a CNN from scratch, we can use a pre-trained model (e.g., ResNet) and fine-tune it for our task. Here, we will use **ResNet-18**, pre-trained on ImageNet, and modify its final layer for CIFAR-10 classification.

  Instead of building a model from scratch, we download *ResNet*, a powerful AI already trained on millions of images. We then replace its final output layer (built for 1,000 categories) with a new layer designed for our 10 categories.
- **Loading and modifying a pre-trained model**:

```
from torchvision import models

# Load a pre-trained ResNet model
model = models.resnet18(pretrained=True)

# Modify the last fully connected layer to match the 10
classes of CIFAR-10
num_ftrs = model.fc.in_features
model.fc = nn.Linear(num_ftrs, 10)
```

- **Freezing layers (optional)**: We can freeze the earlier layers to fine-tune only the last layer while keeping the rest of the network's weights unchanged.

```
# Freeze all layers except the last layer
for param in model.parameters():
    param.requires_grad = False

# Allow training of the final fully connected layer
for param in model.fc.parameters():
    param.requires_grad = True
```

- **Fine-tuning the pre-trained model**: We can now fine-tune the model using a lower learning rate, as you can see in the following code.

  We set up a training loop similar to before, but with a key difference: we use a lower learning rate. Since the pre-trained model is already smart, we do not need to teach it everything; we just gently *fine-tune* it to understand our specific dataset.

```
# Use a lower learning rate for fine-tuning
optimizer = torch.optim.Adam(model.fc.parameters(), lr=0.0001)

# Fine-tuning loop
for epoch in range(10):
    running_loss = 0.0
    model.train()
    for images, labels in trainloader:
        optimizer.zero_grad()
```

```
            outputs = model(images)
            loss = criterion(outputs, labels)
            loss.backward()
            optimizer.step()

            running_loss += loss.item()

        print(f"Epoch {epoch+1}, Loss: {running_loss/len(trainloader)}")
```

Explanation:

- **Pre-trained model**: We use a pre-trained **ResNet-18** model, which has already learned features from the ImageNet dataset. We modify the final layer to output 10 classes (for CIFAR-10).
- **Fine-tuning**: Only the final layer is trained, while the rest of the network remains frozen. This allows us to adapt the model to our specific dataset with minimal training.

LeNet CNN implementation

LeNet, developed by *Yann LeCun* in 1998, was one of the earliest CNN architectures used for handwritten digit recognition. While its architecture is relatively simple and shallow, it laid the foundation for modern CNNs. This section will implement LeNet from scratch, train it on the CIFAR-10 dataset, and compare its performance with the previous standard CNN architecture.

Step 1: Implementing LeNet

In the following code, we implement LeNet from scratch using PyTorch.

This code recreates the classic LeNet architecture. It defines two convolutional layers to detect simple features (like edges) and three fully connected layers to interpret them. We use ReLU to activate the neurons and **max_pool** to shrink the data size, making the calculation more efficient.

```
import torch
import torch.nn as nn
import torch.nn.functional as F

class EnhancedLeNet(nn.Module):
    def __init__(self):
        super(EnhancedLeNet, self).__init__()
        # Convolutional Layers
        self.conv1 = nn.Conv2d(3, 32, kernel_size=5, padding=2)  # Output: 32x32 -> 32x32
        self.conv2 = nn.Conv2d(32, 64, kernel_
size=5)           # Output: 32x32 -> 28x28 -> 14x14

        # Fully Connected Layers
        self.fc1 = nn.Linear(64 * 6 * 6, 512)  # Adjusted for the output of conv2
        self.fc2 = nn.Linear(512, 120)
        self.fc3 = nn.Linear(120, 10)

    def forward(self, x):
```

```
        x = F.relu(self.conv1(x))
        x = F.max_pool2d(x, 2)
        x = F.relu(self.conv2(x))
        x = F.max_pool2d(x, 2)

        # Check the shape before flattening
        #print(x.shape)  # Debugging

        x = x.view(x.size(0), -1)  # Automatically infers correct dimensions
        x = F.relu(self.fc1(x))
        x = F.relu(self.fc2(x))
        x = self.fc3(x)
        return x

# Instantiate the enhanced LeNet
lenet_model = EnhancedLeNet()
```

Step 2: Training LeNet

Use the CIFAR-10 dataset for training and evaluation. Set up the training loop, loss function, and optimizer. We will keep consistency similar to the training setup in the chapter, as you can see in the following code.

This script combines everything into one workflow for LeNet. It prepares the data, defines how we measure error and fix it (loss and optimizer), runs the training loop for 10 epochs, and finally prints out the accuracy score to show how well the model learned.

```
import torch.optim as optim
from torchvision import datasets, transforms
from torch.utils.data import DataLoader

# Data preparation (using CIFAR-10 as in the main chapter)
transform = transforms.Compose([
    transforms.RandomHorizontalFlip(),
    transforms.RandomCrop(32, padding=4),
    transforms.ToTensor(),
    transforms.Normalize((0.5, 0.5, 0.5), (0.5, 0.5, 0.5))
])

trainset = datasets.CIFAR10(root='./data', train=True, download=True, transform=transform)
trainloader = DataLoader(trainset, batch_size=64, shuffle=True)

testset = datasets.CIFAR10(root='./data', train=False, download=True, transform=transform)
testloader = DataLoader(testset, batch_size=64, shuffle=False)

# Loss function and optimizer
criterion = nn.CrossEntropyLoss()
optimizer = optim.SGD(lenet_model.parameters(), lr=0.01, momentum=0.9)
```

```
# Training Loop
epochs = 10
for epoch in range(epochs):
    running_loss = 0.0
    lenet_model.train()
    for images, labels in trainloader:
        optimizer.zero_grad()
        outputs = lenet_model(images)
        loss = criterion(outputs, labels)
        loss.backward()
        optimizer.step()
        running_loss += loss.item()
    print(f"Epoch {epoch + 1}/{epochs}, Loss: {running_loss / len(trainloader)}")
```

Step 3: Evaluating LeNet on the test set

After training, we evaluate the model on the test set to assess its performance, as shown in the following code:

```
correct = 0
total = 0
lenet_model.eval()
with torch.no_grad():
    for images, labels in testloader:
        outputs = lenet_model(images)
        _, predicted = torch.max(outputs, 1)
        total += labels.size(0)
        correct += (predicted == labels).sum().item()

print(f"LeNet Accuracy on CIFAR-10 test set: {100 * correct / total:.2f}%")
```

```
LeNet Accuracy on CIFAR-10 test set: 73.86%
```

As you can see, the results in LeNet are very similar to those of a standard CNN. You can play with fine-tuning or changing settings on these Neural Networks to see what effect it has when you modify the configuration of the layers or the training hyperparameters.

Conclusion

In this chapter, we introduced CNNs and explored how they significantly improve image classification compared to traditional neural networks. By leveraging unique architectural elements such as convolutional and pooling layers, CNNs efficiently capture the spatial hierarchies within images, making them the ideal choice for complex visual tasks. We demonstrated the step-by-step process of building a basic CNN in PyTorch, applying data augmentation and regularization techniques like dropout, and utilizing transfer learning with pre-trained models for enhanced performance. Through this, you now have a foundation to implement CNNs effectively, address overfitting challenges, and build models capable of delivering high accuracy on image classification tasks. This knowledge is a solid base for more advanced topics, like **recurrent neural networks** (**RNNs**) for sequential data, which will be explored in the next chapter.

Exercises

Build and train a CNN on CIFAR-10 with custom architecture.

In this exercise, you will build a custom CNN for classifying images from the CIFAR-10 dataset. The network should have the following requirements:

- **Architecture**:
    - o Start with two convolutional layers, each followed by ReLU activation and max pooling.
    - o Add a fully connected layer with ReLU activation.
    - o Conclude with an output layer appropriate for CIFAR-10's 10-class classification.
- **Data augmentation**: Apply transformations like random cropping and horizontal flipping to increase generalization.
- **Training process**:
    - o Train the network for at least 10 epochs.
    - o Track and print the loss after each epoch.
- **Evaluation**:
    - o Calculate the accuracy of the test set after training.
    - o Save the model after training is complete.
- **Stretch goal (Optional)**:
    - o Add dropout layers in the fully connected layers to prevent overfitting.
    - o Fine-tune a pre-trained ResNet model on CIFAR-10 and compare the performance to the custom CNN.

Multiple choice questions

1. **What is the main advantage of using CNNs for image classification tasks?**
    a. Ability to handle sequential data
    b. Ability to learn spatial hierarchies of features
    c. Faster processing time for all data types
    d. Higher generalization in non-image data
2. **Which layer in a CNN is primarily responsible for reducing the spatial dimensions of feature maps?**
    a. Convolutional layer
    b. Activation layer
    c. Pooling layer
    d. Fully connected layer
3. **What is the key purpose of activation functions like ReLU in CNNs?**
    a. To prevent vanishing gradients
    b. To increase spatial resolution
    c. To initialize weights
    d. To simplify the network
4. **What is an example of a depth-based CNN architecture?**
    a. LeNet
    b. ResNet

   c. VGGNet
   d. Inception network
5. **Which technique can be applied in CNNs to prevent overfitting?**
   a. Max pooling
   b. Dropout
   c. Convolution
   d. Data augmentation
6. **In which scenario would you use a multipath-based architecture like ResNet?**
   a. When you need a shallow network for small datasets
   b. When training a very deep network
   c. For sequential data processing
   d. For textual data processing
7. **What is the primary function of convolutional layers in a CNN?**
   a. Reducing spatial dimensions
   b. Learning hierarchical feature representations
   c. Classifying data into categories
   d. Improving model interpretability
8. **Which dataset is commonly used as a benchmark for training and evaluating CNNs in image classification?**
   a. ImageNet
   b. MNIST
   c. CIFAR-10
   d. COCO
9. **What is typically modified to adapt a pre-trained CNN for a new task in transfer learning?**
   a. Convolutional layers
   b. Initial layer weights
   c. Final fully connected layer
   d. Pooling layers
10. **What does the term data augmentation refer to in CNN training?**
   a. Adding more filters to convolutional layers
   b. Increasing the number of layers
   c. Artificially expanding the dataset through transformations
   d. Freezing layers in a pre-trained model

Answers

1.	b.
2.	c.

3.	a.
4.	c.
5.	b, d
6.	b.
7.	b.
8.	b, c
9.	c.
10.	c.

Key terms

- **CNN**: A type of neural network optimized for processing grid-like data, especially images, by learning spatial hierarchies of features.
- **Convolutional layer**: A layer that applies filters to detect local patterns, such as edges or textures, in small regions of the input data.
- **Pooling layer**: A layer that reduces the spatial dimensions of feature maps to increase computational efficiency and reduce overfitting.
- **Activation function**: A function (e.g., ReLU) applied to introduce non-linearity, aiding the network in learning complex patterns.
- **Vanishing gradient problem**: It is challenging in deep networks where gradients diminish during backpropagation, making training difficult. It is mitigated in CNNs by using activation functions like ReLU.
- **Depth-based CNNs**: CNNs that increase layer depth to capture complex patterns, like VGGNet.
- **Width-based CNNs**: CNNs that widen architectures using parallel paths to capture multi-scale features, exemplified by Inception networks.
- **Multipath-based CNNs**: CNNs that use skip connections to facilitate gradient flow across layers, like in ResNet.
- **Data augmentation**: Techniques applied to artificially increase the size of a training dataset, improving generalization.
- **Transfer learning**: Leveraging a pre-trained model on a new task by adapting its final layers to the specific requirements of the new task.

References

1. *LeCun, Y., Bottou, L., Bengio, Y., & Haffner, P. (1998). Gradient-based learning applied to document recognition. Proceedings of the IEEE, 86(11), 2278-2324.*
2. *He, K., Zhang, X., Ren, S., & Sun, J. (2016). Deep residual learning for image recognition. In Proceedings of the IEEE conference on computer vision and pattern recognition (pp. 770-778).*
3. *Krizhevsky, A. (2009). Learning multiple layers of features from tiny images. Technical report, University of Toronto.*
4. *PyTorch Documentation.* **https://pytorch.org/docs/stable/index.html**
5. *Simonyan, K., & Zisserman, A. (2015). Very deep convolutional networks for large-scale image recognition.*

Join our Discord space

Join our Discord workspace for latest updates, offers, tech happenings around the world, new releases, and sessions with the authors:

https://discord.bpbonline.com

CHAPTER 12
Recurrent Neural Networks with PyTorch

Introduction

In the previous chapter, we explored **convolutional neural networks** (**CNNs**) and their powerful capabilities for processing grid-like data such as images. While CNNs excel at capturing spatial patterns and hierarchies, many real-world problems involve sequential data, where the order and context of information matter critically.

Consider how you are reading this text right now. You do not process each word in isolation—instead, you understand each word in the context of what came before it. This ability to process and understand sequential information is something traditional neural networks struggle with, but it is precisely what **recurrent neural networks** (**RNNs**) were designed to handle.

RNNs have been instrumental in advancing various fields through their ability to process sequences, which involves natural language processing (sentiment analysis, translation, chatbots), time series analysis (stock prices, weather forecasting), speech recognition, music generation, DNA sequence analysis, and video processing.

Traditional neural networks face several limitations when dealing with sequential data, as they require fixed input sizes, they process each input independently, and they cannot maintain context or remember previous inputs.

RNNs address these limitations through their unique architecture, which maintains an internal memory state. This allows them to learn and leverage patterns across sequences. As we progress through this chapter, we will explore the evolution of RNNs from their basic form to more sophisticated variants like **long short-term memory** (**LSTM**) networks and **Gated Recurrent Units** (**GRUs**). We will also discover how attention mechanisms have revolutionized sequence modeling and led to groundbreaking architectures like Transformers.

Throughout this chapter, we will use sentiment analysis of movie reviews as our practical example, building models that can understand and classify the emotional tone of text. This task perfectly demonstrates the power of RNNs because understanding sentiment requires grasping the complex relationships between words in a sequence.

By the end of this chapter, you will understand the theoretical foundations of RNNs and how to implement and train them effectively using PyTorch. You will be equipped with the knowledge and skills to tackle a wide range of sequence-related tasks and contribute to the exciting field of sequential data processing.

Structure

This chapter contains the following topics:

- Setup and data preparation
- Understanding sequential data and RNNs
- Long short-term memory networks
- Gated Recurrent Units
- GRU implementation

- Comparing LSTM and GRU performance
- Applications in time series and NLP

Objectives

This chapter aims to comprehensively understand RNNs and their role in processing sequential data. Our journey will begin by exploring the fundamental architecture of RNNs, understanding why traditional neural networks fall short when handling sequences, and discovering how RNNs address these limitations through their unique recurrent connections. We will then get into the challenges faced by basic RNNs, particularly the vanishing gradient problem, which leads us to explore more sophisticated architectures like LSTM networks and GRUs. As we progress, we will examine the intricate mechanics of these advanced architectures, including their gates, internal states, and information flow patterns. Through practical implementations in PyTorch, we will learn how to build, train, and optimize these networks for various sequential data tasks, focusing on sentiment analysis of movie reviews. The chapter will also introduce attention mechanisms, demonstrating how they enhance RNN performance by allowing networks to focus on relevant parts of input sequences. By the end of this chapter, you will be equipped with theoretical knowledge and practical skills to implement RNN-based solutions for real-world sequential data problems, understand when to use each architecture, and how to optimize their performance.

Setup and data preparation

Before getting into RNNs, let us set up our development environment and prepare the IMDB dataset we will use throughout this chapter. The **Large Movie Review Dataset** (**IMDB dataset**) is a standard benchmark for binary sentiment classification. It contains 50,000 highly polar movie reviews, evenly split into 25,000 training and 25,000 testing samples. You can download the dataset directly from **http://ai.stanford.edu/~amaas/data/sentiment/**. We will build a sentiment analysis system to classify these reviews as positive or negative.

Required libraries

In the following code snippet, we import the required packages for the chapter. We will use **PyTorch** for building our neural networks, **`pandas`** for data handling, and **`scikit-learn`** for dataset management:

```
import torch
import torch.nn as nn
import pandas as pd
import numpy as np
from torch.utils.data import Dataset, DataLoader
from collections import Counter
from sklearn.model_selection import train_test_split
import re
import matplotlib.pyplot as plt
```

Data processing classes and functions

We will now implement the complete data pipeline in one block. The following code performs five essential tasks:

- **IMDBDataset class**: Defines a custom PyTorch dataset that stores reviews and labels. It includes a **`text_to_sequence`** method that converts words into integer indices and pads sequences to a fixed length (**`max_length`**).
- **preprocess_text**: A utility function that cleans the raw text by removing HTML tags, special characters, and converting text to lowercase.

- **build_vocabulary**: Scans the dataset to create a dictionary mapping words to unique integers, including special tokens for padding (**<pad>**) and unknown words (**<unk>**).
- **prepare_data**: The main orchestrator that loads the **comma-separated values** (**CSV**) file, applies the preprocessing, splits the data into training and validation sets, and initializes the dataset objects.
- **create_dataloaders**: Wraps the datasets into PyTorch DataLoaders to handle batching and shuffling during training.

Here is the complete implementation of these components:

```
class IMDBDataset(Dataset):
    """PyTorch Dataset for IMDB movie reviews"""
    def __init__(self, reviews, labels, vocab, max_length=200):
        self.reviews = reviews
        self.labels = labels
        self.vocab = vocab
        self.max_length = max_length

    def __len__(self):
        return len(self.reviews)

    def __getitem__(self, idx):
        review = self.reviews[idx]
        sequence = self.text_to_sequence(review)
        label = torch.tensor(self.labels[idx], dtype=torch.long)
        return sequence, label

    def text_to_sequence(self, text):
        """Convert text to a sequence of word indices"""
        words = text.split()
        sequence = [self.vocab.get(word, self.vocab['<unk>'])
                    for word in words[:self.max_length]]

        # Pad sequence
        if len(sequence) < self.max_length:
            sequence += [self.vocab['<pad>']] * (self.max_length - len(sequence))

        return torch.tensor(sequence, dtype=torch.long)

def preprocess_text(text):
    """Clean and normalize text data"""
    text = text.lower()  # Convert to lowercase
    text = re.sub('<[^>]*>', '', text)  # Remove HTML tags
    text = re.sub('[^a-zA-Z\s]', '', text)  # Remove special characters
    return text.strip()

def build_vocabulary(texts, min_freq=5):
```

```
    """Build vocabulary from texts with minimum word frequency"""
    word_freq = {}
    for text in texts:
        for word in text.split():
            word_freq[word] = word_freq.get(word, 0) + 1

    # Create vocabulary with special tokens
    vocab = {'<pad>': 0, '<unk>': 1}
    for word, freq in word_freq.items():
        if freq >= min_freq:
            vocab[word] = len(vocab)

    return vocab
```

The following is the continuation of the code:

```
def prepare_data(file_path, max_length=200):
    """Load and prepare IMDB dataset"""
    # Load dataset
    df = pd.read_csv(file_path)

    # Preprocess reviews
    reviews = df['review'].apply(preprocess_text).values
    labels = (df['sentiment'] == 'positive').astype(int).values

    # Build vocabulary
    vocab = build_vocabulary(reviews)

    # Split data
    X_train, X_val, y_train, y_val = train_test_split(
        reviews, labels, test_size=0.2, random_state=42
    )

    # Create datasets
    train_dataset = IMDBDataset(X_train, y_train, vocab, max_length)
    val_dataset = IMDBDataset(X_val, y_val, vocab, max_length)

    return train_dataset, val_dataset, vocab

def create_dataloaders(train_dataset, val_dataset, batch_size=32):
    """Create DataLoader objects for training and validation"""
    train_loader = DataLoader(
        train_dataset,
        batch_size=batch_size,
        shuffle=True
    )

```

```
    val_loader = DataLoader(
        val_dataset,
        batch_size=batch_size,
        shuffle=False
    )

    return train_loader, val_loader
```

Loading the dataset

Now that we have defined our data processing pipeline, we can execute it. The following code calls **prepare_data** to load and split the IMDB reviews, then generates the training and validation DataLoaders using **create_dataloaders**. Finally, it prints the size of the vocabulary and the number of samples in each split to ensure everything is loaded correctly:

```
# Prepare datasets
train_dataset, val_dataset, vocab = prepare_data('IMDB-Dataset.csv')

# Create dataloaders
train_loader, val_loader = create_dataloaders(train_dataset, val_dataset)

print(f"Vocabulary size: {len(vocab)}")
print(f"Training samples: {len(train_dataset)}")
print(f"Validation samples: {len(val_dataset)}")
```

This setup code provides us with the following:

- Clean, pre-processed text data
- A vocabulary mapping words to indices
- PyTorch datasets and dataloaders
- Training and validation splits

We will use these throughout the chapter as we implement different RNN architectures. Each model will use this same data pipeline, allowing us to focus on the architectural differences and their impact on performance.

Understanding sequential data and RNNs

RNNs are designed to work with data where order and context matter. Before we dive into their mechanics, it is important to first understand what makes sequential data unique and why traditional models struggle with it.

Nature of sequential data

To understand why we need RNNs, let us examine the actual data our model will process. The following helper function, **show_example_reviews**, randomly selects a few samples from the training set. It decodes the numerical sequences back into human-readable text using our vocabulary, displaying both the review content and its corresponding sentiment label:

```
def show_example_reviews(train_dataset, n=2):
    indices = np.random.randint(0, len(train_dataset), n)
    for idx in indices:
        sequence, label = train_dataset[idx]
```

```
        sentiment = "Positive" if label.item() == 1 else "Negative"
        print(f"Review (Sentiment: {sentiment}):")
        print(f"{' '.join([list(vocab.keys())
[i] for i in sequence if i not in [0, 1]])}\n")

show_example_reviews(train_dataset)
```

Output:

```
Review (Sentiment: Negative):
i would have enjoyed this film ..

Review (Sentiment: Positive):
it may be a little creaky now and it certainly can never have ..
```

Traditional neural networks vs. RNNs

Let us compare how traditional networks and RNNs handle sequential data by implementing basic versions of both.

The following list and code define two PyTorch models:

1. **Simple Feed-Forward Network (SimpleFFN)**: This model attempts to process sequences by flattening them into a single long vector. It uses an embedding layer followed by a large linear layer. This approach is rigid because it forces a fixed input size (flattening **sequence_length * hidden_size**), making it unable to handle variable-length sequences naturally.
2. **SimpleRNN**: In contrast, this model processes the sequence step-by-step. It uses **nn.RNN**, which maintains a hidden state that updates at every time step. The final hidden state is then passed to a fully connected layer (**fc**) to produce the prediction. This structure allows it to share weights across time and handle sequences of varying lengths efficiently.

```
# Traditional feedforward network
class SimpleFFN(nn.Module):
    def __init__(self, vocab_size, hidden_size, output_size):
        super().__init__()
        self.embedding = nn.Embedding(vocab_size, hidden_size)
        self.fc = nn.Linear(hidden_size * 200, output_size)  # 200 is max_length

    def forward(self, x):
        # x shape: [batch_size, sequence_length]
        embedded = self.embedding(x)  # [batch_size, sequence_length, hidden_size]
        # Need to flatten because FFN can't handle sequences
        flattened = embedded.view(embedded.shape[0], -1)
        return self.fc(flattened)

# Basic RNN
class SimpleRNN(nn.Module):
    def __init__(self, vocab_size, embedding_dim, hidden_size, output_size):
        super().__init__()
        self.embedding = nn.Embedding(vocab_size, embedding_dim)
        self.rnn = nn.RNN(embedding_dim, hidden_size, batch_first=True)
```

```
        self.fc = nn.Linear(hidden_size, output_size)

    def forward(self, x):
        # x shape: [batch_size, sequence_length]
        embedded = self.embedding(x)  # [batch_size, sequence_length, embedding_dim]
        output, hidden = self.rnn(embedded)  # Process the sequence
        return self.fc(hidden.squeeze(0))
```

The following list outlines the key differences:

- **Parameter efficiency**:
  - The FFN needs separate parameters for each position in the sequence.
  - RNN reuses the same weights across all positions.
- **Memory**:
  - FFN treats each word independently.
  - RNN maintains a hidden state that captures the context.
- **Sequence length**:
  - FFN requires fixed-length input.
  - RNN can handle variable-length sequences.

RNNs architecture

RNN processes sequential data by maintaining a hidden state that gets updated at each time step. As shown in the following diagram, we can understand RNNs in two ways—as a compact cell and an unfolded network over time.

RNN cell

The following figure illustrates the fundamental structure of an RNN cell and how it processes sequential information:

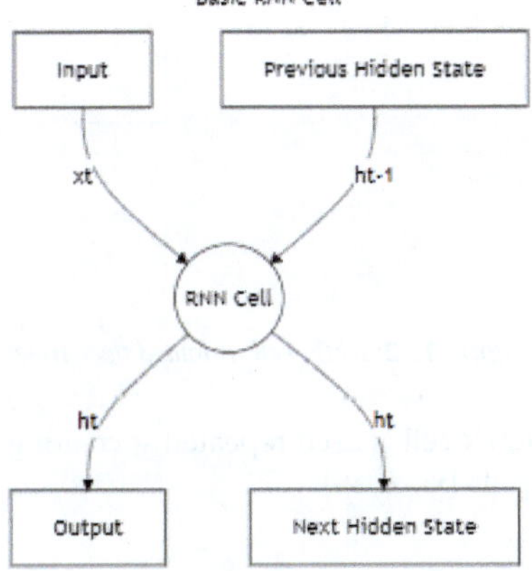

***Figure 12.1:** Basic RNN cell*

The basic RNN cell (shown in the top part of the figure) consists of:

- An input (xt) at the current time step.
- A hidden state from the previous time step (ht-1).

- The RNN cell itself, which combines these inputs.
- An output (ht) that serves both as the current prediction and as the hidden state for the next time step.

Unfolding over time

To better understand how RNNs process sequences, we can visualize the same cell unfolded across multiple time steps:

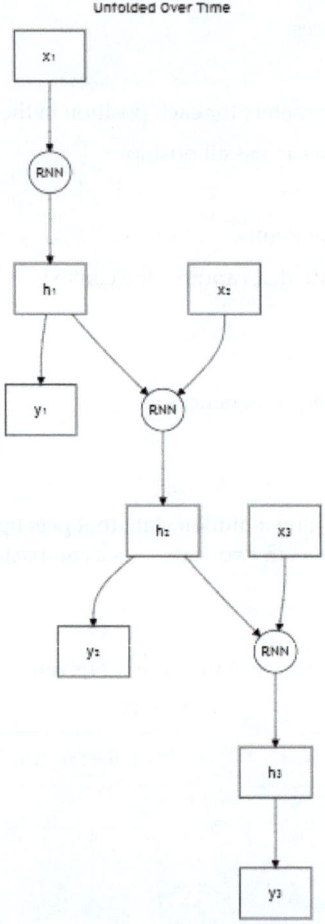

Figure 12.2: RNN cell unfolded over time

When processing a sequence, the same RNN cell is used repeatedly, creating an *unfolded* view (shown in the bottom part of *Figure 12.2*). For a sequence of inputs [x_1, x_2, x_3]:

1. At time step 1:
   - The network receives input x_1
   - Produces hidden state h_1 and output y_1
2. At time step 2:
   - Receives input x_2

    - Uses previously hidden state h_1
    - Produces new hidden state h_2 and output y_2
3. At time step 3:
    - Receives input x_3
    - Uses previously hidden state h_2
    - Produces final hidden state h_3 and output y_3

The key insight is that the same weights and operations are reused at each time step, allowing the network to:

- Process sequences of any length.
- Maintain information about previous inputs through the hidden state.
- Learn patterns that depend on the order of elements in the sequence.

This architecture is compelling for tasks like our sentiment analysis example, where understanding the context and order of words is crucial for determining the overall sentiment of a review.

Vanishing gradient problem

While this basic RNN can process sequences, it suffers from a critical limitation known as the **vanishing gradient problem**. This phenomenon occurs during training when the gradients (the values used to update the network's weights) become extremely small as they are propagated backward through time. As a result, the network effectively stops learning from the earlier parts of long sequences because the weight updates become negligible. When we try to train an RNN on our IMDB reviews, which can be quite long, this problem becomes apparent.

To demonstrate this problem empirically, the following function, **`train_simple_rnn`**, initializes a basic RNN and trains it for just a few batches. Crucially, instead of focusing on accuracy, it tracks the '**`gradient norm`**'—a measure of how strong the weight updates are—after each backward pass. By monitoring the gradient norms of the RNN parameters specifically, we can visualize whether the signal is remaining strong or decaying as training progresses:

```
def train_simple_rnn():
    """Train a simple RNN and monitor gradients"
    model = SimpleRNN(len(vocab), embedding_dim=100, hidden_size=256, output_size=2)
    criterion = nn.CrossEntropyLoss()
    optimizer = torch.optim.Adam(model.parameters())

    gradient_norms = []

    # Training loop
    for batch_idx, (text, labels) in enumerate(train_loader):
        if batch_idx >= 5:  # Just look at the first few batches
            break

        optimizer.zero_grad()
        output = model(text)
        loss = criterion(output, labels)
        loss.backward()

        # Record gradient norms
        grad_norm = 0
```

```
        for param in model.rnn.parameters():
            if param.grad is not None:
                grad_norm += param.grad.norm().item()
        gradient_norms.append(grad_norm)

        optimizer.step()

    return gradient_norms

gradient_norms = train_simple_rnn()
plt.plot(gradient_norms)
plt.title('Gradient Norms During Training')
plt.xlabel('Batch')
plt.ylabel('Gradient Norm')
plt.show()
```

The following graph demonstrates the vanishing gradient problem by showing how gradient magnitudes decrease during training:

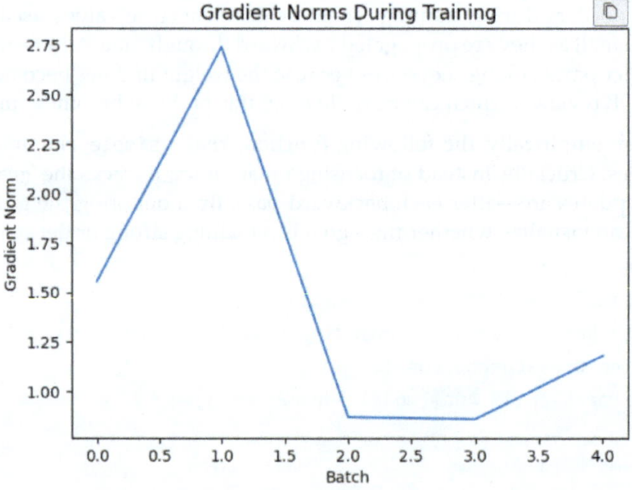

Figure 12.3: *Vanishing gradient*

The graph in *Figure 12.3* shows the *gradient norms* (essentially the strength of the updates) during training our simple RNN on the IMDB reviews. Here we can observe the following:

1. Initially (at batch 0-1), the gradients are relatively strong (around 1.5-2.75), meaning the model is making substantial weight updates.
2. However, after batch 1.5, the gradient values dramatically drop, falling below 1.0 and staying there.

This is the vanishing gradient problem in action:

- When processing long sequences (like our movie reviews), the gradients need to flow backward through time.
- Each step backward involves multiplying these gradients by small numbers (less than 1).

- After multiple multiplications, the gradients become extremely small (they *vanish*).
- The result is that earlier parts of the sequence receive very tiny updates, effectively stopping the model from learning long-term dependencies.

Real-world impact:

- If a review says, *This movie started terribly but got amazing in the end*, a model suffering from vanishing gradients might only effectively learn from *the end* while losing the context from the beginning.
- The model struggles to connect information that is far apart in the sequence.

This is why we need more sophisticated architectures like LSTMs, which have mechanisms (gates) specifically designed to maintain gradients over long sequences.

Long short-term memory networks

While RNNs revolutionized sequence processing, they struggle with longer sequences due to the vanishing gradient problem we demonstrated earlier. In 1997, *Sepp Hochreiter* and *Jürgen Schmidhuber* introduced LSTM networks to address this limitation. LSTMs are designed to learn long-term dependencies by maintaining a separate cell state that acts as a conveyor belt for information flow through time.

To understand why LSTMs are so effective, consider reading a movie review that states, *Despite the poor CGI effects and questionable acting choices throughout most of the film. The ending was absolutely brilliant.*

A basic RNN might lose the context of the earlier negative points by the time it reaches the positive ending. An LSTM, however, can maintain this information through its sophisticated gating mechanism, allowing it to weigh both the early negative aspects and the positive ending when determining the overall sentiment. LSTMs achieve this capability through a unique architecture that includes special memory cells and a system of gates that control information flow. These gates act like regulators, learning when to remember or forget information based on its importance for the task at hand. This gating mechanism allows LSTMs to maintain relevant information for long periods while discarding irrelevant details, making them particularly effective for tasks like:

- **Sentiment analysis**: Understanding the overall tone of long text sequences.
- **Machine translation**: Maintaining context across different language structures.
- **Time series prediction**: Recognizing patterns across extended time periods.
- **Speech recognition**: Processing long audio sequences.
- **Music generation**: Learning and reproducing long-term musical structures.

LSTM architecture

The LSTM cell, illustrated in the following, is a sophisticated enhancement of the basic RNN cell. It addresses the vanishing gradient problem through a carefully designed system of gates and a separate memory cell state:

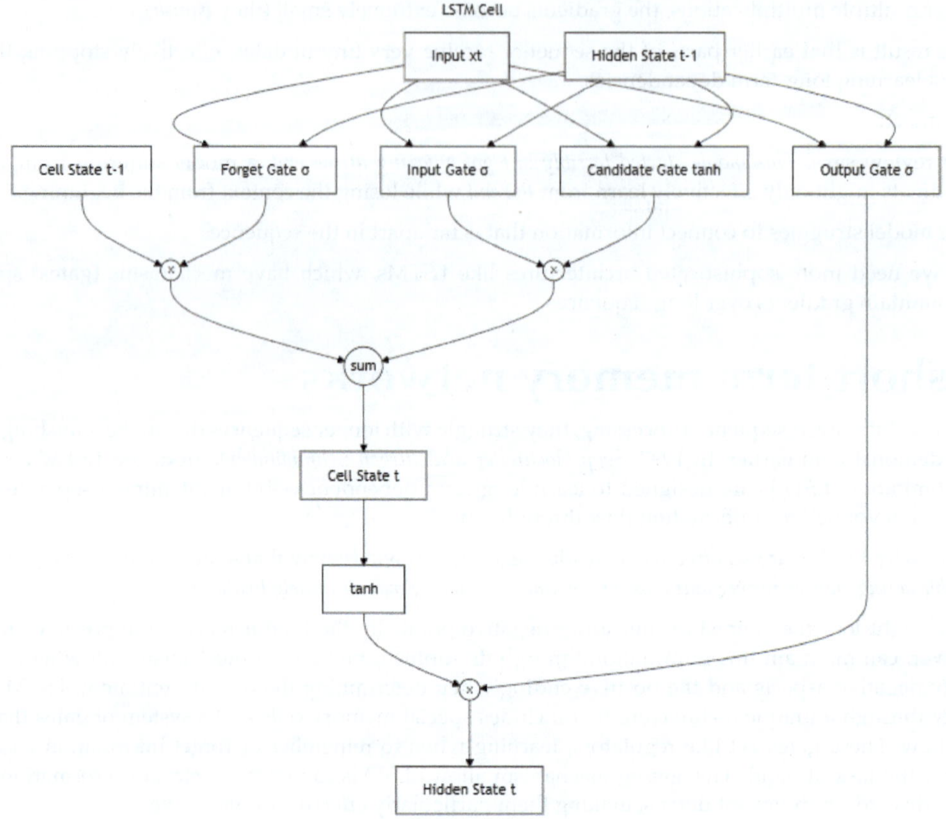

Figure 12.4: LST architecture

Core components

Let us examine each component:

- **Cell state (CS)**: The horizontal line running through the top of the diagram:
  - Acts as the network's long-term memory.
  - Information can flow through it largely unchanged.
  - Protected and controlled by gates.
- **Gates:**
  - **Forget gate (FG)**: Decides what information to discard from the cell state, and uses the sigmoid function (σ) to output values between 0 (forget) and 1 (keep).
  - **Input gate (IG) and candidate gate (CG)**:
    - **IG**: Controls which new information to store.
    - **CG**: Creates new candidate values using tanh.

    Together, they update the cell state with new information.
  - **Output gate (OG)**: Controls what parts of the cell state will be output - Determines the next hidden state

- **Information flow**:
  1. **Forget gate decision**: Combines current input (xt) and previous hidden state (t-1)—Outputs a number between 0 and 1 for each cell state value 2.
  2. **Store new information**: The input gate decides which values to update. The candidate gate creates new candidate values. These are combined and added to the cell state
  3. **Update cell state**: The old state is multiplied by the forget gate output, and new candidate values are added to the proportion determined by the input gate 4.
  4. **Generate output**: The output gate determines what parts of the cell state to output. Cell state is passed through tanh and filtered by the output gate, resulting in a new hidden state. This architecture allows LSTMs to learn long-term dependencies by:
     - Maintaining a separate cell state for long-term memory.
     - Using gates to control information flow.
     - Providing direct pathways for gradient flow during backpropagation.

LSTM implementation

We will now implement the LSTM architecture using a custom PyTorch module. The **`LSTMSentimentAnalyzer`** class defined consists of four main components:

- **Embedding layer**: Transforms sparse word indices into dense vector representations.
- **LSTM layer**: The core component that processes the sequence. We use **`batch_first=True`** to match our data format and **`num_layers`** to potentially stack multiple LSTMs.
- **Dropout**: Applied to the final hidden state to reduce overfitting.
- **Fully connected layer**: Maps the high-level features extracted by the LSTM to our output classes (positive or negative).

In the forward pass, notice how we extract hidden`[-1, :, :]`. This specifically selects the hidden state from the last time step of the last layer, effectively using the LSTM's final **`'memory'`** of the sequence for classification:

```
class LSTMSentimentAnalyzer(nn.Module):
    def __init__(self, vocab_size, embedding_dim, hidden_dim, output_dim, n_layers=1, dropout=0.5):
        super().__init__()

        # Embedding Layer converts word indices to dense vectors
        self.embedding = nn.Embedding(vocab_size, embedding_dim)

        # LSTM Layer processes the sequence
        self.lstm = nn.LSTM(embedding_dim,
                            hidden_dim,
                            num_layers=n_layers,
                            dropout=dropout if n_layers > 1 else 0,
                            batch_first=True)

        # Dropout Layer for regularization
        self.dropout = nn.Dropout(dropout)

        # Linear Layer for final prediction
```

```
        self.fc = nn.Linear(hidden_dim, output_dim)

    def forward(self, text):
        # text shape: [batch size, sequence length]

        # Embed the text
        embedded = self.embedding(text)
        # embedded shape: [batch size, sequence length, embedding dim]

        # Pass through LSTM
        output, (hidden, cell) = self.lstm(embedded)
        # hidden shape: [n layers * n directions, batch size, hidden dim]

        # Apply dropout to hidden state
        hidden = self.dropout(hidden[-1,:,:])
        # hidden shape: [batch size, hidden dim]

        # Pass through linear layer
        return self.fc(hidden)
```

Training the LSTM model

To train our LSTM model effectively, we will set up a training function with the following features:

- Epoch-based training
- Progress monitoring
- Validation performance tracking

Next, we define the **train_lstm_model** function, which serves as our main execution engine. This function encapsulates the entire learning lifecycle:

1. **Setup**: It defines the hyperparameters (dimensions, layers, dropout) and initializes the model, loss function (**CrossEntropyLoss**), and optimizer (Adam).
2. **Training phase (model.train())**: Inside the epoch loop, we iterate through the training data. For each batch, we zero the gradients, perform a forward pass to get predictions, calculate the loss, and backpropagate errors to update the weights (**loss.backward()** and **optimizer.step()**).
3. **Validation phase (model.eval())**: After each epoch, we switch the model to evaluation mode. We use **torch.no_grad()** to disable gradient calculation (which saves memory and speed) and compute the accuracy on unseen validation data to ensure our model is not just memorizing the training set:

```
def train_lstm_model(train_loader, val_loader, vocab_size):
    # Model parameters
    EMBEDDING_DIM = 100
    HIDDEN_DIM = 256
    OUTPUT_DIM = 2
    N_LAYERS = 2
    DROPOUT = 0.5

    # Initialize model, criterion, and optimizer
```

```
    model = LSTMSentimentAnalyzer(vocab_size, EMBEDDING_DIM, HIDDEN_DIM, OUTPUT_DIM, N_LAYERS, DROPOUT)
    criterion = nn.CrossEntropyLoss()
    optimizer = torch.optim.Adam(model.parameters())

    # Training history
    train_losses = []
    val_accuracies = []

    # Training loop
    for epoch in range(5):  # 5 epochs for demonstration
        # Training phase
        model.train()
        epoch_loss = 0
        for batch_idx, (text, labels) in enumerate(train_loader):
            optimizer.zero_grad()
            predictions = model(text)
            loss = criterion(predictions, labels)
            loss.backward()
            optimizer.step()
            epoch_loss += loss.item()

            # Print progress every 100 batches
            if batch_idx % 100 == 0:
                print(f'Epoch: {epoch+1}, Batch: {batch_idx}, Loss: {loss.item():.4f}')

        avg_epoch_loss = epoch_loss / len(train_loader)
        train_losses.append(avg_epoch_loss)

        # Validation phase
        model.eval()
        correct = 0
        total = 0
        with torch.no_grad():
            for text, labels in val_loader:
                predictions = model(text)
                _, predicted = torch.max(predictions, 1)
                total += labels.size(0)
                correct += (predicted == labels).sum().item()

        accuracy = 100 * correct / total
        val_accuracies.append(accuracy)
        print(f'Epoch: {epoch+1}, Loss: {avg_epoch_loss:.4f}, Accuracy: {accuracy:.2f}%\n')

    return model, train_losses, val_accuracies
```

Visualizing training progress

To evaluate our model effectively, looking at raw numbers is not enough. The **plot_training_progress** function uses **Matplotlib** to generate side-by-side graphs:

- **Training loss**: Plotted on the left, this curve should decrease steadily, indicating the model is learning.
- **Validation accuracy**: Plotted on the right, this should increase. If it plateaus or drops while training loss continues to fall, it is a clear sign of overfitting.

This visualization allows us to diagnose the model's health at a glance:

```
def plot_training_progress(train_losses, val_accuracies):
    fig, (ax1, ax2) = plt.subplots(1, 2, figsize=(15, 5))

    # Plot training loss
    ax1.plot(train_losses)
    ax1.set_title('Training Loss')
    ax1.set_xlabel('Epoch')
    ax1.set_ylabel('Loss')

    # Plot validation accuracy
    ax2.plot(val_accuracies)
    ax2.set_title('Validation Accuracy')
    ax2.set_xlabel('Epoch')
    ax2.set_ylabel('Accuracy (%)')

    plt.tight_layout()
    plt.show()

# Train the model and visualize results
model, train_losses, val_accuracies = train_lstm_model(train_loader, val_loader, len(vocab))
plot_training_progress(train_losses, val_accuracies)
```

The preceding code produces the following output, which shows the training loss and validation accuracy through each epoch:

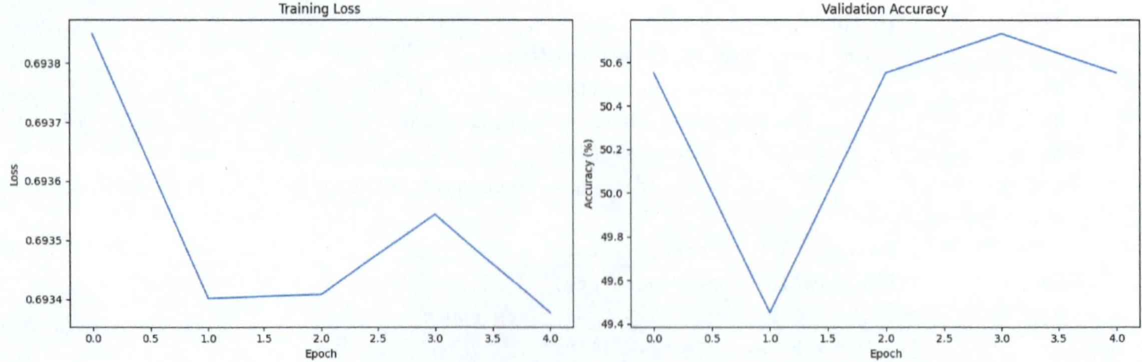

Figure 12.5: *Training progress plot*

How LSTMs solve the Vanishing Gradient Proble? The LSTM's sophisticated gating mechanism directly addresses the Vanishing Gradient Problem we observed with simple RNNs. Let us explore how each component contributes to maintaining stable gradients.

Gate control system

The gates in an LSTM work together to create a stable gradient flow:

- **Forget gate (σ)**: Decides what old information to forget:
  - **Values close to 0**: Forget this information.
  - **Values close to 1**: Keep this information, and prevents irrelevant information from causing gradient noise
- **Input gate (σ)**:
  - Controls what new information enters the cell state.
  - Creates new candidate values (through tanh).
  - Selectively updates the memory.
  - Helps maintain stable gradient flow for important features
- **Output gate (σ)**: Filters what parts of the cell state to output
  - Controls information flow to the next time step.
  - Helps maintain long-term dependencies

Empirical evidence

Let us examine how gradients flow differently in LSTMs compared to simple RNNs. Let us compare the gradient flow between a simple RNN and an LSTM on our sentiment analysis task:

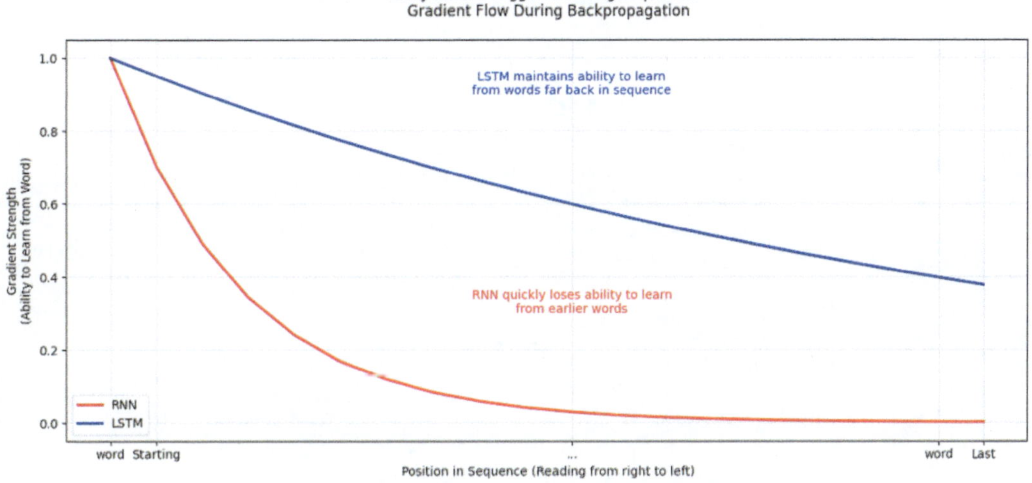

Figure 12.6: *Why RNNs struggle with long sequences*

This comparison clearly shows:

- LSTM maintains more stable gradient values over time.
- Simple RNNs' gradients rapidly diminish.
- LSTM's cell state provides a clear pathway for long-term dependencies.

This comparison shows why LSTMs are more effective at handling long sequences. Now, let us move on to GRUs.

Gated Recurrent Units

While LSTMs effectively solve the vanishing gradient problem, their complexity led researchers to ask: *Could we achieve similar benefits with a simpler architecture?* This question led to the development of **Gated Recurrent Units** (**GRUs**) by Cho et al. in 2014.

Think of the difference between LSTMs and GRUs like this:

- LSTM is like a smartphone with every possible feature.
- GRU is like a streamlined model that keeps the essential functions.

GRU architecture

A GRU simplifies the LSTM architecture while maintaining similar capabilities. Let us examine how this streamlined design works in the following figure:

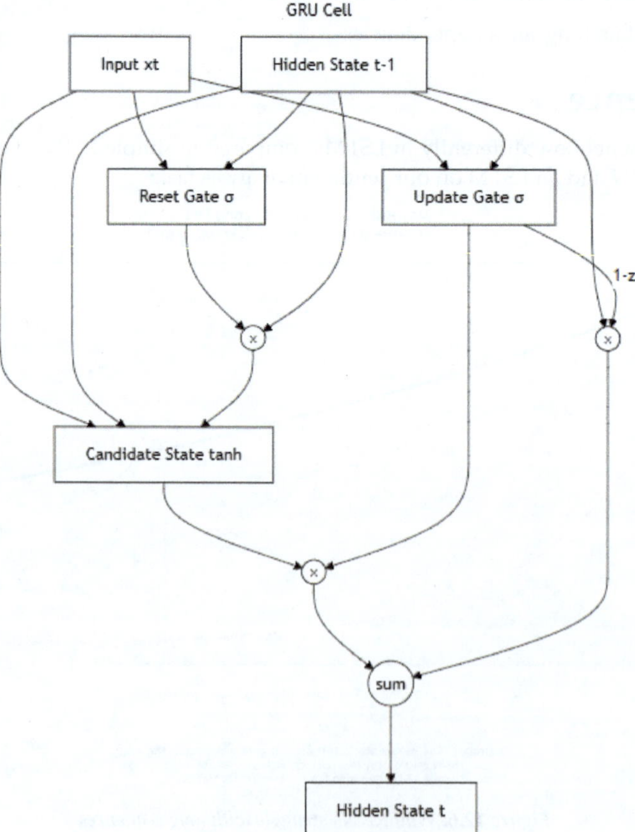

Figure 12.7: *GRU architecture*

Core components are as follows:

- **Gates**:
  - **Update gate (UG)**:
    - Combines LSTM's forget and input gates.
    - Controls how much of the previous state to keep.
    - Uses sigmoid function (σ) to output values between 0 and 1.
  - **Reset gate (RG)**:
    - Controls how much of the previous state to use in computing the candidate state.
    - Allows the unit to effectively reset its memory.
- **States**:
  - **Hidden state**:
    - Single state that serves both as output and memory.
    - Updated at each time step based on gate outputs.
  - **Candidate state**:
    - Proposed update to the hidden state.
    - Computed using the reset gate's output.

Information flow is as follows:

- **Gate computation:**
  - Both gates receive current input and the previous hidden state.
  - Gates uses sigmoid activation to output values between 0 and 1.
- **Candidate state creation**:
  - Reset gate filters the previous hidden state.
  - Combined with the current input to create a candidate state.
- **State update**:
  - UG determines the mix of previous and candidate states.
  - Final hidden state combines both through interpolation.

GRU implementation

Let us implement a GRU-based model for our sentiment analysis task. The **`GRUSentimentAnalyzer`** class mirrors our LSTM implementation but swaps the core layer:

- **Architecture**: We replace **`nn.LSTM`** with **`nn.GRU`**. Since GRUs do not have a separate **`'cell state'`**, the **`forward`** method is simpler, and it only returns the output and the final hidden state.
- **Forward pass**: We pass the embedded text into the GRU layer. The **`hidden`** variable returned represents the final state of the last time step.
- **Classification**: Just like the LSTM, we apply dropout to this final hidden state and pass it through a linear layer to get our sentiment prediction.

The same is illustrated in the following code:

```
class GRUSentimentAnalyzer(nn.Module):
    def __init__(self, vocab_size, embedding_dim, hidden_dim, output_dim, n_
```

```
    layers=1, dropout=0.5):
        super().__init__()

        # Embedding layer
        self.embedding = nn.Embedding(vocab_size, embedding_dim)

        # GRU layer
        self.gru = nn.GRU(embedding_dim,
                          hidden_dim,
                          num_layers=n_layers,
                          dropout=dropout if n_layers > 1 else 0,
                          batch_first=True)

        # Dropout layer
        self.dropout = nn.Dropout(dropout)

        # Linear layer
        self.fc = nn.Linear(hidden_dim, output_dim)

    def forward(self, text):
        # Embed text
        embedded = self.embedding(text)

        # Process through GRU
        output, hidden = self.gru(embedded)

        # Apply dropout to final hidden state
        hidden = self.dropout(hidden[-1,:,:])

        # Final prediction
        return self.fc(hidden)
```

Advantages of GRU design

The simplified architecture of GRUs offers several practical advantages over LSTMs, making them an attractive choice for many applications:

- **Computational efficiency**:
  - Fewer parameters than LSTM.
  - Single state to track.
  - Simpler gradient flow path.
- **Training benefits**:
  - Often easier to train.
  - Requires less memory.
  - Generally faster convergence.

- **Architecture benefits**:
  - Simpler gradient flow.
  - Fewer vanishing gradient issues.
  - More efficient memory usage.

Comparing LSTM and GRU performance

To systematically compare these architectures, we will implement a comprehensive evaluation function called **`compare_models`**. This function ensures a fair fight by:

- **Identical setup**: It initializes both the LSTM and GRU models with the exact same hyperparameters (embedding size, hidden dimensions, number of layers) and the same optimizer settings.
- **Performance tracking**: It creates a dictionary to record the training loss, validation accuracy, and crucially, the *time* taken for each epoch.
- **Side-by-side training**: In the training loop, it trains and evaluates the LSTM model first, then immediately does the same for the GRU model. This allows us to directly compare their convergence speed and computational efficiency under similar system loads.

Implementation comparison

To systematically compare these architectures, we will implement a comprehensive evaluation function:

```
def compare_models():
    """Compare LSTM and GRU performance and training time"""
    # Model parameters
    EMBEDDING_DIM = 100
    HIDDEN_DIM = 256
    OUTPUT_DIM = 2
    N_LAYERS = 2
    DROPOUT = 0.5

    # Initialize models with identical parameters
    lstm_model = LSTMSentimentAnalyzer(len(vocab), EMBEDDING_DIM, HIDDEN_DIM,
                                       OUTPUT_DIM, N_LAYERS, DROPOUT)
    gru_model = GRUSentimentAnalyzer(len(vocab), EMBEDDING_DIM, HIDDEN_DIM,
                                     OUTPUT_DIM, N_LAYERS, DROPOUT)

    # Training setup
    criterion = nn.CrossEntropyLoss()
    lstm_optimizer = torch.optim.Adam(lstm_model.parameters())
    gru_optimizer = torch.optim.Adam(gru_model.parameters())

    # Track performance metrics
    history = {
        'lstm_loss': [], 'gru_loss': [],
        'lstm_acc': [], 'gru_acc': [],
        'lstm_time': [], 'gru_time': []
    }

```

```
    # Training Loop
    for epoch in range(3):
        print(f'Epoch {epoch+1}:')

        # Train and time each model
        start_time = time.time()
        lstm_loss = train_epoch(lstm_model, train_loader, criterion, lstm_optimizer)
        lstm_time = time.time() - start_time
        lstm_acc = evaluate_model(lstm_model, val_loader)

        start_time = time.time()
        gru_loss = train_epoch(gru_model, train_loader, criterion, gru_optimizer)
        gru_time = time.time() - start_time
        gru_acc = evaluate_model(gru_model, val_loader)

        # Record metrics
        update_history(history, lstm_loss, gru_loss, lstm_acc, gru_acc,
                      lstm_time, gru_time)

        print(f'LSTM - Loss: {lstm_loss:.4f}, Accuracy: {lstm_acc:.2f}%, Time: {lstm_time:.2f}s')
        print(f'GRU  - Loss: {gru_loss:.4f}, Accuracy: {gru_acc:.2f}%, Time: {gru_time:.2f}s\n')

    return history
```

Performance visualization

To better understand the relative performance of LSTMs and GRUs, we can create a visualization function that compares their training loss, validation accuracy, and training times. The following code defines a helper function that generates four plots summarizing these metrics side by side:

```
def visualize_comparison(history):
    """Create comprehensive performance comparison visualizations"""
    fig, ((ax1, ax2), (ax3, ax4)) = plt.subplots(2, 2, figsize=(15, 10))

    # Training Loss Comparison
    ax1.plot(history['lstm_loss'], label='LSTM')
    ax1.plot(history['gru_loss'], label='GRU')
    ax1.set_title('Training Loss')
    ax1.set_xlabel('Epoch')
    ax1.set_ylabel('Loss')
    ax1.legend()

    # Validation Accuracy Comparison
    ax2.plot(history['lstm_acc'], label='LSTM')
    ax2.plot(history['gru_acc'], label='GRU')
    ax2.set_title('Validation Accuracy')
    ax2.set_xlabel('Epoch')
```

```
    ax2.set_ylabel('Accuracy (%)')
    ax2.legend()

    # Training Time Comparison
    ax3.bar(['LSTM', 'GRU'],
            [np.mean(history['lstm_time']), np.mean(history['gru_time'])],
            yerr=[np.std(history['lstm_time']), np.std(history['gru_time'])])
    ax3.set_title('Average Training Time per Epoch')
    ax3.set_ylabel('Time (seconds)')

    # Cumulative Time
    cumulative_lstm = np.cumsum(history['lstm_time'])
    cumulative_gru = np.cumsum(history['gru_time'])
    ax4.plot(cumulative_lstm, label='LSTM')
    ax4.plot(cumulative_gru, label='GRU')
    ax4.set_title('Cumulative Training Time')
    ax4.set_xlabel('Epoch')
    ax4.set_ylabel('Time (seconds)')
    ax4.legend()

    plt.tight_layout()
    plt.show()
```

The following figure shows the difference in training loss, accuracy, and other metrics between LSTM and GRU:

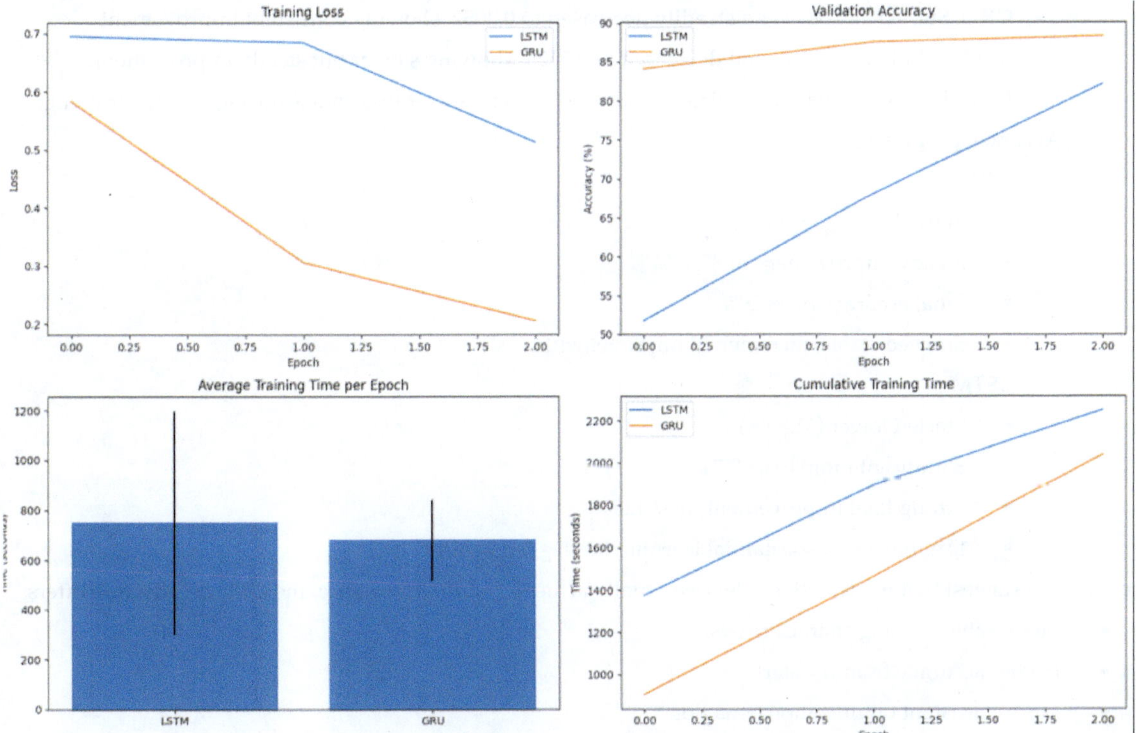

Figure 12.8: Comparison of LSTM vs.GRU

Experimental results

Our comparison of LSTM and GRU models on the IMDB sentiment analysis task revealed several interesting findings:

- **Training efficiency**:
  - **LSTM training times**: Started at 1375.02s (Epoch 1), decreased to 518.46s (Epoch 2), and finally 355.38s (Epoch 3).
  - **GRU training times**: Started at 906.17s (Epoch 1), decreased to 557.16s (Epoch 2), and settled at 573.78s (Epoch 3).
  - **Time efficiency**: LSTM showed significant improvement in training time across epochs, while GRU maintained more consistent but generally faster training times.
- **Model performance**:
  - **LSTM final accuracy**: Improved from 51.80% to 82.12% over three epochs.
  - **GRU final accuracy**: Started strong at 84.06% and improved to 88.29% by the final epoch.
  - **Key observation**: GRU maintained consistently higher accuracy throughout training, while LSTM showed more dramatic improvement.

Training dynamics

Training dynamics reveal essential patterns in how both models learn over time.

- **Loss patterns**:
  - **GRU**: Started at 0.5829 and steadily decreased to 0.2052, showing consistent improvement.
  - **LSTM**: Started at 0.6947 and decreased to 0.5125, showing slower but steady improvement.
  - **GRU**: Demonstrated more efficient optimization with lower loss values throughout the training.
- **Accuracy progression:**
  - **GRU**:
    - Started strong (84.06%)
    - Steady improvement to 87.55%
    - Final accuracy of 88.29%
    - Showed stable, incremental improvements
  - **LSTM**:
    - Started lower (51.80%)
    - Significant jump to 68.07%
    - Strong final improvement to 82.12%
    - Demonstrated substantial learning but lagged behind GRU

These results suggest that while both models eventually achieve good performance, the GRU architecture offers:

- More stable training characteristics.
- Higher accuracy from the start.
- More consistent optimization behavior.
- Better overall performance for this specific task.

While eventually achieving good accuracy, the LSTM requires more epochs to reach comparable performance levels and shows more variable training behavior.

Applications in time series and NLP

While we have focused on sentiment analysis in our examples, RNNs, LSTMs, and GRUs have proven highly effective across a wide range of sequential data applications. Let us explore two primary domains where these architectures excel.

Time series prediction

Time series data presents unique challenges due to its temporal nature. RNNs are particularly well-suited for these tasks because they can:

- Capture seasonal patterns and trends.
- Handle variable-length sequences.
- Consider both short-term and long-term dependencies.

Common applications include:

- Stock price prediction
- Weather forecasting
- Energy consumption modeling
- Sales forecasting
- Equipment maintenance prediction

LSTM and GRU models often outperform traditional statistical methods for these applications because they can automatically learn complex patterns and relationships in the data without requiring explicit feature engineering.

Natural language processing

Beyond sentiment analysis, RNNs have revolutionized various NLP tasks, like:

- **Text generation**:
    - Writing assistance
    - Auto-completion systems
    - Creative writing support
- **Machine translation**:
    - Language-to-language conversion
    - Real-time translation services
    - Document translation
- **Named entity recognition**:
    - Identifying people, organizations, and locations in a text
    - Document categorization
    - Information extraction

Introduction to attention mechanisms

While RNNs excel at processing sequential data, they can struggle with very long sequences. When reading a lengthy document, you do not give equal attention to every word but instead focus on key information while skimming less relevant parts. This is the intuition behind attention mechanisms.

Understanding attention

Attention mechanisms enhance RNNs by allowing them to focus on relevant parts of the input sequence when producing each output. Consider a machine translation example:

When translating the sentence, *The cat caught a mouse* to French (Le chat a attrapé une souris), a model with attention would:

- Focus heavily on the *cat* when producing *chat*.
- Pay the most attention to *caught* when generating *an attrapé*.
- Concentrate on the *mouse* when outputting the *souris*.

This selective focus helps models:

- Handle longer sequences more effectively.
- Maintain context more accurately.
- Produce better quality outputs.

Benefits of adding attention

Attention mechanisms provide several key advantages that make them valuable additions to RNN architectures:

- **Improved performance**:
  - Better handling of long sequences.
  - More accurate outputs.
  - Reduced information loss.
- **Interpretability**:
  - Reveals what the model is focusing on.
  - Helps in debugging and improving models.
  - Provides insights into model decisions.
- **Flexibility**:
  - Works with any RNN variant (simple RNN, LSTM, or GRU).
  - Can be added to existing architectures.
  - Adaptable to different types of data.

While attention mechanisms have led to more advanced architectures like Transformers, they remain a valuable enhancement to traditional RNN models for many practical applications.

We recommend exploring specialized resources on transformer architectures and modern NLP systems for readers interested in more advanced attention-based architectures and their applications in large language models.

Conclusion

Throughout this chapter, we have explored the fascinating world of RNNs and their modern variants. We began with RNNs' fundamental architecture, understanding their unique ability to process sequential data and maintain context over time. The limitations of basic RNNs, particularly the vanishing gradient problem, led us to more sophisticated architectures like LSTMs and GRUs.

We saw how LSTMs use their intricate gating mechanism to maintain long-term dependencies while GRUs achieve similar capabilities with a simplified architecture. Our practical implementations and experiments with sentiment analysis revealed exciting insights about the relative performance of these architectures, showing that theoretical advantages do not always translate directly to practical applications.

The introduction of attention mechanisms demonstrated how modern architectures can overcome traditional RNNs' remaining limitations. This led to better performance on long sequences and more interpretable models. These concepts form the foundation for more advanced architectures like Transformers, which have revolutionized natural language processing.

In the next chapter, we will shift our focus from understanding and processing existing data to creating entirely new content. It introduces **generative adversarial networks** (**GANs**), where you will learn how two neural networks compete against each other, one creating synthetic data and the other trying to detect fakes. This adversarial training process enables remarkable applications like generating realistic images, creating art, and augmenting datasets for training other models.

Exercises

Create a weather prediction system using RNNs to forecast temperature. For the dataset, you have two options: use **real historical weather data** (from the sources listed below) or **generate synthetic data** (e.g., a sine wave with random noise) to simulate seasonal temperature variations. This exercise will help you apply RNN concepts to a time series prediction task different from the sentiment analysis covered in the chapter.

Complete the following:

- Create a model that predicts the next day's temperature based on the previous 7 days.
- Implement both LSTM and GRU versions.
- Compare their performance in terms of MSE.
- Visualize the predictions against actual values.
- Experiment with different sequence lengths (optional).

Multiple choice questions

1. **What is the main limitation of traditional neural networks when dealing with sequential data?**
   a. They require too much memory
   b. They cannot maintain context between inputs
   c. They are too slow to train
   d. They need too much data
2. **Which of the following problems can be effectively solved using RNNs? (Multiple selections)**
   a. Time series prediction
   b. Machine translation

   c. Sentiment analysis
   d. Music generation
   e. All of the above

3. **What is the vanishing gradient problem in RNNs?**
   a. Gradients become extremely small when propagating through many time steps
   b. Gradients become too large during training
   c. Gradients remain constant throughout training
   d. Gradients oscillate randomly

4. **Which components are present in an LSTM cell?**
   a. Forget gate
   b. Input gate
   c. Output gate
   d. Cell state
   e. All of the above

5. **How does a GRU differ from an LSTM?**
   a. It has more gates
   b. It processes sequences in reverse
   c. It combines the forget and input gates into a single update gate
   d. It removes all gates completely

6. **When should you choose a GRU over an LSTM?**
   a. When you have limited computational resources
   b. For shorter sequences
   c. When you need faster training times
   d. For more straightforward sequence tasks
   e. All of the above

7. **What is the purpose of attention mechanisms in RNNs?**
   a. To speed up training
   b. To reduce memory usage
   c. To allow the model to focus on relevant parts of the input sequence
   d. To eliminate the need for gates

8. **Why do we use padding in RNN input sequences?**
   a. To increase model accuracy
   b. To handle variable-length sequences in batches
   c. To reduce memory usage
   d. To speed up training

9. **What advantage does a bidirectional RNN have over a standard RNN?**
   a. Faster training time
   b. Less memory usage
   c. Can process sequences using both past and future context
   d. Simpler architecture
10. **Which of the following is true about RNN training?**
   a. It requires sequential processing of input data
   b. It can benefit from gradient clipping
   c. It often uses backpropagation through time
   d. It typically requires more computation than feedforward networks
   e. All of the above

Answers

1.	b.
2.	e.
3.	a.
4.	e.
5.	c.
6.	e.
7.	c.
8.	b.
9.	c.
10.	e.

Key terms

- **Recurrent neural network (RNN)**: A neural network architecture that processes sequential data by maintaining an internal memory state.
- **The vanishing gradient problem**: It occurs when gradients become extremely small during backpropagation through time, making it difficult for RNNs to learn long-term dependencies.
- **Long short-term memory (LSTM)**: An RNN variant that uses a sophisticated gating mechanism to maintain long-term dependencies and avoid the vanishing gradient problem.
- **Gated Recurrent Unit (GRU)**: A simplified version of LSTM that combines the forget and input gates into a single update gate.
- **Attention mechanism**: A technique that allows neural networks to focus on relevant parts of the input sequence when producing each output.
- **Sequence processing**: Analyzing or generating data sequentially, such as text, time series, or audio.
- **Hidden state**: The internal memory representation in an RNN that captures information about previous inputs.

- **Cell state**: The long-term memory component in an LSTM allows information to flow unchanged through many time steps.
- **Gates**: Neural network components that control the flow of information in LSTM and GRU architectures.
- **Backpropagation through time (BPTT)**: The algorithm used to train RNNs by unrolling the network through time steps and calculating gradients.

These concepts form the foundation of modern sequence processing and continue to evolve as new architectures and techniques are developed.

References

1. **https://en.wikipedia.org/wiki/Recurrent_neural_network**
2. **https://en.wikipedia.org/wiki/Long_short-term_memory**
3. **https://en.wikipedia.org/wiki/Gated_recurrent_unit**
4. **https://en.wikipedia.org/wiki/Attention_(machine_learning)**

CHAPTER 13
Generative Adversarial Networks with PyTorch

Introduction

In previous chapters, we explored neural networks designed for classification, [**convolutional neural network** (**CNNs**)], and sequence processing [**recurrent neural network** (**RNNs**)] tasks. While these architectures excel at understanding and categorizing existing data, they cannot generate new content. This is where **generative adversarial networks** (**GANs**) come into play as they represent a revolutionary approach to creating new, synthetic data that resembles real-world data remarkably well.

Imagine a painter and an art critic working together. The painter learns to produce increasingly convincing artwork by attempting to deceive the critic, while the critic becomes more skilled at distinguishing real from fake paintings. This adversarial dynamic mirrors how GANs operate as they consist of two neural networks (a generator and a discriminator) that compete against each other, resulting in ongoing improvements in generation and discrimination capabilities.

GANs have revolutionized multiple fields through their ability to produce remarkably realistic content. They are widely used in image synthesis to create photorealistic faces, landscapes, and artwork, as well as in data augmentation to expand limited datasets for more effective model training. GANs also enable style transfer by transforming photos into different artistic styles and support domain translation tasks such as converting sketches into photos or simulating facial aging. Beyond visual applications, GANs contribute to drug discovery by generating potential molecular structures and are increasingly applied in fashion design to create innovative clothing designs.

Structure

This chapter will cover the following topics:

- Understanding GAN architecture
- Deep convolutional GAN
- Advanced types of GANs, a beginner's guide
- Practical applications of GANs in real life
- Tips for success with GANs

Objectives

This chapter aims to provide a comprehensive understanding of GANs and their implementation in PyTorch by first exploring the core architecture, the generator and discriminator networks, and the adversarial relationship that drives their learning. Through hands-on implementations, readers will progress from building and training basic GANs to more advanced architectures such as DCGANs, while learning practical techniques to address common training challenges (for example, mode collapse and vanishing gradients) and strategies to improve training stability. Emphasizing real-world applications such as image generation and style transfer, the chapter guides readers in implementing adversarial loss functions, constructing and tuning generator and discriminator models, managing the delicate balance of GAN training, applying stabilization techniques, evaluating GAN performance with appropriate metrics, and developing practical solutions for recurring GAN problems.

Understanding GAN architecture

GANs introduce a novel way of creating new data through what we call *adversarial processes*. Think of it like a game between two players: one tries to create forgeries (the Generator), while the other tries to spot them (the Discriminator). The term *adversarial* comes from this competition between the two networks—they work against each other, but in doing so, both improve at their respective tasks. Observe the following figure:

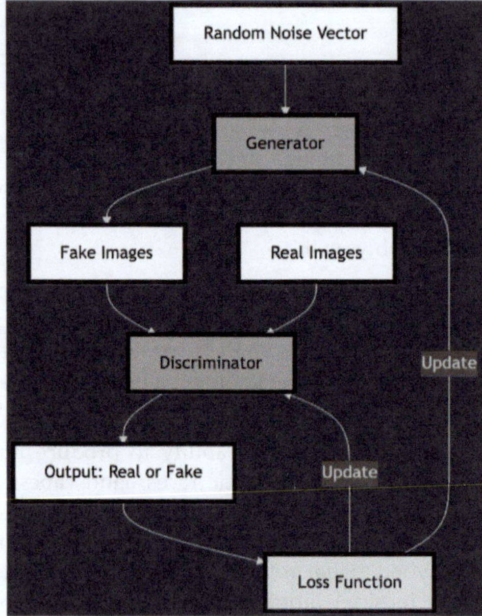

Figure 13.1: *GANs architecture*

Understanding GANs vs text-to-image models

Before implementing, it is essential to understand what GANs can and cannot do. While GANs are powerful generative models, they have specific capabilities and limitations.

GANs can do the following:

- Generate new images that look similar to their training data (e.g., new Simpsons characters that look authentic).
- Learn artistic styles and generate variations.
- Transform images from one domain to another (e.g., photo to painting).
- Create synthetic data for training other models.

GANs cannot do the following:

- Generate images from text descriptions (like *a person with sunglasses*).
- Understand and follow specific prompts.

- Combine concepts they have not seen in training.
- Generate content outside their training domain.

For text-to-image generation (like DALL-E, Stable Diffusion, or Midjourney), more advanced architectures are needed that combine:

- Text understanding models to understand text prompts.
- Diffusion models for image generation.
- Additional components for concept understanding and combination.

While GANs are powerful, they introduce unique challenges related to training and stability. This chapter will guide you through the basics of GAN architecture, implementation in PyTorch, and practical techniques for stable training. By the end, you will grasp how to build and train GANs for various generative tasks, unlocking new opportunities in both creative and practical applications of deep learning.

Core components

Before diving into each part in detail, it is helpful to view a GAN as a small ecosystem composed of three tightly coupled elements, which include the Generator, which proposes samples, the Discriminator, which judges them, and the adversarial loss and training loop that govern their interaction. This lead-in section will outline their roles, how they interact during training, and the practical considerations (loss choices, architecture priors, regularization, and stability techniques) that influence performance. With that foundation, we can examine each component in turn; first, we look at the Generator network.

Generator network

Think of the Generator as an artist learning to paint. At first, this artist starts with random brushstrokes (random noise), having no idea how to create realistic images. Through practice and feedback from the Discriminator, it gradually learns to transform this random input into convincing outputs. Just as an art student might start with basic shapes and gradually learn to create masterpieces, the Generator improves over time by:

- Starting with random numbers (noise).
- Learning patterns from real data.
- Gradually improving its artistic skills.
- Creating increasingly realistic outputs.

Discriminator network

The Discriminator is like an art critic who is shown both real paintings and the Generator's creations. Its job is to study each piece carefully and decide whether it is authentic or fake. Just as a real art critic might look for telltale signs of forgery, the Discriminator learns to:

- Spot subtle differences between real and fake data.
- Identify common mistakes in generated samples.
- Provide feedback that helps the Generator improve.
- Become increasingly sophisticated in its judgment.

Adversarial balance

The concept of adversarial balance is crucial in GANs, and it is like a carefully choreographed dance between the Generator and Discriminator. Here is why it is important:

- **Too strong a discriminator**:
  - If the critic (Discriminator) becomes too good too quickly, the artist (Generator) gets discouraged.
  - The Generator receives only negative feedback and cannot learn effectively.
  - Like a harsh critic who never gives constructive feedback.
- **Too strong a generator**:
  - If the artist becomes too good at fooling a weak critic, he might learn to create only a few *safe* pieces.
  - The Discriminator fails to provide meaningful feedback.
  - Like an art critic who cannot tell good art from bad.
- **Perfect balance**:
  - Both networks should improve gradually together.
  - The Generator gets better at creating realistic data.
  - The Discriminator gets better at spotting fakes.
  - Both push each other to improve, like friendly rivals.

This balance is what makes GANs powerful but also challenging to train. It is a bit like teaching two students who learn from competing. If one gets too far ahead, the other might give up, but if they stay evenly matched, both continue to improve.

Training process, the learning game

Training a GAN is like running a sophisticated training program where both the artist (Generator) and critic (Discriminator) take turns learning. Let us break down this process:

- **Generator training phase**:
  - Start with random noise (like an artist starting with random brushstrokes)
  - Create fake samples (the artist's attempts at creating art)
  - Get feedback from the Discriminator (the critic's review)
  - Adjust techniques to make more convincing creations.
- **Discriminator training phase**:
  - Study a collection of both real art and the Generator's creations.
  - Learn to spot the differences between real and fake.
  - Practice makes perfect em dash get better at telling them apart.
  - Provide meaningful feedback to help the Generator improve.

Think of it as alternating training sessions where each network takes turns learning and improving. The key is that neither should improve too quickly relative to the other.

Loss functions

The loss functions in GANs are like scorecards that tell us how well each network performs its job. Let us break down these mathematical expressions into more understandable terms:

```
# Discriminator loss
d_loss = -torch.mean(torch.log(D(real_data)) + torch.log(1 - D(G(noise))))
```

This means:

- *How well did the Discriminator identify real samples as real?*
- *How well did it spot the Generator's fake samples?*
- The negative sign means we want to minimize mistakes:

```
# Generator loss
g_loss = -torch.mean(torch.log(D(G(noise))))
```

This means:

- *How often did the Generator fool the Discriminator?*
- Lower loss means better forgeries.
- The Generator aims to make the Discriminator guess wrong.

These loss functions work together to create a balanced training process where both networks can improve steadily. Think of them as the rules of the game that ensure fair play and continuous improvement.

Basic GAN implementation

Before writing any model code, this section will walk you through a minimal, working GAN example in PyTorch that you can run end-to-end. We will define the generator and discriminator architectures, choose adversarial losses, implement the training loop (including alternating updates and logging), save model checkpoints, and visualize samples during training. The goal is to create a clear, reproducible pipeline that you can extend (e.g., swap architectures, change losses, add regularization, or scale to other datasets). In the following section, we begin with environment setup and preparing the MNIST data pipeline, where these foundations provide stability to experiments and make the rest of the implementation straightforward.

Setting up the environment and data

Before implementing our GAN, we must configure the hyperparameters and prepare the MNIST dataset. This setup defines the dimensions of our input data and training parameters and creates a data pipeline using PyTorch DataLoader:

```
# Hyperparameters
image_dim = 28 * 28  # MNIST images are 28x28
latent_dim = 100
hidden_dim = 256
batch_size = 128
num_epochs = 30
lr = 0.0002
beta1 = 0.5

# Load MNIST Dataset
transform = transforms.Compose([
    transforms.ToTensor(),
    transforms.Normalize((0.5,), (0.5,))
])

mnist_dataset = torchvision.datasets.MNIST(root='./data',
                                           train=True,
```

```
                                          transform=transform,
                                          download=True)

dataloader = DataLoader(mnist_dataset, batch_size=batch_size,
                        shuffle=True, num_workers=2)
```

The explanation is as follows:

- **image_dim = 28 * 28**: This calculates the total number of pixels in each MNIST image. Since MNIST images are 28x28 pixels, we multiply to get 784 total pixels.
- **latent_dim = 100**: This is the size of the random noise vector that we will use as input to the Generator. Think of it as the *seed* for generating images.
- **hidden_dim = 256**: This defines how many neurons we will have in the hidden layers of our networks.
- **batch_size = 128**: We will process 128 images at a time during training.
- **num_epochs = 30**: We will train through the entire dataset 30 times.
- **lr = 0.0002**: The learning rate—how big steps we take when updating our model (small steps help stability).

The dataset is also loaded in the preceding code snippet; see a quick explanation of the relevant pieces in the following section:

- **transforms.ToTensor()**: Converts images into PyTorch tensors (the format our model needs).
- **transforms.Normalize((0.5,), (0.5,))**: Scales pixel values to be between -1 and 1, which helps training.
- **DataLoader**: Creates batches of our data and can shuffle them (mixing up the order helps training).

Generator architecture

Refer to the following code, where the Generator network takes random noise as input and transforms it into synthetic images. It uses a series of fully connected layers with batch normalization and LeakyReLU activations to build up the features of the output image gradually.

```
class Generator(nn.Module):
    def __init__(self):
        super(Generator, self).__init__()
        self.model = nn.Sequential(
            nn.Linear(latent_dim, hidden_dim),
            nn.BatchNorm1d(hidden_dim),
            nn.LeakyReLU(0.2),

            nn.Linear(hidden_dim, hidden_dim * 2),
            nn.BatchNorm1d(hidden_dim * 2),
            nn.LeakyReLU(0.2),

            nn.Linear(hidden_dim * 2, image_dim),
            nn.Tanh()
        )
```

The following list outlines the detailed architecture:

- **Generator overview**: This network functions as an artist, transforming random noise vectors into fake images through a series of upscaling steps.

- **Input block**: The network takes in 100 random numbers (**`latent_dim`**). A fully connected layer (**`nn.Linear`**) maps these to 256 values (**`hidden_dim`**). This is immediately followed by **`nn.BatchNorm1d`** to stabilize training and `nn.LeakyReLU` to introduce non-linearity.
- **Hidden block**: The 256 features are expanded to 512 values (**`hidden_dim * 2`**) via a second linear layer. This output is again processed through batch normalization and a LeakyReLU activation function.
- **Output block**: The final linear layer maps the 512 features to 784 values (image_dim), representing the total pixels in a 28x28 image.
- **Final activation (nn.Tanh)**: The output passes through a Tanh activation function, squashing the pixel values into a range of -1 to 1. This matches the normalized range of our real MNIST training data.

Discriminator architecture

Refer to the following code, here the Discriminator network analyzes images and determines whether they are real or fake. It employs layer normalization and dropout for training stability, outputting a probability through a sigmoid activation function.

```
class Discriminator(nn.Module):
    def __init__(self):
        super(Discriminator, self).__init__()
        self.model = nn.Sequential(
            nn.Linear(image_dim, hidden_dim * 2),
            nn.LayerNorm(hidden_dim * 2),
            nn.LeakyReLU(0.2),
            nn.Dropout(0.3),
            nn.Linear(hidden_dim * 2, hidden_dim) # Input: 512 -> Output: 256
            nn.LayerNorm(hidden_dim)
            nn.LeakyReLU(0.2)
            nn.Dropout(0.3)
            nn.Linear(hidden_dim, 1),
            nn.Sigmoid()
        )
```

The following list provides a detailed explanation:

- This is our Discriminator network, which tries to tell real images from fake ones.
- The layers work in reverse compared to the Generator.
- **First layer**: Takes a 784-pixel image (**`image_dim`**) and processes it down to 512 values.
- **Final layer**: Outputs a single number between 0 and 1 (probability that the image is real).
- **nn.LayerNorm**: Similar to BatchNorm, helps stabilize training.
- **nn.Dropout**: Randomly turns off 30% of neurons during training to prevent overfitting.
- **nn.Sigmoid**: Makes sure the output is between 0 and 1 (like a probability).

Training loop implementation

The training process alternates between training the Discriminator and Generator networks. The Discriminator learns to distinguish between real and fake images, while the Generator learns to create more convincing fakes based on the Discriminator's feedback. Refer to the following code:

```
def train_gan(generator, discriminator, dataloader, num_epochs, device,
              g_optimizer, d_optimizer, criterion):
    for epoch in range(num_epochs):
        for i, (real_images, _) in enumerate(dataloader):
            batch_size = real_images.size(0)
            real_images = real_images.view(-1, image_dim).to(device)

            # Train Discriminator
            d_optimizer.zero_grad()
            output_real = discriminator(real_images).squeeze()
            d_loss_real = criterion(output_real, real_label)

            noise = torch.randn(batch_size, latent_dim).to(device)
            fake_images = generator(noise)
            output_fake = discriminator(fake_images.detach()).squeeze()
            d_loss_fake = criterion(output_fake, fake_label)

            d_loss = d_loss_real + d_loss_fake
            d_loss.backward()
            d_optimizer.step()

            # Train Generator
            g_optimizer.zero_grad()
            output_fake = discriminator(fake_images).squeeze()
            g_loss = criterion(output_fake, real_label)
            g_loss.backward()
            g_optimizer.step()
```

This function handles the training process, alternating between:

- **Training the Discriminator**:
    - Shows it real images and teaches it to output 1 (real).
    - Shows it generated fake images and teaches it to output 0 (fake).
    - Updates the Discriminator's weights based on its mistakes.
- **Training the Generator**:
    - Creates fake images from random noise.
    - Tries to fool the Discriminator into thinking they are real.
    - Updates the Generator's weights based on how well it fooled the Discriminator.
- **zero_grad()**: It clears out old gradients before calculating new ones.
- **backward()**: Calculates how to update the weights.
- **step()**: It actually updates the weights based on the calculations.
- **detach()**: prevents gradients from flowing back to the Generator during Discriminator training, ensuring we only update the Discriminator weights.

The following graph shows the training losses for the Generator and Discriminator over time. This visualization helps us understand the dynamics between the two networks:

- The blue line represents the Generator's loss, which initially starts high and gradually decreases as it learns to create more convincing fake images.
- The orange line shows the Discriminator's loss, which fluctuates as it continuously adapts to the improving Generator.
- The convergence of both lines towards the middle indicates that the networks have reached a relatively stable adversarial equilibrium.
- The occasional spikes in the losses are normal in GAN training and represent moments where one network temporarily gains an advantage over the other.

  Refer to the following figure, which illustrates the generators and discriminator loss:

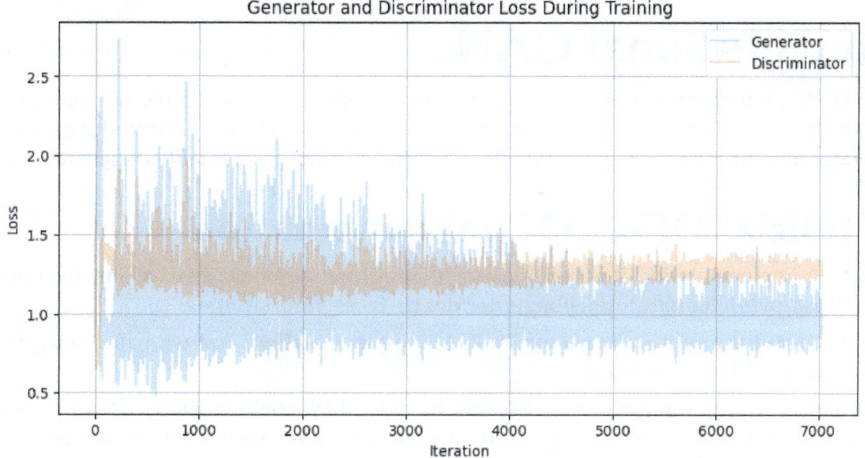

Figure 13.2: *Generator and Discriminator loss*

The following figure shows a grid of MNIST digits generated by our trained GAN. We can observe several essential aspects, which are outlined in the following list:

- The generated numbers show clear digit-like structures, indicating that the Generator has successfully learned key features of handwritten digits.
- There is variety in the samples generated, suggesting that we have avoided mode collapse (where the Generator produces only a limited set of outputs).
- While some digits are very clear and realistic, others may appear slightly blurry or malformed, which is common in basic GAN implementations.
- The quality of these generated images could be improved further with techniques like convolutional layers [**Deep convolutional GANs** (**DC-GANs**)] or more sophisticated architectures.

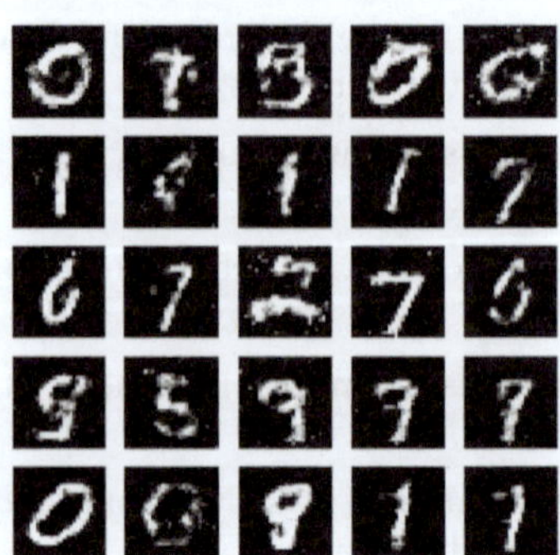

Figure 13.3: MNIST generated images

Deep convolutional GAN

While our basic GAN implementation with fully connected layers works for simple datasets like MNIST, more complex image generation tasks require more sophisticated architectures. DC-GANs introduce convolutional layers to both the generator and discriminator networks, significantly improving the quality of generated images.

PyTorch official DC-GAN implementation

Before discussing our implementation, it is worth noting that PyTorch provides an excellent, well-documented DC-GAN tutorial at **https://pytorch.org/tutorials/beginner/dcgan_faces_tutorial.html**.

This tutorial is considered the gold standard for DC-GAN implementation, and we will discuss it based on their approach while simplifying it for beginners.

The tutorial and the following example use the CelebA dataset, which contains thousands of pictures of people; a training batch would look like the following figure, and the idea, as you already know, is to generate a model that is able to create images based on this dataset.

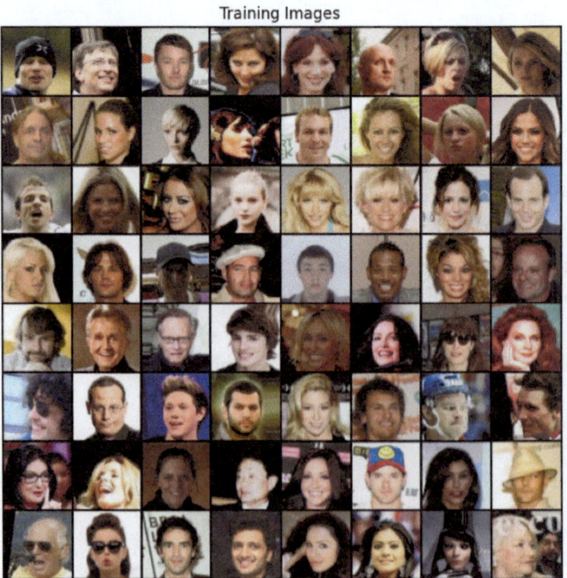

Figure 13.4: Celeba dataset samples

Key architectural improvements

Refer to the following list, which outlines how DC-GANs introduce several crucial improvements over basic GANs:

- **Convolutional layers**: Replace fully connected layers with convolutional layers for both networks.
- **Strided convolutions**: Use strided convolutions instead of pooling layers.
- **Batch normalization**: Add batch normalization in both networks.
- **Activation functions**: Use LeakyReLU in the discriminator and ReLU in the generator.
- **Fully connected layer removal**: Remove fully connected layers in the middle of the network.

Generator architecture

The generator in DC-GAN uses transposed convolutions (sometimes called **deconvolutions**) to upsample from the latent space. Following is a simplified version of the generator:

```
class Generator(nn.Module):
    def __init__(self, ngpu):
        super(Generator, self).__init__()
        self.ngpu = ngpu
        self.main = nn.Sequential(
            # input is Z, going into a convolution
            nn.ConvTranspose2d( nz, ngf * 8, 4, 1, 0, bias=False),
            nn.BatchNorm2d(ngf * 8),
            nn.ReLU(True),
            # state size. ``(ngf*8) x 4 x 4``
            nn.ConvTranspose2d(ngf * 8, ngf * 4, 4, 2, 1, bias=False),
            nn.BatchNorm2d(ngf * 4),
            nn.ReLU(True),
            # state size. ``(ngf*4) x 8 x 8``
            nn.ConvTranspose2d( ngf * 4, ngf * 2, 4, 2, 1, bias=False),
            nn.BatchNorm2d(ngf * 2),
            nn.ReLU(True),
            # state size. ``(ngf*2) x 16 x 16``
            nn.ConvTranspose2d( ngf * 2, ngf, 4, 2, 1, bias=False),
            nn.BatchNorm2d(ngf),
            nn.ReLU(True),
            # state size. ``(ngf) x 32 x 32``
            nn.ConvTranspose2d( ngf, nc, 4, 2, 1, bias=False),
            nn.Tanh()
            # state size. ``(nc) x 64 x 64``
        )

    def forward(self, input):
        return self.main(input)
```

Key differences from the basic GAN generator

When upgrading a basic, fully-connected GAN generator to a convolutional (DCGAN-style) generator, expect the architecture and layer choices to change to model spatial structure; specifically:

- Uses ConvTranspose2d instead of Linear layers.
- Includes BatchNorm2d after each convolutional layer.
- Uses ReLU activations (except for final Tanh).
- Progressively increases spatial dimensions while decreasing feature channels.

Discriminator architecture

The discriminator uses strided convolutions to downsample the input file:

```
class Discriminator(nn.Module):
    def __init__(self, ngpu):
        super(Discriminator, self).__init__()
        self.ngpu = ngpu
        self.main = nn.Sequential(
            # input is ``(nc) x 64 x 64``
            nn.Conv2d(nc, ndf, 4, 2, 1, bias=False),
            nn.LeakyReLU(0.2, inplace=True),
            # state size. ``(ndf) x 32 x 32``
            nn.Conv2d(ndf, ndf * 2, 4, 2, 1, bias=False),
            nn.BatchNorm2d(ndf * 2),
            nn.LeakyReLU(0.2, inplace=True),
            # state size. ``(ndf*2) x 16 x 16``
            nn.Conv2d(ndf * 2, ndf * 4, 4, 2, 1, bias=False),
            nn.BatchNorm2d(ndf * 4),
            nn.LeakyReLU(0.2, inplace=True),
            # state size. ``(ndf*4) x 8 x 8``
            nn.Conv2d(ndf * 4, ndf * 8, 4, 2, 1, bias=False),
            nn.BatchNorm2d(ndf * 8),
            nn.LeakyReLU(0.2, inplace=True),
            # state size. ``(ndf*8) x 4 x 4``
            nn.Conv2d(ndf * 8, 1, 4, 1, 0, bias=False),
            nn.Sigmoid()
        )

    def forward(self, input):
        return self.main(input)
```

Key differences from basic GAN discriminator:

- Uses Conv2d instead of Linear layers.
- Includes BatchNorm2d (except after the first conv layer).
- Uses LeakyReLU activations (except for final Sigmoid).
- Progressively decreases spatial dimensions while increasing feature channels.

Training process

The training process remains similar to the basic GAN but with a few important adjustments:

```
print("Starting Training Loop...")
# For each epoch
for epoch in range(num_epochs):
    # For each batch in the dataloader
    for i, data in enumerate(dataloader, 0):

        ############################
        # (1) Update D network: maximize log(D(x)) + log(1 - D(G(z)))
        ###########################
        ## Train with all-real batch
        netD.zero_grad()
        # Format batch
        real_cpu = data[0].to(device)
        b_size = real_cpu.size(0)
        label = torch.full((b_size,), real_label, dtype=torch.float, device=device)
        # Forward pass real batch through D
        output = netD(real_cpu).view(-1)
        # Calculate loss on all-real batch
        errD_real = criterion(output, label)
        # Calculate gradients for D in backward pass
        errD_real.backward()
        D_x = output.mean().item()

        ## Train with all-fake batch
        # Generate batch of latent vectors
        noise = torch.randn(b_size, nz, 1, 1, device=device)
        # Generate fake image batch with G
        fake = netG(noise)
        label.fill_(fake_label)
        # Classify all fake batch with D
        output = netD(fake.detach()).view(-1)
        # Calculate D's loss on the all-fake batch
        errD_fake = criterion(output, label)
        # Culculule the gradients for this batch, accumulated (summed) with previous gradients
        errD_fake.backward()
        D_G_z1 = output.mean().item()
        # Compute error of D as sum over the fake and the real batches
        errD = errD_real + errD_fake
        # Update D
        optimizerD.step()

```

```
        ############################
        # (2) Update G network: maximize log(D(G(z)))
        ###########################
        netG.zero_grad()
        label.fill_(real_label)  # fake labels are real for generator cost
        # Since we just updated D, perform another forward pass of all-fake batch through D
        output = netD(fake).view(-1)
        # Calculate G's loss based on this output
        errG = criterion(output, label)
        # Calculate gradients for G
        errG.backward()
        D_G_z2 = output.mean().item()
        # Update G
        optimizerG.step()

        # Output training stats
        if i % 50 == 0:
            print('[%d/%d][%d/%d]\tLoss_D: %.4f\tLoss_G: %.4f\tD(x): %.4f\tD(G(z)): %.4f / %.4f'
                  % (epoch, num_epochs, i, len(dataloader),
                     errD.item(), errG.item(), D_x, D_G_z1, D_G_z2))

        # Save Losses for plotting later
        G_losses.append(errG.item())
        D_losses.append(errD.item())

        # Check how the generator is doing by saving G's output on fixed_noise
        if (iters % 500 == 0) or ((epoch == num_epochs-1) and (i == len(dataloader)-1)):
            with torch.no_grad():
                fake = netG(fixed_noise).detach().cpu()
            img_list.append(vutils.make_grid(fake, padding=2, normalize=True))
```

Important implementation tips

The following list outlines several important implementation tips:

- **Input normalization**: Normalize input images to range [-1, 1].
- **Learning rate**: Use 0.0002 for the Adam optimizer.
- **Beta1 parameter**: Set to 0.5 for the Adam optimizer.
- **Batch size**: Typically, 128 or higher works well.
- **Weight initialization**: Initialize weights with mean=0, std=0.02.

After you have trained the model with the preceding code, you now have a model that can be used to generate images. The following code snippet uses the Generator (netG) to create a set of 64 images (8x8), as illustrated in the following code:

```
num_images = 64  # How many images you want to generate
noise = torch.randn(num_images, nz, 1, 1, device=device) # Random noise
with torch.no_grad():
    generated_images = netG(noise).detach().cpu()

# Show generated images
plt.figure(figsize=(8,8))
plt.axis("off")
plt.title("Generated Images")
plt.imshow(np.transpose(vutils.make_grid(generated_
images, padding=2, normalize=True),(1,2,0)))
plt.show()
```

The result would look like the following figure:

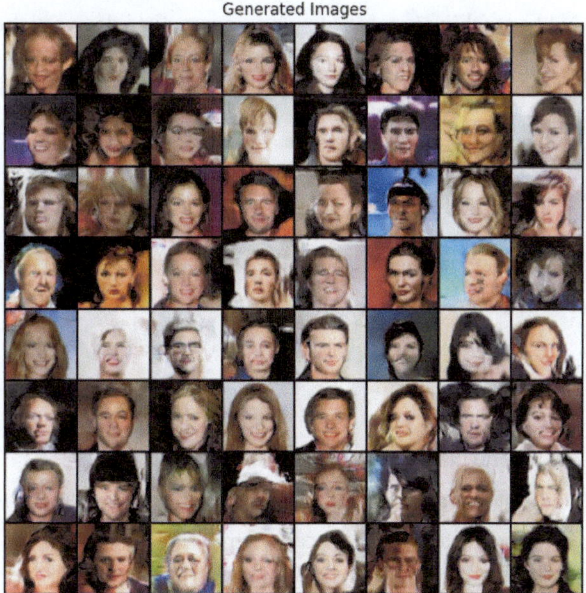

Figure 13.5: *Generated images with DC-GAN*

This model took about 5 hours to be trained on a normal **central processing unit** (**CPU**) device, no **graphics processing unit** (**GPU**), and with only 5 batches, you can see that some of the pictures already start to look realistic, while others are far from perfection.

Practical considerations

When implementing, consider emphasizing DC-GAN:

- GPU memory usage will be higher than basic GANs due to convolutional operations.
- Training time will be longer, but results will be significantly better.
- The architecture is specifically designed for image generation.
- Image size should be a power of 2 (32x32, 64x64, 128x128, etc.).

For a complete working implementation, we highly recommend following the PyTorch official tutorial. It provides extensive documentation, helper functions, and visualization code that will help you understand the full implementation details.

Advanced types of GANs, a beginner's guide

Before understanding specific variants, this section provides a high-level overview of popular GAN families and explains why you might choose one over another. Different GANs are designed to solve various practical problems, including improving training stability, enabling conditional generation, translating between image domains, producing higher-resolution outputs, and learning disentangled factors. In the following section, we will discuss the WGAN explanation, then summarize other important GAN types with a brief description and typical use cases, so you can choose which to study or experiment with next.

Wasserstein GAN, making GANs more stable

Think of training a regular GAN like teaching two kids to play a game. One draws pictures (the Generator), and the other tries to spot the fake ones (the Discriminator). Sometimes this game can get messy as one kid might get too good too quickly, or they might get frustrated and give up. This is where WGAN comes in to make the game fairer and more fun to play.

WGAN is special because:

- **Better balance**: Like having a good referee in a game, WGAN keeps both players (Generator and Discriminator) playing fairly.
- **More reliable training**: It is like having training wheels on a bike—it helps you learn without falling over.
- **Better feedback**: Gives clear scores that tell you how well you are doing.

Real-world example

Imagine you are learning to cook:

- A regular GAN is like someone just saying *good* or *bad* to your dishes.
- WGAN is like getting detailed feedback: *The sauce needs more salt*, or *the pasta is cooked perfectly.*

This better feedback helps you improve faster and more consistently.

Creating more realistic images using StyleGAN

StyleGAN is like having an artist who not only draws pictures but also understands different aspects of what they are drawing. Think of it like building a face in a video game character creator, where you can adjust different features separately.

StyleGAN is special because:

- **Control over different features**:
    - Like having separate sliders for hair style, eye color, and face shape.
    - Can mix and match features from different images.
    - Makes more realistic and controllable results.
- **Gradual learning**:
    - Starts with basic shapes (like a sketch).

- Gradually adds more details (like adding colors, then textures, then fine details).
- Like learning to draw by starting with stick figures and working up to detailed portraits.

Real-world applications of StyleGAN

StyleGAN's high-fidelity synthesis and fine-grained style control make it useful across many practical domains where realistic, editable images are valuable. Examples include:

- **Virtual try-on systems**:
  - See how clothes would look on you without trying them on.
  - Test different hairstyles before getting a haircut.
  - Preview makeup looks.
- **Game development**:
  - Creating unique characters
  - Generating diverse NPC (non-player character) faces.
  - Making realistic textures for objects.
- **Creative tools**:
  - Photo editing and enhancement.
  - Age progression/regression (how someone might look younger or older).
  - Creating artwork and designs.

Practical applications of GANs in real life

Beyond the specific capabilities of StyleGAN, GANs have a broad impact across various industries and creative fields. Their ability to generate realistic data, learn complex distributions, and perform sophisticated transformations makes them powerful tools for solving real-world problems. This section examines some of the most significant practical applications of GANs, showcasing their versatility and potential.

The following list outlines ways of making art and design easier:

- **Photo enhancement**: Making blurry photos clear.
- **Restoring old photos**: Fixing damaged old family pictures.
- **Creating art**: Helping artists try new styles.

Helping with training data

GANs can create extra training examples when you do not have enough real data:

- **Medical training**: Creating more examples of rare conditions.
- **Self-driving cars**: Generating different traffic scenarios.
- **Security systems**: Creating examples of unusual situations.

Fashion and design

The following list outlines how GANs are used in fashion and design:

- **Virtual fashion shows**: Showing how clothes look without making them.
- **Design ideas**: Generating new clothing or furniture designs.
- **Virtual try-on**: Seeing how clothes would look on you.

Entertainment

The following list outlines how GANs are used in entertainment:

- **Video games**: Creating unique characters and textures.
- **Movie effects**: Generating background crowds or environments.
- **Animation**: Helping create in-between frames.

Tips for success with GANs

GAN training is part art, part engineering. Start small, iterate quickly, and treat each change as an experiment you can measure and reproduce. The following section outlines concise and practical recommendations that will help you achieve reliable results faster and avoid the most common pitfalls.

Common problems and solutions

The following list provides a short troubleshooting guide for the most frequent GAN failure modes and quick fixes to try first. Treat these as first-pass checks, change one variable at a time, inspect generated samples and metrics after each change, and keep checkpoints so you can roll back if needed.

- **When the Generator gets stuck**:
    - **Problem**: Keeps making the same few images over and over.
    - **Solution**: Check Hyperparameters (adjust learning rate, batch size, etc) or use different types of GANs (like WGAN) and more diverse training data.
- **When training gets wobbly**:
    - **Problem**: Results keep getting better and worse randomly.
    - **Solution**: Use smaller learning rates and more stable GAN types.
- **Getting better quality**:
    - Start with proven models (like DC-GAN for beginners).
    - Use good-quality training data.
    - Be patient, as training takes time.

Best practices for beginners

The following are some best practices for beginners:

- **Start simple**:
    - Begin with basic GAN projects like generating simple shapes or numbers.
    - Move to more complex projects as you gain confidence.
    - Use pre-made architectures before creating your own.
- **Monitor your training**:
    - Save examples of generated images regularly.
    - Keep track of how long training takes.
    - Watch for signs of problems (like all images looking the same).

- **Use good data**:
    - o Clean and organize your training data.
    - o Make sure all images are the same size.
    - o Use enough examples (usually thousands of images).

Conclusion

In this chapter, we explored the fascinating world of GANs and their ability to create new content. We started with the basic concept: two networks working together like an artist and a critic, and built up to more advanced architectures like DC-GAN, WGAN, and StyleGAN.

Through this chapter, we developed an understanding of how GANs work through simple and relatable analogies, learning how to implement basic GANs and DC-GANs using PyTorch, exploring advanced GAN architectures along with their real-world applications, understanding common challenges associated with GAN training and how to overcome them, and gaining practical experience through hands-on examples.

We have seen how GANs can be used in various real-world applications, from creating art to helping train self-driving cars. While GANs can be challenging to train, the techniques and best practices we have covered will help you build successful GAN projects.

Like learning any new skill, mastering GANs takes practice and patience. Start with simple projects, monitor your training carefully, and gradually work your way up to more complex applications. In the next chapter, we will explore reinforcement learning and its implementation using PyTorch. The chapter will also discuss the fundamental aspects of RL, including agent-environment interactions, reward structures, and the balance between exploration and exploitation.

Exercises

This hands-on project allows you to apply the chapter's concepts in practice: you will build, train, and evaluate a simple GAN that generates face images. The goal is not only to obtain decent samples, but also to learn the complete experiment loop—data preparation, architecture choices, training dynamics, logging, and lightweight evaluation—so you can iterate and troubleshoot systematically.

Project: Create a simple face generator.

Goal: Build a basic GAN that can generate simple face images.

Steps:

1. Start with the DC-GAN code from earlier in the chapter.
2. Use a small dataset of face images (like CelebA). You can download it automatically using torchvision.datasets.CelebA(root='./data', split='train', download=True). Please note sometimes download might hit rate limits by Kaggle/Google, in that case you need to download manually.
3. Train the model for 50 epochs.
4. Document the improvements in image quality over time.
5. Try modifying parameters like learning rate and batch size to see their effects.

Bonus challenge:

- Implement one feature from WGAN (like removing the sigmoid from the discriminator).
- Compare the results with your original implementation.

Multiple choice questions

1. **Which analogy best describes how a GAN works?**
    a. A teacher grading a student's work
    b. An artist and an art critic working together
    c. A computer processing images
    d. A scientist conducting experiments
2. **What is the main job of the Generator in a GAN?**
    a. To classify images
    b. To detect fake images
    c. To create new images from random noise
    d. To store training data
3. **Which of these is not something GANs can do?**
    a. Create new faces that do not exist
    b. Transform photos to look like paintings
    c. Generate images based on text descriptions
    d. Create synthetic training data
4. **What does DC-GAN add to basic GANs?**
    a. Convolutional layers for better image generation
    b. The ability to process text
    c. Faster training speed
    d. The ability to work with smaller datasets
5. **What is the most common problem when training GANs?**
    a. Running out of memory
    b. Finding the right balance between Generator and Discriminator
    c. Processing speed
    d. Dataset size
6. **What makes WGAN special compared to regular GANs?**
    a. It is faster to train
    b. It provides better feedback for training
    c. It uses less memory
    d. It can work with any type of data
7. **Which of these applications best demonstrates StyleGAN's capabilities?**
    a. Text translation
    b. Voice generation
    c. Adjustable face generation with controllable features
    d. Video processing

8. **What should you do if your GAN keeps generating the same image?**
    a. Increase the learning rate
    b. Use a smaller dataset
    c. Use more diverse training data
    d. Train for fewer epochs
9. **When implementing a GAN, what should you check first?**
    a. That your training data is properly preprocessed
    b. Your computer's GPU speed
    c. The network connection
    d. The size of your hard drive
10. **Which is a sign that your GAN is training well?**
    a. The Generator loss keeps increasing
    b. The Discriminator always wins
    c. Both networks improve gradually over time
    d. Training completes very quickly

Answers

1.	b.
2.	c.
3.	c.
4.	a.
5.	b.
6.	b.
7.	c.
8.	c.
9.	a.
10.	c.

Key terms

- **Generative adversarial network (GAN)**: A type of AI model where two networks compete to generate and evaluate new content.
- **Generator**: The part of a GAN that creates new content, like an artist learning to paint.
- **Discriminator**: The part of a GAN that evaluates content, like an art critic judging paintings.
- **DC-GAN**: A type of GAN that uses convolutional layers to create better quality images.
- **Mode collapse**: When a GAN gets stuck generating the same few outputs repeatedly.
- **Training stability**: How well the Generator and Discriminator maintain balance during training.
- **StyleGAN**: An advanced GAN that can control different features of generated images separately.

- **WGAN**: A more stable version of GAN that provides better training feedback.
- **Batch normalization**: A technique that helps stabilize GAN training.
- **Adversarial training**: The process where Generator and Discriminator compete to improve each other.
- **Latent space**: The mathematical space where the Generator's input (random noise) exists.
- **Transfer learning**: Using a pre-trained GAN model as a starting point for your own project.

References

1. **https://pytorch.org/tutorials/beginner/dcgan_faces_tutorial.html.**

Chapter 14
Reinforcement Learning with PyTorch

Introduction

In earlier chapters, we examined specialized neural architectures, **convolutional neural networks** (**CNNs**) for visual data processing, **recurrent neural networks** (**RNNs**) for sequential pattern recognition, and **generative adversarial networks** (**GANs**) for synthetic content creation. While these architectures have proven highly effective at extracting patterns from static datasets, they all share a fundamental constraint: their learning process relies on passive analysis of pre-collected data rather than active engagement with dynamic environments

Reinforcement learning introduces an entirely different approach to machine learning. Instead of learning from labeled examples, reinforcement learning systems learn by doing and experiencing consequences. Think about how you might teach a dog a new trick. You do not show the dog thousands of photos of other dogs performing the trick (that would be supervised learning). Instead, you let the dog try different actions, reward it when it gets closer to the desired behavior, and provide feedback when it makes mistakes. Over time, the dog learns which behaviors lead to treats and praise. This interactive learning process is precisely how reinforcement learning works.

Reinforcement learning has transformed various fields by enabling AI systems to achieve mastery in complex games such as Chess, Go, and various video games, control robots for manufacturing, delivery, and exploration, optimize resources in data centers, energy grids, and supply chains, personalize recommendations and user experiences, navigate autonomous vehicles and drones, and develop trading strategies in finance.

What makes reinforcement learning special is its ability to handle problems where decisions have long-term consequences. Unlike supervised learning, where the *right answer* is provided for each example, reinforcement learning agents must discover good strategies through exploration and experience, just like humans learn many skills.

This chapter introduces reinforcement learning fundamentals through hands-on PyTorch implementations. We will develop autonomous agents that, *operate in dynamic environments* using trial-and-error exploration, *master decision-making* through Q-learning and policy gradient methods, continuously optimize behavior via reward maximization

By the end, you will understand how to create reinforcement learning systems for various applications, combining neural networks with reinforcement learning principles.

Structure

This chapter covers the following topics:

- Understanding reinforcement learning
- Fundamentals of decision processes
- Q-learning, learning from experience
- Combining deep learning with Deep Q-Networks and reinforcement learning

- Policy gradient methods
- Implementing policy gradient methods with PyTorch
- Applications and case studies
- Best practices for reinforcement learning

Objectives

This chapter is a practical introduction to reinforcement learning and its implementation using PyTorch. We will start by dissecting the fundamental aspects of reinforcement learning, including agent-environment interactions, reward structures, and the balance between exploration and exploitation. Following that, we will delve into the basic idea of decision processes, which lay the groundwork for comprehending sequential decision-making challenges.

Much of the chapter focuses on Q-learning and its deep learning extension, **Deep Q-Networks** (**DQNs**), explaining how neural networks can help reinforcement learning agents handle complex environments. We will implement and train DQNs from scratch using PyTorch, applying them to solve classical control problems. The chapter also covers Policy Gradient methods, which offer an alternative approach for training reinforcement learning agents and are especially useful for continuous action spaces.

In this chapter, we will focus on practical applications in PyTorch, demonstrating how to organize your code, craft network architectures, and resolve typical problems in reinforcement learning. By the conclusion of this chapter, you will have the skills to design, implement, and train reinforcement learning agents for diverse uses, including gaming, robotics, and resource optimization.

Understanding reinforcement learning

Reinforcement learning centers on improving decision-making skills. In contrast to other machine learning techniques, reinforcement learning is characterized by an agent engaging with an environment, obtaining feedback through rewards, and adjusting its actions to increase those rewards as it progresses.

The reinforcement learning framework consists of these key components:

- **Agent**: The entity that makes decisions and interacts with the environment (for example, a robot, a game-playing AI, or any other decision-making system).
- **Environment**: The world with which the agent interacts. For example, a game, a simulation, or the real world.
- **State**: Information about the current situation. Consider what the agent can observe about the environment at a given moment.
- **Action**: A decision made by the agent that shapes the outcome environment. This can include moving left or right, pressing a button, or changing a setting.
- **Reward**: Feedback from the environment indicating how good the agent's action was. Rewards can be positive (like points in a game) or negative (like penalties).
- **Policy**: The agent's strategy for selecting actions based on what it observes. This is what the agent is trying to improve through learning.

Learning process a continuous cycle

Let us go over the step-by-step process of reinforcement learning:

1. The agent perceives the existing condition of its surroundings (what it can see or sense).
2. Based on this state, the agent chooses an action according to its current policy.

3. The environment changes to a new state based on the agent's action.
4. The environment rewards the agent based on the action and the new state.
5. The agent uses this experience to improve its policy for future decisions.
6. This cycle repeats, with the agent continuously learning better strategies.

This process reflects how people develop different skills. For example, when learning to ride a bike, you explore different actions, see how they work, and slowly improve. Your technique uses feedback (staying upright acts as a reward, while falling provides a penalty).

Major obstacles in reinforcement learning

Reinforcement learning presents several distinct challenges that make it difficult to design agents capable of learning effectively in complex environments. Let us discuss them in detail in the following sections.

Dilemma of exploration vs. exploitation

A key challenge in reinforcement learning is finding the right balance between exploration and exploitation.

- **Exploration**: Experimenting with different actions to uncover more effective strategies.
- **Exploitation**: Leveraging established effective actions to optimize rewards.

Imagine visiting a new restaurant. *Do you opt for a familiar dish you enjoy (exploitation), or do you venture out to try something new that could be even better (exploration)?* Reinforcement learning agents regularly encounter this dilemma.

Delayed rewards

In many reinforcement learning problems, the consequences of actions are not immediately obvious:

- An action might not yield an immediate reward but could be essential for obtaining larger rewards later.
- For example, sacrificing a piece in chess might seem bad immediately, but could lead to winning the game many moves later.
- This makes it difficult to determine which actions were most responsible for eventual success or failure.

Learning from changing data

As the agent learns and changes its behavior, the data it experiences also changes:

- This makes learning more challenging than supervised learning, where the data distribution is fixed.
- Neural networks, built to learn from fixed datasets, often face challenges with this aspect of reinforcement learning.

Let us implement a simple example to illustrate the reinforcement learning process in a basic environment. We will create a simple grid world where an agent learns to navigate to a goal while avoiding obstacles. On the GitHub repository, for *Chapter 14, Reinforcement Learning with PyTorch*, find this snippet and execute/read the code.

The following snippet is just a small preview:

```
import numpy as np
import matplotlib.pyplot as plt

# Define a simple treasure hunt environment
class TreasureHunt:
```

```
    """
    A simple 4x4 grid world where an agent (blue circle) must find the treasure (gold star)
    while avoiding traps (red squares).

    The grid is structured as follows:
    - The agent starts in the top-left corner (0,0)
    - The treasure is in the bottom-right corner (3,3)
    - There are two traps at positions (1,1) and (2,2)

    Actions:
        0: Move up
        1: Move right
        2: Move down
        3: Move left

    Rewards:
        +10: Finding the treasure (success)
        -10: Falling into a trap (failure)
        -1: Each move (encourages finding the shortest path)
    «»»
    def __init__(self):
        self.width = 4
        self.height = 4
        self.agent_position = (0, 0)  # Start at top-left corner
        self.treasure_position = (3, 3)  # Treasure at bottom-right corner
        self.traps = [(1, 1), (2, 2)]  # Traps in the middle

    def reset(self):
        """Reset the environment to initial state"""
        self.agent_position = (0, 0)
        print("Game reset! Agent is back at the starting position (0,0).")
        return self.agent_position

```

In the book's GitHub repo, *Chapter 14, Reinforcement Learning with PyTorch*, you can see the detailed step-by-step instructions for the agent. *Figure 14.1* demonstrates the example of *Step 9*, where the agent fell into a trap. As the steps are random, when the reader runs the code, the steps taken and the output might be different.

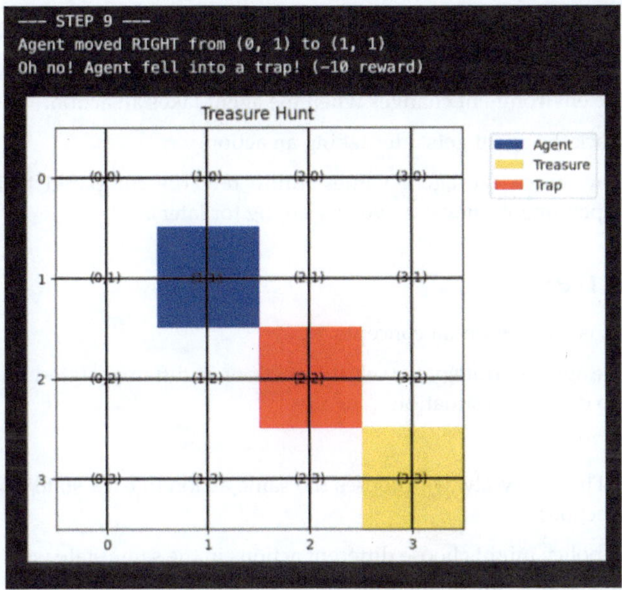

***Figure 14.1**: Step output for the Treasure Hunt Example*

This simple example demonstrates the essential components of reinforcement learning:

- An environment (TreasureHunt) with states, actions, and rewards.
- An agent (RandomExplorer) that interacts with the environment.
- A cycle of choosing actions, transitioning states, and receiving rewards.

Although this random agent does not learn and merely chooses actions at random, it demonstrates the reinforcement learning framework. In the following sections, we will develop agents that learn from their experiences.

Fundamentals of decision processes

To understand reinforcement learning more deeply, we need to grasp the concept of decision processes, particularly **Markov Decision Processes** (**MDPs**). Do not worry about the fancy name; the idea is intuitive and provides a framework for thinking about sequential decision-making problems.

Decision process

A decision process describes a situation where:

- An agent makes decisions (takes actions).
- These decisions affect the state of the environment.
- The agent receives rewards based on states and actions.
- The agent must make a series of choices, rather than a single one.

The *Markov* part means that the future depends only on the current state, not on the history of how the agent got there. This is like saying, *what matters is where you are now, not how you got here.*

Key elements of decision processes

Let us break down the key components using simple language:

- **States**: All the possible situations the agent can find itself in.
- **Actions**: The choices available to the agent.
- **Transitions**: How the environment changes when the agent takes an action.
- **Rewards**: The feedback the agent gets after taking an action.
- **Discount factor**: How much the agent values future rewards compared to immediate ones (like the difference between spending money now versus saving for later).

Policies and values

In reinforcement learning, we use two essential concepts:

- **Policy**: A policy is the agent's strategy for selecting actions in different states. It is like having a guidebook that tells you what to do in each situation.

  Policies can be:

  - **Deterministic**: The policy always chooses the same action in each state (like always turning right at a specific intersection)
  - **Stochastic**: The policy might choose different actions in the same state with specific probabilities (like sometimes going straight and sometimes turning at an intersection)
- **Value**: Value functions tell us how good it is to be in a particular state or to take a specific action:
  - **State value**: How much total reward can the agent expect if it starts in each state and follows its policy
  - **Action value**: How much total reward can the agent expect if it takes a specific action in each state and then follows its policy

These values help the agent decide which states to aim for and which actions to take.

Simple decision process example

Let us implement a simplified version of a decision process with a small grid world.

On the GitHub repository, find this snippet and execute/read the code. The following snippet is just a small preview:

```
import numpy as np
import matplotlib.pyplot as plt

def create_treasure_grid():
    """
    Create a simple 3x4 treasure hunt grid with:
    - A goal/treasure (top-right corner) giving +10 reward
    - A trap (middle-right) giving -10 reward
    - An obstacle (middle-left) that can›t be entered
    - Regular cells that give -1 reward (representing the cost of taking time)

    Grid layout (visual representation):
```

```
    [ 0,0 ][ 0,1 ][ 0,2 ][GOAL]
    [ 1,0 ][WALL][ 1,2 ][TRAP]
    [ 2,0 ][ 2,1 ][ 2,2 ][ 2,3]
    «»»
    # Initialize grid values with zeros
    values = np.zeros((3, 4))

    # Define special states
    goal = (3, 0)      # Treasure: x=3, y=0 (top-right)
    trap = (3, 1)      # Trap: x=3, y=1 (middle-right)
    obstacle = (1, 1)  # Wall: x=1, y=1 (middle-left)

    # Mark obstacle as not accessible
    values[obstacle[1], obstacle[0]] = np.nan

    # Initialize policy (which action to take in each state)
    # 0: up, 1: right, 2: down, 3: left
    policy = np.zeros((3, 4), dtype=int)

    # Return initial setup
    return values, policy, goal, trap, obstacle
```

Example output of one iteration: This output shows what the agent does at each iteration:

```
All actions evaluated: ['-1.00', '-1.00', '-1.00', '-1.00']
  Best action: UP with value -1.00
  Value updated from 0.00 to -1.00 (change: 1.0000)
Cell (3,2): Trying all possible actions from this state
  - Action UP: Moves to (3,1)
    * Immediate reward: -10 (terminal state, no future value)
  - Action RIGHT: Hits boundary/wall, stays at (3,2)
    * Immediate reward: -1, Future value: 0.00
    * Total value of this action: -1.00
  - Action DOWN: Hits boundary/wall, stays at (3,2)
    * Immediate reward: -1, Future value: 0.00
    * Total value of this action: -1.00
  - Action LEFT: Moves to (2,2)
    * Immediate reward: -1, Future value: 0.00
    * Total value of this action: -1.00
  All actions evaluated: ['-10.00', '-1.00', '-1.00', '-1.00']
  Best action: RIGHT with value -1.00
  Value updated from 0.00 to -1.00 (change: 1.0000)

Iteration 1 complete. Maximum value change: 10.0000
```

The execution of the preceding code will provide an output visualization as shown here:

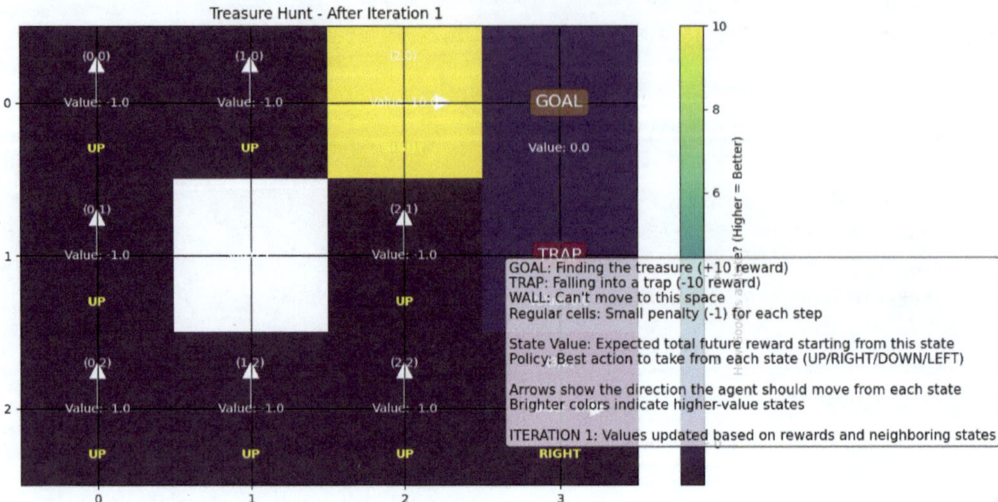

Figure 14.2: *Intermediate agent and its environment*

The following list provides an explanation of the figure:

- The highest values near the goal state (where the agent wants to go).
- Lower values near the trap state (which the agent wants to avoid).
- Arrows indicate the optimal action to take in each state.
- The obstacle is marked with an X.

This simple model forms the foundation for understanding reinforcement learning algorithms. In the next section, we will explore Q-learning, a powerful method that allows agents to learn optimal policies through experience without knowing the environment's dynamics.

Q-learning, learning from experience

Although the value iteration method we discussed is effective when we fully understand the environment, many real-world scenarios do not provide this prior knowledge. Q-learning presents a robust alternative: it learns directly from experiences without needing an environmental model.

Understanding Q-learning

Q-learning is an algorithm in reinforcement learning in which an agent assesses the value of each action for every state. In this context, *Q* represents the quality of an action in a specific state, essentially indicating its usefulness in that scenario.

The core idea behind Q-learning is simple:

- Try an action
- See what reward you get
- Update your estimate of how good that action is
- Repeat

Over time, these estimates (Q-values) converge to the true values, allowing the agent to make optimal decisions.

Understanding how Q-learning works

Q-learning maintains a *Q-table* with estimated values for each state-action pair. For example, in our grid world, we might have:

```
Q[(0,0), UP] = -3.2
Q[(0,0), RIGHT] = -2.1
Q[(0,0), DOWN] = -4.5
Q[(0,0), LEFT] = -5.0
```

These values tell us about the expected total future reward for taking each action in each state.

The learning process works as follows:

1. Observe the current state
2. Choose an action (using an exploration-exploitation strategy)
3. Observe the reward and the next state
4. Update the Q-value using the Q-learning update rule
5. Repeat

Exploration strategy

A key part of Q-learning is balancing exploration (experimenting with different actions to uncover effective strategies) with exploitation (leveraging known good actions to optimize rewards). To manage this balance, we use the epsilon-greedy (ε-greedy) strategy.

The ε-greedy strategy is an algorithm that allows the agent to switch between trying new things and sticking to what works based on a specific probability parameter, ε (epsilon).

The strategy works is outlined in the following list:

- **With probability ε(epsilon) (Exploration)**: The agent ignores its learned values and chooses a random action. This ensures the agent discovers new states and rewards it has not seen before.
- **With probability 1- ε(epsilon) (Exploitation)**: The agent becomes *greedy* and chooses the action with the highest Q-value currently in its table. This maximizes the rewards based on what the agent already knows.
- **Epsilon decay**: In the beginning, we want the agent to explore widely, so we typically start with a high ε (e.g., ε =1.0). As the agent learns more about the environment, we gradually decrease ε (a process called decay). This shifts the agent's behavior from pure exploration to exploitation, allowing it to perfect the optimal policy it has discovered.

Implementing tabular Q-learning

Let us implement Q-learning for our grid world example, as shown here:

```
import numpy as np
import matplotlib.pyplot as plt
import random
from collections import defaultdict

class QLearningAgent:
    def __init__(self, actions, learning_rate=0.1, discount_factor=0.9, exploration_rate=0.1):
```

```
        self.actions = actions # List of possible actions
        self.alpha = learning_rate  # How quickly we update our Q-values
        self.gamma = discount_factor  # How much we value future rewards
        self.epsilon = exploration_rate  # How often we explore vs. exploit

        # Initialize Q-table with zeros for all state-action pairs
        self.q_table = defaultdict(lambda: np.zeros(len(actions)))

    def select_action(self, state):
        # Epsilon-greedy action selection
        if random.random() < self.epsilon:
            # Explore: select a random action
            return random.choice(self.actions)
        else:
            # Exploit: select the action with highest Q-value
            return np.argmax(self.q_table[state])

    def learn(self, state, action, reward, next_state, done):
        # Q-learning update formula

        # Current estimate of state-action value
        current_q = self.q_table[state][action]

        if done:
            # If this is a terminal state, there's no next action
            max_next_q = 0
        else:
            # Best possible value from the next state
            max_next_q = np.max(self.q_table[next_state])

        # Target Q-value based on reward and future value
        target_q = reward + self.gamma * max_next_q

        # Update Q-value towards the target
        self.q_table[state][action] += self.alpha * (target_q - current_q)
```

This code demonstrates a complete Q-learning implementation. The agent learns to navigate the grid world, avoid the trap, and reach the goal. Over time, the rewards per episode increase as the agent discovers better strategies.

The key aspects of Q-learning demonstrated here are:

- The Q-table that stores action values for each state.
- The epsilon-greedy strategy for balancing exploration and exploitation.
- The Q-learning update rule that improves estimates based on experience.
- The decay of the exploration rate as the agent learns.

Q-learning is powerful because it makes no assumptions about the environment, it learns purely from experience.

Combining deep learning with Deep Q-Networks and RL

Although Q-learning performs effectively in small, discrete state spaces, it faces challenges in complex environments with large or continuous state spaces. This is where Deep Q-Networks offer a solution, merging the strengths of deep learning and reinforcement learning.

Need for Deep Q-Networks

Imagine we are trying to train an agent to play Atari games using pixel inputs. The screen resolution might be 210×160 pixels with 3 color channels, leading to 3^(210×160) possible states, far too many for a traditional Q-table!

Deep Q-Networks solve this problem by approximating the Q-function using a neural network. Instead of storing Q-values in a table, we train a network to predict them.

Deep Q-Network architecture

A Deep Q-Network typically consists of:

- **Input layer**: Takes the state representation (e.g., game screen pixels).
- **Hidden layers**: Several convolutional and / or fully connected layers.
- **Output layer**: Produces Q-values for each possible action.

Key innovations in DQNs

DQNs introduced several important innovations that significantly advanced the field of deep reinforcement learning by making training more stable and efficient:

- **Experience replay**: Instead of learning only from the current experience, DQNs store experiences in a replay buffer and sample randomly from this buffer during training. This helps break the correlation between consecutive samples and stabilizes the training.
- **Target network**: DQNs use a separate *target network* to calculate target Q-values. This network is updated less frequently than the main network, which helps stabilize training by providing a consistent target.
- **Reward clipping**: To help the network focus on meaningful rewards, DQN often clips rewards to be within a fixed range (e.g., [-1, 1]).

Understanding Gymnasium for reinforcement learning

Before implementing our DQN in PyTorch, let us understand what Gymnasium is and why we use it in reinforcement learning.

Gymnasium (formerly known as **Gym**) is a toolkit for developing and comparing reinforcement learning algorithms. It provides a standard **application programming interface** (**API**) for communicating with reinforcement learning environments and pre-built environments for testing algorithms.

History of Gymnasium:

- **OpenAI Gym**: Introduced by OpenAI in 2016, this toolkit is designed for creating and evaluating reinforcement learning algorithms.
- **Transfer to Farama Foundation**: In 2022, OpenAI transferred the maintenance of the Gym to the Farama Foundation, a non-profit organization dedicated to maintaining open-source reinforcement learning tools.

- **Rebranding as Gymnasium**: The Farama Foundation rebranded the Gym as Gymnasium while maintaining backward compatibility and adding new features.

Functioning of Gymnasium

Gymnasium provides a simple interface between your reinforcement learning agent and the environment:

- **Environment creation**: Create an environment using `gym.make('EnvironmentName')`
- **Agent-environment loop**:
    - o The agent receives a state from the environment.
    - o The agent performs an action based on the state.
    - o The environment returns a new state, reward, and whether the episode is done.
- **Reset**: When an episode ends, the environment is reset to start a new episode

Key environments in the Gymnasium are as follows:

- **Classic control**: Simple physics-based environments like CartPole, MountainCar, and Pendulum.
- **Atari games**: Classic Atari games like Breakout, Pong, and Space Invaders.
- **Box2D**: Physics-based environments using the Box2D engine.
- **MuJoCo**: Environments for continuous control tasks.
- **Custom environments**: You can also create your environments by implementing the Gymnasium API.

Relationship between Gymnasium and PyTorch

Gymnasium and PyTorch serve different purposes in reinforcement learning:

- **Gymnasium**: Provides the environment for your agent to interact with.
- **PyTorch**: Provides the tools for building and training the neural networks that power your agent.

Together, they form a powerful combination for implementing deep reinforcement learning algorithms:

- Gymnasium handles the environment simulation and interaction.
- PyTorch handles the neural network training and inference.

This division of responsibilities enables organized code and adaptability in implementation.

Implementing a Deep Q-Networks in PyTorch

Now that we understand the relationship between PyTorch and Gymnasium, let us implement a Deep Q-Network to solve the CartPole environment. First, we need to install the required packages:

CartPole environment

CartPole is a classic benchmark problem in reinforcement learning and control theory. It involves a pole attached by an unactuated joint to a cart, which moves along a frictionless track. The goal is to prevent the pole from falling over by applying forces to move the cart left or right. This environment is widely used to test and demonstrate reinforcement learning algorithms due to its simplicity and clear objective, as shown:

- **State space**: 4-dimensional vector (cart position, cart velocity, pole angle, pole angular velocity)
- **Action space**: 2 discrete actions (push cart left or right)
- **Reward**: +1 for each time step the pole remains upright
- **Episode end**: The pole leans past 15 degrees, or the cart shifts further. than 2.4 units from the center

Let us begin by installing the required packages:

```
%pip install gymnasium matplotlib torch
```

Now, let us implement our DQN:

```
import gymnasium as gym
import numpy as np
import matplotlib.pyplot as plt
import random
from collections import deque
import torch
import torch.nn as nn
import torch.optim as optim
import torch.nn.functional as F

# Set random seeds for reproducibility
random.seed(42)
np.random.seed(42)
torch.manual_seed(42)

# Check if CUDA is available
device = torch.device("cuda" if torch.cuda.is_available() else "cpu")
print(f"Using device: {device}")

# Create the CartPole environment
env = gym.make("CartPole-v1")

# Define the DQN network architecture
class DQN(nn.Module):
    def __init__(self, state_size, action_size):
        super(DQN, self).__init__()
        self.fc1 = nn.Linear(state_size, 64)  # First fully connected layer
        self.fc2 = nn.Linear(64, 64)         # Second fully connected layer
        self.fc3 = nn.Linear(64, action_size) # Output layer

    def forward(self, x):
        x = F.relu(self.fc1(x))  # Apply ReLU activation to first layer
        x = F.relu(self.fc2(x))  # Apply ReLU activation to second layer
        return self.fc3(x)       # Return Q-values for each action
```

Let us break down this neural network:

- It takes the state (4 values for CartPole) as input.
- It has two hidden layers with 64 neurons each, and ReLU activation.
- It outputs Q-values for each possible action (2 for CartPole).

Now, let us implement the experience replay buffer:

```
# Define the replay buffer for experience replay
class ReplayBuffer:
```

```
    def __init__(self, capacity):
        self.buffer = deque(maxlen=capacity) # Fixed-size buffer

    def add(self, state, action, reward, next_state, done):
        # Add experience to buffer
        self.buffer.append((state, action, reward, next_state, done))

    def sample(self, batch_size):
        # Randomly sample a batch of experiences
        batch = random.sample(self.buffer, batch_size)

        # Separate the components of the experiences
        states, actions, rewards, next_states, dones = zip(*batch)

        # Convert to PyTorch tensors
        states = torch.FloatTensor(np.array(states)).to(device)
        actions = torch.LongTensor(np.array(actions)).to(device)
        rewards = torch.FloatTensor(np.array(rewards)).to(device)
        next_states = torch.FloatTensor(np.array(next_states)).to(device)
        dones = torch.FloatTensor(np.array(dones)).to(device)

        return states, actions, rewards, next_states, dones

    def __len__(self):
        return len(self.buffer)
```

The replay buffer:

- Stores experiences (**state**, **action**, **reward**, **next_state**, **done**).
- Has a fixed capacity (old experiences are discarded when the buffer is full).
- Can randomly sample batches of experiences for training.

Next, let us implement the DQN agent:

```
# Define the DQN Agent
class DQNAgent:
    def __init__(self, state_size, action_size):
        self.state_size = state_size
        self.action_size = action_size

        # Main Q-network for making decisions
        self.q_network = DQN(state_size, action_size).to(device)

        # Target Q-network for stable learning targets
        self.target_network = DQN(state_size, action_size).to(device)
        self.target_network.load_state_dict(self.q_network.state_dict())
        self.target_network.eval() # Set to evaluation mode

```

```
        # Hyperparameters
        self.gamma = 0.99            # Discount factor
        self.epsilon = 1.0           # Initial exploration rate
        self.epsilon_min = 0.01      # Minimum exploration rate
        self.epsilon_decay = 0.995   # Epsilon decay rate
        self.learning_rate = 0.001   # Learning rate
        self.update_target_frequency = 10  # How often to update target network

        # Replay buffer
        self.replay_buffer = ReplayBuffer(capacity=10000)
        self.batch_size = 64

        # Optimizer
        self.optimizer = optim.Adam(self.q_network.parameters(), lr=self.learning_rate)

    def select_action(self, state):
        # Epsilon-greedy action selection
        if random.random() < self.epsilon:
            return random.randrange(self.action_size)  # Explore: random action
        else:
            state = torch.FloatTensor(state).unsqueeze(0).to(device)
            with torch.no_grad():
                action_values = self.q_network(state)
            return torch.argmax(action_values).item()  # Exploit: best action

    def learn(self):
        # If not enough samples in the buffer, skip learning
        if len(self.replay_buffer) < self.batch_size:
            return

        # Sample a batch from the replay buffer
        states, actions, rewards, next_states, dones = self.replay_buffer.sample(self.
batch_size)

        # Get Q-values for current states and chosen actions
        q_values = self.q_network(states).gather(1, actions.unsqueeze(1)).squeeze(1)

        # Get maximum Q-values for next states using the target network
        next_q_values = self.target_network(next_states).max(1)[0]

        # Calculate target Q-values
        targets = rewards + self.gamma * next_q_values * (1 - dones)

        # Calculate loss
        loss = F.mse_loss(q_values, targets)
```

```

        # Optimize the model
        self.optimizer.zero_grad()
        loss.backward()
        self.optimizer.step()

        # Decay epsilon
        self.epsilon = max(self.epsilon_min, self.epsilon * self.epsilon_decay)

        return loss.item()

    def update_target_network(self):
        # Update the target network with the main network's weights
        self.target_network.load_state_dict(self.q_network.state_dict())

    def save(self, filename):
        # Save the trained model
        torch.save(self.q_network.state_dict(), filename)

    def load(self, filename):
        # Load a pre-trained model
        self.q_network.load_state_dict(torch.load(filename))
        self.target_network.load_state_dict(self.q_network.state_dict())
```

This Deep Q-Networks agent implements the key innovations we discussed:

- **Experience replay**: Stores experiences in a replay buffer and learns from random batches.
- **Target network**: Uses a separate network for calculating target Q-values.
- **Epsilon-greedy exploration**: Balances exploration and exploitation.

Now, let us implement the training function:

```
# Training function
def train_dqn(env, agent, num_episodes=500):
    scores = []
    losses = []
    eps_history = []

    print("Starting DQN training...")
    for episode in range(num_episodes):
        state, _ = env.reset()  # Reset environment at start of episode
        score = 0
        done = False

        while not done:
            # Select and perform an action
            action = agent.select_action(state)
            next_state, reward, terminated, truncated, _ = env.step(action)
```

```
            done = terminated or truncated

            # Store the transition in the replay buffer
            agent.replay_buffer.add(state, action, reward, next_state, done)

            # Learn from experience
            loss = agent.learn()
            if loss:
                losses.append(loss)

            # Move to the next state
            state = next_state
            score += reward

        # Update the target network periodically
        if episode % agent.update_target_frequency == 0:
            agent.update_target_network()
            print(f"Episode {episode}: Updated target network")

        # Save statistics
        scores.append(score)
        eps_history.append(agent.epsilon)

        # Print progress
        if episode % 10 == 0:
            avg_score = np.mean(scores[-10:])
            print(f"Episode {episode}: Score = {score}, Average Score = {avg_score:.2f}, Epsilon = {agent.epsilon:.2f}")

        # If we achieve a high enough score, consider the task solved
        if np.mean(scores[-100:]) >= 195.0:
            print(f"Environment solved in {episode} episodes!")
            agent.save("dqn_cartpole_solved.pth")
            break

    return scores, losses, eps_history
```

Finally, a function to test our trained agent:

```
# Test function to see how our trained agent performs
def test_agent(env, agent, num_episodes=10, render=False):
    scores = []

    for episode in range(num_episodes):
        state, _ = env.reset()
        score = 0
        done = False
```

```

        while not done:
            # Choose the best action (no exploration)
            state_tensor = torch.FloatTensor(state).unsqueeze(0).to(device)
            with torch.no_grad():
                action_values = agent.q_network(state_tensor)
            action = torch.argmax(action_values).item()

            # Take the action
            next_state, reward, terminated, truncated, _ = env.step(action)
            done = terminated or truncated

            # Update state and score
            state = next_state
            score += reward

            # Render the environment if requested
            if render:
                env.render()

        scores.append(score)
        print(f"Test Episode {episode+1}: Score = {score}")

    print(f"Average Test Score: {np.mean(scores):.2f}")
    return scores
```

Now, let us put it all together and train our agent:

```
# Main execution
state_size = env.observation_space.shape[0]  # 4 for CartPole
action_size = env.action_space.n  # 2 for CartPole (left or right)

agent = DQNAgent(state_size, action_size)

# Train the agent
scores, losses, eps_history = train_dqn(env, agent, num_episodes=500)

# Plot the training results
plt.figure(figsize=(15, 5))

plt.subplot(1, 3, 1)
plt.plot(scores)
plt.title('Episode Scores')
plt.xlabel('Episode')
plt.ylabel('Score')

plt.subplot(1, 3, 2)
```

```
plt.plot(losses)
plt.title('Loss over Time')
plt.xlabel('Training Step')
plt.ylabel('Loss')

plt.subplot(1, 3, 3)
plt.plot(eps_history)
plt.title('Epsilon over Time')
plt.xlabel('Episode')
plt.ylabel('Epsilon')

plt.tight_layout()
plt.show()

# Test the trained agent
test_scores = test_agent(env, agent)

# Close the environment
env.close()
```

Analysis of Deep Q-Networks performance on CartPole

After training our Deep Q-Networks agent on the CartPole environment, we can analyze its performance.

Note: When the reader executes this code, the output might be different.

Refer to the following figure:

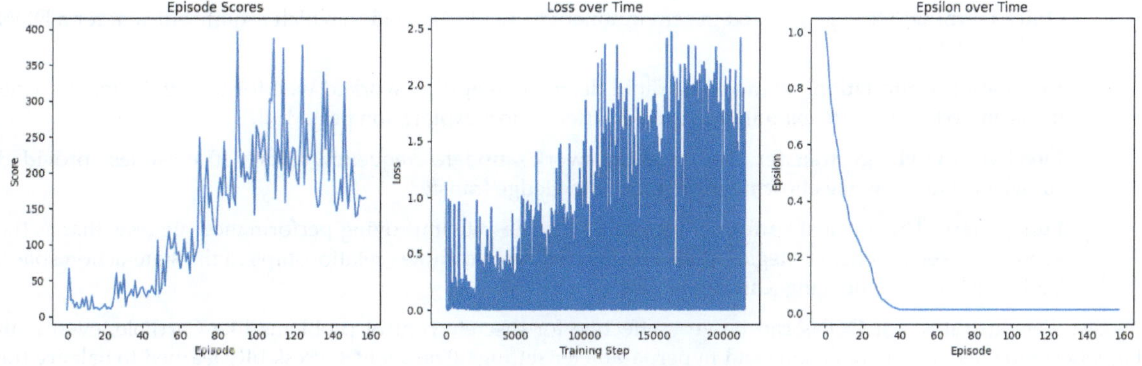

***Figure 14.3:** Results of the DQN training*

We can see several interesting patterns in how the DQN agent learned to solve the CartPole environment:

- **Episode scores (Left graph)**: The scores represent how long the pole stays balanced in each episode (higher is better):
    - **Initial performance (Episodes 0-40)**: The agent starts with low scores (around 10-40), which is expected as it is mostly taking random actions with a high epsilon value.

  - **Rapid improvement phase (Episodes 40-90)**: We see a dramatic increase in performance, with scores jumping from around 40 to over 200. This coincides with epsilon reaching its minimum value of 0.01, meaning the agent is now primarily exploiting its learned knowledge.
  - **Peak performance (Episodes 90-130)**: The agent achieves its best scores during this period, with several episodes reaching nearly 400 (the maximum score for CartPole-v1 is 500).
  - **Slight decline (Episodes 130-157)**: There is some variability and a slight downward trend in the final phase, which is common in reinforcement learning as the agent continues to learn and adapt.
  - **Solution reached**: The environment was solved at episode 157, indicating the agent achieved an average score of 195 or higher over 100 episodes.
- **Loss over time (Middle graph)**: The loss graph shows the prediction error of the Q-network:
  - **Initial low loss**: The loss begins unexpectedly low, probably due to the initial random predictions lacking structure for the network to learn from.
  - **Increasing loss trend**: As training progresses, we see the loss growing rather than decreasing, which is unusual compared to supervised learning but can happen in reinforcement learning.
  - **High variability**: Loss exhibits significant fluctuations throughout training, indicating that Q-values are consistently adjusted as the agent explores new states and refines its policy.
  - **Stabilization at elevated level**: Following training, the loss settles between 1.5 and 2.5, showing that the network has reached a stable learning state.
- **Epsilon over time (Right graph)**: This chart illustrates the rate of exploration:
  - **Rapid initial decay**: Epsilon decreases very quickly from 1.0 to near 0.01 in just the first 20-30 episodes, meaning the agent transitions from mostly random exploration to mainly exploitation quite early.
  - **Minimum value plateau**: After around episode 40, epsilon remains constant at 0.01, allowing for a small amount of exploration throughout the rest of the training.

Key findings from the implementation:

- **Quick learning**: The agent solved the environment in just 157 episodes, which is quite efficient for a DQN implementation.
- **Exploration-exploitation balance**: The rapid decrease in epsilon worked well for this problem, allowing the agent to transition to exploitation quickly after a short exploration period.
- **Effective knowledge transfer**: The target network's update frequency (every 10 episodes) provided sufficient stability while allowing for regular knowledge transfer.
- **Loss pattern**: The unusual pattern of increasing loss despite improving performance suggests that as the agent discovered better strategies, it also uncovered more complex relationships in the state-action space, leading to more challenging learning targets.

This case demonstrates that DQNs can be very effective for discrete control problems like CartPole, even with relatively simple network architectures and hyperparameter settings. The agent successfully learned to balance the pole for extended periods despite the task's inherent instability.

Policy gradient methods

While DQNs work well for environments with discrete action spaces, many real-world problems require continuous actions. For example, a robot might need to control motors with continuous torque values, or a trading algorithm might need to decide how much of an asset to buy or sell. This is where policy gradient methods come in.

Understanding policy gradient methods

Policy Gradient methods take a fundamentally different approach from Q-learning:

- **Direct policy learning**: Instead of learning value functions and deriving policies, these methods directly learn the policy function.
- **Stochastic policies**: They often output probability distributions over actions rather than deterministic actions.
- **Gradient-based optimization**: They use gradient ascent to maximize expected rewards.

The core idea is simple: adjust the policy parameters in the direction that increases the expected reward.

REINFORCE a basic policy gradient algorithm

One of the simplest policy gradient methods is REINFORCE (also known as **Monte Carlo Policy Gradient**). The algorithm works as follows:

- Sample trajectories (sequences of states, actions, and rewards) by running the current policy.
- Compute returns (sum of discounted rewards) for each time step.
- Update the policy parameters to increase the probability of actions that led to high returns.

The policy network typically outputs probabilities for each action, and actions are sampled from this distribution during training.

Advantages of policy gradient methods

Policy gradient methods offer several advantages:

- **Continuous action spaces**: They naturally handle continuous action spaces.
- **Stochastic policies**: They can learn stochastic policies, which can be beneficial in some environments.
- **More straightforward reward signals**: They can learn from sparse rewards more effectively than value-based methods.

Implementing policy gradient methods with PyTorch

While we would not provide a complete implementation here, the key components of implementing a policy gradient method in PyTorch include:

- A policy network that outputs action probabilities.
- A function to sample actions from the policy.
- A method to compute returns from rewards.
- A loss function that encourages actions that lead to high returns.

The policy network can be a simple neural network that maps states to action probabilities as follows:

```
class PolicyNetwork(nn.Module):
    def __init__(self, state_size, action_size):
        super(PolicyNetwork, self).__init__()
        self.fc1 = nn.Linear(state_size, 128)
        self.fc2 = nn.Linear(128, action_size)

```

```
    def forward(self, x):
        x = F.relu(self.fc1(x))
        x = self.fc2(x)
        return F.softmax(x, dim=1)
```

The loss function for REINFORCE is designed to maximize the log probability of actions multiplied by their returns:

```
def compute_loss(policy_network, states, actions, returns):
    action_probs = policy_network(states)
    selected_action_probs = action_probs.gather(1, actions.unsqueeze(1)).squeeze(1)
    log_probs = torch.log(selected_action_probs)
    return -torch.mean(log_probs * returns)
```

This loss function encourages the policy to increase the probability of actions that led to high returns and decrease the likelihood of actions that led to low returns.

Applications and case studies

Reinforcement learning has been applied to various problems across different domains. Let us explore some key applications:

- **Game playing**: One of the most visible applications of reinforcement learning has been in game playing:
  - **Chess and Go**: DeepMind's AlphaGo and AlphaZero used a combination of deep learning and reinforcement learning to master these complex board games.
  - **Video games**: It is fantastic to see how reinforcement learning agents have shown incredible skills in popular games like Atari, Dota 2, StarCraft II, and more!
  - **Card games**: Reinforcement learning is a fascinating tool for developing clever strategies for poker and many other card games.
- **Robotics and control**: Reinforcement learning is gaining traction in robotics and control systems.
  - **Robot manipulation**: Instructing robots to seize objects, use tools, and execute intricate tasks.
  - **Locomotion**: Creating controllers for robotic movement, including walking and running.
  - **Self-driving cars**: Educating autonomous vehicles to maneuver through intricate surroundings.
- **Resource management**: Reinforcement learning is being applied to optimize resource allocation in various systems:
  - **Data center cooling**: Google employs reinforcement learning to enhance cooling efficiency in its data centers, achieving a 40% reduction in energy usage.
  - **Traffic light control**: Reinforcement learning can optimize traffic light timing to reduce congestion.
  - **Electricity grid management**: Balancing supply and demand in electricity grids.
- **Healthcare**: Reinforcement learning is beginning to find applications in healthcare:
  - **Treatment planning**: Optimizing treatment regimens for diseases like cancer.
  - **Drug discovery**: Enhancing the efficiency of the drug discovery process through the systematic identification of novel molecules.
  - **Patient monitoring**: Optimizing alarm systems to reduce false alarms while ensuring patient safety.

Best practices for reinforcement learning

Reinforcement learning can be challenging to work with due to its high variance and sensitivity to hyperparameters. Here are some best practices to keep in mind:

- **Algorithm selection**:
  - **Consider the environment**: Value-based methods like DQN often work well for discrete action spaces. For continuous action spaces, policy gradient methods or actor-critic methods are more appropriate.
  - **Start simple**: Begin with the simplest algorithm that might work for your problem before moving to more complex methods.
- **Environment design**:
  - Take your time crafting a thoughtful reward function. This part is essential in reinforcement learning because it shapes how the agent learns and acts. By aligning it with your goals, you ensure the agent truly grasps your expected behavior.
  - Uniformly adjusting rewards boosts learning stability.
  - **Consider the duration of the episodes**: Although brief episodes provide more regular learning chances, they may overlook significant long-term connections.
- **Training process:**
  - **Evaluate performance by looking** at your context's average reward, variability, and other essential metrics.
  - **Implement proper exploration**: Ensure your agent explores the environment sufficiently, especially in the early stages of learning.
  - **Use experience replay**: Even for policy gradient methods, experience replay can improve sample efficiency.

Debugging and troubleshooting

The following are some points to consider:

- **Check your environment**: Test it with straightforward policies to confirm it operates as intended.
- **Check for gradients**: Large or Vanishing gradients might indicate problems with your network's architecture or learning rate.
- **Monitoring**: Regularly monitor your agent's actions to gain insight into how it learns.

Conclusion

This chapter took us from theory to code, showing how reinforcement learning flips the script on traditional machine learning. Instead of learning from static datasets, we have built agents that learn by doing, chasing rewards in grid worlds or balancing virtual poles. Through PyTorch implementations, we have seen firsthand how Q-learning and policy gradients turn trial-and-error into smart decision-making.

The field of RL is not just growing, it is exploding. While we have covered the essentials (enough to get you building functional agents!), the rabbit hole goes much deeper. *Want to train AI teams that collaborate like pro gamers?* Check out multi-agent systems. Curious about how robots learn complex tasks step-by-step? That is hierarchical RL. And if you are the meta type, there is even RL that knows how to learn.

Here is the secret sauce: RL mastery is not about memorizing equations. Fire up those Jupyter Notebooks. Break (then fix) your DQN's hyperparameters. PyTorch auto grad and GPU support turn even wild ideas into testable code, whether you are optimizing delivery routes or training NPCs for games.

Exercises

Modifying the Treasure Hunt Environment as follows:

- **Exercise statement**: This chapter introduces a straightforward treasure-hunt setting where an agent moves through a grid to locate treasure and dodge traps. Your task for this exercise is to enhance the environment by adding a new element: teleporters.

  Your task:

  - Modify the *TreasureHunt* class to include two teleporter cells.
  - When the agent steps on a teleporter, they should be transported to the other teleporter.
  - Track and display the number of times the agent uses teleporters during an episode.
  - Run the environment with the *RandomExplorer* agent to demonstrate the teleporter functionality.
- **Requirements:**
  - Place teleporters at positions (0,2) and (2,3).
  - Teleporters should be visually distinct (use a different color).
  - Add appropriate logging when the agent uses a teleporter.
  - The rest of the environment should function as before.
- **Starting code**: You can use the TreasureHunt environment code from the chapter as your starting point. Focus on modifying only the necessary parts to add the teleporter functionality.

Multiple choice questions

1. **What distinguishes reinforcement learning from supervised learning?**
   a. Reinforcement learning requires more data than supervised learning
   b. Reinforcement learning learns from labeled examples
   c. Reinforcement learning learns through interaction with an environment
   d. Reinforcement learning only works with neural networks
2. **In reinforcement learning, what is a policy?**
   a. The rules that define how the environment changes
   b. The agent's strategy for selecting actions based on states
   c. The method for calculating rewards
   d. The technique for saving neural network weights
3. **What is the exploration-exploitation dilemma in reinforcement learning?**
   a. The challenge of choosing between using known good actions and trying new actions
   b. The difficulty of designing appropriate reward functions
   c. The tradeoff between training speed and model accuracy
   d. The challenge of working with limited computational resources

4. **What does the Q in Q-learning stand for?**
   a. Quotient
   b. Quality
   c. Query
   d. Quantity
5. **What is the purpose of the epsilon (ε) parameter in an epsilon-greedy strategy?**
   a. To control the learning rate of the agent
   b. To set the discount factor for future rewards
   c. To determine how often the agent explores versus exploits
   d. To calculate the value of terminal states
6. **Why do we need DQNs instead of tabular Q-learning for many problems?**
   a. DQNs always converge faster than tabular methods
   b. DQNs are easier to implement
   c. DQNs can handle environments with large or continuous state spaces
   d. DQNs require less memory to run
7. **What is experience replay in DQN?**
   a. A technique that replays successful episodes to speed up learning
   b. A method for storing and randomly sampling past experiences
   c. A visualization tool that allows researchers to review the agent's behavior
   d. A form of transfer learning
8. **What is the purpose of the target network in DQN?**
   a. To provide a behavioral example for the agent to imitate
   b. To maintain a separate network for exploration
   c. To provide stable learning targets
   d. To speed up computation by distributing the workload
9. **How do policy gradient methods differ from value-based methods like Q-learning?**
   a. Policy gradient methods do not require a neural network
   b. Policy gradient methods directly learn the policy function
   c. Policy gradient methods always converge to the optimal solution
   d. Policy gradient methods can only be used for discrete action spaces
10. **What is the relationship between Gymnasium and PyTorch in reinforcement learning?**
    a. Gymnasium provides environments, while PyTorch provides tools for neural networks
    b. Gymnasium is a subset of PyTorch specifically designed for RL
    c. Gymnasium handles neural network training, while PyTorch handles environment simulation
    d. They are competing frameworks and should not be used together

Answers

1.	c.
2.	b.
3.	a.
4.	b.
5.	c.
6.	c.
7.	b.
8.	c.
9.	b.
10.	a.

Key terms

- **Agent**: The decision-maker in reinforcement learning interacts with the environment, selecting actions based on observations and learning from feedback.
- **Environment**: The setting in which the agent operates, providing states and rewards in relation to the agent's actions.
- **State**: Details regarding the current circumstances that the agent can perceive in the environment.
- **Action**: A choice by the agent that impacts the environment.
- **Reward**: Feedback from the environment indicating how good or bad the agent's action was.
- **Policy**: The agent's strategy for selecting actions based on states.
- **Exploration-exploitation dilemma**: The balance between trying new actions to discover potentially better strategies (exploration) and using known good actions to maximize rewards (exploitation).
- **Markov Decision Process (MDP)** is a helpful framework designed to model decision-making challenges. In these scenarios, outcomes involve a mix of random events and choices made by a decision-maker.
- **Value function**: A function that estimates the expected future reward from a state or state-action pair.
- **Q-learning** is a fascinating reinforcement learning algorithm that helps us understand how valuable specific actions can be in different situations!
- **Q-table**: A lookup table that stores the estimated value of each state-action pair in Q-learning.
- **Epsilon-greedy strategy**: An exploration strategy that selects the best-known action most of the time but occasionally chooses a random action.
- **Deep Q-Network (DQN)**: A neural network approximating the Q-function in reinforcement learning, enabling learning in large state spaces.
- **Experience replay**: A technique in DQN that stores and randomly samples past experiences to improve learning stability and efficiency.
- **Target network**: A separate network used in DQN to provide stable learning targets, updated less frequently than the leading network.
- **Gymnasium**: A toolkit (formerly OpenAI Gym) that provides standardized environments for developing and comparing reinforcement learning algorithms.

- **Policy gradient methods**: Reinforcement learning algorithms that directly optimize the policy by computing gradients concerning expected returns.
- **REINFORCE algorithm**: A basic policy gradient method that updates policy parameters in proportion to the return times and the gradient of the action probabilities.
- **Reward clipping**: A technique used in DQN to limit the range of rewards, improving learning stability.
- **Discount factor**: This is a helpful little parameter that shows how much the agent treasures future rewards in relation to those immediate ones.

References

1. *Gymnasium Documentation* **https://gymnasium.farama.org/index.html**
2. *PyTorch Reinforcement Learning (PPO) Tutorial* **https://pytorch.org/tutorials/intermediate/reinforcement_ppo.html**
3. *TorchRL GitHub Repository* **https://github.com/pytorch/rl**
4. *Safety-Gymnasium Documentation* **https://safety-gymnasium.readthedocs.io**
5. *Sutton and Barto's Reinforcement Learning: An Introduction (Online Book)* **http://incompleteideas.net/book/the-book-2nd.html**
6. *Reinforcement Learning with Gymnasium: A Practical Guide* **https://www.datacamp.com/tutorial/reinforcement-learning-with-gymnasium**
7. *Policy Gradient Theorem Explained* **https://www.datacamp.com/tutorial/policy-gradient-theorem**
8. *DQN Explained – Papers with Code* **https://paperswithcode.com/method/dqn**
9. *Farama Foundation's Gymnasium (GitHub Repository)* **https://github.com/Farama-Foundation/Gymnasium**

Chapter 15
Advanced Deep Learning Topics

Introduction

In preceding chapters, we have examined foundational architectures in the realm of deep learning: **convolutional neural networks** (**CNNs**) utilized for image processing and **recurrent neural networks** (**RNNs**) employed for sequential data. **Generative adversarial networks** (**GANs**) for content creation, and reinforcement learning for decision making. These approaches have transformed numerous fields, from computer vision to natural language processing, and continue to be important topics of modern AI systems.

Deep learning is evolving quickly. Researchers and practitioners are constantly pushing the limits and developing new techniques to solve ever more complicated problems. This chapter takes you beyond the fundamentals and into the cutting edge of deep learning research.

We will talk about transformative architectures like Transformers, which have revolutionized natural language processing and are now being applied across diverse domains. We will explore **graph neural networks** (**GNNs**), which can learn from relational data structures beyond the features of traditional neural networks. We will examine Bayesian approaches that bring uncertainty quantification to deep learning and self-supervised methods that leverage vast amounts of unlabeled data for more efficient learning.

These advanced techniques are not just theoretical constructs; they form the backbone of today's most powerful AI systems. Transformers power large language models like GPT and **Bidirectional Encoder Representations from Transformers** (**BERT**), which have redefined what is possible in language understanding and generation. GNNs enable breakthrough applications in drug discovery, social network analysis, and recommendation systems. Self-supervised learning has unlocked new computer vision and language modeling features, reducing dependence on labeled data.

By mastering these cutting-edge approaches, you will be equipped to tackle some of the most challenging problems in machine learning, from processing complex structured data to designing models that learn efficiently from limited supervision. You will gain insights into the techniques driving state-of-the-art performance across multiple domains and develop a deeper understanding of the principles guiding ongoing innovation in deep learning.

This chapter will focus on practical implementations in PyTorch, providing code examples you can adapt and extend for your applications. Whether interested in research, application development, or staying at the forefront of AI advancements, exploring advanced deep learning topics will expand your technical toolkit and deepen your understanding of what is possible with modern neural networks.

Structure

This chapter covers the following topics:

- Transformers and attention mechanisms
- Graph neural networks

- Bayesian neural networks
- Neural architecture search
- Self-supervised learning
- Advanced optimization techniques
- Combining multiple advanced techniques

Objectives

In this chapter, we are going to expand your grasp of deep learning by talking about some exciting, advanced architectures and techniques that go well beyond the traditional neural networks you might already know. We will talk about the theories that underpin these innovative approaches, all while keeping things grounded with practical examples and easy-to-follow instructions.

We will start by unraveling the fascinating architecture of Transformers. You will discover how attention mechanisms work and why they have changed the game across so many different fields. Next, we will explore GNNs, which are designed to handle non-Euclidean data and make sense of relational information. This opens up new avenues for applications, such as analyzing social networks and modeling molecules.

We will also look into Bayesian neural networks, which introduce uncertainty estimation into deep learning predictions. This is especially important for decision-making in critical areas like healthcare and autonomous systems, where understanding risk is crucial.

Another concept we will discuss is **neural architecture search** (**NAS**). This method automates the design of neural networks, which can save you a lot of time and technical know-how in developing effective models. We will not stop there, as self-supervised learning techniques will also be on our agenda, as they allow models to learn from unlabeled data. This breakthrough has significantly impacted fields such as computer vision and natural language processing.

Lastly, we will cover advanced optimization techniques designed to enhance training stability and convergence. This means you will be able to train models that are not only effective but also efficient.

Throughout this chapter, we will provide straightforward guidance on when and how to apply these advanced techniques to tackle real-world challenges. By the end, you will be well-equipped to navigate state-of-the-art deep learning systems and stay ahead in the ever-evolving world of AI innovation.

Transformers and attention mechanisms

Transformers have revolutionized natural language processing and are now applied across diverse domains, including computer vision, audio processing, and reinforcement learning. In this section, we will explore the architecture of Transformers and how they leverage attention mechanisms to achieve remarkable performance.

Understanding attention mechanisms

At the heart of Transformers is the attention mechanism, which allows a model to focus on different input parts when producing each output element. Unlike RNNs that process sequences step by step, attention enables direct connections between any positions in a sequence, regardless of their distance.

The fundamental intuition behind attention is asking: For each element in my sequence, *which other elements should we focus on to understand better or process it?*

The attention mechanism works through a concept of queries, keys, and values:

- **Query (Q)**: *What are you looking for?*
- **Key (K)**: *What you match against?*
- **Value (V)**: *What do you retrieve if there is a match?*

The process can be summarized in these steps:

1. For each position, compute query, key, and value vectors.
2. For each query, calculate a compatibility score with all keys.
3. Convert these scores to weights using Softmax.
4. Multiply each value by its corresponding weight.
5. Sum the weighted values to get the attention output.

Self-attention as the foundation

Self-attention (also called intra-attention) relates different positions of a single sequence to compute a representation of the sequence. The following code calculates how different sequence elements relate to each other. It computes similarity scores, converts them to weights, and produces a context-aware representation.

```
def self_attention(query, key, value):
    # Compute attention scores
    scores = torch.matmul(query, key.transpose(-2, -1))

    # Scale scores
    d_k = query.size(-1)
    scores = scores / math.sqrt(d_k)

    # Apply softmax to get attention weights
    weights = F.softmax(scores, dim=-1)

    # Compute output as weighted sum of values
    output = torch.matmul(weights, value)

    return output
```

This seemingly simple mechanism has profound implications, allowing models to capture long-range dependencies without the sequential computational bottleneck of RNNs.

Transformer architecture

The Transformer architecture, introduced in the paper *Attention is All You Need* by *Vaswani* et al., consists of an encoder and a decoder, each containing multiple layers of self-attention and feed-forward neural networks.

The key components include:

1. **Multi-head attention**: Instead of performing a single attention function, this computes multiple attention outputs in parallel and concatenates them.
2. **Positional encoding**: Since Transformers do not have inherent sequence ordering, positional encodings are added to embeddings to provide information about token positions.
3. **Layer normalization**: Applied after each sub-layer to stabilize training.
4. **Residual connections**: Help with gradient flow during training.
5. **Feed-forward networks**: Applied to each position separately and identically.

Multi-head attention

Multi-head attention allows the model to jointly attend to information from different representation subspaces at different positions. This implementation enables parallel attention patterns by splitting inputs into multiple *heads*. Each head learns different relationship aspects before combining the results.

```
# Simplified multi-head attention concept
def multi_head_attention(query, key, value, num_heads):
    # Split Q, K, V into multiple heads
    batch_size = query.size(0)
    head_dim = query.size(-1) // num_heads

    # Reshape for multiple heads
    query = query.view(batch_size, -1, num_heads, head_dim).transpose(1, 2)
    key = key.view(batch_size, -1, num_heads, head_dim).transpose(1, 2)
    value = value.view(batch_size, -1, num_heads, head_dim).transpose(1, 2)

    # Apply attention for each head
    output = self_attention(query, key, value)

    # Combine heads
    output = output.transpose(1, 2).contiguous().view(batch_size, -1, num_heads * head_
dim)

    return output
```

Transformer applications

Transformers have had a profound impact across many domains. Let us discuss each of these in detail in the following sections.

Natural language processing

In **natural language processing** (NLP), Transformers have revolutionized how machines understand and generate human language:

- BERT revolutionized language understanding.
- GPT models transformed text generation.
- T5 and others enabled sophisticated text-to-text tasks.

Computer vision

In computer vision, Transformers have introduced new architectures that rival or surpass traditional convolutional methods:

- **Vision Transformer** (ViT) achieved state-of-the-art performance in image classification.
- DETR reimagined object detection.
- Swin Transformer introduced a hierarchical representation for vision.

Multimodal models

In multimodal models, Transformers have enabled seamless integration of different data types, such as text and images:

- CLIP connects text and images.
- DALL-E generates images from text descriptions.
- Flamingo integrates vision and language.

Using Transformers with HuggingFace

Most developers use pre-trained models from libraries like HuggingFace's Transformers. Here is a brief example of using a pre-trained BERT model:

```
from transformers import BertModel, BertTokenizer

# Load pre-trained model and tokenizer
tokenizer = BertTokenizer.from_pretrained('bert-base-uncased')
model = BertModel.from_pretrained('bert-base-uncased')

# Tokenize input text
inputs = tokenizer("Hello, my dog is cute", return_tensors="pt")

# Get model outputs
outputs = model(**inputs)

# Use the outputs for your task
last_hidden_states = outputs.last_hidden_state
```

Graph neural networks

Traditional neural networks excel at processing data with a grid-like topology (images) or a sequential structure (text). Still, many real-world problems involve data best represented as graphs: social networks, molecular structures, recommendation systems, and knowledge bases. GNNs extend deep learning to these non-Euclidean domains.

Understanding graph data

A graph consists of:

- **Nodes (or vertices)**: Individual entities
- **Edges**: Connections between nodes
- **Node features**: Attributes of nodes
- **Edge features**: Attributes of connections

Unlike images or sequences, graphs have no fixed structure; they can have varying numbers of nodes and connections.

Working principles of GNNs

The core idea behind GNNs is to learn node representations by aggregating information from neighboring nodes. This message-passing mechanism allows information to flow across the graph structure.

The general framework involves:

- Initialize node representations with node features.
- For each layer, update node representations by aggregating neighbor information.
- Use the final node representations for downstream tasks.

Types of GNNs

Several GNN architectures have been developed, each with different message-passing schemes.

Graph convolutional networks

Graph convolutional networks (**GCNs**) apply convolutional operations to graph data by aggregating information from immediate neighbors. This basic GCN propagates information between connected nodes. It updates node features using neighbor information through two convolutional layers:

```
import torch
import torch.nn as nn
import torch.nn.functional as F
from torch_geometric.nn import GCNConv

class GCN(nn.Module):
    def __init__(self, num_features, hidden_dim, num_classes):
        super(GCN, self).__init__()
        self.conv1 = GCNConv(num_features, hidden_dim)
        self.conv2 = GCNConv(hidden_dim, num_classes)

    def forward(self, data):
        x, edge_index = data.x, data.edge_index

        x = self.conv1(x, edge_index)
        x = F.relu(x)
        x = F.dropout(x, p=0.5, training=self.training)
        x = self.conv2(x, edge_index)

        return F.log_softmax(x, dim=1)
```

Graph attention networks

Graph attention networks (**GATs**) introduce attention mechanisms to weigh the importance of different neighbors. GATs weigh neighbor importance using attention mechanisms. This allows dynamic focus on relevant connections during information aggregation:

```
from torch_geometric.nn import GATConv

class GAT(nn.Module):
    def __init__(self, num_features, hidden_dim, num_classes, heads=8):
        super(GAT, self).__init__()
        self.conv1 = GATConv(num_features, hidden_dim, heads=heads)
```

```
        self.conv2 = GATConv(hidden_dim*heads, num_classes)

    def forward(self, data):
        x, edge_index = data.x, data.edge_index

        x = F.dropout(x, p=0.6, training=self.training)
        x = self.conv1(x, edge_index)
        x = F.elu(x)
        x = F.dropout(x, p=0.6, training=self.training)
        x = self.conv2(x, edge_index)

        return F.log_softmax(x, dim=1)
```

Applications of GNNs

GNNs have shown impressive results across diverse applications.

Molecular property prediction

GNNs can predict the properties of molecules by treating atoms as nodes and bonds as edges:

```
# Example of molecular graph representation
# Atoms as nodes, bonds as edges
molecule_graph = Data(
    x=torch.tensor(atom_features, dtype=torch.float),
    edge_index=torch.tensor(bond_connections, dtype=torch.long),
    edge_attr=torch.tensor(bond_features, dtype=torch.float),
    y=torch.tensor([[molecular_property]], dtype=torch.float)
)
```

Recommendation systems

GNNs can model user-item interactions for more sophisticated recommendations:

```
# Bipartite graph of users and items
user_nodes = torch.tensor(user_features, dtype=torch.float)
item_nodes = torch.tensor(item_features, dtype=torch.float)
edges = torch.tensor(interactions, dtype=torch.long)  # [user_indices, item_indices]

# Learn embeddings through GNN layers
user_embeddings, item_embeddings = gnn_model(user_nodes, item_nodes, edges)

# Make recommendations based on learned embeddings
recommendations = torch.matmul(user_embeddings, item_embeddings.T)
```

Social network analysis

GNNs excel at tasks like community detection, influence prediction, and node classification in social networks.

Using PyTorch Geometric for GNNs

PyTorch Geometric (PyG) is a library built on PyTorch that provides implementations of various GNN architectures:

```
# Installation
# pip install torch-geometric

from torch_geometric.datasets import Planetoid
from torch_geometric.transforms import NormalizeFeatures

# Load a standard graph dataset (Cora)
dataset = Planetoid(root='/tmp/Cora', name='Cora', transform=NormalizeFeatures())
data = dataset[0]  # Get the graph

# Define and train GNN model
device = torch.device('cuda' if torch.cuda.is_available() else 'cpu')
model = GCN(dataset.num_features, 16, dataset.num_classes).to(device)
data = data.to(device)
optimizer = torch.optim.Adam(model.parameters(), lr=0.01)

model.train()
for epoch in range(200):
    optimizer.zero_grad()
    out = model(data)
    loss = F.nll_loss(out[data.train_mask], data.y[data.train_mask])
    loss.backward()
    optimizer.step()
```

Bayesian neural networks

Standard neural networks provide point estimates of parameters and predictions without quantifying uncertainty. **Bayesian neural networks (BNNs)** bring probabilistic modeling to deep learning, offering uncertainty quantification crucial for decision-making in critical applications.

From deterministic to probabilistic

Instead of learning single-weight values, BNNs learn distributions over weights:

- **Standard NN**: $w = [w_1, w_2, ..., w_n]$
- **Bayesian NN**: $w \sim N(\mu, \sigma^2)$ for each weight.

This allows the model to express uncertainty in its predictions.

The following list outlines the importance of uncertainty:

- **Safety-critical applications (healthcare, autonomous driving)**: Imagine a self-driving car encountering a blizzard. A standard network might confidently mistake white noise for a clear road. A Bayesian network detects high variance (σ^2) in its weights, realizes it is uncertain, and hands control back to the human driver or slows down. In healthcare, this means a diagnostic model can flag difficult cases for human review rather than guessing a diagnosis.

- **Active learning (selecting informative samples)**: When labeling data is expensive (e.g., hiring doctors to read X-rays), you do not want to label random images. You want to label the ones the model finds confusing. Uncertainty estimates highlight these *informative samples*, allowing the model to ask for help exactly where it needs it most to improve faster.
- **Out-of-distribution detection**: If a model trained only on cats and dogs is shown a picture of a giraffe, a standard model will be forced to classify it as either a cat or a dog (often with high confidence). A Bayesian model effectively says, *This data looks nothing like what I learned*, producing high uncertainty and alerting the user that the input is an anomaly.
- **Exploration in reinforcement learning**: An agent (like a robot or game player) needs to decide whether to stick to what it knows (exploitation) or try something new (exploration). Uncertainty acts as a *curiosity signal*. If the agent is uncertain about the outcome of an action, it is motivated to try that action to reduce its uncertainty, leading to better discovery of new strategies.

Methods for Bayesian deep learning

Several techniques have been developed to incorporate uncertainty estimation into deep learning models. These methods enable models to not only make predictions but also quantify their confidence, which is critical for reliable decision-making in many applications. Let us discuss some of the most widely used approaches.

- **Monte Carlo Dropout**: The simplest approach leverages dropout as a Bayesian approximation. This network uses dropout during inference to estimate uncertainty. Multiple forward passes create prediction distributions showing model confidence:

```
class MCDropoutNet(nn.Module):
    def __init__(self, input_dim, hidden_dim, output_dim, dropout_rate=0.1):
        super(MCDropoutNet, self).__init__()
        self.fc1 = nn.Linear(input_dim, hidden_dim)
        self.fc2 = nn.Linear(hidden_dim, hidden_dim)
        self.fc3 = nn.Linear(hidden_dim, output_dim)
        self.dropout = nn.Dropout(dropout_rate)

    def forward(self, x):
        x = F.relu(self.fc1(x))
        x = self.dropout(x)
        x = F.relu(self.fc2(x))
        x = self.dropout(x)
        return self.fc3(x)

    def predict_with_uncertainty(self, x, num_samples=10):
        self.train()  # Enable dropout during inference
        predictions = []

        for _ in range(num_samples):
            predictions.append(self(x).unsqueeze(0))

        predictions = torch.cat(predictions, dim=0)
        mean = predictions.mean(dim=0)
        variance = predictions.var(dim=0)
```

```

        return mean, variance
```

- **Variational inference**: More sophisticated BNNs use variational inference to learn weight distributions. This Bayesian layer learns weight distributions instead of fixed values. It samples parameters during forward passes and tracks uncertainty through KL divergence:

```
class BayesianLinear(nn.Module):
    def __init__(self, in_features, out_features):
        super(BayesianLinear, self).__init__()

        # Parameters for weight, mean , and variance
        self.weight_mu = nn.Parameter(torch.Tensor(out_features, in_features))
        self.weight_rho = nn.Parameter(torch.Tensor(out_features, in_features))

        # Parameters for bias, mean , and variance
        self.bias_mu = nn.Parameter(torch.Tensor(out_features))
        self.bias_rho = nn.Parameter(torch.Tensor(out_features))

        # Initialize parameters
        self.reset_parameters()

        # KL divergence
        self.kl = 0

    def reset_parameters(self):
        nn.init.kaiming_normal_(self.weight_mu)
        nn.init.constant_(self.weight_rho, -5)
        nn.init.constant_(self.bias_mu, 0)
        nn.init.constant_(self.bias_rho, -5)

    def forward(self, input):
        # Sample weights and calculate KL divergence
        weight_sigma = torch.log1p(torch.exp(self.weight_rho))
        weight = self.weight_mu + weight_sigma * torch.randn_like(self.weight_mu)

        bias_sigma = torch.log1p(torch.exp(self.bias_rho))
        bias = self.bias_mu + bias_sigma * torch.randn_like(self.bias_mu)

        # Calculate KL divergence
        self.kl = self._kl_divergence(weight, self.weight_mu, weight_sigma) + \
                  self._kl_divergence(bias, self.bias_mu, bias_sigma)

        return F.linear(input, weight, bias)

    def _kl_divergence(self, sample, mu, sigma):
        # Prior: N(0, 1)
```

```
        kl = 0.5 * (sigma.pow(2) + mu.pow(2) - 2 * torch.log(sigma) - 1)
        return kl.sum()
```

Practical BNN applications

BNNs are particularly valuable in:

- **Medical diagnosis**: Providing uncertainty estimates alongside predictions helps clinicians make informed decisions:

```
# Example of predicting disease with uncertainty
diagnosis, uncertainty = bayesian_model.predict_with_uncertainty(patient_data)
print(f"Diagnosis: {diagnosis}, Confidence: {1 - uncertainty}")
```

- **Autonomous systems**: Uncertainty awareness helps self-driving cars know when they do not know:

```
# Action selection with uncertainty consideration
steering_angle, uncertainty = bayesian_model.predict_with_uncertainty(sensor_data)
if uncertainty > safety_threshold:
    # Fall back to conservative driving behavior
```

Neural architecture search

NAS automates the design of neural network architectures, which has traditionally been a manual process requiring domain expertise. NAS uses optimization techniques to find optimal architectures for specific tasks.

NAS framework

NAS consists of three components:

1. **Search space**: Defines possible architectures.
2. **Search strategy**: Method to explore the search space.
3. **Performance estimation strategy**: *How to evaluate candidate architectures?*

Let us explore various search strategies of NAS.

Reinforcement learning-based NAS

A controller network learns to generate architectures that maximize task performance. This conceptual implementation uses a neural network to generate architectures. The controller learns through reinforcement learning to propose high-performing designs:

```
# Conceptual example of RL-based NAS
class NASController(nn.Module):
    def __init__(self, num_layers, num_ops):
        super(NASController, self).__init__()
        self.lstm = nn.LSTMCell(num_ops, 100)
        self.classifier = nn.Linear(100, num_ops)

    def forward(self, x, hidden):
        hx, cx = self.lstm(x, hidden)
        logits = self.classifier(hx)
```

```
        return logits, (hx, cx)

    def sample_architecture(self, num_layers):
        # Sample architecture based on controller outputs
        architectures = []
        hidden = (torch.zeros(1, 100), torch.zeros(1, 100))

        for i in range(num_layers):
            input = torch.zeros(1, self.num_ops)
            logits, hidden = self(input, hidden)
            op_id = torch.multinomial(F.softmax(logits, dim=-1), 1).item()
            architectures.append(op_id)

        return architectures
```

Evolutionary algorithms

Uses genetic algorithms to evolve network architectures. This pseudocode demonstrates architecture evolution through genetic algorithms. It selects top performers and creates new designs via mutation/crossover:

```
# Pseudocode for evolutionary NAS
def evolve_architectures(population_size, generations):
    # Initialize random population
    population = [random_architecture() for _ in range(population_size)]

    for generation in range(generations):
        # Evaluate fitness (accuracy) of each architecture
        fitness = [evaluate(arch) for arch in population]

        # Select parents based on fitness
        parents = selection(population, fitness)

        # Create new population through crossover and mutation
        new_population = []
        while len(new_population) < population_size:
            parent1, parent2 = random.sample(parents, 2)
            child = crossover(parent1, parent2)
            child = mutate(child)
            new_population.append(child)

        population = new_population

    # Return best architecture
    return population[np.argmax([evaluate(arch) for arch in population])]
```

Differentiable architecture search

Differentiable architecture search (DARTS) makes the architecture search space continuous and differentiable:

```
class MixedOp(nn.Module):
    def __init__(self, operations):
        super(MixedOp, self).__init__()
        self.ops = nn.ModuleList(operations)
        self.weights = nn.Parameter(torch.randn(len(operations)))

    def forward(self, x):
        weights = F.softmax(self.weights, dim=0)
        return sum(w * op(x) for w, op in zip(weights, self.ops))
```

Practical implementations

While full NAS implementations are complex, libraries like AutoPyTorch and DARTS simplify usage:

```
# Example using Auto-PyTorch
from autoPyTorch.api.tabular_classification import TabularClassificationTask

# Initialize the task
api = TabularClassificationTask()

# Find the best neural architecture for your data
api.search(
    X_train=X_train,
    y_train=y_train,
    X_test=X_test,
    y_test=y_test,
    optimize_metric='accuracy',
    total_walltime_limit=3600,
    func_eval_time_limit=300
)

# Use the final model
y_pred = api.predict(X_test)
```

Self-supervised learning

Self-supervised learning reduces dependency on labeled data by creating *pseudo-labels* from the data. This approach has led to breakthroughs in representation learning across domains.

Self-supervised learning involves:

- Creating a pretext task using only unlabeled data.
- Training a model to solve this task.
- Using the learned representations for downstream tasks.

Contrastive learning

Contrastive learning is a specific approach to self-supervised learning where the *pretext task* is instance discrimination. Instead of using human labels, the model generates its own supervision by creating multiple views of the same data point.

The process works as follows:

- **Positive pairs**: The system takes an image (e.g., a dog) and applies random augmentations (cropping, color jitter) to create two different versions of it. Since they come from the same original source, the model knows they are a *match* (positive pair).
- **Negative pairs**: It compares these against augmented versions of *other* images in the batch, which it knows are *non-matches* (negative pairs).
- **The learning goal**: The model is trained to pull the representations of matching pairs closer together while pushing the representations of non-matching pairs apart.

By solving this task, the model learns to understand high-level features (like the shape of an ear or the texture of fur) that remain constant despite changes in color or orientation, effectively learning useful representations without ever seeing a manual label. The following code illustrates various examples:

```
# SimCLR-style contrastive learning
class ContrastiveLearning(nn.Module):
    def __init__(self, encoder, projection_dim=128):
        super(ContrastiveLearning, self).__init__()
        self.encoder = encoder
        self.projector = nn.Sequential(
            nn.Linear(encoder.output_dim, projection_dim),
            nn.ReLU(),
            nn.Linear(projection_dim, projection_dim)
        )

    def forward(self, x):
        h = self.encoder(x)
        z = self.projector(h)
        return h, z

def contrastive_loss(z_i, z_j, temperature=0.5):
    # Normalize embeddings
    z_i = F.normalize(z_i, dim=1)
    z_j = F.normalize(z_j, dim=1)

    # Concatenate representations
    representations = torch.cat([z_i, z_j], dim=0)

    # Compute similarity matrix
    similarity_matrix = F.cosine_similarity(representations.unsqueeze(1),
                                            representations.unsqueeze(0),
                                            dim=2)

```

```
    # Define positive pairs
    batch_size = z_i.shape[0]
    pos_mask = torch.zeros((2 * batch_size, 2 * batch_size), dtype=torch.bool)
    for i in range(batch_size):
        pos_mask[i, batch_size + i] = 1
        pos_mask[batch_size + i, i] = 1

    # Compute loss
    sim = torch.exp(similarity_matrix / temperature)
    neg_sim = sim.clone()
    neg_sim[pos_mask] = 0

    pos_sim = sim[pos_mask].reshape(2 * batch_size, 1)

    loss = -torch.log(pos_sim / (pos_sim + neg_sim.sum(dim=1, keepdim=True)))

    return loss.mean()
```

Masked data modeling

This is a generative approach to self-supervised learning, most famously used in models like BERT. While contrastive learning discriminates between images, masked modeling creates a supervisory signal by intentionally corrupting the input.

The process involves:

- **Masking**: The system takes a sentence (or image) and hides a portion of it (e.g., replacing `"dog"` with `[MASK]`).
- **Reconstruction**: The model must use the remaining visible context to predict the exact original value of the masked part.
- **Self-supervision**: The `"ground truth"` label is simply the original unmasked data, meaning no human labeling is required.

The following is an example code:

```
# Example of masked language modeling with PyTorch
from transformers import BertForMaskedLM, BertTokenizer
import torch

tokenizer = BertTokenizer.from_pretrained('bert-base-uncased')
model = BertForMaskedLM.from_pretrained('bert-base-uncased')

# Prepare masked input
text = "The quick brown [MASK] jumps over the lazy dog."
inputs = tokenizer(text, return_tensors="pt")

# Get predictions
with torch.no_grad():
    outputs = model(**inputs)
```

```

# Get predictions for the masked token
mask_token_index = torch.where(inputs["input_ids"] == tokenizer.mask_token_id)[1]
predictions = outputs.logits[0, mask_token_index]
predicted_token_id = torch.argmax(predictions).item()
predicted_token = tokenizer.decode(predicted_token_id)

print(f"Predicted word: {predicted_token}")
```

Applications of self-supervised learning

Self-supervised learning has emerged as a powerful paradigm that enables models to learn useful representations from unlabeled data by creating surrogate tasks. This approach has led to significant advances across various domains, particularly in computer vision and natural language processing, where labeled data can be scarce or expensive to obtain.

The following sections discuss these significant advances in detail.

Computer vision

Self-supervised learning has transformed visual representation learning by removing the need for massive, manually labeled datasets like ImageNet. Instead of teaching a model, this is a cat via labels; we teach it to understand the *structure* of visual data.

The primary technique used here is **instance discrimination** (often via contrastive learning). The model learns that two different *views* of the same image (e.g., one cropped and rotated, one black-and-white) represent the same underlying object, while any other image in the batch is different.

By forcing the model to match these different views, the neural network learns robust features, such as shapes, textures, and object parts, that are invariant to lighting, color, or orientation changes.

The following code demonstrates the critical data augmentation pipeline used in frameworks like SimCLR. It generates the *positive pairs* required for the model to learn these robust representations:

```
# Data augmentation pipeline for contrastive learning
transform = transforms.Compose([
    transforms.RandomResizedCrop(224),
    transforms.RandomHorizontalFlip(),
    transforms.RandomApply([transforms.ColorJitter(0.4, 0.4, 0.4, 0.1)], p=0.8),
    transforms.RandomGrayscale(p=0.2),
    transforms.ToTensor(),
    transforms.Normalize([0.485, 0.456, 0.406], [0.229, 0.224, 0.225])
])

# Create two augmented views of the same image
def get_contrastive_pair(image):
    return transform(image), transform(image)
```

Natural language processing

Self-supervised learning has revolutionized NLP by enabling models to learn rich language representations from large unlabeled text corpora. These pretrained models can then be fine-tuned on specific downstream tasks with relatively small, labeled datasets, achieving state-of-the-art performance. The following example demonstrates fine-tuning a pretrained BERT model for a text classification task:

```
# Fine-tuning a pretrained BERT model
from transformers
import BertForSequenceClassification, Trainer, TrainingArguments

model = BertForSequenceClassification.from_pretrained('bert-base-uncased', num_labels=2)

training_args = TrainingArguments(
    output_dir='./results',
    num_train_epochs=3,
    per_device_train_batch_size=16,
    per_device_eval_batch_size=64,
    warmup_steps=500,
    weight_decay=0.01,
    logging_dir='./logs',
)

trainer = Trainer(
    model=model,
    args=training_args,
    train_dataset=train_dataset,
    eval_dataset=eval_dataset
)

trainer.train()
```

So far, we have looked at specialized architectures (like Transformers and GNNs) and learning paradigms (like self-supervised learning). However, regardless of which architecture or method you choose, you still need to train these models effectively. This brings us to our final major topic: the optimization tools that help *all* deep learning models learn faster and more stably.

Advanced optimization techniques

Training deep neural networks involves navigating complex optimization landscapes. Advanced optimization techniques help models converge faster and achieve better performance.

Learning rate scheduling

Learning rate schedulers adjust the learning rate during training. This adaptive scheduler adjusts rates based on validation performance. It reduces rates when progress plateaus to enable finer optimization:

```
# Learning rate scheduler example
optimizer = torch.optim.Adam(model.parameters(), lr=0.001)
scheduler = torch.optim.lr_scheduler.ReduceLROnPlateau(
    optimizer, mode='min', factor=0.1, patience=10, verbose=True
)

```

```
# In the training loop
for epoch in range(epochs):
    train_loss = train_one_epoch(model, train_loader, optimizer)
    val_loss = validate(model, val_loader)

    # Adjust learning rate based on validation loss
    scheduler.step(val_loss)
```

Gradient clipping

Gradient clipping prevents exploding gradients:

```
# Gradient clipping example
optimizer = torch.optim.Adam(model.parameters(), lr=0.001)

# In the training loop
for epoch in range(epochs):
    for batch in dataloader:
        optimizer.zero_grad()
        outputs = model(batch)
        loss = criterion(outputs, targets)
        loss.backward()

        # Clip gradients
        torch.nn.utils.clip_grad_norm_(model.parameters(), max_norm=1.0)

        optimizer.step()
```

Mixed precision training

Mixed precision reduces memory usage and speeds up training. This implementation accelerates training while conserving memory. It uses lower-precision calculations for most operations with careful gradient scaling:

```
# Mixed precision training with PyTorch
from torch.cuda.amp import autocast, GradScaler

model = YourModel().cuda()
optimizer = torch.optim.Adam(model.parameters())
scaler = GradScaler()

for epoch in range(epochs):
    for batch in dataloader:
        optimizer.zero_grad()

        # Forward pass with autocast
        with autocast():
            outputs = model(batch)
            loss = criterion(outputs, targets)
```

```

        # Backward pass with gradient scaling
        scaler.scale(loss).backward()
        scaler.step(optimizer)
        scaler.update()
```

Optimizer selection and customization

Different optimizers are suited for different tasks:

```
# Adam with weight decay (AdamW)
optimizer = torch.optim.AdamW(
    model.parameters(),
    lr=0.001,
    betas=(0.9, 0.999),
    weight_decay=0.01
)

# SGD with momentum and weight decay
optimizer = torch.optim.SGD(
    model.parameters(),
    lr=0.01,
    momentum=0.9,
    weight_decay=0.0001
)
```

Combining multiple advanced techniques

Real-world deep learning systems often combine multiple advanced techniques to achieve state-of-the-art performance. This section explores how these approaches can work together synergistically.

Case study: Modern image classification

This example demonstrates a state-of-the-art training pipeline by combining three distinct advanced techniques. It uses a ViT architecture initialized with self-supervised pre-trained weights, allowing the model to leverage previously learned visual features instead of training from scratch. To maximize efficiency, the training loop integrates advanced optimization: it uses mixed precision (via **autocast** and **GradScaler**) to speed up math operations and reduce memory, alongside a learning rate scheduler (cosine annealing) to fine-tune the model's convergence. Check the following code example:

```
# Vision Transformer with self-supervised pretraining
from transformers import ViTForImageClassification

# Load pretrained (self-supervised) Vision Transformer
model = ViTForImageClassification.from_pretrained('google/vit-base-patch16-224-in21k')

# Fine-tune with mixed precision and learning rate scheduling
optimizer = torch.optim.AdamW(model.parameters(), lr=3e-5, weight_decay=0.01)
```

```
scheduler = torch.optim.lr_scheduler.CosineAnnealingLR(optimizer, T_max=num_epochs)
scaler = GradScaler()

for epoch in range(num_epochs):
    for images, labels in train_loader:
        optimizer.zero_grad()

        with autocast():
            outputs = model(images)
            loss = criterion(outputs, labels)

        scaler.scale(loss).backward()
        scaler.step(optimizer)
        scaler.update()

    scheduler.step()
```

Case study: Natural language understanding

This implementation enhances a standard **BERT transformer** by converting it into a **Bayesian neural network** to quantify uncertainty. By using **Monte Carlo Dropout**—keeping dropout active during inference—the model generates multiple varying predictions for the same input rather than a single fixed answer. The variance between these predictions provides a measure of **uncertainty**, allowing the system to flag low-confidence results, which is essential for safe decision-making in critical applications. Check the following code example:

```
# Transformer with Bayesian uncertainty estimation
from transformers import BertModel, BertTokenizer
import torch.nn.functional as F

class BayesianBERT(nn.Module):
    def __init__(self, num_classes):
        super(BayesianBERT, self).__init__()
        self.bert = BertModel.from_pretrained('bert-base-uncased')
        self.dropout = nn.Dropout(0.3)
        self.classifier = nn.Linear(768, num_classes)

    def forward(self, input_ids, attention_mask):
        outputs = self.bert(input_ids=input_ids, attention_mask=attention_mask)
        pooled_output = outputs.pooler_output
        pooled_output = self.dropout(pooled_output)
        logits = self.classifier(pooled_output)
        return logits

    def predict_with_uncertainty(self, input_ids, attention_mask, num_samples=10):
        self.train() # Enable dropout during inference
        predictions = []

```

```
        for _ in range(num_samples):
            with torch.no_grad():
                logits = self(input_ids, attention_mask)
                predictions.append(F.softmax(logits, dim=1).unsqueeze(0))

        predictions = torch.cat(predictions, dim=0)
        mean_pred = predictions.mean(dim=0)
        uncertainty = predictions.var(dim=0).sum(dim=1)

        return mean_pred, uncertainty
```

Conclusion

This chapter explored cutting-edge deep learning techniques that extend beyond traditional approaches. With their attention mechanisms, Transformers have revolutionized NLP and are expanding to other domains. GNNs enable learning on graph-structured data, opening new applications in various fields. BNNs provide uncertainty quantification essential for critical applications. NAS automates the design of optimal architectures. Self-supervised learning reduces dependency on labeled data, and advanced optimization techniques improve training efficiency.

By understanding these advanced topics, you can tackle complex machine-learning challenges and stay at the forefront of AI innovation. While we have provided high-level overviews and implementation examples, each topic represents an active research area with ongoing developments. The practical PyTorch implementations shared throughout this chapter give you starting points to explore these techniques in your projects.

The next chapter will apply some of these concepts to build a practical recommendation system, demonstrating how these advanced techniques translate into real-world applications.

Exercises

The following exercises cover the key concepts from this chapter.

1. **Attention mechanism**:
   - **Topic**: Transformers and attention

     This exercise helps understand the core of transformer models.
   - **Problem**:
     - Create a function that takes Q, K, V matrices as input.
     - Compute attention scores as QK^T / sqrt(d_k).
     - Apply softmax to normalize the weights.
     - Return both the attention output and weights.
2. **Node classification with GNN**:
   - **Topic**: GNNs

     This exercise introduces message passing on graphs.
   - **Problem**:
     - Take node features and edge index as input.
     - Create a normalized adjacency matrix with self-loops.
     - Apply the GCN update: H' = A_norm @ H @ W.
     - Return updated node features.

3. **Contrastive learning setup:**
    - **Topic**: Self-supervised learning

    This exercise demonstrates learning without labels.
    - **Problem:**
        - Create two augmented views of the same image.
        - Use a shared encoder for both views.
        - Implement NT-Xent contrastive loss.
        - Train to maximize similarity between views.

Multiple choice questions

1. **What is the key innovation in Transformer architectures that allows them to process sequences more efficiently than RNNs?**
    a. They use more layers
    b. Attention mechanisms
    c. They only process important tokens
    d. They require less memory.
2. **What is the primary mechanism for learning node representations in GNNs?**
    a. Message passing between neighboring nodes
    b. Pooling operations across the entire graph
    c. Random walk sampling
    d. Edge weight optimization.
3. **Which of the following is not a component in a typical Transformer architecture?**
    a. Multi-head attention
    b. Positional encoding
    c. Recurrent layers
    d. Feed-forward networks
4. **What distinguishes Bayesian neural networks from standard neural networks?**
    a. They use different activation functions
    b. They learn distributions over weights rather than point estimates
    c. They require less training data
    d. They only work with continuous data
5. **Which technique uses dropout during inference time to approximate Bayesian uncertainty?**
    a. Variational inference
    b. Monte Carlo Dropout
    c. Ensemble methods
    d. Gradient boosting
6. **What are the three main components of NAS?**
    a. Search space, search strategy, performance estimation
    b. Model size, training time, accuracy

   c. Hardware requirements, dataset size, model complexity
   d. Gradient computation, weight optimization, validation strategy

7. **What is the main advantage of self-supervised learning?**
   a. It works only with labeled data
   b. It creates pseudo-labels from unlabeled data
   c. It requires fewer computational resources
   d. It consistently outperforms supervised methods

8. **Which of these is not a common approach to self-supervised learning?**
   a. Contrastive learning
   b. Masked data modeling
   c. Reinforcement learning
   d. Data augmentation

9. **What is the purpose of gradient clipping in deep learning optimization?**
   a. To speed up model training
   b. To prevent exploding gradients
   c. To improve model accuracy
   d. To reduce memory consumption

10. **Which advanced optimization technique helps reduce memory usage while potentially speeding up training?**
   a. Mixed precision training
   b. Learning rate scheduling
   c. Gradient accumulation
   d. Weight decay

Answers

1.	b.
2.	a.
3.	c.
4.	b.
5	b.
6.	a.
7.	b.
8.	c.
9.	b.
10.	a.

Key terms

- **Attention mechanism**: A technique that allows models to focus on different input parts when producing each output element.
- **Graph neural network (GNN)**: Neural network architecture designed to work with graph-structured data.
- **Bayesian neural network (BNN)**: A Neural network that learns distributions overweighs to quantify prediction uncertainty.
- **Neural architecture search (NAS)**: Automated process for designing neural network architectures.
- **Self-supervised learning**: An Approach that creates supervisory signals from unlabeled data itself.
- **Contrastive learning**: A self-supervised method that learns by comparing similar and dissimilar pairs.
- **Mixed precision training**: Technique using lower precision format (e.g., float16) during parts of training to improve speed and memory usage.
- **Gradient clipping**: A Technique to prevent exploding gradients by limiting their magnitude.

References

1. *Vaswani, A. et al. (2017). "Attention is All You Need."*
2. *Kipf, T. N., & Welling, M. (2017). "Semi-Supervised Classification with Graph Convolutional Networks."*
3. *Veličković, P., et al. (2018). "Graph Attention Networks."*
4. *Gal, Y., & Ghahramani, Z. (2016). "Dropout as a Bayesian Approximation."*
5. *Liu, H., et al. (2018). "DARTS: Differentiable Architecture Search."*
6. *Chen, T., et al. (2020). "A Simple Framework for Contrastive Learning of Visual Representations."*
7. *Devlin, J., et al. (2019). "BERT: Pre-training of Deep Bidirectional Transformers for Language Understanding."*
8. *You, Y. et al. (2020). "Large Batch Optimization for Deep Learning: Training BERT in 76 minutes."*

Chapter 16
Building a Recommendation System

Introduction

Every day, we face an overwhelming number of choices-millions of products on e-commerce websites, countless movies and series on streaming services, and an endless stream of posts on social media. Recommendation systems assist in navigating this sea of information by forecasting what content will be most pertinent or interesting to a user. From suggesting the next song on a playlist to recommending a book you might like, these systems personalize content to our tastes and have become integral to modern digital experiences.

A recommendation system (or recommender system) filters and ranks items (products, movies, songs, articles, etc.) for a user based on available data. The aim is to offer users tailored recommendations they will appreciate or find valuable. Successful recommendation systems improve user satisfaction and key business metrics, such as click-through rates, time spent on the platform, and sales, which is why they are crucial for services like Netflix, Amazon, YouTube, and Spotify. Significant areas where recommendation systems are applied include e-commerce, suggesting products a customer might purchase based on their browsing and purchase history (e.g., *Customers who viewed this item also viewed* on Amazon); media streaming involves recommending movies, TV shows, songs, or videos tailored to a user's past consumption (Netflix, YouTube, Spotify); social media analyzes user interactions and preferences (Facebook, Twitter, LinkedIn) to personalize the feed or suggest new connections/pages, and content platforms recommend news articles, blog posts, or courses that align with the user's interests (news sites, e-learning platforms).

Behind these varied applications, most recommendation systems rely on a few core techniques. In this chapter, we will explore the two fundamental approaches, which include **collaborative filtering** (**CF**), which leverages usage data (like user ratings or clicks), and content-based filtering, which leverages information about the items (like genre, tags, or text). We will also examine hybrid systems combining both approaches to overcome their limitations.

In recent years, deep learning has increasingly been applied to recommendation tasks, improving accuracy by capturing complex patterns in data. We will learn how deep neural networks (using PyTorch) can enhance recommender systems, from simple embeddings to advanced architectures like sequence models and graph neural networks.

Before diving into implementations, it is important to note some challenges unique to recommendation systems: data sparsity (each user only interacts with a tiny fraction of items, so the user-item matrix is empty primarily), cold start problems (how to recommend for new users with no history, or new items with no interactions), and the need for evaluation methods beyond traditional accuracy (recommendations are often evaluated with metrics like Precision@K, Recall@K, or **root mean squared error** (**RMSE**) for rating predictions, and ultimately via A/B testing in production). These challenges will be addressed through the techniques we explore in this chapter.

Structure

This chapter covers the following topics:

- Introduction to recommendation systems
- Collaborative filtering techniques

- Content-based filtering techniques
- Hybrid recommendation systems
- Recommenders

Objectives

By the end of this chapter, you will have a solid understanding of how to build various recommendation systems and the reasoning behind each approach. We will start with the basics of recommendation algorithms, implementing collaborative and content-based filtering from scratch to see how they work. Hands-on PyTorch code examples will teach you how to implement a simple matrix factorization model for collaborative filtering and use vector similarities for content-based filtering. Building on these fundamentals, we will create a hybrid model combining collaborative and content information, illustrating how to alleviate cold start problems by incorporating item features into the recommendation process. As we progress, you will see how deep learning can take these ideas further: we will implement a neural network-based recommender to learn complex patterns from interaction data.

The focus will remain practical throughout the chapter. You will get experience with typical PyTorch workflows applied to recommendation: defining nn.Module classes for models, training them with suitable loss functions, and using the trained models to produce recommendations.

Introduction to recommendation systems

What is a recommendation system, and how does it frame the problem of suggesting items to users? At its core, a recommendation system operates on a **utility matrix** (often called a user-item matrix or ratings matrix). This matrix is conceptual, with **rows** representing users and **columns** representing items. An entry in this matrix encodes a particular user's preference for a specific item. This preference could be explicit (like a rating of 1-5 stars a user gave a movie) or implicit (like whether the user clicked on or purchased an item, how many seconds of a song they listened to, etc.). Most entries in this matrix are unknown—any given user has only rated or interacted with a small fraction of all items available. The job of a recommender system is to **predict the missing entries**: that is, estimate how much a user would like items they have not yet interacted with, and then suggest the items with the highest predicted preferences.

There are two primary paradigms for doing this prediction: CF and content-based filtering. The following are the details:

- **CF**: This method is based on the principle that *people who agreed in the past tend to agree in the future*. In other words, CF assumes that if two users have similar past preferences, they will likely have similar future preferences. CF methods use the collective behavior of many users (hence *collaborative*) to make recommendations—for example, by finding users with tastes similar to yours and recommending items that similar users liked (this is known as **user-based CF**), or by finding items that are similar to the ones you have enjoyed in the past and recommending those (item-based CF). Importantly, CF methods do not require information about the items (such as genre or description); they rely purely on the user-item interaction data (the patterns of ratings or clicks). This can be very powerful, as CF can uncover surprising or non-obvious associations (e.g., people who read Alice in Wonderland also tend to buy a particular brand of cookbook, something you would not guess from content alone). However, CF struggles with **cold start** scenarios, for example, if a new user has no interactions, or a new item has no ratings, collaborative methods have no data for those. We will discuss ways to mitigate this later (such as hybrid approaches).
- **Content-based filtering**: This method recommends items **similar in content** to what the user has liked. It assumes we have descriptors or features for items. For a movie, features might include its genre, director, cast, or a textual synopsis; for a product, features might be its category, price, brand, or textual description; for a song, perhaps its genre or acoustic characteristics. A content-based system uses these item profiles to build a **user profile** (representing the user's preferences regarding content features) and

then recommends new items with similar profiles. For example, if a user likes sci-fi movies, a content-based system will recommend other sci-fi movies. Content-based filtering does not require other users' data–it is all about matching the user's history and the item information. This means content-based methods can handle the cold start for new items (if item features are known), and a brand-new movie can be recommended if its content is similar to what the user likes. However, content-based methods can be limited by the expressiveness of the item features; they might miss recommending something outside the user's established interests (known as serendipity), and they cannot leverage the *wisdom of the crowd* in the way CF can.

To summarize, CF bases recommendations on similar users/items using interaction data, while content-based filtering bases recommendations on similar content/features using item metadata. Often, the best systems combine both approaches to determine the strengths of each and mitigate weaknesses. These are **hybrid systems**, which we will cover after exploring pure CF and content-based methods.

Another dimension to categorize recommendation systems is whether they produce predictions as **ratings** (predicting the numerical rating a user would give an item) or as **rankings** (directly producing a list of top N items to recommend). Classical approaches like matrix factorization often focus on predicting ratings (which can be evaluated by error metrics like RMSE). In contrast, many modern approaches focus on ranking (evaluated by metrics like Precision@K, Recall@K, NDCG, etc.). In practice, even if a model predicts scores, you use those to rank items for a user.

In the following sections, we will understand each approach. We will start with CF, which has historically been one of the most successful and popular recommendation techniques (famously, the Netflix Prize competition in 2006-2009 brought much attention to matrix factorization, a collaborative filtering method).

Collaborative filtering techniques

CF uses the power of the community's preferences to inform individual recommendations. There are two broad categories of CF techniques: **memory-based** and **model-based**. The following are the details:

- Memory-based collaborative filtering (neighborhood-based CF) directly leverages the user-item data to find neighbors (similar users or items) and make predictions. These methods operate on the principle of similarity; they find users like the target user, or items like the target item, using some similarity metric computed from the rating matrix. They are relatively straightforward to implement and interpret.
- Model-based collaborative filtering uses machine learning models to learn latent factors or patterns from the data, which can generalize better. Rather than using the raw data directly at prediction time, these methods train a model (such as a matrix factorization model or a neural network) on the user-item interaction data. The model learns to predict how a user would rate an item, and after training, the model can produce recommendations quickly. Model-based methods often yield better accuracy and can incorporate additional techniques like regularization to handle sparsity.

We will explore both categories. Let us begin with memory-based techniques, specifically user-based and item-based collaborative filtering.

Memory-based collaborative filtering

There are 2 types of memory-based CF:

- **User-user CF**: In user-based CF, for a given target user (say User A), we find other users who have historically had similar preferences to User A. Once we have these similar users (often called the neighborhood for User A), we can recommend items that those users liked, which User A has not seen yet. The critical part here is defining *similar preferences*. Typically, we represent each user by their vector of item ratings (or interactions). Then we compute a similarity measure between two users' rating vectors. Standard similarity measures include cosine similarity (treating the rating vectors as coordinates and measuring the cosine of the angle between them) and Pearson correlation (a normalized measure of linear correlation between the two users' rating patterns). Cosine similarity is widespread for implicit feedback (like binary interactions) or when magnitudes matter; Pearson correlation is popular for explicit ratings, as it captures relative preferences (adjusting for users who might consistently give higher or lower ratings overall).

We can use a straightforward method to make a prediction using a user-user similarity matrix. To estimate how much User A would appreciate Item X, we examine the users who are most like User A and calculate a weighted average of their ratings for Item X. The similarity scores between User A and these similar users serve as the weights for the average. Typically, we focus on the top K users who are most like User A, making the prediction based on these closest neighbors. Additionally, we may adjust the ratings to account for each user's average rating, which helps normalize the differences in how users rate items.

- **Item-item CF**: This is analogous but flips the problem, which is to recommend for User A, we look at items that User A has already liked or interacted with. So, we compute similarity between **items** based on the users who rated them. For example, if two movies tend to be enjoyed by the same set of users, those movies are considered similar. If User A loved Movie M, then item-based CF would recommend the film most similar to Movie M (which User A has not seen yet). Item-based methods also use cosine similarity or correlation, but now each item is represented as a vector of ratings (from all users who rated it). To predict User A's rating for Item X, we can take an average of User A's ratings for similar items, weighted by those items' similarity to X.

  Item-based CF is very popular in the industry (Amazon's famous recommendation engine in the early 2000s was largely item-item CF) because item similarities are often more stable and interpretable (item properties do not change as fast as user preferences might). Also, an item-based approach can be efficient if you have significantly more users than items; you precompute the similarity between every pair of items offline, then online, for a given user, you look up the items they liked and pull the precomputed similar items.

Computing similarities

Let us illustrate how we might compute similarity between items with a small example. We will use cosine similarity. Suppose we have a user-item rating matrix where missing values are represented as 0.0, because treating *unrated* as a literal zero skews our math, we will use a masking approach in PyTorch. This ensures we only calculate the similarity between two items based on users who have actively rated both:

```
import torch

# Example rating matrix: rows = users, cols = items
# 0.0 indicates no rating (unknown)
ratings = torch.tensor([
    [5.0, 4.0, 0.0, 1.0, 0.0],  # User 0
    [0.0, 2.0, 3.0, 0.0, 0.0],  # User 1
    [1.0, 0.0, 2.0, 5.0, 0.0],  # User 2
    [0.0, 0.0, 5.0, 4.0, 3.0]   # User 3
])

num_users, num_items = ratings.shape

# 1. Create a boolean mask where True (1.0) means a rating exists
mask = (ratings > 0).float()
```

```

# 2. Initialize an empty similarity matrix
sim_matrix = torch.zeros((num_items, num_items))

# 3. Compute masked cosine similarity
for i in range(num_items):
    for j in range(num_items):
        # Find users who rated BOTH item i and item j
        co_rated = mask[:, i] * mask[:, j]

        if co_rated.sum() > 0:
            # Mask the vectors to only include co-rated users
            vec_i = ratings[:, i] * co_rated
            vec_j = ratings[:, j] * co_rated

            # Compute dot product and norms ONLY on valid overlapping ratings
            dot_product = (vec_i * vec_j).sum()
            norm_i = torch.norm(vec_i)
            norm_j = torch.norm(vec_j)

            # Prevent division by zero
            if norm_i > 0 and norm_j > 0:
                sim_matrix[i, j] = dot_product / (norm_i * norm_j)

# Print similarity matrix (rounded for readability)
print("Item-Item Cosine Similarity (Masked):\n", sim_matrix.round(decimals=2))

# Find the item most similar to item 0
item0_similarities = sim_matrix[0].clone()
# Exclude item 0 itself by setting its similarity to -1.0 temporarily
item0_similarities[0] = -1.0

most_similar_item = torch.argmax(item0_similarities).item()
print(f"Most similar item to Item 0 is Item {most_similar_item}")
```

In this code, we set up a simple ratings matrix for 4 users and 5 items. Using a cosine similarity method, we calculated how similar each pair of items is. This resulted in a 5x5 matrix called **sim_matrix**, where each entry shows the similarity score between two items. For example, an item's similarity score is 1 (meaning it is identical to itself). The printout will reveal which items are most alike. Additionally, the code finds the item most similar to Item 0. (In real situations, we would usually look for the top K items that are similar to each item.)

After we have the similarity scores, we can make recommendations for a user based on item-based CF. For instance, to suggest an item that a user has not rated yet, we can look at all the items the user has rated. We then calculate an average score for the unrated item, considering how similar each rated item is to the unrated one. This method helps us predict which items the user might like based on their past ratings.

However, using memory-based methods like this can have some issues:

- They can be affected by unusual preferences from a single user, which can skew the results.
- As the number of users and items grows, calculating and storing similarity scores can become resource-intensive and impractical.
- These methods typically do not readily incorporate other important information, like when the interaction occurred or details about the items.

To overcome these challenges, we can look to model-based CF, especially techniques like matrix factorization, which can better handle sparse data.

Model-based CF and MF

Matrix factorization (**MF**) is a powerful model-based technique designed to handle the high sparsity of the user-item interaction matrix. In a typical recommendation scenario, the vast majority of items have not been rated by most users, leaving the matrix mostly empty.

Instead of operating directly on this massive, sparse matrix, MF decomposes the data into two smaller, dense matrices:

- **User embeddings**: A matrix where each user is represented by a low-dimensional vector.
- **Item embeddings**: A matrix where each item is represented by a low-dimensional vector of the same size.

The values within these vectors are known as **latent factors**. Rather than relying on pre-defined attributes like a movie's genre or a user's age, the model learns these factors directly from the interaction patterns. For instance, a learned latent factor might implicitly capture a movie's balance of action versus romance, while the corresponding value in the user's vector captures how much they prefer that specific trait.

To predict a user's rating for an unseen item, the model calculates the **dot product** of the user's embedding vector and the item's embedding vector. This mathematical operation measures the alignment between what the user likes and what the item offers.

To make these predictions more accurate, we typically add **bias terms**:

- **User bias**: Accounts for a user's general tendency to rate items higher or lower than the global average.
- **Item bias**: Accounts for an item's overall popularity or baseline quality, independent of individual user tastes.

To implement this in a framework like PyTorch, we treat the user vectors, item vectors, and their respective biases as learnable parameters. We initialize them randomly and use an optimization algorithm, such as Adam, to iteratively adjust their values, minimizing the error between our model's predicted ratings and the actual known ratings.

Let us build a basic matrix factorization model and see how it works, refer to the following code:

```
import torch.nn as nn
import torch.optim as optim

# Suppose we have the following known ratings (user_id, item_id, rating):
ratings = [
    (0, 0, 5.0), (0, 1, 4.0), (0, 3, 1.0),
    (1, 1, 2.0), (1, 2, 3.0),
    (2, 0, 1.0), (2, 2, 2.0), (2, 3, 5.0),
    (3, 2, 5.0), (3, 3, 4.0), (3, 4, 3.0)
]
```

```
num_users = 4    # users 0 through 3
num_items = 5 # items 0 through 4

# Define latent factor dimension
K = 3  # small number of latent features

class MatrixFactorization(nn.Module):
    def __init__(self, num_users, num_items, num_factors):
        super(MatrixFactorization, self).__init__()
        # Embedding layers for users and items
        self.user_emb = nn.Embedding(num_users, num_factors)
        self.item_emb = nn.Embedding(num_items, num_factors)
        # Initialize embeddings (optional): We can initialize to small random values
        nn.init.normal_(self.user_emb.weight, std=0.1)
        nn.init.normal_(self.item_emb.weight, std=0.1)
        # Bias terms for users and items
        self.user_bias = nn.Embedding(num_users, 1)
        self.item_bias = nn.Embedding(num_items, 1)
        nn.init.zeros_(self.user_bias.weight)
        nn.init.zeros_(self.item_bias.weight)

    def forward(self, user_ids, item_ids):
        # Look up the embedding vectors for given user IDs and item IDs
        u_vecs = self.user_emb(user_ids)     # shape: [batch_size, K]
        i_vecs = self.item_emb(item_ids)     # shape: [batch_size, K]
        # Compute dot product for each user-item pair in the batch
        dot = (u_vecs * i_vecs).sum(dim=1)   # shape: [batch_size]
        # Add user and item bias
        u_bias = self.user_bias(user_ids).squeeze() # shape: [batch_size]
        i_bias = self.item_bias(item_ids).squeeze() # shape: [batch_size]
        # We can optionally add a global bias term as well, but we'll omit it here for simplicity
        return dot + u_bias + i_bias
```

In this code, we constructed a `MatrixFactorization` model with user and item embeddings of size `K=3`. We included user and item bias terms to account for systematic differences in ratings. We then trained the model on our small dataset. We printed the **mean squared error** (**MSE**) loss every 100 epochs to see the training progress (on a real dataset, you would use a validation set and more epochs as needed). After training, we printed out the learned embedding vectors for users and items (in a real scenario, these numbers are not directly meaningful to interpret, but we could examine relative distances or use them for clustering).

Finally, we demonstrated how to use the trained model to recommend items for a given user. For user 0, we computed the model's predicted score for every item (0 through 4). We then excluded the items that user 0 has already rated (since presumably they have already *experienced* those) and picked the top 2 items with the highest predicted scores. The output will show which item IDs are recommended. In a realistic situation, you would map these IDs back to actual item names or titles for presentation. Even with this tiny dataset, this demonstrates the entire pipeline, training a collaborative filtering model, and using it to produce recommendations.

MF model like this, with low-dimensional embeddings, can capture some underlying structure in the user-item interactions. For example, it might determine that User 0 and User 2 have similar tastes if their learned embedding vectors are close in the K-dimensional space, and similarly for items. This approach was at the heart of many early success stories in recommendation systems, including Netflix's move to a big latent factor model for its movie ratings.

Generalizations and improvements

There are many extensions to this basic MF model. The following list outlines a few examples:

- The **Singular Value Decomposition** (**SVD++**) algorithm is an advanced method that builds on the idea of matrix factorization, which was initially developed for the Netflix Prize. It considers ratings and other user interactions with items (even those not rated).
- In MF, regularization is essential to minimize overfitting, which happens when our model learns too much from the training data and does not perform well on new, unseen data. We achieve this by limiting the number of factors we use and applying specific training techniques.
- Some methods, like **alternating least squares** (**ALS**), can be more effective than simple methods for calculating error. For cases where we have implicit feedback (like clicks or views rather than ratings), we might use weighted methods to reflect better how much each interaction informs our recommendations.

Additionally, we can adjust how much each interaction matters in our calculations, recognizing that some may carry more weight than others based on user behavior. The limitation of basic matrix factorization is that it relies purely on the user-item interaction matrix. If a user or item is new (cold start), we have no embeddings for them until they get some interactions. This is where **content** and **hybrid** methods come into play, as we will see next.

However, before moving on, understand how CF (both memory-based and model-based) naturally produces a notion of **similarity**:

- In memory-based CF, we explicitly computed similarity.
- In model-based CF (MF), similarity is implicit: for example, dot products between learned item factor vectors give a measure of item similarity (in fact, if you take the item embedding matrix from our model, you can compute cosine similarity between those embedding vectors just like we did with raw ratings; the embedding space may even be better at grouping similar items than the raw rating vectors were, because the model learned to position them in a meaningful way).

When to use CF? If you have a lot of user-item interaction data and it is reliable (e.g., users rate movies or click songs, etc.), CF can capture complex taste patterns. It excels when user behavior is the primary signal, mainly when many users contribute information that helps recommend to each other. It is less valuable when you have very little interaction data (few users or items), or when content is the main clue (e.g., recommending brand-new items, or when recommendations must be based on specific item attributes for some reason). In such cases, content-based methods shine.

Content-based filtering techniques

Content-based filtering provides a complementary approach to recommendations by leveraging item information. Instead of looking for behavior patterns among users, we focus on items' descriptive attributes and users' preferences in terms of those attributes.

The essential components of a content-based system are as follows:

- **Item profiles**: A structured description or feature vector for each item. This could be a vector of keywords for a document, a one-hot or multi-hot encoding of genres for a movie, or a set of attributes like brand, price, and category for a product. You can also use learned features (for example, embedding vectors from **natural language processing** (**NLP**) or image models for text or image items).

- **User profile**: A representation of the user's preferences in the same feature space as item profiles. This is typically built by analyzing the content of items the user has interacted with. For instance, if a user has liked 10 articles, and 7 of them are about machine learning and 3 about cooking, the user's profile might weight technology-related keywords highly as a reflection of interest in machine learning.

The recommendation is then made by matching the user profile against candidate item profiles, essentially finding items whose content resembles what the user likes.

For example, suppose we are building a movie recommender. For content, each movie might have features like what genres it belongs to (Action, Comedy, Drama, Sci-Fi, etc.), maybe the year, director, or a plot summary. A user profile could be a vector that says, for example, this user is 70% into Sci-Fi, 30% into Action, and not at all into Romance or Drama. If a new sci-fi/action movie comes along, a content-based system would likely recommend it to this user because its genre profile matches the user's profile.

The most common technique for measuring similarity between the user profile and item profile (or between items) is **cosine similarity**, the formula we used earlier, but now applied to feature vectors in content space instead of rating patterns.

Another common approach is to use a **nearest neighbors** search in the feature space—for instance, find the top K items whose features are closest (in Euclidean distance or cosine distance) to the user's liked item features.

Let us demonstrate a simple content-based recommendation using a toy example. We will create some fake item features (imagine these could be like genre indicators or other attributes), build a user profile from items the user likes, then compute cosine similarity to find new items for the user, using the following code:

```
# Example: 5 movies, each with 3 content features (genres: [Action, Sci-Fi, Romance])
item_features = torch.tensor([
    [1.0, 1.0, 0.0],  # Item 0: Action & Sci-Fi (e.g., The Matrix)
    [1.0, 0.0, 1.0],  # Item 1: Action & Romance (e.g., Mr. & Mrs. Smith)
    [0.0, 1.0, 1.0],  # Item 2: Sci-Fi & Romance (e.g., The Time Traveler's Wife)
    [1.0, 1.0, 1.0],  # Item 3: Action, Sci-Fi, & Romance (e.g., The Fifth Element)
    [0.0, 1.0, 0.0]   # Item 4: Pure Sci-Fi (e.g., Arrival)
])

# Let's say our user has liked item 0 and item 2 in the past.
liked_items = [0, 2]

# Build the user profile by averaging the feature vectors of liked items (one simple strategy).
user_profile = item_features[liked_items].mean(dim=0)
print("User profile vector:", user_profile.tolist())

# Compute cosine similarity between the user profile and each item's features
norm_user = torch.norm(user_profile)
item_norms = torch.norm(item_features, dim=1)
# Compute dot product between user profile and each item feature vector
dot_scores = item_features @ user_profile  # shape: (num_items,)
cosine_sim = dot_scores / (item_norms * norm_user + 1e-8)

```

```
print("Cosine similarity of each item to the user profile:", cosine_sim.tolist())

# Exclude the items the user already liked
mask = torch.ones(item_features.size(0), dtype=torch.bool)
mask[liked_items] = False
unseen_similarity = cosine_sim * mask  # zero out seen items

# Recommend the top item based on similarity
recommended_item = torch.argmax(unseen_similarity).item()
print(f"Top recommended item for the user (content-based): Item {recommended_item}")

```

In this example, we had 5 items with 3 features each. We assumed the user liked items 0 and 2. We built the user's profile as the average of item 0's and item 2's feature vectors (essentially saying the user equally likes whatever characteristics those two items have). Then we computed the cosine similarity between this user profile vector and each item's feature vector. The item with the highest similarity (the user does not already like that) is recommended.

If you run this code, you will see the user profile and the similarity scores. The recommended item will be the one with the highest cosine similarity. Content-based logic would interpret that as *the recommended item shares many features with what the user already enjoyed.*

The following list outlines a few things to note about content-based systems:

- **Feature selection/engineering is crucial**: The quality of recommendations is directly tied to how informative the item features are. If important aspects of the items are not captured in the features, the recommender cannot use them. In our simple example, features were abstract, but imagine they were genres, and if the user likes two sci-fi movies, the profile is heavy on Sci-Fi, and we would recommend other sci-fi movies. If the user has diverse tastes, the profile can be a mix.
- **User profiles can incorporate weighting**: We used a simple average of the features that were liked. In practice, you weigh more recent interactions more heavily, or weight by how much the user wanted an item (if ratings are available, an item rated 5 stars contributes more strongly to the profile than an item rated 3 stars). There are also learning-based approaches where you train a classifier for each user based on item content (treating it like a classification or regression problem: given item content, predict the user's rating or like).
- **Cold start for users vs items**: Content-based has an advantage for new items, even if no user has seen an item, as long as it has features, it can be recommended to users whose profiles match it. However, suppose a new user arrives with no history. In this situation, a purely content-based approach cannot create a profile unless the user willingly shares their preferences or demographics that might align with item features. Typically, new users are encouraged to rate a few items or select some genres they enjoy to help get their profile started.
- **Avoiding narrow recommendations**: One pitfall of content-based systems is that they can become *too narrow,* only recommending similar items and not introducing diversity. For instance, if a user has only watched action movies, they might never see a recommendation for an acclaimed documentary because their profile does not align with it, even if they like it. Some systems address this by injecting a bit of serendipity or using exploration-based methods (e.g., occasionally recommend something outside the profile, or diversify the recommendation list).

Content-based filtering is often used in tandem with CF. For example, if a user is new (no interactions), the system might fall back to content-based recommendations using whatever information is known about them (like their stated genre preferences or the popularity of items in categories they are interested in). If an item is new, content-based methods can ensure it still gets recommended to the right users by matching features, rather than waiting for enough interactions to accumulate.

However, content-based methods alone cannot tell *how much* a user will like an item beyond what the profile suggests. CF can sometimes pick up signals like *this user might also like this* surprisingly different *item because other users with similar tastes did*, which content-based filtering would miss. This is why hybrid systems are valuable; they combine both approaches to get the best of both worlds.

Hybrid recommendation systems

Hybrid recommendation systems aim to combine collaborative and content-based filtering to mitigate their weaknesses and improve overall recommendations. There are many ways to design a hybrid:

- **Weighted hybrid**: Combine CF and content-based recommendation scores (e.g., a weighted sum) to produce a final score or ranking.
- **Switching hybrid**: Use one approach or the other based on certain conditions (for example, if the user is new or has very few interactions, rely more on content-based; otherwise, use collaborative).
- **Feature-augmented models**: Use outputs of one method as features in another, or incorporate content features into a collaborative model (this is common in model-based hybrids, where you might add item content features into the MF model).
- **Unified models**: Build a single model using interaction and content data. Many modern approaches do this by feeding both kinds of information into a machine learning model (for example, a deep neural network might take as input a user ID embedding and item content features together).

A classic example of a hybrid is the *Content-boosted CF*, where content-based predictions are used to fill in some of the missing entries of the user-item matrix to do CF. Another example is factorization machines and their deep learning variants (DeepFM, etc.), which can incorporate arbitrary features (user features, item features, and interactions) into a factorized model.

In this section, we will demonstrate one simple hybrid approach: building a model that uses user IDs (collaborative signal) and item features (content signal) to predict a rating or preference. This could be seen as a simplified version of what is sometimes called a **broad** and deep model (like Google's Wide and Deep approach for recommender systems), where one part of the model memorizes collaborative patterns (the embedding lookup for user IDs, akin to a collaborative filtering component). Another part generalizes based on content features (the layers processing item features).

Our hybrid model will be a neural network in PyTorch that does the following:

- **Input**: A user ID and an item feature vector.
- The model has an embedding for the user ID (capturing that user's latent preferences, like in MF).
- The model combines the user embedding with the item's feature vector and processes it through some layers to output a predicted rating or score.

This way, the model can learn from interactions (user ID being part of the input means it can memorize if a user likes some specific items beyond what features predict). It can generalize to new items by relying on item features (even if the item ID is new, as long as its features are there, the network can output something reasonable from the features and the user's embedding).

Let us implement and train a simple hybrid model on our toy data. We will reuse the small dataset of user-item ratings and the item features we defined earlier for a content-based example. For demonstration, our item features are just three-dimensional as before, as shown in the following code:

```
import torch.nn.functional as F

# Assume we have `ratings` list and `item_features` tensor defined from before.
# (ratings: list of (user, item, rating), item_features: tensor of shape [num_items, num_
```

```
features])

num_features = item_features.size(1)
hidden_dim = 8 # number of hidden units for our neural network

import torch.nn as nn
import torch.nn.functional as F

# Assume we have ratings list and item_features tensor defined from before
num_features = item_features.size(1)
hidden_dim = 8 # number of hidden units for our neural network

class HybridRecommender(nn.Module):
    def __init__(self, num_users, num_item_features, hidden_dim, dropout_rate=0.2):
        super(HybridRecommender, self).__init__()

        # 1. Collaborative Part: Embedding for user IDs
        self.user_emb = nn.Embedding(num_users, hidden_dim)
        nn.init.normal_(self.user_emb.weight, std=0.1)

        # 2. Content Part: Project item features to match the hidden -
dimension
        self.item_proj = nn.Linear(num_item_features, hidden_dim)

        # 3. Feed-forward network for combining user and item representations
        # Input dimension is hidden_dim * 2 (concatenated user and item vectors)
        self.fc1 = nn.Linear(hidden_dim * 2, hidden_dim)

        # Normalization and Regularization Layers
        self.bn1 = nn.BatchNorm1d(hidden_dim)
        self.dropout = nn.Dropout(dropout_rate)

        # Final output layer
        self.fc2 = nn.Linear(hidden_dim, 1)

    def forward(self, user_ids, item_feats):
        # user_ids: tensor of shape [batch_size]
        # item_feats: tensor of shape [batch_size, num_item_features]

        u_vecs = self.user_emb(user_ids) # [batch_size, hidden_dim]

        # Feature Fusion: Process item features through projection layer
        i_vecs = F.relu(self.item_proj(item_feats)) # [batch_size, hidden_dim]

```

```
        # Concatenate user embedding and processed item features
        x = torch.cat([u_vecs, i_vecs], dim=1)

        # Pass through MLP with Batch Normalization and Dropout
```

The following is a continuation of the preceding code:

```
        x = self.fc1(x)
        x = self.bn1(x)
        x = F.relu(x)
        x = self.dropout(x)

        # Output a single score (rating)
        x = self.fc2(x)
        return x.squeeze() # return 1D tensor (batch of scores)

# Instantiate model
hybrid_model = HybridRecommender(num_users, num_features, hidden_dim)
optimizer = optim.Adam(hybrid_model.parameters(), lr=0.01)
loss_fn = nn.MSELoss()

# Prepare data (same ratings list, but now need item feature for each
  example)
user_ids = torch.tensor([u for u, i, r in ratings])
item_ids = [i for u, i, r in ratings]
item_feats_tensor = torch.stack([item_features[i] for i in item_ids])
ratings_tensor = torch.tensor([r for u, i, r in ratings])

# Training loop for the hybrid model
hybrid_model.train()
for epoch in range(501):
    pred = hybrid_model(user_ids, item_feats_tensor)
    loss = loss_fn(pred, ratings_tensor)
    optimizer.zero_grad()
    loss.backward()
    optimizer.step()
    if epoch % 100 == 0:
        print(f"Epoch {epoch}: MSE = {loss.item():.4f}")

# Let's use the trained hybrid model to predict user 3's rating for item 0 (as an example)
hybrid_model.eval()
test_user = torch.tensor([3])
test_item_feat = item_features[0].unsqueeze(0)  # features for item 0
predicted_rating = hybrid_model(test_user, test_item_feat).item()
print(f"Predicted rating for User 3 on Item 0: {predicted_rating:.2f}")
```

Output:

```
Epoch 0: MSE = 11.3953
Epoch 100: MSE = 0.7215
Epoch 200: MSE = 1.3665
Epoch 300: MSE = 0.5481
Epoch 400: MSE = 0.9767
Epoch 500: MSE = 0.5969
Predicted rating for User 3 on Item 0: 3.45
```

In this hybrid architecture, we treat the user part as an embedding (allowing the model to learn each user's latent preferences) and represent the items using their concrete features. Notice that we did not just pass raw features into the network; instead, we introduced a projection layer (`self.item_proj`) to transform the item features into the same dimensional space as the user embeddings. This enables a more sophisticated feature fusion when we concatenate them.

To make this model robust and production-ready, we also integrated two critical components:

- **Batch normalization (nn.BatchNorm1d)**: Normalizes the activations between layers, which stabilizes and accelerates the training process.
- **Dropout (nn.Dropout)**: A regularization technique that randomly zeroes out a percentage of neurons during training. This prevents the network from relying too heavily on any single feature, combating overfitting.

While our toy dataset is incredibly small, these additions represent the standard blueprint for building scalable deep learning recommenders.

After training, we tested the model by asking: *What rating would user 3 give to item 0, according to the model?* The model will produce a prediction. We could similarly query any user-item pair, including ones not in the original dataset. For example, if an item had no ratings in the training set, the model could still predict it because it can rely on the item's features in combination with the user embedding. Similarly, for a new user (not in training), we would not have an embedding learned (this simple model cannot handle a genuinely new user ID it never saw—that is still a cold start issue for the user side unless we incorporate user features or have an approach to initialize new user embeddings). However, one can imagine extending this hybrid, and if we had user features (like age, location, etc.), we could include them in the input alongside or instead of user ID embedding, which would help with new users.

The output of training shows the MSE dropping as it learns. Given its flexibility (we have more parameters than data points), this hybrid model likely will overfit our tiny dataset, but in practice, one would regularize and tune it.

Real-world use of hybrids

Most production systems are hybrid in some way. For instance, Netflix uses a mix of algorithms: matrix factorization, neural networks, and metadata-based models, blended in an ensemble. Amazon's recommender might primarily use item-item CF and incorporate content-based rules for new products or categories. Spotify famously combines collaborative filtering on listening behavior with audio content analysis of songs to recommend music popular among similar users and sonically similar to what you like.

Hybrid systems can also be multi-stage: a typical pattern is a *candidate generation* stage followed by a *ranking* stage. For example, the first stage might use a fast collaborative filtering method to retrieve 500 candidate items for the user (these could be reasonably personalized but not heavily content-based). The second stage might then re-rank those 500 using a more complex model that includes content features, business rules, and fine-grained predictions to pick the top 5 to show. This two-tier approach (often CF for candidate generation and a hybrid or feature-rich model for ranking) is used by YouTube and others as it balances scalability and accuracy.

Having explored collaborative, content-based, and a simple hybrid, let us move on to the frontier. Using deep learning more extensively in recommendation systems. Our hybrid example was already a simple neural network.

Next, we will expand on deep learning techniques for recommender systems, including more advanced architectures that have been developed.

Deep learning for recommendation systems

Deep learning has made significant inroads into recommender systems over the past decade. Many modern recommenders use deep neural networks to capture non-linear relationships better and handle complex input data (such as text, images, or sequential user behavior) that earlier methods struggled with. Using neural networks for recommendation can be seen as a natural extension of what we have already done:

- The MF model we built can be viewed as a straightforward neural network, and the user and item embeddings are like the first layer (lookups) with a dot product and biases producing the output. It is essentially a linear model in the latent space.
- The hybrid model we just built is a small feed-forward neural network taking user embeddings and item features as input.

Deep learning allows us to create models that combine many sources of information and learn complex functions. Let us highlight a few deep learning approaches for recommendation:

- **Neural Collaborative Filtering** (**NCF**): This framework generalizes matrix factorization by replacing the simple dot product with a multi-layer neural architecture. For example, you take the user embedding and item embedding, concatenate them, and pass them through multiple fully connected layers to predict a score. This can learn an arbitrary function of the latent features, potentially capturing more complex interactions than a dot product. A well-known paper (*Neural Collaborative Filtering by He et al., 2017*) proposed a model called **Neural Matrix Factorization** (**NeuMF**), which is an ensemble of a dot-product (matrix factorization) component and a multi-layer perceptron component.
- **Deep hybrid models**: Neural networks can easily incorporate content features and IDs. We saw a simple example. More elaborate versions might involve multiple input towers—one for the user [which could even be a **recurrent neural network** (**RNN**) processing the user's sequence of actions or attributes] and one for the item (processing item attributes, text, etc.)—that are then combined.
- **Autoencoders for recommendation**: An autoencoder is a neural network that tries to reconstruct its input. In recommendation, one approach is to train an autoencoder to rebuild a user's interaction vector (e.g., a binary vector of which items they interacted with, of length equal to the total number of items). The hidden layer of the autoencoder becomes a dense representation of the user's preferences, and the output layer's reconstruction can be seen as predicted affinities for all items. The autoencoder is learning something akin to latent factors, but with non-linearity. Denoising and variational autoencoders have been applied to recommendations (such as the **multi-variational autoencoders** (**VAE**) model for implicit feedback recommendations, a state-of-the-art approach for specific tasks).
- **Using pre-trained networks for content**: If you have rich content, you can use deep learning to process it into features. For example, **convolutional neural networks** (**CNNs**) can extract features from product images, or **Bidirectional Encoder Representations from Transformers** (**BERT**) can embed product descriptions or movie plots and then feed those into a recommender model. This is a form of deep content-based recommendation.

Let us implement an NCF-style model to simplify our exploration. We will use only user and item IDs as inputs (no additional content) and build a multi-layer neural network to predict a rating or interaction. We already have a small dataset, and it is too small to demonstrate the full power of such a model, but we can still illustrate how you would code it:

```
class NeuralCF(nn.Module):
    def __init__(self, num_users, num_items, embed_dim, hidden_dims):
        super(NeuralCF, self).__init__()
```

```
        # Embedding layers for user and item
        self.user_emb = nn.Embedding(num_users, embed_dim)
        self.item_emb = nn.Embedding(num_items, embed_dim)
        nn.init.normal_(self.user_emb.weight, std=0.1)
        nn.init.normal_(self.item_emb.weight, std=0.1)
        # Fully connected layers for the MLP part
        # We'll create a sequential model from the list of hidden_dims
        layers = []
        input_dim = embed_dim * 2  # since we will concatenate user and item embedding
        for h in hidden_dims:
            layers.append(nn.Linear(input_dim, h))
            layers.append(nn.ReLU())
            input_dim = h
        layers.append(nn.Linear(input_dim, 1))  # final output layer
        self.mlp = nn.Sequential(*layers)

    def forward(self, user_ids, item_ids):
        u = self.user_emb(user_ids)
        v = self.item_emb(item_ids)
        # Concatenate user and item embedding vectors
        x = torch.cat([u, v], dim=1)
        # Pass through MLP
        out = self.mlp(x)
        return out.squeeze()  # return a scalar prediction

# Instantiate the neural CF model
ncf_model = NeuralCF(num_users, num_items, embed_dim=5, hidden_dims=[20, 10])
optimizer = optim.Adam(ncf_model.parameters(), lr=0.01)
loss_fn = nn.MSELoss()

user_tensor = torch.tensor([u for u, i, r in ratings])
item_tensor = torch.tensor([i for u, i, r in ratings])
rating_tensor = torch.tensor([r for u, i, r in ratings])

# Training loop
ncf_model.train()
for epoch in range(501):
    pred = ncf_model(user_tensor, item_tensor)
    loss = loss_fn(pred, rating_tensor)
    optimizer.zero_grad()
    loss.backward()
    optimizer.step()
    if epoch % 100 == 0:
        print(f"Epoch {epoch}: MSE = {loss.item():.4f}")

```

```
# Example prediction: user 0 on item 2 (which user 0 has not
  rated in our data)
ncf_model.eval()
test_user = torch.tensor([0])
test_item = torch.tensor([2])
score = ncf_model(test_user, test_item).item()
print(f"Neural CF predicted score for User 0 on Item 2: {score:.3f}")
```

In this `NeuralCF` class:

- We created user and item embeddings of size **`embed_dim`** (I set 5 in the instantiation, just as an example).
- We then define a sequence of fully connected layers as specified by **`hidden_dims`**. In this case, **`[20, 10]`** means two hidden layers: the first takes the concatenated 10-dim input (5+5 from user and item embed), maps to 20, then ReLU, then to 10, ReLU, then final output to 1.
- This is a relatively small network. In a real scenario, you may choose dimensions based on your dataset size (and include dropout or batch norm as needed).
- We train it on the known ratings with MSE loss. (If we were doing implicit feedback instead of ratings, we might train with a different loss like binary cross-entropy and have the data as 0/1 indicating interaction or not.)
- After training, we test the model's prediction for a user-item pair that was not in the training set (User 0 on Item 2). The model will output a score (which, in this case, loosely corresponds to a predicted rating).

Even though our dataset is tiny, the idea is clear: the neural network can learn any function of the user and item latent features, rather than just a linear dot product. If there are non-linear patterns (e.g., maybe a user likes *comedy and drama together* but not each alone, a weird pattern that a linear model might not capture), a neural model might. On a larger scale, NCF models have been shown to improve accuracy on benchmark datasets over traditional MF in some cases. However, they can be trickier to train and require more data to generalize because they have more parameters and flexibility.

When to apply deep learning in recommendation systems? Not every recommendation task needs deep learning. Traditional CF (like matrix factorization or nearest neighbors) remains a strong baseline. However, deep learning becomes particularly useful when:

- You have **rich features** (e.g., textual descriptions, images, audio, knowledge graph info) to combine with interaction data.
- You want to capture a **sequence of user actions** (we will cover this in the next section on advanced techniques).
- You have a large-scale problem where specialized deep models (like the two-tower **deep neural networks (DNNs)** for candidate retrieval) are needed for speed and scalability.
- Deep models are capable of multi-task learning to predict intricate or multiple goals successfully. This allows them to optimize for clicks and dwell time simultaneously through various outputs. You may notice that simpler models fail to capture particular interaction effects, possibly due to numerous feature interactions that a deep factorization model can better handle.

Deep learning models in recommendation systems also integrate well with modern training hardware [**graphics processing units (GPUs/tensor processing units (TPUs)**] and can be trained end-to-end. In contrast, some traditional methods might require more manual feature engineering or do not scale as well with more data without distributed computing frameworks.

In practice, many production systems will use deep learning in some components. For example, a user embedding might be learned by an RNN over their sequence of events (deep model) and then used in a simple dot product with item embeddings for scoring (CF), or vice versa, a deep image model might learn item embeddings if the items are images, and then be used in CF. The possibilities are endless, but the guiding principle is to use the right level of model complexity for the problem at hand.

Now that we understand the core approaches and basic deep learning implementations, let us move to **advanced techniques** that push recommendation systems further. These include sequence-aware recommendations and other cutting-edge methods often requiring deep learning.

Recommenders

Recommenders is one of the most comprehensive and mature open-source ecosystems for production-grade recommendation engines. It is part of the Linux Foundation and was initially developed at Microsoft. This repository offers a curated collection of algorithms, utilities, and best practices that bridge the gap between academic research and industrial deployment.

Overview and philosophy

The Recommenders project contributes significantly to the recommendation systems community, providing a unified framework that addresses many practical challenges when building real-world recommender systems. Under *Miguel Fierro's* and his colleagues' stewardship, the project has evolved into a model zoo of collaborative filtering, content-based, hybrid, and deep learning approaches, all designed with production scalability in mind.

What distinguishes Recommenders from other recommendation libraries is its focus on industrial-scale data handling, polished PyTorch models, and deployment pipelines that can adapt rather than require rebuilding from scratch. The repository is a learning resource for practitioners new to recommendation systems and a production-ready toolkit for experienced engineers looking to implement state-of-the-art algorithms.

Integration with PyTorch

The relationship between Recommenders and PyTorch exemplifies modern machine learning engineering practices. While the toolkit supports multiple frameworks, PyTorch is a first-class citizen for implementing NCF, deep learning models, and advanced architectures. The repository provides pre-trained weights and optimized training scripts that leverage PyTorch's dynamic computation graphs and GPU acceleration capabilities.

For practitioners working through the concepts covered in this chapter, Recommenders offers ready-to-use PyTorch implementations that can serve as reference implementations and starting points for custom development. Rather than implementing MF or NCF from scratch, developers can import these battle-tested modules directly into their projects, swap datasets, and reuse the training infrastructure.

Practical applications and evaluation framework

The repository addresses several critical gaps in the recommendation systems landscape, particularly around evaluation methodology and production deployment considerations. Recommenders provide standardized evaluation protocols, benchmark datasets, and metrics that align with industry best practices, moving beyond simple accuracy measures to consider factors like diversity, novelty, and computational efficiency.

Miguel Fierro's stewardship has ensured continuous updates aligned with current research, including optimizations for modern hardware architectures, integration with cloud services, and support for large-scale distributed training. The project's emphasis on reproducible research and fair comparison between algorithms makes it an invaluable resource for academic researchers and industry practitioners.

Reasons to consider Recommenders

For readers of this chapter working on recommendation systems, Recommenders is a natural next step after understanding the fundamental concepts. Rather than reinventing established algorithms, the repository allows practitioners to focus on domain-specific challenges, data preprocessing, and system integration while leveraging proven implementations for core recommendation logic. The project's commitment to maintaining compatibility with evolving PyTorch versions and incorporating emerging techniques ensures that systems built on this foundation remain current with the rapidly advancing field of recommendation systems.

Quick study guide

The following list is a quick guide to answer the question regarding where to go next:

- **Advanced deep learning for RecSys**: Move beyond dot products by replacing them with multilayer perceptrons (e.g., NCF/NeuMF). Experiment with *two-tower* (user + item) architectures or wide and deep models that mix memorization and generalization. TorchRec, TensorFlow Recommenders, and Google's DLRM codebase provide ready templates at an industrial scale. Pay special attention to embedding-table sharding, feature crosses, and multi-task losses (click-through **and** dwell time).
- **Sequence-aware/session-based models**: Treat the user's recent interaction history as a sentence and predict the *next word*. Start with GRU4Rec or SASRec (self-attention) and compare to plain RNNs; open benchmarks include **MovieLens-1M** sequences and **RecSys Challenge** logs. Evaluate with Recall@K and MRR on sliding windows, then add temporal & contextual features (time-of-day, device)
- **Graph-based recommendations**: Model the data as a bipartite user-item graph (plus side-info nodes) and run message-passing with a GNN (e.g., PinSage, LightGCN). Libraries such as **PyTorch Geometric** and **DGL** abstract away sampling and neighbor aggregation. Use contrastive losses or dot-product scoring to rank items; observe gains on sparse catalogs and cold-start items.
- **Reinforcement learning for recommendation systems**: Frame recommendation as a sequential decision process where each suggestion is an *action* and clicks, watch-time, or purchases are rewards. Start with contextual bandits (ε-greedy, Thompson Sampling) for live A/B tests, then investigate Deep Q-Networks or policy-gradient methods (Slate-Q, REINFORCE) to maximize long-term user value. Simulated user environments help before deploying online.

Conclusion

Recommendation systems are where data science meets user delight. In this chapter, you implemented the core families of recommenders-collaborative, content-based, and hybrid- and saw how each addresses cold-start, sparsity, and scalability differently. You also explored how deep-learning models can capture subtle nonlinear signals hidden in large-scale interaction logs, from simple multilayer perceptrons to sequence-aware architectures. Armed with these techniques, you can prototype a recommender in a Jupyter Notebook, harden it for production with TorchRec or ANN-based retrieval, and monitor it with the right online metrics. Your next challenge is choosing the model complexity level matching your data and latency budget while never losing sight of user value and ethical considerations such as fairness and privacy.

In the next chapter, we shift from understanding user preferences to processing human language by exploring NLP with PyTorch. You will discover how to transform messy text into machine-readable data through tokenization and word embeddings, and how revolutionary Transformer architectures empower applications like sentiment analysis and chatbots.

Exercises

In this exercise, you will build a hybrid recommendation system using PyTorch. A hybrid recommender combines collaborative and content-based filtering to leverage user–item interactions and items. You will create a small toy dataset of users, items, and item features (e.g., genre tags), then train a simple PyTorch model that takes a user ID, an item ID, and the item's content features to predict a user's item rating. Finally, you will use the trained model to generate recommendations for a user by predicting and ranking unrated items.

Steps:

1. **Dataset setup**: Define a small dataset with a few users, items, and known ratings. Also, create a feature vector (e.g., binary tags or genres) for each item.
2. **Model definition**: Implement a PyTorch model that embeds user IDs and item IDs (collaborative filtering) and also processes item content features (content-based). For example, concatenate the user embedding, item embedding, and content features, then pass through a small feed-forward network to output a rating.
3. **Training**: Use MSE loss to train the model on the known ratings in your toy dataset.
4. **Recommendation**: After training, pick a user and predict ratings for all items the user has not rated. Sort these predictions to output the top recommended items for that user.

Multiple choice questions

1. **Chapter-level challenges highlighted for recommender systems include:**
   a. Cold-start for new users
   b. Data sparsity in the user-item matrix
   c. Determinantal point processes
   d. Over-fitting in CNNs
2. **To predict an unseen rating with user-based memory CF, you need:**
   a. A similarity score between the target user and neighbors
   b. Neighbor users' ratings on the target item
   c. The item's complete content profile
   d. Pearson or cosine normalization of similarities
3. **The chapter names these similarity measures for neighborhood CF:**
   a. Cosine similarity
   b. Jaccard index
   c. Pearson correlation
   d. Euclidean distance
4. **Matrix factorization, as presented, learns:**
   a. Latent user vectors (embeddings)
   b. Latent item vectors (embeddings)
   c. Pre-defined genre tags as factors
   d. Optional user and item bias terms

5. **A pure content-based recommender relies on:**
   a. Item feature vectors (profiles)
   b. A user profile built from previously liked items
   c. Other users' interaction histories
   d. Cosine similarity in feature space
6. **Which approaches can alleviate cold-start for items according to the chapter?**
   a. Content-based filtering
   b. Hybrid models mixing content and CF
   c. User-user neighborhoods alone
   d. Dot-product matrix factorization without features
7. **Hybrid-system designs explicitly described include:**
   a. Weighted blending of CF and content scores
   b. Switching between methods based on data availability
   c. Feature-augmented or unified neural models
   d. Sequence-aware Transformers
8. **For evaluation, the chapter distinguishes:**
   a. RMSE and MAE as rating-oriented metrics
   b. Recall@K and NDCG@K as ranking-oriented metrics
   c. Precision@K as a rating-error metric
   d. Offline metrics versus A/B testing in production
9. **In deployment, the chapter contrasts** batch **versus** real-time **inference by stating:**
   a. Batch generation pre-computes recommendations offline
   b. Real-time scoring adapts to the user's current context
   c. Batch methods inherently require ANN indices
   d. Real-time methods must meet strict latency budgets
10. **The chapter's simple hybrid neural model accepts as direct inputs:**
   a. A learnable user-ID embedding
   b. The item's feature vector
   c. The complete sequence of past interactions
   d. An explicit dwell-time signal

Answers

1.	a,b.
2.	a,b,d.
3.	a,c.
4.	a,b,d.
5.	a,b.
6.	a,b.
7.	a,b,c.

8.	a,b.
9.	a,b,d.
10.	a,b.

Key terms

- **User-item matrix**: Sparse grid of user interactions (ratings, clicks, etc.) with items.
- **Cold-start problem**: Lack of history for a new user or item, hampering personalization.
- **Cosine similarity**: Angle-based measure used to compare rating or feature vectors.
- **Pearson correlation**: Centered similarity measure for explicit-rating CF.
- **Latent factor/embedding**: A low-dimensional vector learned for each user or item in MF and neural models.
- **MF**: Model-based CF decomposes the interaction matrix into user and item embeddings plus biases.
- **Content-based filtering**: Recommends items whose content features match a user's derived profile.
- **Hybrid recommendation system**: Combines collaborative and content signals via weighting, switching, or unified models.
- **Batch vs. real-time serving**: Offline pre-computation versus on-the-fly scoring, trading freshness against latency.
- **RMSE/MAE vs. Recall@K/NDCG**: Rating-error metrics versus ranking-quality metrics used for evaluation.

References

1. *He, X., Liao, L., Zhang, H., Nie, L., Hu, X., & Chua, T.-S. (2017). Neural Collaborative Filtering. WWW '17.*
2. *Koren, Y., Bell, R., & Volinsky, C. (2009). Matrix Factorization Techniques for Recommender Systems. IEEE Computer, 42(8), 30-37.*
3. *Rendle, S., Freudenthaler, C., Gantner, Z., & Schmidt-Thieme, L. (2012). BPR: Bayesian Personalized Ranking from Implicit Feedback. UAI '09.*
4. *Covington, P., Adams, J., & Sargin, E. (2016). Deep Neural Networks for YouTube Recommendations. RecSys '16.*
5. *Hidasi, B., Karatzoglou, A., Baltrunas, L., & Tikk, D. (2016). Session-based Recommendations with Recurrent Neural Networks. ICLR '16.*
6. *Ying, R. et al. (2018). Graph Convolutional Neural Networks for Web-Scale Recommender Systems (PinSage). KDD '18.*
7. *Wang, X. et al. (2019). LightGCN: Simplifying and Powering Graph Convolution Network for Recommendation. SIGIR '20.*
8. *Zarifis, G. et al. (2020). TorchRec: Facebook's Open-Source Library for Large-Scale Recommendation Systems. Meta AI Blog.*
9. *Zhao, S. et al. (2019). Deep Reinforcement Learning for List-wise Recommendations. arXiv:1905.12926.*
10. *Ricci, F., Rokach, L., & Shapira, B. (Eds.). (2022). Recommender Systems Handbook (3rd ed.). Springer.*

CHAPTER 17
Natural Language Processing with PyTorch

Introduction

Imagine talking to your phone's virtual assistant, searching for a song by typing a few words, or translating a text message into another language. Behind these seemingly magical feats lies the power of **natural language processing** (**NLP**), a field that allows computers to read, understand, and even generate human language.

For humans, language comes as naturally as breathing. But language is like an alien landscape for computers: ambiguous, messy, and full of hidden meaning. NLP is the bridge that helps machines cross this landscape, enabling them to transform strings of characters into knowledge, sentiment, or action.

This chapter will explore how machines learn to process, analyze, and understand text using deep learning, specifically with PyTorch. You will discover how simple tools like tokenization and embeddings allow a computer to *see* text as numbers, and how revolutionary models like Transformers have enabled applications such as chatbots, translation, and sentiment analysis. We will use well-known, manageable datasets and explain each concept with practical code and visual analogies.

Whether you dream of building chatbots, intelligent search engines, or translation tools, this chapter will give you the foundation to start with NLP in the deep learning era.

Structure

This chapter covers the following topics:

- NLP pipeline from raw text to insight
- Splitting text into meaningful pieces using tonkenization
- Embeddings give meaning to words
- Neural network models for NLP through the ages
- Attention mechanisms in neural networks
- Transformers
- Practical NLP applications or mini projects

Objectives

By the end of this chapter, you will clearly understand the essential steps and concepts that power modern NLP systems. You will see how raw text is transformed into structured data that neural networks can understand, learn why word embeddings are so robust for capturing meaning, and discover how transformer-based models have enabled machines to tackle language tasks with unprecedented accuracy. Through hands-on PyTorch code and real datasets, you will develop the skills to preprocess text, apply embeddings, use pre-trained transformer models, and evaluate your results. Whether aiming to classify text, analyze sentiment, or understand the latest advances in NLP, this chapter will equip you with the practical knowledge and confidence to experiment with language data in your projects.

NLP pipeline from raw text to insight

Have you ever wondered how a search engine finds the correct answer to your question, or how your phone autocorrects your message just as you type? A well-worn path called the NLP pipeline is at the heart of these applications. Think of this as a recipe: starting with raw text, the pipeline processes and transforms language, step by step, into something a neural network can learn from or act upon.

The NLP pipeline transforms raw, messy text into structured data that neural networks can process. Let us visualize this step-by-step journey by referring to the following figure:

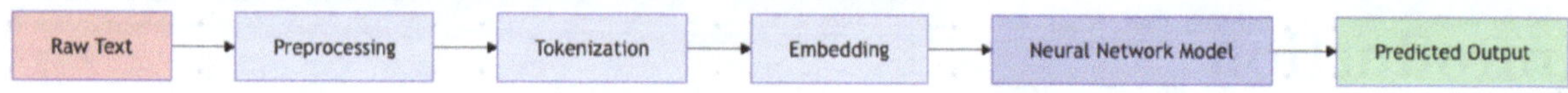

***Figure 17.1:** The journey from raw text to machine understanding*

Text preprocessing getting text ready for machines

Text in the wild is messy. People use slang, typos, emojis, and inconsistent punctuation. To help a computer *see* the structure, we first need to clean things up, a process called **preprocessing**.

Imagine trying to learn a new language by reading handwritten notes with coffee stains and doodles. Cleaning the page and straightening the lines makes learning a lot easier.

Common preprocessing steps are as follows:

1. **Lowercasing**: Makes everything uniform (e.g., *Apple* and *apple* are treated the same).
2. **Removing punctuation and special characters**: This helps avoid confusion caused by unnecessary symbols.
3. **Stripping extra spaces and HTML tags**: Cleans up digital text.
4. **(Optional) Removing stop words**: Avoid prevalent words like *the* or *is*.

Simple text cleaning

Here is how you might clean up a sentence using Python:

```
import re

def preprocess_text(text):
    # Lowercase
    text = text.lower()
    # Remove HTML tags
    text = re.sub(r'<[^>]+>', '', text)
    # Remove punctuation and numbers
    text = re.sub(r'[^a-z\s]', '', text)
    # Remove extra spaces
    text = re.sub(r'\s+', ' ', text).strip()
```

```
    return text

sample = "Hello! <br> This is an Example, with Numbers 123 and symbols :-)"
print(preprocess_text(sample))
```

This function takes any text, converts it to lowercase, and removes **Hypertext Markup Language (HTML)**, punctuation, numbers, and extra spaces. The result is a clean, machine-friendly string.

Splitting text into meaningful pieces using tokenization

After cleaning, we need to break text into smaller units called **tokens**, usually words or subwords. This is called **tokenization**.

Think of tokenization as slicing a loaf of bread. A loaf is hard to eat whole, but slices are just the right size.

Word vs. subword tokenization

When tokenizing text, you have two main approaches to choose from, each with distinct advantages:

- **Word tokenization**: Splits by spaces. Simple but can miss important parts (like *can't*).
- **Subword tokenization**: Splits into smaller, more reusable pieces (*unbelievable* | *un, believ, able*).

This is important for modern models that handle new words and typos.

Tokenizing text

Let us use the popular **`nltk`** library for word tokenization:

```
import nltk
nltk.download('punkt')

from nltk.tokenize import word_tokenize

text = "Natural Language Processing (NLP) is fun!"
tokens = word_tokenize(text)
print(tokens)
```

Here is how a sentence gets split into individual tokens:

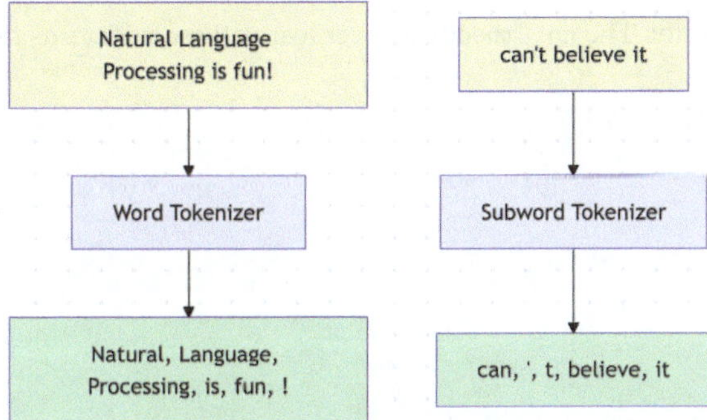

Figure 17.2: *Tokenization process*

We use library tokenizers from Hugging Face's **`transformers`** for more advanced models.

Embeddings give meaning to words

Computers cannot *understand* words as we do. They need numbers! **Embeddings** are special vectors that represent the meaning of words in a high-dimensional space.

Imagine plotting every word in English on a giant map. Words with similar meanings (*cat* and *dog*) end up close together, while unrelated words (*apple* and *democracy*) are far apart.

Beyond Simple Numerical IDs

Assigning each word a unique number (like **`cat = 1`**, **`dog = 2`**) loses all sense of meaning. **`Cat`** and **`dog`** are just as different as **`cat`** and **`refrigerator`**. Embeddings solve this by placing similar words close together.

Classic embeddings, Word2Vec, and GloVe

These methods learn word vectors from large text corpora:

- **Word2Vec**: Learns to predict a word from its context (and vice versa).
- **GloVe**: Focuses on global word co-occurrence statistics.

We usually use embeddings as part of a larger model, but understanding the idea is key.

Using PyTorch embeddings

Here is how to turn word indices into vectors in PyTorch:

```
import torch
import torch.nn as nn

# Let's say we have 10 words in our vocabulary, and we want 5-dimensional embeddings
embedding = nn.Embedding(num_embeddings=10, embedding_dim=5)

# Example sentence: [2, 8, 1] (these are word indices)
input = torch.LongTensor([2, 8, 1])
output = embedding(input)
print(output)
```

Each index is mapped to a 5D vector. The **`nn.Embedding`** layer learns these vectors as the model trains.

Word embeddings place similar words close together in high-dimensional space. The following figure shows how words with related meanings cluster together:

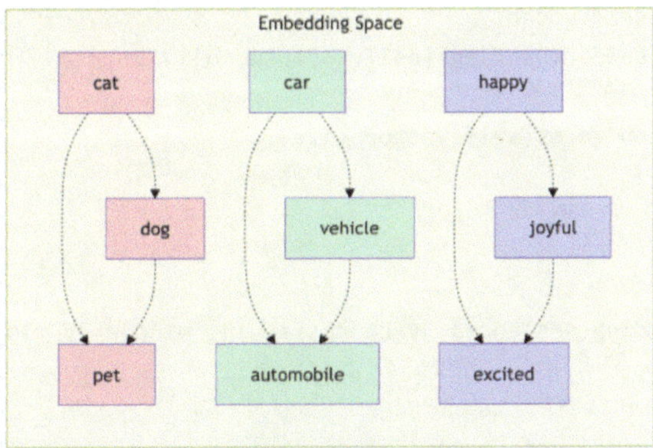

***Figure 17.3:** Similar words cluster together in embedding space*

Training your word embeddings

While most real-world word embeddings are learned from large text corpora using specialized libraries like **`gensim`** or **`torchtext`**, it is helpful first to understand the mechanics behind the scenes. The following example shows how to build a simple word embedding model from scratch, assign random vectors to each word, and visualize these embeddings in two dimensions using **t-Distributed Stochastic Neighbor Embedding** (**t-SNE**). This approach is purely for illustration and helps demystify what is happening inside more complex embedding models.

```
# Alternative Word2Vec implementation without gensim dependency issues
import numpy as np
from collections import defaultdict, Counter
import matplotlib.pyplot as plt
from sklearn.manifold import TSNE

class SimpleEmbedding:
    def __init__(self, sentences, vector_size=10, window=2, min_count=1):
        self.vector_size = vector_size
        self.window = window
        self.min_count = min_count

        # Build vocabulary
        word_counts = Counter()
        for sentence in sentences:
            word_counts.update(sentence)

        # Filter words by min_count
        self.vocab = {word: idx for idx, (word, count) in enumerate(word_counts.items())
                      if count >= min_count}

        # Initialize random embeddings
        vocab_size = len(self.vocab)
        self.embeddings = np.random.randn(vocab_size, vector_size) * 0.1
```

```

    def get_vector(self, word):
        if word in self.vocab:
            return self.embeddings[self.vocab[word]]
        else:
            return np.zeros(self.vector_size)

# Example usage
sentences = [["this", "is", "a", "cat"], ["dog", "embeddings", "are",
"useful"]]
model = SimpleEmbedding(sentences, vector_size=10, window=2, min_count=1)

# Get embedding for a word
embedding_vector = model.get_vector('embeddings')
print(f"Embedding for 'embeddings': {embedding_vector}")

# Visualize embeddings
words = list(model.vocab.keys())
vectors = [model.get_vector(word) for word in words]

# Convert vectors list to numpy array for t-SNE
vectors_array = np.array(vectors)

# Use t-SNE for dimensionality reduction
tsne = TSNE(n_components=2, random_state=0, perplexity=max(1, min(3, len(words)-1)))
Y = tsne.fit_transform(vectors_array)

plt.figure(figsize=(10, 8))
plt.scatter(Y[:, 0], Y[:, 1])
for i, word in enumerate(words):
    plt.annotate(word, (Y[i, 0], Y[i, 1]), fontsize=12)
plt.title('Word Embeddings Visualization')
plt.xlabel(‘t-SNE Component 1’)
plt.ylabel(‘t-SNE Component 2’)
plt.show()
```

In this example, we create a simple class that assigns a random vector to each word in a small vocabulary. We then use t-SNE to reduce these high-dimensional vectors to two dimensions for visualization. Notice that similar words like **cat** and **dog** may not appear close together because the vectors are random and not learned from data. In real embedding models, the training process adjusts these vectors so that words with similar meanings cluster together in the embedding space. This code helps you understand the basic mechanics of word embeddings and how they can be visualized, setting the stage for more advanced, data-driven approaches.

Neural network models for NLP through the ages

Earlier in *Chapter 12, Recurrent Neural Networks with PyTorch,* we explored how RNNs and their advanced cousin, the **long short-term memory (LSTM)** network, enable computers to process sequential data such as sentences and paragraphs. As a quick recap: RNNs keep track of immediate context, while LSTMs use special gates to remember long-term dependencies across longer texts. If you want a deeper refresher on the mechanics behind this, feel free to revisit the sections *Understanding sequential data* and *RNNs and LSTM networks* in *Chapter 12, Recurrent Neural Networks with PyTorch*. However, for this chapter, just knowing that they process text sequentially is enough.

Moving beyond recurrent neural networks

RNNs and LSTMs were a massive leap for NLP, but they struggled with long texts and were slow to train. It is like reading a book word by word and remembering every detail from the beginning, complex for humans, and even more challenging for computers.

To illustrate how RNNs and LSTMs can be used in practice, let us look at a minimal example of an LSTM for binary sentiment classification. Refer to the following code, and it will give you a hands-on feel for how these models process sequential data, even though they have limitations compared to more modern architectures like Transformers.

```
import torch
import torch.nn as nn

# Example: 5 words in vocab, 3-dim embeddings, 4 hidden units
class SentimentLSTM(nn.Module):
    def __init__(self):
        super().__init__()
        self.embedding = nn.Embedding(5, 3)
        self.lstm = nn.LSTM(3, 4, batch_first=True)
        self.fc = nn.Linear(4, 1)
    def forward(self, x):
        x = self.embedding(x)
        _, (h, _) = self.lstm(x)
        return torch.sigmoid(self.fc(h[-1]))

model = SentimentLSTM()
sample_input = torch.tensor([[0, 1, 2, 3]])  # Example input: batch of 1, 4 tokens
output = model(sample_input)
print(output)  # Output: tensor([[0.5...]], grad_fn=<SigmoidBackward0>)
```

This code defines a simple **`SentimentLSTM`** class that inherits from **`nn.Module.`** The model consists of an embedding layer (to convert word indices into vectors), an LSTM layer (to process the sequence), and a fully connected layer (to predict sentiment). The **`forward`** method defines how the input data flows through the model. We then create an instance of the model and pass a sample input through it. The output is a probability (between 0 and 1) representing the sentiment of the input text. This example demonstrates the basic structure of an LSTM-based sentiment classifier, even though it is a simplified version for demonstration purposes.

Attention mechanisms in neural networks

Imagine reading a long paragraph. You do not remember every word; your mind zooms in on the most critical parts. This is the idea behind the attention mechanism.

Attention lets the model decide which words in the sequence are most relevant to the current prediction, focusing computational power where it matters. The following diagram illustrates the core components of a Transformer block, showing how information flows through the attention and feedforward layers:

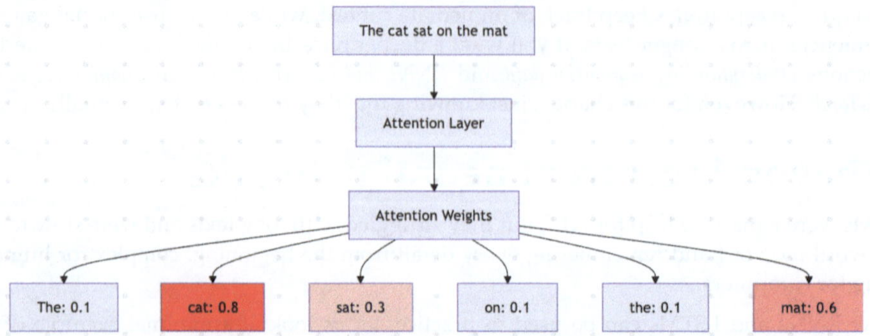

Figure 17.4: Attention highlights the essential words for each task

Transformers

While attention started as a helper for RNNs, the **Transformer** architecture (introduced in the paper *Attention is All You Need*, 2017) ditched recurrence entirely. Instead, Transformers use layers of self-attention and feedforward networks to process sequences in parallel, allowing them to scale up and learn complex patterns.

If RNNs read a book one word at a time, Transformers read the whole page instantly, instantly picking out connections between words, no matter how far apart they are.

Key features of Transformers

What makes Transformers so revolutionary? Three core innovations set them apart from earlier architectures:

- **Self-attention**: Each word can *look* at every other word.
- **Parallel processing**: Faster to train.
- **Scalable**: The backbone of today's state-of-the-art models (like GPT, BERT, etc.).

The NLP pipeline transforms raw, messy text into structured data that neural networks can process. The following figure traces this transformation journey from initial input through each processing stage to the final output:

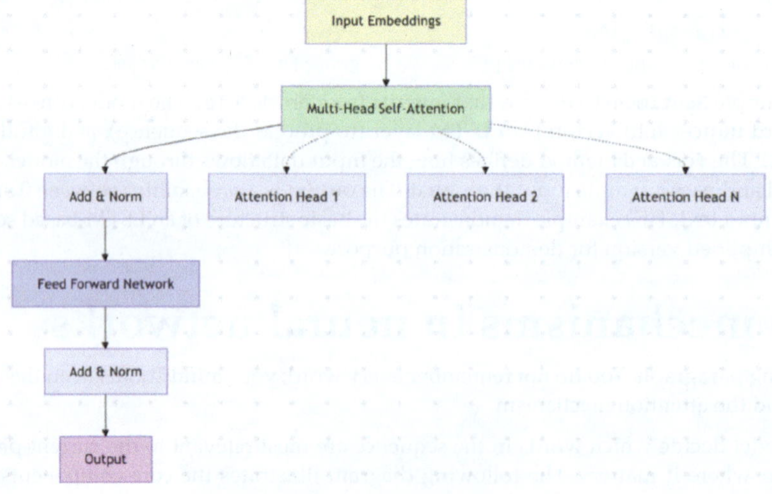

Figure 17.5: The core of a Transformer block

Using Transformers in practice

Thanks to libraries like Hugging Face's transformers, you do not need to build a Transformer from scratch. Pre-trained models can be used for classification, sentiment analysis, translation, and more.

The beauty of pre-trained Transformers lies in their versatility and accessibility. Models like BERT, GPT, and RoBERTa have already learned rich language representations from billions of words, capturing grammar, context, and even some world knowledge. You can leverage this learning in two ways: either use it directly through simple pipelines for common tasks, or fine-tune it on your specific dataset to adapt its knowledge to your particular domain.

The Hugging Face ecosystem has democratized access to state-of-the-art NLP by providing thousands of pre-trained models through a unified interface. Whether you need to analyze customer reviews, translate documents, answer questions, or generate text, there is likely a pre-trained model ready to use. This approach saves weeks or months of training time and requires far fewer computational resources than training from scratch.

In the following sections, we will explore how to use these models through high-level pipelines and how to fine-tune them for custom tasks. Even if you are working on a unique problem, starting with a pre-trained Transformer typically yields better results than building a model from the ground up.

Practical application of pre-trained Transformers for sentiment analysis

Let us see how all these pieces fit together. Using a pre-trained DistilBERT model, we will use the IMDB movie reviews dataset or randomly written reviews to classify sentiment, positive or negative.

Here is how you can perform sentiment analysis with just a few lines of code:

```
from transformers import pipeline

# Load a sentiment-analysis pipeline with a pre-trained DistilBERT model
classifier = pipeline("sentiment-analysis")

results = classifier([
    "I absolutely loved this movie, it was fantastic!",
    "This was the worst film I've ever seen."
])

for result in results:
    print(f"Label: {result['label']}, Score: {result['score']:.2f}")
```

The pipeline handles preprocessing, tokenization, embedding, and prediction for you.

You can swap in your dataset and experiment with other models (e.g., distilbert-base-uncased for smaller/faster runs).

Fine-tuning on custom data

If you want to adapt a model to a new dataset (fine-tuning), use a few more lines with PyTorch and Hugging Face. However, the above pattern works out of the box for most cases.

Fine-tuning is the process of taking a pre-trained model and continuing its training on your specific dataset. This allows the model to adapt its general language understanding to your particular domain, whether that is medical texts, legal documents, customer support tickets, or social media posts. The pre-trained model provides a strong foundation, and fine-tuning helps it specialize.

The key advantage of fine-tuning over training from scratch is efficiency. While training a Transformer from scratch might require millions of examples and weeks of GPU time, fine-tuning can achieve excellent results with just thousands (or even hundreds) of labeled examples and a few hours of training. The model already understands language structure; you are simply teaching it the nuances of your specific task.

When fine-tuning, you typically freeze some of the lower layers of the model (which capture general language features) and update only the upper layers and the task-specific head. This prevents overfitting on small datasets while still allowing the model to adapt to your domain. You also use a smaller learning rate than you would for training from scratch, making careful adjustments rather than dramatic changes to the pre-trained weights.

The Hugging Face Trainer **application programming interface (API)** simplifies this process significantly. It handles the training loop, evaluation, checkpointing, and logging with minimal code. For most applications, you can achieve strong performance by loading a pre-trained model, adding a task-specific classification head, and fine-tuning on your labeled data for just a few epochs.

Fine-tuning BERT for custom tasks

With Hugging Face Transformers, you can fine-tune BERT for classification in just a few lines. Here is a minimal example for inference (fine-tuning requires a dataset and more setup):

```
from transformers import pipeline

classifier = pipeline("sentiment-analysis")
result = classifier("PyTorch makes NLP easy!")
print(result)  # Output: [{'label': 'POSITIVE', 'score': 0.99...}]
```

Practical NLP applications or mini-projects

Now that you understand the fundamental concepts and tools of NLP, it is time to see them in action. The following mini-projects demonstrate how to apply pre-trained Transformer models to real-world language tasks using just a few lines of code. Each project addresses a common NLP challenge and shows you how to leverage the power of models like BERT without needing extensive training data or computational resources.

These examples are intentionally concise and practical. They use Hugging Face's pipeline API, which abstracts away much of the complexity while still delivering production-quality results. As you work through each mini-project, pay attention to how the same underlying Transformer architecture adapts to completely different tasks, from extracting entities to generating summaries. This versatility is what makes modern NLP so powerful.

You can run these examples immediately on your own text data, making them perfect starting points for your own projects. Whether you are analyzing customer feedback, building a chatbot, or extracting information from documents, these patterns will serve as your foundation.

Mini-project 1: Named entity recognition

Extracting names of people, organizations, and locations from news articles or documents is crucial for information retrieval, search engines, and knowledge graphs.

Let us use a pre-trained model to identify and categorize entities in a sentence automatically. The following code demonstrates how to load a NER pipeline and apply it to sample text:

```
from transformers import pipeline

ner = pipeline("ner", grouped_entities=True)
print(ner("Hugging Face is based in New York City."))
```

This code uses Hugging Face's NER pipeline to find, and group named entities in the input text. The output will show which words are recognized as organizations or locations, making extracting structured information from unstructured text easy.

Mini-project 2: Text summarization

Automatically summarizing long articles or reports helps users quickly grasp the main points without reading the entire text.

Using a pre-trained summarization model, here is how to generate a concise summary of a longer text:

```
from transformers import pipeline

summarizer = pipeline("summarization")
text = "Machine learning is a field of artificial
intelligence that uses statistical techniques to give computer
systems the ability to learn from data."
print(summarizer(text))
```

The summarization pipeline condenses the input text into a shorter version, highlighting the most critical information. This is especially useful for news aggregation, research, and content curation.

Mini-project 3: Sentiment analysis

Understanding customer opinions in reviews or social media posts helps businesses monitor brand reputation and improve products.

Let us analyze the sentiment of a sentence to determine if it is positive or negative using the following code:

```
from transformers import pipeline

classifier = pipeline(«sentiment-analysis»)
result = classifier("I love using PyTorch for deep learning!")
print(result)
```

This code classifies the sentiment of the input text as positive or negative, along with a confidence score. It is a quick way to gauge public opinion or customer satisfaction from text data.

Mini-project 4: Question answering

Building systems that can answer questions from documents or FAQs is essential for chatbots, virtual assistants, and customer support.

Using a pre-trained model, here is how to extract an answer to a specific question from a given context.

```
from transformers import pipeline

qa = pipeline("question-answering")
context = "PyTorch is an open-source machine learning library based on the Torch library."
question = "What is PyTorch based on?"
print(qa(question=question, context=context))
```

The question-answering pipeline takes a question and a context paragraph and returns the most relevant answer in the text. This is the foundation for building intelligent Q&A systems.

Mini-project 5: Text generation

Generating text automatically is valid for creative writing, chatbots, and content creation tools. Let us develop a short text given a prompt using a language model.

```
from transformers import pipeline

generator = pipeline("text-generation", model="distilgpt2")
prompt = "Deep learning with PyTorch is"
print(generator(prompt, max_length=20, num_return_sequences=1))
```

This code uses a pre-trained language model to continue the given prompt. The model predicts the following words, creating coherent and contextually relevant text, which can be used for brainstorming, dialogue systems, or creative applications.

Conclusion

NLP is the secret sauce behind many innovative daily applications, from search engines to translation apps, chatbots, and beyond. In this chapter, you have learned how text is transformed from messy raw data into structured inputs for neural networks, how embeddings give meaning to words, and why Transformer models have become the backbone of modern NLP.

Armed with PyTorch, Hugging Face, and your new knowledge, you are ready to explore language tasks ranging from sentiment analysis to question answering. As you dive deeper, remember that language is rich and ever-evolving. The tools you have learned are your compass for exploring this exciting landscape.

In the next chapter, we shift from understanding language to understanding images, exploring computer vision techniques with PyTorch. You will learn how to classify images, detect objects, and segment scenes using powerful pre-trained models and transfer learning.

Exercises

Complete the following exercises to test your understanding:

1. **Text preprocessing challenge**: Take the following messy text and write a preprocessing function to clean it: "Hello!!! This is a <b>GREAT</b> example with 123 numbers & symbols @#$%"

   Your function should remove HTML tags, convert to lowercase, remove numbers and special characters, and normalize whitespace.
2. **Custom tokenization**: Write a simple tokenizer that splits text by spaces and punctuation. Test it on: *Don't you think NLP is amazing?*
3. **Embedding exploration**: Using the SimpleWord2Vec class from the chapter, create embeddings for a larger vocabulary (at least 20 words) and visualize them. Try to include words from different categories (animals, colors, emotions).
4. **LSTM modification**: Modify the SentimentLSTM class to:
   - Accept variable vocabulary size as a parameter.
   - Add a dropout layer for regularization.
   - Return both the prediction and the hidden state.
5. **Pipeline comparison**: Compare the results of sentiment analysis on the exact text using different pre-trained models:
   - "*sentiment-analysis*" (default)

- "*cardiffnlp/twitter-roberta-base-sentiment-latest*"
- Test on: "*The movie was okay, not great but not terrible either.*"

6. **Multi-task NLP**: Create a function that takes a text input and returns:
    - Sentiment analysis result
    - Named entities found
    - A summary (if the text is long enough)
    - Test it on a news article or product review.
7. **Custom question-answering**: Create a simple FAQ system using the question-answering pipeline. Prepare a context about PyTorch and test various questions about it.

Multiple choice questions

1. **What is the primary purpose of text preprocessing in NLP?**
    a. To make text shorter
    b. To convert text into a format suitable for machine learning models
    c. To translate text into different languages
    d. To generate new text
2. **Which tokenization approach is better for handling out-of-vocabulary words?**
    a. Word-level tokenization
    b. Character-level tokenization
    c. Subword tokenization
    d. Sentence-level tokenization
3. **What is the main advantage of word embeddings over one-hot encoding?**
    a. They are faster to compute
    b. They capture semantic relationships between words
    c. They use less memory
    d. They are easier to interpret
4. **What does a high attention weight indicate in the attention mechanism?**
    a. The word is longer
    b. The word appears frequently
    c. The word is more relevant for the current prediction
    d. The word is at the beginning of the sentence
5. **What is the key innovation of the Transformer architecture?**
    a. Using convolutional layers
    b. Processing sequences in parallel with self-attention
    c. Using only recurrent layers
    d. Eliminating the need for embeddings

6. **Which of the following is not a common NLP task?**
   a. Sentiment analysis
   b. Named entity recognition
   c. Image classification
   d. Text summarization
7. **What does fine-tuning a pre-trained model mean?**
   a. Adjusting hyperparameters
   b. Training the model from scratch
   c. Adapting a pre-trained model to a specific task with additional training
   d. Reducing the model size
8. **What does the embedding layer do in the context of LSTM for NLP?**
   a. Reduces the sequence length
   b. Converts word indices to dense vectors
   c. Applies attention mechanism
   d. Generates the final prediction
9. **Which Hugging Face pipeline would you use for extracting people and organization names from text?**
   a. "sentiment-analysis"
   b. "question-answering"
   c. "ner"
   d. "text-generation"
10. **What is the main limitation of RNNs compared to Transformers?**
    a. RNNs cannot handle text data
    b. RNNs process sequences sequentially, making them slower and less effective for long sequences
    c. RNNs require more memory
    d. RNNs cannot be trained with backpropagation

Answers

1.	b.
2.	c.
3.	b.
4.	c.
5.	b.
6.	c.
7.	c.
8.	b.
9.	c.
10.	b.

Key terms

- **Natural language processing (NLP)**: A field of artificial intelligence focused on enabling computers to understand, interpret, and generate human language.
- **Text preprocessing**: The process of cleaning and preparing raw text data for analysis or modeling, including steps like lowercasing, removing punctuation, and tokenization.
- **Tokenization**: The process of splitting text into smaller units, such as words, subwords, or characters, for easier analysis.
- **Word embeddings**: Dense vector representations of words that capture semantic meaning and relationships between words.
- **Word2Vec**: A popular algorithm for learning word embeddings based on predicting context words from a target word (or vice versa).
- **GloVe**: (Global Vectors for Word Representation) An unsupervised learning algorithm for obtaining vector representations for words by aggregating global word-word co-occurrence statistics.
- **Recurrent neural network (RNN)**: A type of neural network designed to process sequential data by maintaining a hidden state across time steps.
- **Long short-term memory (LSTM)**: An advanced RNN architecture that helps models remember information over long sequences and mitigates the vanishing gradient problem.
- **Attention mechanism**: A neural network component that allows models to focus on specific parts of the input sequence when making predictions.
- **Transformer**: A deep learning architecture that relies on self-attention mechanisms to process sequences in parallel, enabling efficient modeling of long-range dependencies.
- **Bidirectional Encoder Representations from Transformers (BERT)**: A pre-trained Transformer-based model widely used for various NLP tasks.
- **Fine-tuning**: The process of adapting a pre-trained model to a specific task or dataset by continuing training on new data.
- **Named entity recognition (NER)**: An NLP task that identifies and classifies entities (such as people, organizations, and locations) in text.
- **Sentiment analysis**: The process of determining the emotional tone or opinion expressed in a piece of text.
- **Text summarization**: Automatically generating a concise summary of a longer text document.
- **Question answering**: An NLP task where a model extracts or generates answers to questions based on a given context.

References

1. *Vaswani, A., Shazeer, N., Parmar, N., Uszkoreit, J., Jones, L., Gomez, A. N., ... & Polosukhin, I. (2017).* **https://arxiv.org/abs/1706.03762**
2. *Mikolov, T., Chen, K., Corrado, G., & Dean, J. (2013).* **https://arxiv.org/abs/1301.3781**.
3. *Pennington, J., Socher, R., & Manning, C. D. (2014).* **https://nlp.stanford.edu/pubs/glove.pdf**. *Proceedings of the 2014 Conference on Empirical Methods in Natural Language Processing (EMNLP).*
4. *Devlin, J., Chang, M. W., Lee, K., & Toutanova, K. (2018).* **https://arxiv.org/abs/1810.04805**
5. *Wolf, T., Debut, L., Sanh, V., Chaumond, J., Delangue, C., Moi, A., ... & Rush, A. M. (2020).* **https://arxiv.org/abs/1910.03771** *Proceedings of the 2020 Conference on Empirical Methods in Natural Language Processing: System Demonstrations.*

6. *PyTorch Documentation:* **https://pytorch.org/docs/stable/index.html**
7. *Hugging Face Transformers Documentation:* **https://huggingface.co/docs/transformers/index**
8. *Jurafsky, D., & Martin, J. H. (2023). Speech and Language Processing* (3rd ed.). **https://web.stanford.edu/~jurafsky/slp3/**

CHAPTER 18
Computer Vision with PyTorch

Introduction

In previous chapters, we explored how neural networks process structured data, text, and sequences. *However, what about the world of images?* Computer vision is one of artificial intelligence's most exciting and impactful fields, from recognizing faces in photos to enabling self-driving cars to see the road.

Computer vision enables machines to interpret and understand the visual world. With the help of deep learning and PyTorch, we can now build systems that classify images, detect objects, and even segment every pixel in a scene. This chapter will embark on a hands-on journey through computer vision's foundations and practical applications, focusing on accessible, real-world examples.

This chapter builds upon foundational concepts introduced in earlier chapters, such as image classification and transfer learning (refer to *Chapter 10, Training Neural Networks with PyTorch,* for a detailed introduction). Here, we revisit these techniques with a focus on practical applications in computer vision using PyTorch, including object detection and image segmentation. Readers familiar with the basics may skip the initial sections and focus on the advanced topics and mini-projects.

Structure

This chapter covers the following topics:

- Setup and data preparation
- Downloading and organizing data
- Understanding image data
- Data augmentation and preprocessing
- Transfer learning for image classification
- Object detection with pre-trained models
- Image segmentation with pre-trained models
- Visualizing model predictions
- Working with custom dataset
- Evaluating model performance
- Troubleshooting and best practices
- Object detection with a pre-trained model

Objectives

This chapter aims to provide a comprehensive, beginner-friendly introduction to computer vision using PyTorch. We will start by understanding how images are represented as data, then move on to essential preprocessing and augmentation techniques. You will learn how to leverage powerful pre-trained models for classification, detection, and segmentation tasks, and how to visualize and interpret their predictions. Through a hands-on mini project, you will gain practical experience building your computer vision applications. By the end, you will have the knowledge and confidence to tackle real-world vision problems and continue your journey in this exciting field.

Setup and data preparation

Before diving into computer vision tasks, setting up our environment with the right tools is essential. PyTorch and torchvision provide the core deep learning and vision functionality, while **Python Imaging Library** (**PIL**) and matplotlib help us load and visualize images. Setting up these libraries ensures we can efficiently handle image data, perform transformations, and display results throughout this chapter.

Import the required libraries using the following code:

```
import torch
import torchvision
import torchvision.transforms as transforms
from torchvision.datasets import ImageFolder
from torch.utils.data import DataLoader
from PIL import Image
import matplotlib.pyplot as plt
import numpy as np
```

Downloading and organizing data

For our hands-on examples, we will use the CIFAR-10 dataset. The **Canadian Institute for Advanced Research** (**CIFAR-10**) is a popular benchmark in computer vision. CIFAR-10 contains 60,000 color images across 10 different classes, such as airplanes, cars, birds, and cats. This dataset is ideal for beginners because it is small, well-labeled, and easy to work with. We will also apply normalization to standardize the pixel values, which helps the model learn more effectively.

We will also apply normalization to standardize the pixel values. Because we will later use models pre-trained on the ImageNet dataset, we must normalize our CIFAR-10 images using ImageNet's specific mean and standard deviation across the RGB channels. This ensures the pre-trained model interprets our new images correctly:

```
# Download and load the CIFAR-10 dataset.
transform = transforms.Compose([
    transforms.ToTensor(),
    transforms.Normalize((0.485, 0.456, 0.406), (0.229, 0.224, 0.225))
])

trainset = torchvision.datasets.CIFAR10(root='./data', train=True,
                                        download=True, transform=transform)
trainloader = DataLoader(trainset, batch_size=32, shuffle=True)

testset = torchvision.datasets.CIFAR10(root='./data', train=False,
```

```
                                         download=True, transform=transform)
testloader = DataLoader(testset, batch_size=32, shuffle=False)
```

This code downloads the CIFAR-10 dataset, applies normalization to each image, and prepares the data for training and testing using PyTorch's DataLoader. The DataLoader handles batching and shuffling, which are essential for efficient training and ensuring the model sees a good mix of images in each epoch.

Understanding image data

Before training any model, it is crucial to understand the structure of your data. In computer vision, images are represented as grid pixels, with each pixel containing color information. In PyTorch, images are stored as tensors with the shape (channels, height, width), where the channels correspond to **Red, Green, and Blue** (**RGB**) values. Visualizing a few images from the dataset helps us verify that the data is loaded correctly and gives us an intuition for what the model will see.

Let us visualize a few images generated from the following dataset:

```
# Lead-in: Display a batch of images from CIFAR-10.
dataiter = iter(trainloader)
images, labels = next(dataiter)

def imshow(img):
    img = img / 2 + 0.5 # unnormalize
    npimg = img.numpy()
    plt.imshow(np.transpose(npimg, (1, 2, 0)))
    plt.show()

imshow(torchvision.utils.make_grid(images[:4]))
```

The following are the results:

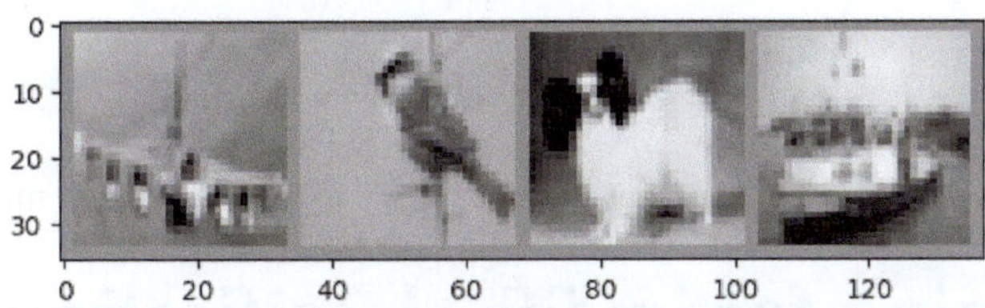

***Figure 18.1:** Random subset from CIFAR*

By displaying the first four images in a batch, we can quickly check for any data loading or preprocessing issues. This step also helps us spot potential problems, such as mislabeled images or class imbalance, before we start training.

Data augmentation and preprocessing

Data augmentation techniques such as random flipping and cropping were introduced in *Chapter 9, Building Blocks of Neural Networks in PyTorch*. This chapter extends these concepts with additional augmentations and demonstrates their impact on more complex vision models.

Data augmentation is a powerful technique that artificially increases the diversity of your training data by applying random transformations to the images. This simulates real-world variations, such as changes in orientation, lighting, or scale, and helps the model generalize better to new data. Augmentation is significant when you have a limited dataset, as it reduces the risk of overfitting.

Augmentation is significant when you have a limited dataset, as it reduces the risk of overfitting:

```
# Define a data augmentation pipeline.
augment_transform = transforms.Compose([
    transforms.RandomHorizontalFlip(),
    transforms.RandomRotation(10),
    transforms.ColorJitter(brightness=0.2, contrast=0.2),
    transforms.ToTensor(),
    # Use standard ImageNet statistics here too!
    transforms.Normalize(mean=[0.485, 0.456, 0.406],
                         std=[0.229, 0.224, 0.225])
])
```

The augmentation pipeline above randomly flips, rotates, and adjusts the brightness and contrast of each image before converting it to a tensor. Depending on your specific dataset and task, you can customize this pipeline to include other transformations, such as cropping or adding noise, as shown in the following figure:

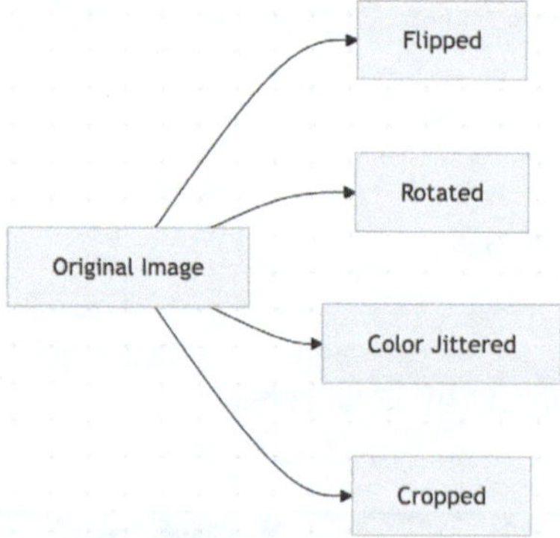

Figure 18.2: *Data augmentation*

Data augmentation creates new training samples by transforming the original images, making models more robust.

Transfer learning for image classification

As introduced in *Chapter 10, Training Neural Networks with PyTorch*, transfer learning leverages pre-trained models like ResNet to accelerate training on new datasets. Here, we briefly recap this process with PyTorch, emphasizing its application in computer vision tasks beyond simple classification, such as object detection and segmentation.

Using a pre-trained model

The CIFAR-10 dataset and basic image classification pipeline were covered in *Chapters 9, Building Blocks of Neural Networks in PyTorch, and Chapter 10, Training Neural Networks with PyTorch.* We include a concise example to set the stage for more advanced computer vision tasks. Readers familiar with this can proceed to the object detection and segmentation sections.

The following code demonstrates how to benefit from a model's prior knowledge by loading a pre-trained ResNet-18, freezing its layers, and customizing the final layer for a specific classification problem:

```
# Load a pre-trained ResNet-18 and adapt it for CIFAR-10.
import torch.nn as nn
from torchvision.models import resnet18, ResNet18_Weights

# 1. Specify the weights to load (DEFAULT gets the best available ImageNet weights)
weights = ResNet18_Weights.DEFAULT

# 2. Load the model using the weights parameter instead of pretrained=True
model = resnet18(weights=weights)

for param in model.parameters():
    param.requires_grad = False # Freeze all layers

num_classes = 10
model.fc = nn.Linear(model.fc.in_features, num_classes) # Replace final layerl
```

In this example, we load a pre-trained ResNet-18 model. Notice that instead of using the older, deprecated **`pretrained=True`** argument, we explicitly pass **`weights=ResNet18_Weights.DEFAULT`**. This modern approach ensures PyTorch downloads the most up-to-date and accurate weights available. We then freeze its existing layers to retain the learned features, and replace the final fully connected layer to match the number of classes in CIFAR-10.

Training the model

Since we are using transfer learning, we only need to train the final layer of the model. The optimizer updates the weights of this layer based on the loss function, which measures how well the model's predictions match the actual labels. This focused training speeds up the process and helps prevent overfitting:

```
# Lead-in: Train only the final layer of the model.
import torch.optim as optim

criterion = nn.CrossEntropyLoss()
optimizer = optim.Adam(model.fc.parameters(), lr=0.001)

# Training loop (simplified for demonstration)
for epoch in range(2):  # Use more epochs for real training
    for images, labels in trainloader:
        optimizer.zero_grad()
        outputs = model(images)
        loss = criterion(outputs, labels)
        loss.backward()
        optimizer.step()
```

This training loop updates only the final layer's weights, allowing the model to adapt to the new dataset quickly. In practice, you would train for more epochs and monitor the loss and accuracy to ensure the model learns effectively. If the model is not improving, consider adjusting the learning rate or trying different data augmentations.

Object detection with pre-trained models

Object detection is a key task in computer vision, enabling models to locate and classify multiple objects within an image. Real-world applications include autonomous vehicles, security systems, and medical imaging. PyTorch provides powerful pre-trained models like Faster **Region-based Convolutional Neural Network (R-CNN)**, which can detect a wide variety of objects with high accuracy. *(Note: To run the following examples, ensure you have cloned this book's official GitHub repository and your working directory is set to this chapter's folder, where* sample.jpg *and* sample2.jpg *are provided.)* Let us see this in action:

```
#  Use a pre-trained Faster R-CNN to detect objects in an image.
from torchvision.models.detection import fasterrcnn_resnet50_fpn
import matplotlib.pyplot as plt
import matplotlib.patches as patches

detector = fasterrcnn_resnet50_fpn(pretrained=True)
detector.eval()

img = Image.open('sample.jpg')
transform = transforms.Compose([transforms.ToTensor()])
img_tensor = transform(img)
with torch.no_grad():
    prediction = detector([img_tensor])[0]
print("Detected classes:", prediction['labels'])
print("Bounding boxes:", prediction['boxes'])

# Add visualization with minimal code changes
fig, ax = plt.subplots(1, figsize=(12, 8))
ax.imshow(img)

# Filter detections by confidence (optional)
confidence_threshold = 0.5
scores = prediction['scores']
boxes = prediction['boxes']
labels = prediction['labels']

# Draw bounding boxes
for box, score, label in zip(boxes, scores, labels):
    if score > confidence_threshold:  # Only show confident detections
        x1, y1, x2, y2 = box
        width = x2 - x1
        height = y2 - y1

        # Create rectangle patch
        rect = patches.Rectangle((x1, y1), width, height,
                                 linewidth=2, edgecolor='red', facecolor='none')
```

```
            ax.add_patch(rect)

            # Add label
            ax.text(x1, y1-5, f'Class {label.item()}: {score:.2f}',
                    bbox=dict(boxstyle="round,pad=0.3", facecolor='yellow', alpha=0.7),
                    fontsize=10)

ax.axis('off')
plt.title('Object Detection Results')
plt.tight_layout()
plt.show()
```

Results show the detected classes in tensor format. For each detected object, we also get the bounding boxes (X, Y coordinates), which, in tensor format, are basically an array of pixel coordinates:

```
Detected classes: tensor([ 2,  1, 31, 62,  1, 31,  1, 33,  1,  1, 31, 19, 27, 33,  1,  1,  7, 31,
        31, 62, 62,  1,  1, 15, 51,  1, 62,  1,  2, 62, 62,  1, 31, 27, 21,  1,
        62,  1, 31, 33, 62,  1, 31, 31,  2,  2, 31, 31,  1,  1, 31,  1,  1, 62,
         1,  1,  1, 18, 22,  1,  1,  1, 15,  1,  1,  1,  1, 31, 62,  1, 62])
Bounding boxes: tensor([[4.1036e+02, 9.6325e+02, 9.7937e+02, 1.3198e+03],
        [4.7454e+02, 6.2220e+02, 6.4234e+02, 9.8298e+02],
```

The image shows the regions where objects are detected with the preceding code:

Figure 18.3: *Resulting image with bounding boxes for object detection*

This code uses a pre-trained Faster R-CNN model to detect objects in an image and visualize the results. The model outputs each detected object's bounding boxes, class labels, and confidence scores. We can focus on the most reliable predictions by filtering detections based on confidence. You can experiment with different images or adjust the confidence threshold to see how the model performs in various scenarios.

Image segmentation with pre-trained models

While object detection draws boxes around objects, image segmentation goes further by labeling each pixel in the image. Semantic segmentation assigns a class to every pixel, allowing for precise scene understanding. This is especially useful in medical imaging, autonomous driving, and robotics applications, as shown in the following code:

```
from torchvision.models.segmentation import deeplabv3_resnet50
import matplotlib.pyplot as plt
import numpy as np
from PIL import Image

# Load and preprocess the image
img = Image.open('sample2.jpg').convert('RGB')
transform = transforms.Compose([transforms.ToTensor()])
img_tensor = transform(img).unsqueeze(0)

# Get the segmentation mask
segmenter = deeplabv3_resnet50(pretrained=True)
segmenter.eval()
with torch.no_grad():
    output = segmenter(img_tensor)['out'][0]
mask = output.argmax(0).byte().cpu().numpy()

# Convert original image to numpy and resize to match mask
img_np = np.array(img)
# Resize the original image to match the mask size
img_resized = np.array(Image.fromarray(img_np).resize((mask.shape[1], mask.shape[0])))

# Create a color mask with random colors for each class
np.random.seed(42)
num_classes = mask.max() + 1
colors = np.random.randint(0, 255, size=(num_classes, 3), dtype=np.uint8)
color_mask = colors[mask]

# Blend the resized image and the color mask
alpha = 0.5
overlay = (alpha * img_resized + (1 - alpha) * color_mask).astype(np.uint8)

plt.figure(figsize=(10, 6))
plt.imshow(overlay)
plt.axis('off')
plt.title('Segmentation Overlay (All Classes)')
plt.show()
```

The following figure illustrates the results:

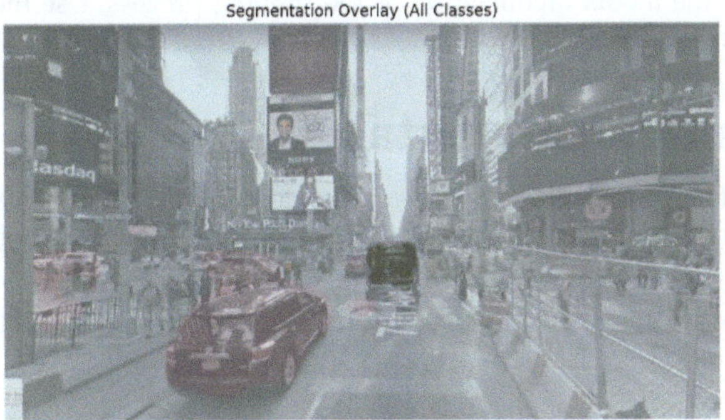

Figure 18.4: *Image segmentation results*

This code demonstrates how to visualize image segmentation results by overlaying the predicted mask on top of the original image. First, the image is loaded and preprocessed, then passed through a pre-trained DeepLabV3 model to obtain a segmentation mask, where each pixel is assigned a class label. Since the output mask may not match the original image's size, the code resizes the image to align with the mask's dimensions. To make the segmentation visually clear, each class in the mask is assigned a random color, creating a colorful mask that highlights different regions the model identifies. The original image and the color mask are then blended using a transparency factor, resulting in an overlay that allows both the original content and the segmentation results to be seen simultaneously. Finally, the combined image is displayed, providing an intuitive and informative visualization of how the model interprets and segments the scene. This approach works with any image, as long as the objects present are among the classes the model was trained to recognize.

Visualizing model predictions

Visualizing the model's predictions is an essential step in evaluating its performance. We can quickly spot patterns, strengths, and weaknesses in the model's behavior by comparing the predicted labels to the actual images. This hands-on inspection complements quantitative metrics and helps build intuition about the model's decision-making process.

The following code prints the predicted class and shows a mini grid with the image previews:

```
# Lead-in: Show images with predicted labels.
outputs = model(images)
_, predicted = torch.max(outputs, 1)
imshow(torchvision.utils.make_grid(images[:4]))
print('Predicted:', ' '.join(f'{trainset.classes[p]}' for p in predicted[:4]))
```

The following figure illustrates the result:

```
Predicted: airplane, deer, ship, airplane
```

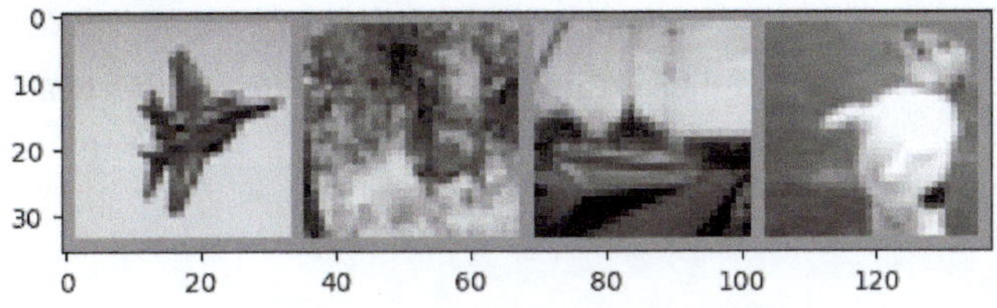

Figure 18.5: *Image classification prediction*

The output shows the predicted class for each image in the batch. Consistent errors or misclassifications may indicate issues with the data, the model architecture, or the training process. Use these insights to guide further experimentation and improvement.

Working with custom datasets

You will want to train a model on your images in many real-world projects rather than a standard dataset. PyTorch's **ImageFolder** class makes this process straightforward, as long as your photos are organized into folders by class. This approach is flexible and works for any image classification task.

The following code shows how to create DataLoaders for train and validation datasets based on relative paths on your drive:

```
data/
        train/
                cats/
                dogs/
        val/
                cats/
                dogs/
```

Refer to the following code to load your custom dataset:

```
from torchvision.datasets import ImageFolder
from torch.utils.data import DataLoader
# For this code to run, you need the folders and class folders inside each train and val folders, with images inside each folder

train_data = ImageFolder('data/train', transform=transform)
val_data = ImageFolder('data/val', transform=transform)

train_loader = DataLoader(train_data, batch_size=32, shuffle=True)
val_loader = DataLoader(val_data, batch_size=32, shuffle=False)
```

Ensure your folder structure matches the expected format, with each class in its subfolder. This setup allows you to easily adapt the code in this chapter to your data and tasks, whether you are classifying animals, plants, or everyday objects.

Evaluating model performance

Evaluating your model's performance goes beyond just measuring accuracy. Metrics like precision, recall, and the confusion matrix provide deeper insights into how well the model distinguishes between different classes. A confusion matrix, in particular, helps you identify which classes are most often confused and where the model might need improvement.

The following code calculates accuracy and then creates a confusion matrix with a heatmap to show the predicted classes vs the real classes:

```
# Calculate accuracy
correct = 0
total = 0
with torch.no_grad():
```

```
    for images, labels in testloader:
        outputs = model(images)
        _, predicted = torch.max(outputs, 1)
        total += labels.size(0)
        correct += (predicted == labels).sum().item()
print(f'Accuracy: {100 * correct / total:.2f}%')

# Confusion matrix
from sklearn.metrics import confusion_matrix
import seaborn as sns

all_preds = []
all_labels = []
with torch.no_grad():
    for images, labels in testloader:
        outputs = model(images)
        _, predicted = torch.max(outputs, 1)
        all_preds.extend(predicted.numpy())
        all_labels.extend(labels.numpy())

cm = confusion_matrix(all_labels, all_preds)
sns.heatmap(cm, annot=True, fmt='d')
plt.xlabel('Predicted')
plt.ylabel('True')
plt.title('Confusion Matrix')
plt.show()
```

A confusion matrix shows how often predictions match the proper labels for each class. Diagonal values are correct predictions; off-diagonal values show misclassifications. For each label, it keeps track of the correct and incorrect predictions, and a small figure to explain the following concept:

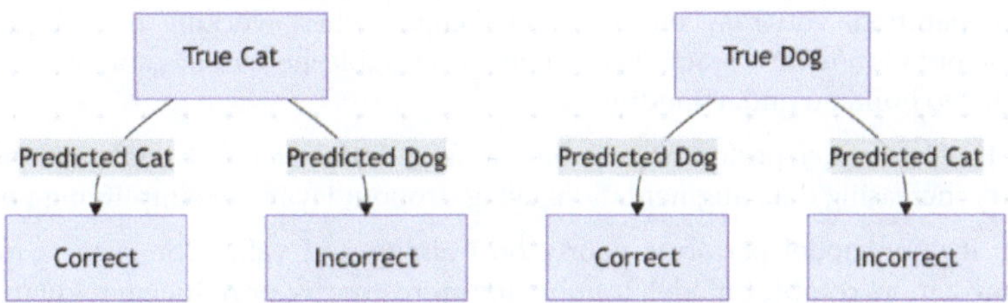

***Figure 18.6:** How a confusion matrix gets its data*

In the following confusion matrix, we can see the full results of the preceding code snippet:

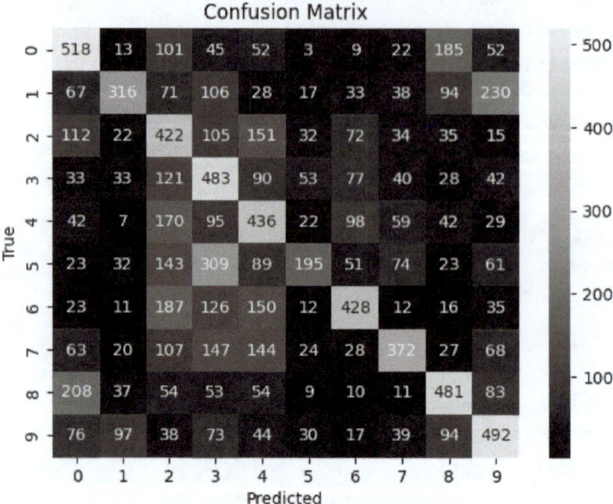

***Figure 18.7**: Confusion matrix for true labels vs predicted labels*

In the preceding matrix, each row represents the actual class (the `true` label), while each column represents the class predicted by the model. The diagonal cells (from top left to bottom right) show the number of times the model correctly predicted each class. For example, the value in row 0, column 0 (518) means the model correctly identified 518 images of class 0. Off-diagonal cells indicate misclassifications; for instance, the value in row 0, column 8 (185) means that 185 images of class 0 were incorrectly predicted as class 8. Ideally, most values should be concentrated along the diagonal, indicating high accuracy. The confusion matrix not only reveals the overall accuracy but also highlights which classes are most often confused with each other, helping you identify specific weaknesses in your model and guiding further improvements.

Troubleshooting and best practices

Even with the best preparation, you may encounter challenges when working on computer vision projects. Understanding common pitfalls and best practices will help you troubleshoot issues and build more robust models. Refer to the following list to build an understanding:

- **Overfitting**: If your model performs well on training data but poorly on validation data, it may be overfitting. Try increasing data augmentation, using dropout layers, or simplifying your model.
- **Underfitting**: If your model performs poorly on training and validation data, it may be underfitting. Consider using a more complex model, training for more epochs, or reducing regularization.
- **Imbalanced data**: If some classes have far more images than others, the model may become biased. Use class weights in your loss function or collect more data for underrepresented classes.
- **Device errors**: Ensure your model and data are on the same device [**central processing unit** (**CPU**) or **graphics processing unit** (**GPU**)]. Use .to(device) to move tensors and models as needed.
- **Learning rate issues**: If your model's loss is not decreasing, try lowering the learning rate. If training is too slow, try increasing it slightly.

Best practices

The following list outlines the best practices:

- Always visualize your data and predictions.
- Monitor both training and validation metrics.
- Save your best model checkpoints.
- Experiment with different architectures and hyperparameters.

Object detection with a pre-trained model

Next, let us use a pre-trained faster R-CNN model to detect objects in a sample image. The image is just a random image found on the internet:

```
import torch
from torchvision.models.detection import fasterrcnn_resnet50_fpn
from torchvision.transforms import ToTensor
from PIL import Image
import matplotlib.pyplot as plt
import matplotlib.patches as patches
import requests
from io import BytesIO

# 1. Download a sample image from the web
url = "https://c7.alamy.com/comp/2JAM4K4/shoeshine-stand-on-42nd-stgreet-at-5th-avenue-
outside-the-new-york-public-library-in-manhattan-2JAM4K4.jpg"
response = requests.get(url)
img = Image.open(BytesIO(response.content)).convert("RGB")

# 2. Convert to tensor
img_tensor = ToTensor()(img)

# 3. Load pre-trained object detector
model = fasterrcnn_resnet50_fpn(pretrained=True)
model.eval()

# 4. Run detection
with torch.no_grad():
    prediction = model([img_tensor])[0]

# 5. Visualization
fig, ax = plt.subplots(1, figsize=(12, 8))
ax.imshow(img)
for box, score, label in zip(prediction['boxes'],
prediction['scores'], prediction['labels']):
    if score > 0.7:
```

```
        x1, y1, x2, y2 = box
        rect = patches.Rectangle((x1, y1), x2 - x1, y2 - y1, linewidth=2, edgecolor='red', facecolor='none')
        ax.add_patch(rect)
        ax.text(x1, y1 - 10, f'Class {label.item()}: {score:.2f}', color='yellow',
                fontsize=10, bbox=dict(facecolor='red', alpha=0.5))
ax.axis('off')
plt.title('Object Detection Results')
plt.show()
```

The following list illustrates the result:

Figure 18.8: *Mini project object detection*

In this mini-project, we demonstrate how to use a pre-trained Faster R-CNN model to detect objects in a real-world image. To keep the example fully self-contained and easy to run, the code downloads a sample image from the web at runtime, so you do not need to download or label any data manually.

The process begins by fetching an image using the `requests` library and loading it into memory with Pillow (`PIL`). We then convert the image into a tensor format suitable for PyTorch models. Next, we load the Faster R-CNN model pre-trained on the **Common Objects in Context** (**COCO**) dataset, which can detect everyday objects such as people, cars, and animals.

The model processes the image and outputs predictions including bounding boxes, class labels, and confidence scores for each detected object. We filter out predictions with confidence scores below 0.7 to focus on the most reliable detections. Finally, we visualize the results by drawing bounding boxes and labels on the original image using Matplotlib.

This example illustrates the power and convenience of transfer learning and pre-trained models in computer vision. By leveraging models trained on large datasets, you can quickly build applications that detect objects in images without needing to collect or label your data. The approach can be easily adapted to other photos by changing the **Uniform Resource Locator** (**URL**) or loading local files.

Conclusion

This chapter revisits key concepts such as image classification and transfer learning, building on earlier chapters to explore their application in advanced computer vision tasks. Readers are encouraged to review *Chapters 9, Building Blocks of Neural Networks in PyTorch*, and *Chapter 10, Training Neural Networks with PyTorch*, for foundational knowledge and use this chapter as a bridge to more complex models and real-world applications.

You learned the foundations and practical computer vision techniques in this chapter with PyTorch. You explored how to prepare and augment image data, leverage transfer learning, perform object detection and segmentation, and evaluate model performance. By working through hands-on projects and troubleshooting common issues, you have gained the skills to tackle real-world vision problems.

In the next chapter, we will shift our focus from spatial data to temporal sequences by exploring time series analysis with PyTorch. You will learn how to handle data where the order of observations is critical, such as stock prices or heart rate measurements. We will delve into building specialized architectures like LSTMs and GRUs to capture long-term dependencies, implement attention mechanisms for more precise predictions, and master multi-step forecasting techniques to predict far into the future. This will equip you with a new set of tools to tackle real-world challenges where time is the most important dimension.

Exercises

The readers have to build a multi-class image classifier using transfer learning, where:

- **Objective**: Create a multi-class image classifier using transfer learning with a pre-trained ResNet model on the CIFAR-10 dataset. This exercise will test your understanding of data preparation, transfer learning, data augmentation, training, and evaluation—all the key concepts covered in this chapter.
- **Task**: Write code that accomplishes the following:
  - Load and prepare the CIFAR-10 dataset with data augmentation
  - Use a pre-trained ResNet-18 model and adapt it for CIFAR-10's 10 classes
  - Train the model for 3 epochs
  - Evaluate the model's performance with accuracy and a confusion matrix
  - Visualize sample predictions

  The code should be completely self-contained and executable without any manual data preparation.

Multiple choice questions

1. **What is the main benefit of transfer learning in computer vision?**
   a. It requires less data.
   b. It always improves accuracy.
   c. It uses knowledge from pre-trained models.
   d. It eliminates the need for GPUs.
2. **Which of the following are common data augmentation techniques?**
   a. Horizontal flip
   b. Random rotation
   c. Adding noise
   d. Changing image resolution

3. **What does an object detection model output?**
    a. Bounding boxes
    b. Class labels
    c. Segmentation masks
    d. Confidence scores
4. **What does a confusion matrix show?**
    a. Model architecture
    b. Correct and incorrect predictions
    c. Training loss
    d. Class relationships
5. **Which tasks can be solved with semantic segmentation?**
    a. Assigning a label to each pixel
    b. Drawing bounding boxes
    c. Counting objects
    d. Image classification
6. **Why is normalization important in image preprocessing?**
    a. It speeds up training
    b. It standardizes pixel values
    c. It increases the dataset size
    d. It helps the model learn better
7. **What is overfitting?**
    a. The model performs well on training but poorly on new data
    b. The model performs well on both training and new data
    c. The model is too simple
    d. The model is too complex for the data
8. **How can you address class imbalance?**
    a. Use class weights
    b. Collect more data for rare classes
    c. Ignore the problem
    d. Use data augmentation
9. **Which library provides pre-trained vision models in PyTorch?**
    a. torchvision
    b. Scikit-learn
    c. PIL
    d. Numpy

10. **What is the main purpose of the DataLoader class?**
    a. To batch and shuffle data
    b. To visualize images
    c. To train models
    d. To preprocess text

Answers

1.	a,c.
2.	a,b,c.
3.	a,b,d.
4.	b.
5.	a.
6.	b,d.
7.	a,d.
8.	a,b,d.
9.	a.
10.	a.

Key terms

- **Computer vision**: The field of AI focused on enabling machines to interpret visual information.
- **Transfer learning**: Using a model trained on one task as the starting point for a related task.
- **Data augmentation**: Techniques to increase dataset diversity by applying random transformations.
- **Object detection**: Identifying and localizing objects within an image.
- **Semantic segmentation**: Assigning a class label to every pixel in an image.
- **Confusion matrix**: A table used to evaluate the performance of a classification model.
- **Overfitting**: When a model learns the training data too well, it fails to generalize.
- **DataLoader**: A PyTorch utility for batching and shuffling data during training.

References

1. *PyTorch Documentation, "torchvision.models," 2024. Provides the official API reference and usage examples for PyTorch's vision models, including ResNet, Faster R-CNN, and Mask R-CNN.*
2. *TorchVision Library, PyTorch, 2024. A key resource offering pre-trained models, datasets, and data transformation functions tailored for computer vision tasks.*
3. *Antiga, L., Stevens, E., & Viehmann, T. (2020). Deep Learning with PyTorch. Manning Publications. This comprehensive guide covers the basics to advanced techniques in PyTorch, with practical examples that include image classification and transfer learning.*

4. *Avendi, M. (2022). PyTorch Computer Vision Cookbook. Packt Publishing. It focuses on solving real-world computer vision problems using PyTorch, with step-by-step recipes for tasks like image classification, object detection, and segmentation.*

5. *Pointer, I. (2019). Programming PyTorch for Deep Learning. O'Reilly Media. A beginner-friendly reference that introduces PyTorch's API while covering essential computer vision tasks.*

6. *Dosovitskiy, A., et al. (2020). An Image is Worth 16x16 Words: Transformers for Image Recognition at Scale. arXiv:2010.11929. Introduces Vision Transformers (ViT) and represents a foundational shift in how computer vision models are built—this work is widely implemented in PyTorch.*

7. *Ultralytics. YOLOv5: Real-Time Object Detection. GitHub Repository, 2024. The repository for YOLOv5 provides a cutting-edge example of object detection using PyTorch and is highly regarded for its efficiency in real-time detection applications.*

8. *Kirillov, A., et al. (2023). Segment Anything. arXiv:2304.02643. Details the Segment Anything Model (SAM), an influential work in interactive segmentation tasks with extensive PyTorch implementations.*

9. *PyTorch Tutorials: Transfer Learning for Computer Vision. PyTorch.org, 2024. This is an official tutorial that walks through the process of adapting pre-trained vision models for new tasks and datasets via transfer learning.*

10. *PyTorch Tutorials: Object Detection and Instance Segmentation. PyTorch.org, 2024. A practical resource illustrating how to implement object detection and instance segmentation models using PyTorch's visualization and model-building tools.*

CHAPTER 19
Time Series Analysis with PyTorch

Introduction

In the previous chapters, we explored advanced neural network architectures and their applications in various domains. While we have covered image processing with **convolutional neural networks** (**CNNs**) and sequential data with **recurrent neural networks** (**RNNs**), a specialized area of **machine learning** (**ML**) deserves dedicated attention, which is time series analysis. Time series data is everywhere around us, from stock prices fluctuating throughout the day to your heart rate measurements during exercise, from weather patterns changing over seasons to website traffic varying by hour.

Time series analysis represents one of the most practical and widely used ML applications in the real world. Unlike static datasets, where each sample is independent, time series data has a temporal dimension that creates unique challenges and opportunities. The value at any given time point is often influenced by previous values, making patterns, trends, and dependencies that traditional machine learning approaches struggle to capture effectively.

Think of time series data like a story unfolding over time. As you need to read previous chapters to understand the current plot, time series models must consider historical data points to predict future values accurately. This temporal dependency is what makes time series analysis both fascinating and challenging.

PyTorch provides excellent tools for time series analysis, offering the flexibility to build everything from simple forecasting models to complex anomaly detection systems. The framework's dynamic computation graph and extensive neural network modules make it well-suited for the sequential nature of time series data.

This chapter explores a range of approaches to time series analysis, beginning with fundamental concepts and advancing toward more sophisticated techniques. It covers classical decomposition methods, modern neural network architectures such as RNNs and **long short-term memory** (**LSTM**) networks tailored for temporal data, and state-of-the-art models like **Temporal Convolutional Networks** (**TCNs**). Practical applications include forecasting future values, identifying trends, and detecting anomalies within sequential datasets. Time series analysis finds broad use across multiple industries—finance employs it for stock price prediction, risk assessment, and algorithmic trading; healthcare uses it for patient monitoring, epidemic forecasting, and evaluating drug effectiveness; manufacturing applies it to predictive maintenance, quality control, and supply chain optimization; the energy sector leverages it for load forecasting, renewable generation prediction, and grid management; while retail and technology domains rely on it for demand forecasting, inventory management, user behavior modeling, and performance optimization.

By the end of this chapter, you will have a comprehensive understanding of time series analysis techniques and the practical skills to implement them using PyTorch. You will be equipped to tackle real-world temporal data challenges, from building accurate forecasting models to detecting unusual patterns that might indicate system failures or opportunities.

Structure

This chapter covers the following topics:

- Understanding time series data and patterns
- Data preprocessing for time series
- Creating sequences for neural networks
- Building LSTM models with PyTorch
- Advanced model GRU with attention
- Multi-step forecasting
- Practical implementation tips

Objectives

This chapter aims to comprehensively understand time series analysis using PyTorch, equipping you with theoretical knowledge and practical implementation skills for temporal data processing. We will begin by exploring the fundamental characteristics of time series data, including trends, seasonality, and cyclical patterns, while understanding how these differ from traditional ML datasets. Our journey will cover essential preprocessing techniques such as time series decomposition, normalization, and feature engineering that are crucial for preparing temporal data for analysis. We will then delve into the application of RNNs and LSTM networks specifically for time series tasks, understanding how their memory mechanisms make them particularly suitable for capturing temporal dependencies. Moving beyond traditional recurrent architectures, we will explore TCNs, which offer advantages in parallelization and long-range dependency modeling. The chapter will provide hands-on experience with various forecasting techniques, teaching you to predict future values and evaluate model performance using appropriate metrics for time series data. Finally, we will examine anomaly detection methods that can identify unusual patterns or outliers in temporal data, which is crucial for applications like fraud detection, system monitoring, and quality control. Through practical implementations and real-world examples, you will develop the expertise to choose appropriate architectures for different time series problems and understand the trade-offs between various approaches.

Understanding time series data

Time series data consists of observations recorded at regular time intervals. The key characteristic distinguishing time series from other data types is the temporal ordering - the sequence of observations matters, and there is typically a correlation between consecutive data points.

Components of time series

Let us visualize the main components that make up a time series to better understand what we are working with:

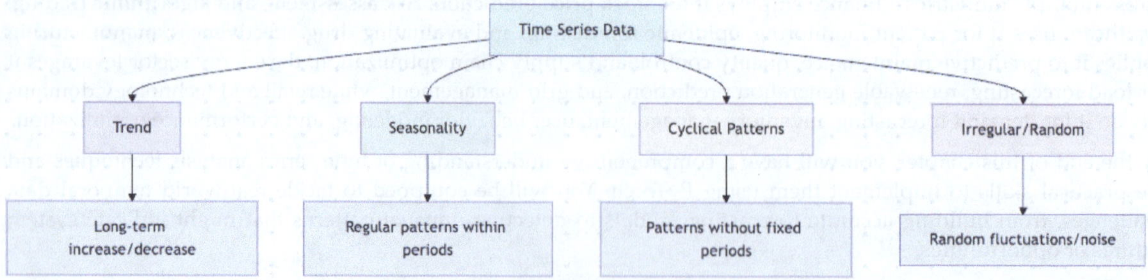

Figure 19.1: Components of time series

Figure 19.1 illustrates the four main components that typically comprise any time series data. Understanding these components is crucial because different modeling approaches work better for various patterns. The trend shows the overall direction of the data over time. Seasonality represents regular patterns that repeat at fixed intervals. Cyclic patterns are similar to seasonality but do not have fixed periods. Incremental components represent random variations or noise in the data.

Types of time series problems

Before we start building models, let us understand the different types of problems we can solve with time series analysis:

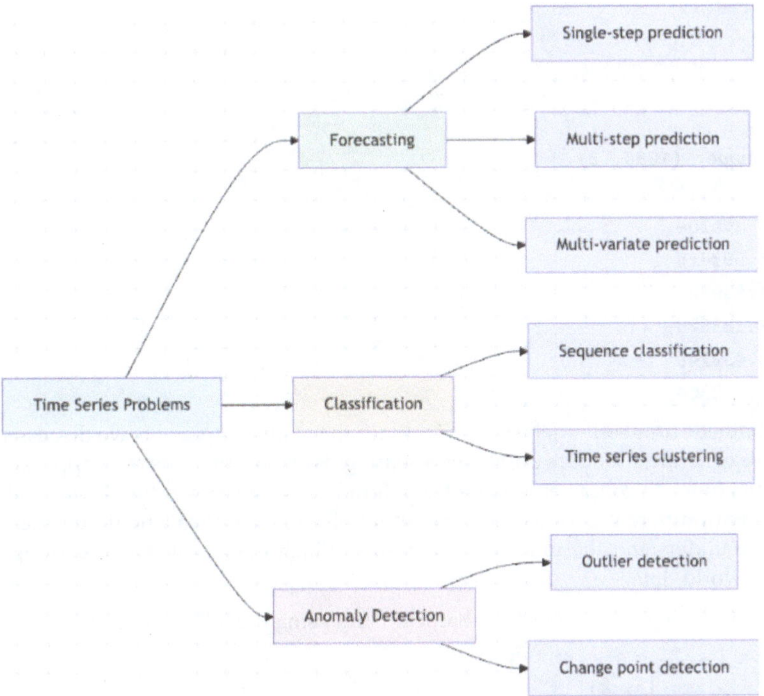

***Figure 19.2**: Types of time series problems*

This flowchart shows the main categories of time series problems you will encounter. Forecasting involves predicting future values, classification categorizes time series sequences, and anomaly detection focuses on identifying unusual patterns or outliers. Each type requires different modeling approaches and evaluation strategies.

Data preprocessing for time series

Proper data preprocessing is crucial for successful time series analysis. Let us start by loading and examining a sample time series dataset to understand the preprocessing steps.

Note: To keep this chapter focused on the core machine learning concepts, we have omitted standard library imports (like numpy and pandas) and the implementation details of several custom helper functions (such as `generate_time_series`, `detect_outliers`, `handle_missing_values`, and `train_test_split_temporal`). The complete, runnable code—including all helper functions and imports—is available in the accompanying Jupyter Notebook in this book's GitHub repository. We highly encourage you to follow along using the notebook!

The following code demonstrates how to load and initially examine time series data. We will use a synthetic dataset to illustrate the key concepts:

```
# Generate the data
data = generate_time_series(1000)
dates = pd.date_range(start='2020-01-01', periods=len(data), freq='D')
df = pd.DataFrame({'date': dates, 'value': data})

print("Time series data shape:", df.shape)
print("\nFirst few rows:")
print(df.head())
print("\nBasic statistics:")
print(df['value'].describe())
```

Output:

```
Time series data shape: (1000, 2)
 First few rows:
        date      value
 0 2020-01-01  55.993428
 1 2020-01-02  55.839720
 2 2020-01-03  58.203809
 3 2020-01-04  60.432148
 4 2020-01-05  57.108364
```

This code creates a synthetic time series dataset that includes the main components we discussed: trend, seasonality, and random noise. We generate 1000 data points representing daily observations over approximately 2.7 years. The **generate_time_series** function combines a linear trend (gradual increase over time), seasonal patterns (using sine and cosine functions with different periods), and random noise to create realistic time series data. This synthetic approach allows us to understand the underlying patterns, which is helpful when learning the concepts before applying them to real-world data.

Now, let us visualize this data to understand its characteristics using the following code:

```
# Visualize the time series data
plt.figure(figsize=(15, 8))

# Plot the full time series
plt.subplot(2, 2, 1)
plt.plot(df['date'], df['value'], linewidth=1)
plt.title('Complete Time Series')
plt.xlabel('Date')
plt.ylabel('Value')
plt.xticks(rotation=45)
```

The following visualization illustrates the synthetic time series data generated in the preceding step. It provides a clear view of how the trend, seasonality, and random noise interact over time. By examining the chart, we can observe the gradual upward movement introduced by the trend, the repeating oscillations produced by the seasonal component, and the irregular fluctuations caused by random variation. Together, these elements create a dataset that closely resembles real-world temporal behavior, serving as a foundation for the modeling techniques explored later in this chapter.

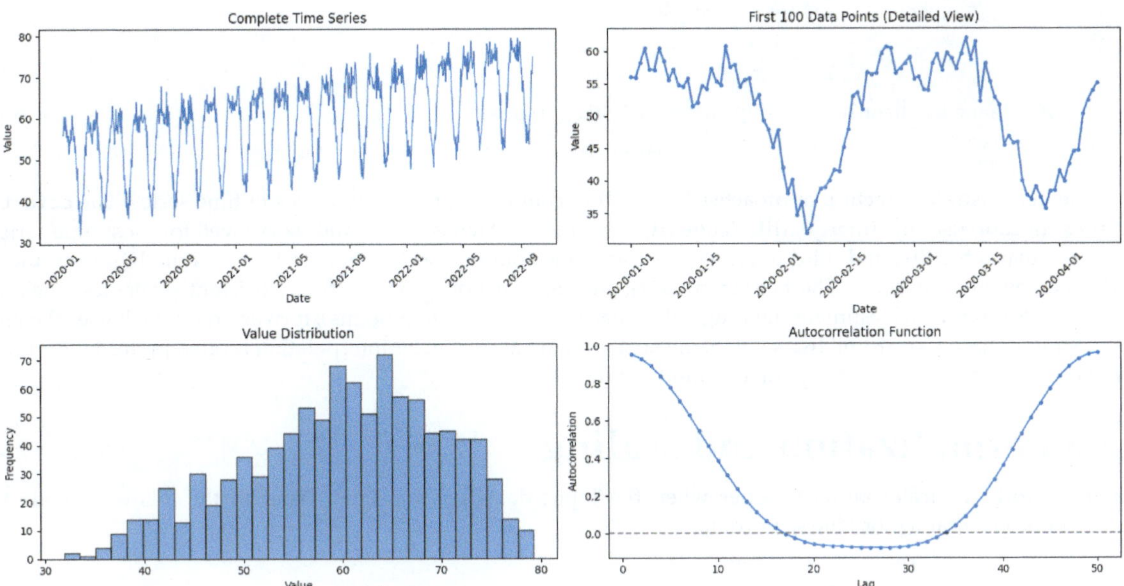

Figure 19.3: Time series visualization

This visualization code creates four plots to help us understand our time series data from multiple perspectives. The complete time series plot shows the overall pattern and trends, while the detailed view of the first 100 points helps us see the short-term fluctuations and seasonal patterns. The distribution histogram reveals whether our data follows a normal distribution or has any skewness, and the autocorrelation plot shows how strongly the current values are related to past values at different time lags. High autocorrelation at certain lags indicates strong seasonal or cyclical patterns.

Handling missing values and outliers

Real-world time series data often contains missing values and outliers that must be addressed before modeling. Let us implement functions to detect and handle these issues using the following code:

```
# Introduce some missing values and outliers for demonstration
df_with_issues = df.copy()

# Add some missing values
missing_indices = np.random.choice(df.index, size=20, replace=False)
df_with_issues.loc[missing_indices, 'value'] = np.nan

# Add some outliers
outlier_indices = np.random.choice(df.index, size=10, replace=False)
df_with_issues.loc[outlier_indices, 'value'] *= 3  # Make values 3x larger

print(f"Missing values: {df_with_issues['value'].isna().sum()}")

# Detect outliers
outliers = detect_outliers(df_with_issues['value'].dropna())
```

```
print(f"Detected outliers: {outliers.sum()}")

# Handle missing values
df_cleaned = handle_missing_values(df_with_issues)
print(f"Missing values after cleaning: {df_cleaned['value'].isna().sum()}")
```

This code demonstrates practical approaches to handling common data quality issues in time series. The **detect_outliers** function uses the **interquartile range** (**IQR**) method, which is robust and works well for most time series data. It calculates the first and third quartiles, then identifies points that fall outside 1.5 times the IQR from these quartiles as potential outliers. The **handle_missing_values** function provides three different strategies, such as linear interpolation (which estimates missing values based on surrounding points), forward fill (which uses the last known value), and backward fill (which uses the next known value). Linear interpolation is often preferred for time series because it maintains the temporal continuity of the data.

Data normalization and scaling

Neural networks typically perform better when the input data is normalized. Refer to the following code to implement proper scaling for time series data:

```
# Apply scaling to our cleaned data
scaler = TimeSeriesScaler(method='minmax')
scaler.fit(df_cleaned['value'])
scaled_values = scaler.transform(df_cleaned['value'])

print("Original data range:", df_cleaned['value'].min(), "to", df_cleaned['value'].max())
print("Scaled data range:", scaled_values.min(), "to", scaled_values.max())
```

The custom **TimeSeriesScaler** class in the GitHub repository provides a clean interface for scaling time series data while maintaining the ability to inverse transform predictions back to the original scale. This is crucial for time series analysis because we often must interpret our forecasts in the original units. The class supports min-max scaling (which scales values to a 0-1 range) and Standard scaling (which centers the data around zero with unit variance). Min-Max scaling is often preferred for neural networks because it ensures all values are in a bounded range, which helps with gradient stability during training.

Feature engineering for time series

Feature engineering is crucial for time series analysis as it helps models understand temporal patterns. Let us create various types of features that capture different aspects of the time series using the following code:

```
# Start with time features
df_with_features = create_time_features(df_scaled)
print(f"After time features: {df_with_features.shape}")

# Add lag features
df_with_features = create_lag_features(df_with_features)
print(f"After lag features: {df_with_features.shape}")

# Add rolling features
df_with_features = create_rolling_features(df_with_features)
print(f"After rolling features: {df_with_features.shape}")
```

```

# Display feature names
feature_columns = [col for col in df_with_features.columns if col not in ['date', 'value']]
print(f"\nCreated {len(feature_columns)} features:")
for i, col in enumerate(feature_columns):
    print(f"{i+1:2d}. {col}")
```

Output:

```
Creating comprehensive feature set...
After time features: (1000, 14)
After lag features: (1000, 20)
After rolling features: (1000, 36)

Created 34 features:
 1. year
 2. month
 3. day
 4. dayofweek
...
31. value_rolling_mean_30
32. value_rolling_std_30
33. value_rolling_min_30
34. value_rolling_max_30
```

This comprehensive feature engineering approach creates multiple features that help neural networks understand different temporal patterns. Time-based features like month, day, and day of week help capture calendar effects. The cyclical features using sine and cosine transformations are significant because they represent cyclical patterns (like months or days of the week) in a way that neural networks can easily understand. For example, December (month 12) and January (month 1) are close in time, and the cyclical encoding captures this relationship. Lag features provide the model with direct access to previous values, while rolling features capture local trends and volatility patterns over different time windows.

Let us visualize some of these features to understand their relationships using the following code snippet:

```
# Visualize feature relationships
plt.figure(figsize=(15, 10))

# Plot original value vs some key features
plt.subplot(2, 3, 1)
plt.scatter(df_with_features['value_lag_1'].dropna(),
           df_with_features['value'].dropna()[1:], alpha=0.5)
plt.xlabel(‘Value (t-1)’)
plt.ylabel(‘Value (t)’)
plt.title('Current vs Previous Value')
```

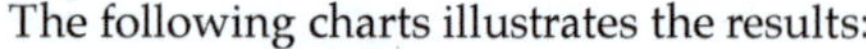

The following charts illustrates the results:

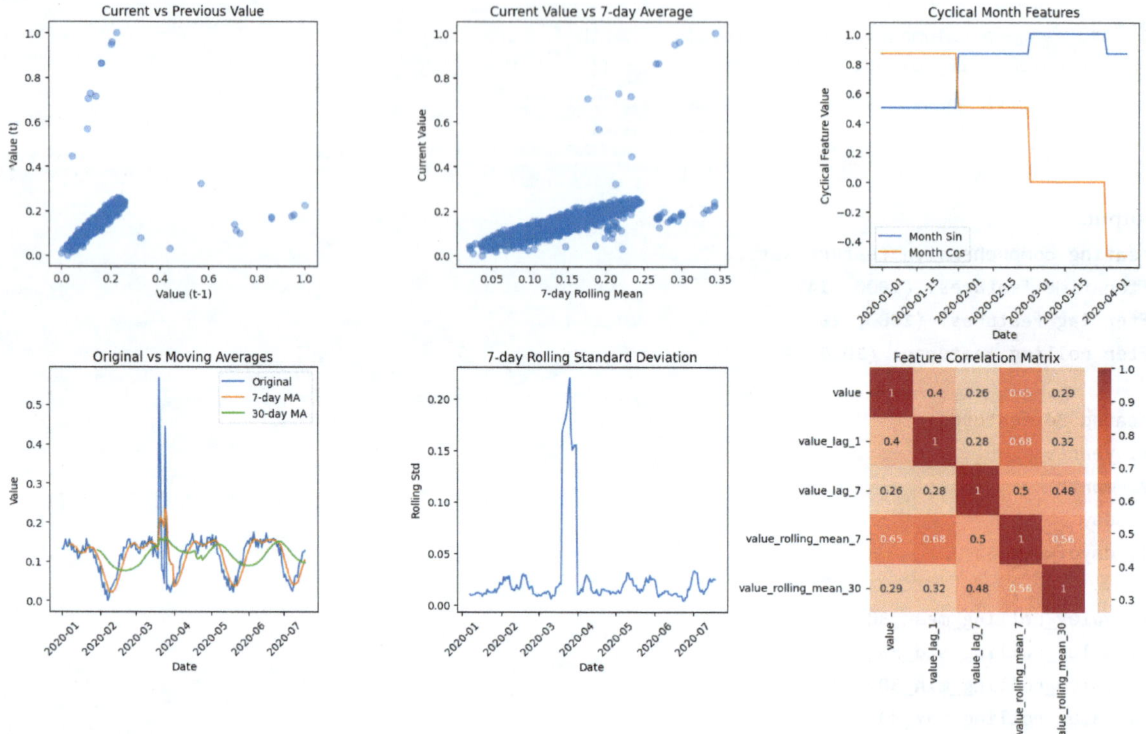

Figure 19.4: Feature engineering

These visualizations help us understand how different features relate to our target variable and each other. The scatter plots show the strength of relationships between current values and lagged or rolling features. Strong linear relationships indicate that these features will be helpful for prediction. The cyclical features plot demonstrates how sine and cosine transformations create smooth, continuous representations of cyclical patterns. The correlation matrix helps identify which features are most predictive and whether we have redundant features that might not add value to our model.

Creating sequences for neural networks

Neural networks for time series analysis typically work with data sequences rather than individual points. Let us create a function to convert our time series data into sequences suitable for training using the following code snippet:

```
X, y = create_sequences(df_with_features, sequence_length,
                        target_col='value', feature_cols=selected_features)

print(f"Input sequences shape: {X.shape}")
print(f"Target values shape: {y.shape}")
print(f"Each sequence contains {X.shape[1]} time steps with {X.shape[2]} features")
```

Output:

```
Creating sequences with length 30...
Input sequences shape: (940, 30, 10)
Target values shape: (940,)
Each sequence contains 30 time steps with 10 features
```

This sequence creation function is fundamental to time series neural networks. It transforms our tabular data into sequences where each input consists of multiple consecutive time steps, and each target is the value we want to predict. The function creates overlapping data windows - for example, if we use a sequence length of 30, the first sequence uses time steps 0-29 to predict step 30, the second sequence uses steps 1-30 to predict step 31, and so on. This sliding window approach maximizes the training data we can extract from our time series. The resulting 3D array has dimensions (number of sequences, sequence length, number of features), the expected input format for PyTorch's RNN layers.

Because temporal splitting is crucial for time series analysis (we must never use future information to predict past values), we cannot use a standard random split. Instead, we use a simple temporal split that slices the data sequentially. Here is the implementation we will use throughout the chapter:

```python
def train_test_split_temporal(X, y, test_size=0.2):
    split_idx = int(len(X) * (1 - test_size))

    X_train, X_test = X[:split_idx], X[split_idx:]
    y_train, y_test = y[:split_idx], y[split_idx:]

    return X_train, X_test, y_train, y_test
```

Let us split our data into training and testing sets using the following code snippet, while carefully maintaining temporal order:

```python
# Split the data
X_train, X_test, y_train, y_test = train_test_split_temporal(X, y, test_size=0.2)

print("Training set:")
print(f"  X_train shape: {X_train.shape}")
print(f»  y_train shape: {y_train.shape}»)
print("\nTest set:")
print(f"  X_test shape: {X_test.shape}")
print(f"  y_test shape: {y_test.shape}")

# Convert to PyTorch tensors
X_train_tensor = torch.FloatTensor(X_train)
y_train_tensor = torch.FloatTensor(y_train)
X_test_tensor = torch.FloatTensor(X_test)
y_test_tensor = torch.FloatTensor(y_test)

print(f"\nPyTorch tensors created successfully")
print(f"Training data device: {X_train_tensor.device}")
```

Output:

```
Training set:
  X_train shape: (752, 30, 10)
```

```
  y_train shape: (752,)

Test set:
  X_test shape: (188, 30, 10)
  y_test shape: (188,)

PyTorch tensors created successfully
Training data device: cpu
```

The temporal split is crucial for time series analysis because we must never use future information to predict past values. Unlike traditional ML, where we can randomly shuffle data, time series requires that our test set contains only data points after our training set in time. This simulates the real-world scenario where we train on historical data and make predictions. Converting to PyTorch tensors prepares our data for neural network training and allows us to move data to the GPU easily if available.

Building LSTM Models with PyTorch

Now, let us build our first neural network model for time series prediction. We will start with an LSTM network, which is particularly well-suited for time series data:

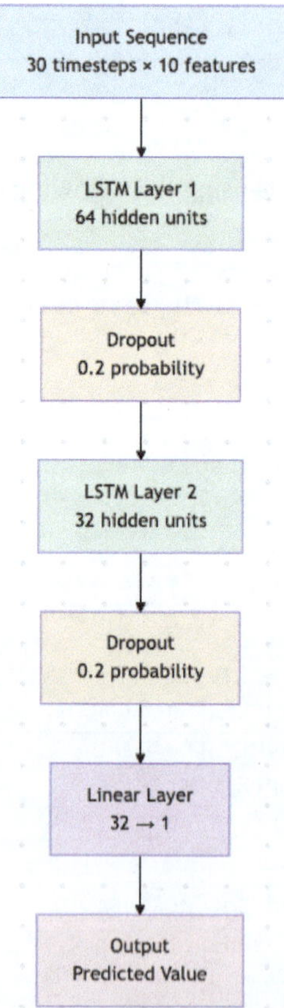

Figure 19.5: LSTM for time series with PyTorch

This architecture diagram shows the flow of data through our LSTM model. The input sequence contains 30 timesteps (our lookback window) with 10 features at each timestep. The data flows through two LSTM layers with decreasing hidden units (64 then 32), with dropout layers in between to prevent overfitting. Finally, a linear layer maps the LSTM output to a single predicted value. This architecture balances model complexity with the risk of overfitting, making it suitable for most time series prediction tasks.

Let us implement this LSTM model using the following code snippet:

```
# Model parameters
input_size = X_train.shape[2]  # Number of features
hidden_size = 64
num_layers = 2
output_size = 1
dropout = 0.2

# Create the model
model = LSTMTimeSeriesModel(input_size, hidden_size, num_layers, output_size, dropout)

print("Model Architecture:")
print(model)
print(f"\nTotal parameters: {sum(p.numel() for p in model.parameters()):,}")
print(f"Trainable parameters: {sum(p.numel() for p in model.parameters() if p.requires_grad):,}")
```

Output:

```
Model Architecture:
LSTMTimeSeriesModel(
  (lstm): LSTM(10, 64, num_layers=2, batch_first=True, dropout=0.2)
  (dropout): Dropout(p=0.2, inplace=False)
  (linear): Linear(in_features=64, out_features=1, bias=True)
)

Total parameters: 52,801
Trainable parameters: 52,801
```

This LSTM model implementation includes several essential design choices. The **batch_first=True** parameter makes the input format more intuitive (**batch_size**, **sequence_length**, **features**). We initialize the hidden states (**h0** and **c0**) to zeros for each batch, which is standard practice. The model takes the output from the last timestep of the LSTM sequence, applies dropout for regularization, and then uses a linear layer to produce the final prediction. The model is designed to be flexible with configurable hidden size, number of layers, and dropout rate.

Refer to the following code to set up the training process with a proper loss function and optimizer:

```
# Training setup
device = torch.device('cuda' if torch.cuda.is_available() else 'cpu')
print(f"Using device: {device}")

model = model.to(device)
X_train_tensor = X_train_tensor.to(device)
y_train_tensor = y_train_tensor.to(device)
X_test_tensor = X_test_tensor.to(device)
```

```
y_test_tensor = y_test_tensor.to(device)

# Loss function and optimizer
criterion = nn.MSELoss()
optimizer = torch.optim.Adam(model.parameters(), lr=0.001, weight_decay=1e-5)

# Learning rate scheduler
scheduler = torch.optim.lr_scheduler.ReduceLROnPlateau(optimizer, mode='min',
                                                      factor=0.5,
    patience=10)

print("Starting model training...")
train_losses, test_losses = train_model(model, X_train_tensor, y_train_tensor,
                                        X_test_tensor, y_test_tensor, epochs=100, batch_
    size=32)
```

Output:

```
Using device: cpu
Starting model training...
Epoch [10/100], Train Loss: 0.006960, Test Loss: 0.009116
Epoch [100/100], Train Loss: 0.004596, Test Loss: 0.008567
```

This training function implements several best practices for training neural networks on time series data. We use batch processing to make training more efficient, but we set **shuffle=False** to maintain the temporal order within each epoch. Gradient clipping prevents the exploding gradient problem that can occur with RNNs. The learning rate scheduler automatically reduces the learning rate when the validation loss stops improving, which helps the model converge to a better solution. We track both training and validation losses to monitor for overfitting.

Let us visualize the training progress and evaluate our model using the following code:

```
# Make predictions
model.eval()
with torch.no_grad():
    train_predictions = model(X_train_tensor).cpu().numpy().squeeze()
    test_predictions = model(X_test_tensor).cpu().numpy().squeeze()

# Convert back to original scale
train_predictions_original = scaler.inverse_transform(train_predictions)
test_predictions_original = scaler.inverse_transform(test_predictions)
y_train_original = scaler.inverse_transform(y_train)
y_test_original = scaler.inverse_transform(y_test)

# Calculate metrics
train_mse = mean_squared_error(y_train_original, train_predictions_original)
test_mse = mean_squared_error(y_test_original, test_predictions_original)
train_mae = mean_absolute_error(y_train_original, train_predictions_original)
test_mae = mean_absolute_error(y_test_original, test_predictions_original)
```

Output:

```
Model Performance:
Training MSE: 147.5354
Test MSE: 290.4995
Training MAE: 4.7529
Test MAE: 7.4213
```

The visualization chart for the preceding code is illustrated in the following figure:

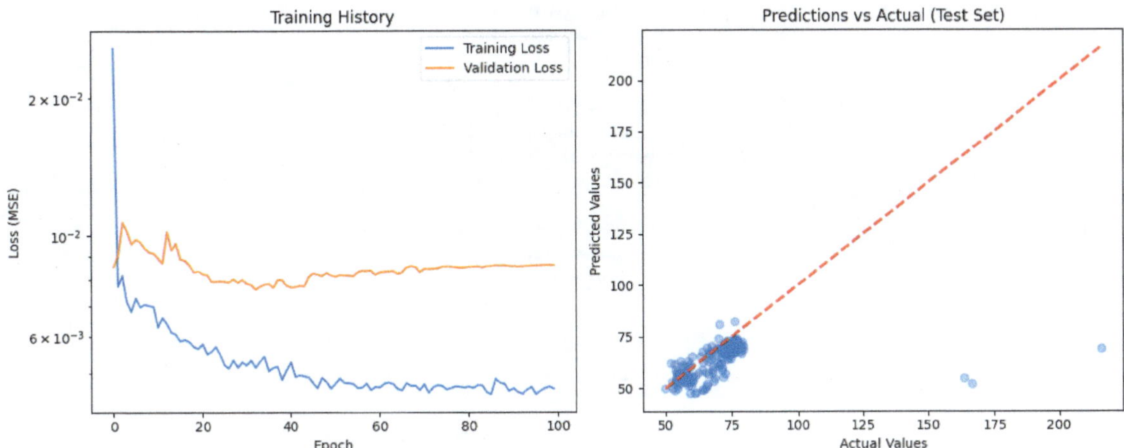

Figure 19.6: *Training loop results visualization*

This evaluation code provides comprehensive insights into our model's performance. The training history plot helps us identify whether the model is overfitting (if validation loss starts increasing while training loss continues to decrease) or underfitting (if both losses remain high). We convert predictions to the original scale for meaningful interpretation and calculate **mean squared error** (**MSE**) and **mean absolute error** (**MAE**) metrics. The scatter plot of predictions vs actual values shows how well our model captures the relationship—points close to the diagonal line indicate accurate predictions.

Advanced model GRU with attention

Let us implement a more sophisticated model that combines **Gated Recurrent Unit** (**GRU**) layers with an attention mechanism. This approach can capture more complex temporal patterns:

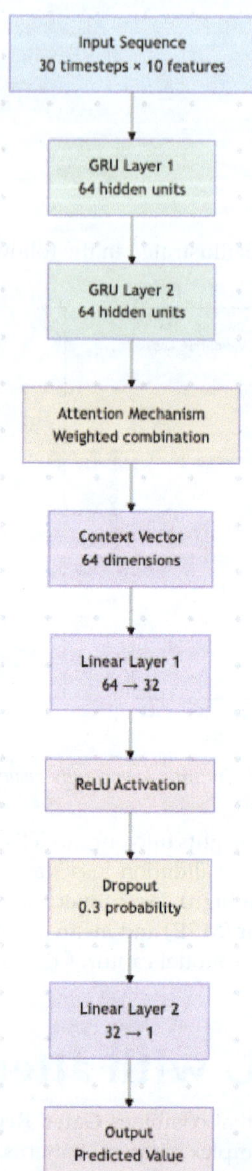

Figure 19.7: *GRU with attention*

This advanced architecture incorporates an attention mechanism that allows the model to focus on the most relevant parts of the input sequence when making predictions. The attention mechanism computes weights for each timestep in the sequence, creating a context vector that emphasizes the most essential information. This is particularly useful for time series where certain past events might be more relevant than others for predicting future values.

Here is the implementation of the GRU model with attention:

```
# Create the advanced model
advanced_model = GRUWithAttention(input_size, hidden_size=64, num_layers=2,
                                   output_size=1, dropout=0.3)
```

```
advanced_model = advanced_model.to(device)

print("Advanced Model Architecture:")
print(advanced_model)
print(f"\nTotal parameters: {sum(p.numel() for p in advanced_model.parameters()):,}")
```

```
Advanced Model Architecture:
GRUWithAttention(
  (gru): GRU(10, 64, num_layers=2, batch_first=True, dropout=0.3)
  (attention): AttentionLayer(
    (attention): Linear(in_features=64, out_features=1, bias=False)
  )
  (fc1): Linear(in_features=64, out_features=32, bias=True)
  (relu): ReLU()
  (dropout): Dropout(p=0.3, inplace=False)
  (fc2): Linear(in_features=32, out_features=1, bias=True)
)

Total parameters: 41,729
```

This advanced model introduces several improvements over the basic LSTM. The GRU layers are often more efficient than LSTM while maintaining similar performance. The attention mechanism allows the model to dynamically focus on different parts of the input sequence, which is particularly valuable for time series with varying patterns or when certain historical events are more predictive than others. The two-layer output network with ReLU activation provides additional nonlinear transformation capability.

Let us train this advanced model and compare its performance using the following code:

```
print("Training advanced model...")
advanced_train_losses, advanced_test_losses = train_advanced_model(
    advanced_model, X_train_tensor, y_train_tensor, X_test_tensor, y_test_
tensor, epochs=100)
```

Output:

```
Training advanced model...
Epoch [10/100], Train Loss: 0.007553, Test Loss: 0.011929
..
Epoch [100/100], Train Loss: 0.006476, Test Loss: 0.014792
```

The training process for the advanced model is similar to the basic LSTM, but we need to handle the fact that the model returns both predictions and attention weights. This training function is designed to work with the more complex output structure while maintaining the same best practices for gradient clipping and learning rate scheduling.

Now, let us evaluate both models and visualize the attention mechanism using the following code:

```
# Evaluate the advanced model
advanced_model.eval()
with torch.no_grad():
    advanced_train_pred, _ = advanced_model(X_train_tensor)
    advanced_test_pred, test_attention = advanced_model(X_test_tensor)

```

```
        advanced_train_pred = advanced_train_pred.cpu().numpy().squeeze()
        advanced_test_pred = advanced_test_pred.cpu().numpy().squeeze()
        test_attention = test_attention.cpu().numpy()

# Convert to original scale
advanced_train_pred_orig = scaler.inverse_transform(advanced_train_pred)
advanced_test_pred_orig = scaler.inverse_transform(advanced_test_pred)

# Calculate metrics for advanced model
advanced_train_mse = mean_squared_error(y_train_original, advanced_train_pred_orig)
advanced_test_mse = mean_squared_error(y_test_original, advanced_test_pred_orig)
advanced_train_mae = mean_absolute_error(y_train_original, advanced_train_pred_orig)
advanced_test_mae = mean_absolute_error(y_test_original, advanced_test_pred_orig)

print("Model Comparison:")
print("="*50)
print("Basic LSTM Model:")
print(f"  Training MSE: {train_mse:.4f}, MAE: {train_mae:.4f}")
print(f"  Test MSE: {test_mse:.4f}, MAE: {test_mae:.4f}")
print("\advanced GRU + Attention Model:")
print(f"  Training MSE: {advanced_train_mse:.4f}, MAE: {advanced_train_mae:.4f}")
print(f"  Test MSE: {advanced_test_mse:.4f}, MAE: {advanced_test_mae:.4f}")
```

Output:

```
Model Comparison:
==================================================
Basic LSTM Model:
  Training MSE: 147.5354, MAE: 4.7529
  Test MSE: 290.4995, MAE: 7.4213

Advanced GRU + Attention Model:
  Training MSE: 204.4590, MAE: 8.1417
  Test MSE: 501.5878, MAE: 15.3331
```

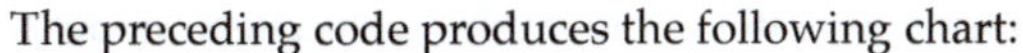

The preceding code produces the following chart:

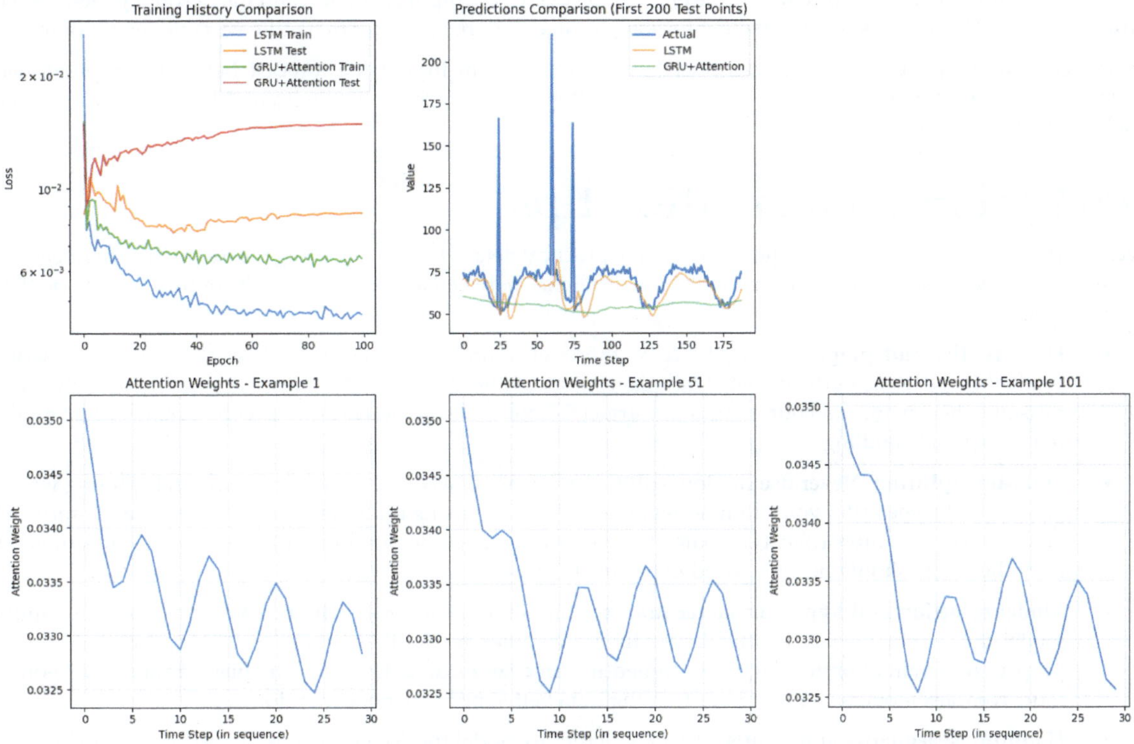

Figure 19.8: *GRU + Attention vs. LSTM*

This comprehensive comparison shows us several important insights. The comparison of training history helps us understand which model converges faster and achieves better performance. The comparison of predictions visualizes how well each model captures the actual patterns in the test data. The attention weight plots are exciting as they show which parts of the input sequence the model considers most important for each prediction. High attention weights at specific time steps indicate that those historical points are crucial for the current prediction.

Multi-step forecasting

Multi-step forecasting involves predicting multiple time steps into the future, which is often more challenging than single-step forecasting. Several approaches to multi-step forecasting exist, each with its advantages and trade-offs.

The recursive approach uses a model repeatedly trained for one-step-ahead prediction. We predict the next time step, add it to our input sequence, and use this extended sequence to indicate the following time step. This approach is simple to implement but can accumulate errors over multiple steps, leading to degraded performance for longer forecast horizons.

The direct approach trains separate models for each forecast horizon. For example, if we want to predict 5 steps, we train 5 different models, one to predict 1 step, another to predict 2 steps, and so on. This approach can be more accurate but requires training multiple models and does not capture dependencies between different forecast horizons.

The multi-output approach trains a single model to predict all future time steps simultaneously. This approach can capture dependencies between different forecast horizons and is computationally efficient, but it can be more challenging to train and may not perform well for very long forecast horizons.

Sequence-to-sequence models, borrowed from natural language processing, offer another approach. These models use an encoder-decoder architecture where the encoder processes the input sequence, and the decoder generates the output sequence. This approach is compelling for longer forecast horizons and can handle variable-length outputs.

The choice of approach depends on your specific requirements, including the forecast horizon, computational constraints, and accuracy requirements. In practice, it is often worth experimenting with multiple approaches to see which works best for your problem.

Practical implementation tips

Successful time series models require attention to many practical details beyond choosing the exemplary architecture. Here are some key considerations that can make the difference between a model that works in theory and one that works in practice:

- **Data quality and preprocessing**: Start by thoroughly understanding your data. Plot your time series to identify patterns, outliers, and data quality issues. Check for missing values and know why they are missing - this can inform your imputation strategy. Look for structural breaks or regime changes that might require special handling.
- **Train-test splitting**: Never use random splitting for time series data. Always use temporal splitting where your test set comes after your training set in time. Consider using multiple validation sets or walk-forward validation to get a more robust estimate of model performance. Be careful about data leakage—information from the future should never be used to predict the past.
- **Model selection and hyperparameter tuning**: Start simple and gradually increase complexity. A simple model that works reliably is often better than a complex model that is hard to tune and maintain. Use proper cross-validation techniques designed for time series data. Consider the bias-variance trade-off—more complex models might fit your training data better, but may not generalize well.
- **Handling seasonality and trends**: Decide whether to model these components explicitly or let the neural network learn them implicitly. Explicit modeling (like detrending or seasonal decomposition) can make learning easier, but requires domain knowledge. Implicit modeling is more flexible but may require more data and careful architecture design.
- **Evaluation metrics**: Choose metrics that align with your business objectives. MAE and **root mean square error** (**RMSE**) are typical. Still, metrics like **mean absolute percentage error** (**MAPE**) should be considered for interpretability or custom metrics that reflect your specific use case. Continually evaluate on multiple horizons if you are doing multi-step forecasting.
- **Computational considerations**: Time series models can be computationally expensive, especially for long sequences or when doing hyperparameter tuning. Consider using techniques like gradient checkpointing to reduce memory usage or distributed training for large datasets. Also, consider inference time requirements—a model that takes too long to generate predictions may not be practical for real-time applications.
- **Monitoring and maintenance**: Time series models can degrade as the underlying data distribution changes. Implement monitoring to detect when model performance is declining and have a strategy for retraining or updating your models. Consider online learning approaches for scenarios where the data distribution is constantly evolving.
- **Handling multiple time series**: If you are working with multiple related time series, consider whether to train separate models for each or a single model for all series. Global models can be more robust and can leverage patterns across different series, but they may not capture series-specific patterns as well as individual models.

- **Incorporating external features**: External features like weather data, economic indicators, or promotional activities can significantly improve forecasting accuracy. However, be careful about feature availability at prediction time—you can only use features that will be available when you need to make predictions.
- **Uncertainty quantification**: Point forecasts are often insufficient—decision makers must understand the uncertainty surrounding predictions. Consider approaches like quantile regression, Monte Carlo dropout, or ensemble methods to provide prediction intervals along with point forecasts.

Conclusion

Time series analysis with PyTorch opens up powerful possibilities for forecasting and understanding temporal patterns in data. Throughout this chapter, we have explored the fundamental concepts that make time series data unique and learned how to adapt neural network architectures to handle sequential information effectively.

We began by understanding the special characteristics of time series data—the temporal dependencies, trends, seasonality, and cycles that distinguish it from traditional machine learning problems. We learned why the order of observations matters and how concepts like stationarity and autocorrelation help us better understand our data.

We then explored various neural network architectures suitable for time series analysis, like LSTMs and GRUs. Each offers different advantages depending on your specific problem requirements. The key insight is that the temporal structure of your data should guide your choice of architecture.

Data preprocessing emerged as a critical success factor. Proper normalization, sequence creation, and feature engineering can distinguish between a model that struggles to learn and one that achieves excellent performance. We emphasized the importance of understanding your data thoroughly before applying any modeling techniques.

Multi-step forecasting gave us several strategic choices, from recursive approaches that reuse single-step models to sophisticated sequence-to-sequence architectures. The choice depends on your forecast horizon, accuracy requirements, and computational constraints. We learned that there is rarely a one-size-fits-all solution, and experimentation is often necessary to find the best approach.

The practical implementation tips highlighted the gap between theoretical knowledge and real-world application. Issues like proper train-test splitting, handling data quality problems, computational efficiency, and model monitoring are crucial for building systems that work reliably in production environments.

Perhaps most importantly, we learned that successful time series modeling is as much about understanding your domain and data as it is about choosing the right algorithms. The best model is not necessarily the most sophisticated one, but the one that reliably solves your specific problem while being maintainable and interpretable.

As you apply these concepts to your time series problems, remember to start simple and gradually increase complexity as needed. Focus on understanding your data, choose appropriate evaluation metrics, and always validate your models properly. With these foundations, you can tackle various time series forecasting challenges using PyTorch.

The field of time series analysis continues to evolve rapidly, with new architectures and techniques being developed regularly. The principles and practices covered in this chapter provide a solid foundation to serve you well as you explore more advanced topics and stay current with the latest developments in this exciting field. In the next chapter, we will learn to deploy the machine learning models.

Exercises

Aim: Build a complete time series forecasting pipeline using PyTorch and LSTM networks.

Create a time series forecasting model that:

- Generates a synthetic time series with trend and seasonality.
- Preprocesses the data using sliding windows.

- Trains an LSTM model to predict future values.
- Forecasts the next 50 time steps.
- Evaluates performance using MAE and RMSE metrics.
- Visualizes the results with actual vs. predicted values.

Multiple choice questions

1. **Which of the following are key characteristics that distinguish time series data from regular tabular data? (Select all that apply)**
   a. Temporal dependencies between observations
   b. Independence of data points
   c. Presence of trends and seasonality
   d. Random ordering of observations
2. **What are the main advantages of using LSTM networks over basic RNNs for time series analysis? (Select all that apply)**
   a. Better handling of long-term dependencies
   b. Faster training time
   c. Ability to avoid the vanishing gradient problem
   d. Simpler architecture
3. **Which preprocessing steps are typically important for time series data before training neural networks? (Select all that apply)**
   a. Random shuffling of data points
   b. Proper normalization or scaling
   c. Temporal train-test splitting
   d. Creating sequences from the time series
4. **What is the main challenge with the recursive approach to multi-step forecasting?**
   a. It requires training multiple models
   b. Error accumulation over multiple prediction steps
   c. It cannot handle long forecast horizons
   d. It is computationally too expensive
5. **Why is proper train-test splitting crucial in time series analysis?**
   a. To prevent data leakage from the future to the past
   b. To ensure the random distribution of data
   c. To balance the dataset
   d. To reduce computational complexity
6. **Which of the following are valid approaches for multi-step time series forecasting? (Select all that apply)**
   a. Recursive forecasting
   b. Random forest regression

c. Direct multi-step forecasting

d. Sequence-to-sequence models

7. **What should you consider when choosing evaluation metrics for time series models? (Select all that apply)**

a. Alignment with business objectives

b. Interpretability of the metric

c. Computational efficiency only

d. Performance across different forecast horizons

8. **Which factors are essential for the practical implementation of time series models? (Select all that apply)**

a. Data quality and preprocessing

b. Model complexity only

c. Computational considerations

d. Monitoring and maintenance strategies

9. **What is stationarity in time series analysis?**

a. When statistical properties of the series remain constant over time

b. When the series has no trend

c. When the series has regular seasonality

d. When the series has no missing values

10. **Which approach is generally recommended when starting a new time series forecasting project?**

a. Begin with simple models and gradually increase complexity

b. Start with the most complex model available

c. Use the same model that worked for other projects

d. Focus only on the latest research techniques

Answers

1.	a,c.
2.	a,c.
3.	b,c,d.
4.	b.
5.	a.
6.	a,c,d.
7.	a,b,d.
8.	a,c,d.
9.	a.
10.	a.

Key terms

- **Autocorrelation**: It is the correlation of a time series with itself at different time lags, measuring how past values influence current values.
- **LSTM**: A recurrent neural network architecture designed to handle long-term dependencies in sequential data through gating mechanisms.
- **Multi-step forecasting**: The task of simultaneously predicting multiple future time steps instead of just the next single time step.
- **RNN**: A class of neural networks designed for sequential data, where connections between nodes form cycles allowing information to persist.
- **Seasonality**: Regular, predictable patterns in time series data that repeat over known periods (daily, weekly, monthly, yearly).
- **Sequence-to-sequence model**: An encoder-decoder architecture that processes an input sequence and generates an output sequence, useful for multi-step forecasting.
- **Stationarity**: A property of time series where statistical characteristics (mean, variance, autocorrelation) remain constant over time.
- **Time series**: A sequence of data points collected or recorded regularly, where the temporal order contains essential information.
- **Trend**: The long-term movement or direction in time series data, representing gradual increases or decreases over time.
- **Vanishing gradient problem**: A difficulty in training deep neural networks where gradients become exponentially small, making it hard to learn long-term dependencies.

References

1. *Hochreiter, S., & Schmidhuber, J. (1997). Long Short-Term Memory. Neural Computation, 9(8), 1735-1780. The foundational paper introduces LSTM networks and explains their architecture and advantages for sequence modeling.*
2. *Brownlee, J. (2018). Deep Learning for Time Series Forecasting. Machine Learning Mastery. A practical guide covering LSTM and other deep learning methods for time series forecasting, including preprocessing and evaluation.*
3. *Goodfellow, I., Bengio, Y., & Courville, A. (2016). Deep Learning. MIT Press. Comprehensive textbook covering deep learning fundamentals, including recurrent neural networks and sequence modeling.*
4. *PyTorch Documentation. (2024). Official PyTorch API documentation for LSTM modules and data handling utilities used in time series modeling. https://pytorch.org/docs/stable/nn.html#lstm*
5. *Brown, T., et al. (2020). Attention Is All You Need - Neural Information Processing Systems (NeurIPS) advances. Introduces the attention mechanism, which is also discussed in the chapter in the context of GRU with attention.*
6. *Hyndman, R. J., & Athanasopoulos, G. (2018). Forecasting: Principles and Practice (2nd ed.). A widely used textbook on time series forecasting, covering classical and modern methods, evaluation, and practical considerations.*
7. *Chollet, F. (2017). Deep Learning with Python. Manning Publications. It includes practical examples of LSTM and sequence modeling, which help understand implementation details.*

CHAPTER 20
Deploying Machine Learning Models

Introduction

Up to this point, we have learned how to build and train machine learning models using PyTorch (and earlier, Scikit-learn). Now comes the crucial next step: deployment. Deploying a model involves taking the trained model out of the research or training environment and making it available for real-world use, typically as a service that provides predictions on new data in real-time. In practical terms, deployment bridges the gap between your offline model training and an online application (for example, a web service or mobile app) that uses the model's predictions.

Why does deployment matter? Without deployment, even the most accurate model remains isolated—it is not accessible to end users or integrated into products. Deployment allows us to serve the model's predictions to users, automate decision-making in production systems, and continually deliver value from our machine learning efforts. It also involves considerations such as scalability (handling a large number of requests), reliability, and maintenance (updating the model as data changes). In short, deployment is the process by which machine learning models transition from a notebook to the real world.

In this chapter, we will walk through a step-by-step guide to deploying a PyTorch model for real-time inference using **Azure Machine Learning** (**Azure ML**). We will use the same SimpleNN model for **Modified National Institute of Standards and Technology** (**MNIST**) that we developed earlier in the book (as discussed in *Chapter 9, Building Blocks of Neural Networks in PyTorch*, where we built and trained a simple neural network on the MNIST dataset). By reusing this model, we bring our journey full circle, taking a familiar model from training to a deployed endpoint that can predict handwritten digits on demand.

While our focus is on Azure ML as the deployment platform, it is worth noting that the general principles also apply to other cloud services. Platforms such as *AWS SageMaker* and *Google Cloud Vertex AI* offer similar capabilities for hosting models as live endpoints. Azure ML provides a convenient, integrated environment for our demonstration. By the end of this chapter, you will have the foundation to explore deployment on any platform.

We will cover the entire deployment pipeline—preparing and optimizing the model (including optional steps like pruning and quantization for efficiency), packaging the model and its environment, registering it with Azure ML, writing a scoring script (Azure's term for the inference code), deploying the model to a managed online endpoint, and finally calling the deployed model through a **representational state transfer application programming interface** (**REST API**) to get predictions. Along the way, we will explain key concepts in plain language, such as what a scoring script does, what real-time endpoints are, how Azure utilizes Docker and container registries under the hood, and how to manage different versions of models during deployment.

By the end of this chapter, you will have deployed a PyTorch model and made it available as a web service, gaining valuable insight into the *production side of machine learning*. This is a significant step in any machine learning project: it is where models begin to perform real work for real users.

Structure

This chapter covers the following topics:

- Model deployment
- Preparing the model for deployment
- Registering the model in Azure ML
- Creating an Azure ML environment or Docker environment
- Writing the scoring script
- Deploying to a real-time endpoint on Azure ML
- Testing the deployed model for real-time inference
- Model versioning and updating deployments

Objectives

By the end of this chapter, you will know how to take a trained machine learning model and turn it into a live web service on a cloud platform. You will learn how to prepare a PyTorch model for production by saving its state and optionally applying optimizations, such as quantization and pruning, to reduce size and latency. You will understand how to use Azure ML to register models (creating a versioned record of your model in the cloud) and define a reproducible environment using *Conda* and *Docker*. We will make a scoring script that instructs the service on how to initialize the model and respond to prediction requests. You will then deploy the model to a real-time endpoint in Azure ML and make test predictions via a REST API call. Along the way, we will explain key deployment concepts, such as the difference between an endpoint and a deployment, the role of Azure's Container Registry and Docker images in serving models, and how model versioning enables you to manage updates. After completing this chapter, you will be equipped not only to deploy our MNIST model but also to tackle deploying your models and explore other cloud deployment options with confidence.

Model deployment

In machine learning workflows, model deployment refers to making a trained model available for use in an environment outside of the training context. Typically, this means hosting the model on a server (or cloud service) so that predictions can be requested via some interface (for example, an API). Deployment is essential because it is the step where a model transitions from an experimental artifact to a usable tool integrated into applications or processes.

Think of model deployment as similar to deploying an application or website. Just as you would host a web app on a server so that users can interact with it, we host our machine learning model on a server (or a managed service) so that other software or users can send data to it and receive predictions in return.

The following list outlines two ways to deploy models:

- **Batch processing**: It is where a model is used on a schedule or on demand to make predictions on a large batch of inputs (not covered in this chapter, but common for offline analytics).
- **Real-time (online) deployment**: It is where the model is always up and running behind a REST API (or similar interface), ready to handle one-off prediction requests with low latency. *This is our focus in this chapter.*

We will specifically deploy our model as a real-time inference service on Azure ML. This means we will create a **web endpoint** [a **Hypertext Transfer Protocol** (**HTTP**) **Uniform Resource Locator** (**URL**)] that clients can call with new data (in our case, an image of a handwritten digit) and that will respond with a prediction (the digit the model identifies as the picture represents). Azure ML's managed endpoints simplify a lot of the heavy lifting: Azure handles provisioning servers or containers, scaling up as needed, and exposes a secure web service for us.

Why Azure ML? Azure ML is one of several cloud platforms that support model deployment. We chose it here for its seamless integration with Python and support for PyTorch, as well as the rich features it provides, such as versioning and monitoring. However, it is worth noting that the concepts are very similar on other platforms. The details are as follows:

- *AWS SageMaker* offers model hosting endpoints where you can deploy PyTorch models using SageMaker's **software development kit** (**SDK**) or console.
- *Google Cloud Vertex AI* allows deploying models to endpoints and offers similar model registry and versioning capabilities.
- Even outside of cloud providers, you can deploy a model by hosting it on your server (using *Flask*, *FastAPI*, or *TorchServe*). However, you would then be responsible for managing scaling and infrastructure yourself.

Regardless of the platform, the typical steps for real-time deployment are to save the trained model, provide an environment for it to run (including libraries and OS dependencies), write a service or function to handle incoming requests, and start that service on a server. Managed services, such as Azure ML, automate the server and scaling aspects for you, allowing you to focus on the model and code.

In the following sections, we will prepare our model and environment, and then discuss the deployment to Azure ML.

The following flowchart outlines the end-to-end workflow for deploying our MNIST model on Azure ML, from training to serving real-time predictions:

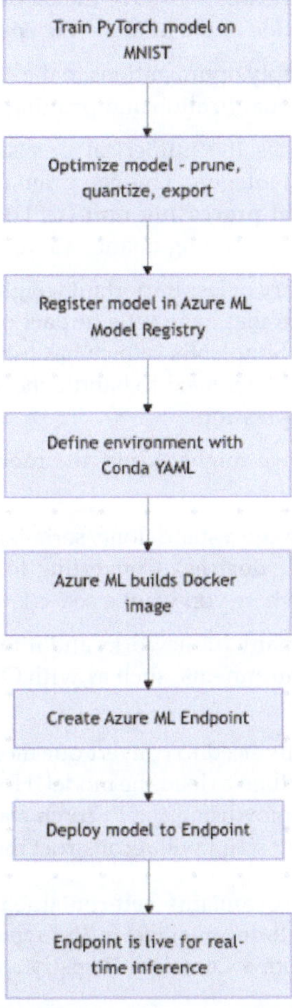

Figure 20.1: *Deployment process*

This figure illustrates the sequence of steps for deploying our trained model. We start by teaching the PyTorch model and then apply any optimizations or conversions [such as pruning, quantization, or exporting to TorchScript or **Open Neural Network Exchange** (**ONNX**) format] to prepare it for production. Next, we register the model with Azure ML, which stores the model file in the cloud and assigns it a version. We also specify an environment (using a `Conda YAML` file) listing the dependencies needed to run the model. Azure ML uses this to build a Docker container image, which is saved to **Azure's Container Registry** (**ACR**) behind the scenes. We then create a managed online endpoint, which is essentially a URL that will serve as the interface to our model. Finally, we deploy the model to the endpoint by tying together the model, environment, and our scoring code into a deployment instance. Once deployed, the endpoint is live and can serve predictions in real time to any client that sends an HTTP request.

With the big picture in mind, let us now understand the details, starting with preparing our trained model for deployment.

Preparing the model for deployment

Before deploying a model, it is essential to save and package it properly. In *Chapter 9, Building Blocks of Neural Networks in PyTorch*, we trained a SimpleNN on the MNIST dataset. Assuming you have retrained or have the final model (perhaps improved through subsequent chapters), the first step is to save the model's weights so they can be deployed. In PyTorch, the recommended practice is to save the model's state dictionary (containing the learned parameters) rather than a complete Python pickle of the model. This ensures better compatibility and flexibility.

We also have the opportunity at this stage to apply optimizations to the model, making it more efficient for inference. Standard post-training optimizations include quantization and pruning, the details are as follows:

- **Quantization:** This technique reduces the numerical precision of the model's weights (and possibly activations) from 32-bit floats to 8-bit integers. This can dramatically shrink the model's size and improve inference speed, especially on **central processing unit** (**CPU**), with only a minor impact on accuracy (if done correctly). PyTorch supports post-training quantization, which we can apply to our trained model.
- **Pruning:** Pruning removes unnecessary or less important weights from the model (for example, eliminating connections in neural network layers that have little impact on outputs). This results in a sparser model that can be smaller and faster. In our SimpleNN (which has fully connected layers), pruning can zero out a percentage of the weights. We would later need to handle the sparse model appropriately, but it serves as a good demonstration of model compression.

Additionally, for maximum interoperability, we might export the model to standard formats like *TorchScript* or *ONNX*:

- **TorchScript**: It is PyTorch's way to create a standalone, serializable model that can run without the Python interpreter (e.g., in C++ or on mobile devices). Converting to TorchScript via tracing or scripting can be helpful in deployment in scenarios where you want a self-contained model.
- **ONNX**: It is a format supported by many frameworks and inference engines. Exporting to ONNX enables the model to be used in various environments, such as with ONNX Runtime for optimized serving or on other platforms.

For deployment on Azure ML, we do not strictly need to convert our model to TorchScript or ONNX. Azure ML can deploy a PyTorch state dict just fine by using Python to load the model. However, it is still valuable to be aware of these formats. In this example, we will primarily deploy using the PyTorch state dict (the file **`simple_nn_state_dict.pth`** containing our trained weights), and our scoring script will reconstruct the model class and load these weights.

Note: This chapter in our GitHub repository contains self-contained scripts with all the code shown in the following sections. These scripts are also well-documented in the repository. Remember that you must have an Azure Subscription, an Azure ML resource with a Container Registry created upfront; creating these resources is a procedure outside the scope of this chapter.

Refer to the following steps to prepare the model:

1. Save the model state dictionary. In your training code, after training is complete, save the weights:

```
# After training the model (SimpleNN)
torch.save(model.state_dict(), "models/simple_nn_state_dict.pth")
```

   - This creates a file **simple_nn_state_dict.pth** containing the model parameters. We will use this file for deployment.
   - We may also optionally save other formats:

```
torch.save(model, "models/simple_nn_complete.pth")

# (Optional) Convert to TorchScript and save
traced_model = torch.jit.trace(model, torch.randn(1, 1, 28, 28))
traced_model.save("models/simple_nn_traced.pt")

# (Optional) Export to ONNX
torch.onnx.export(model, torch.randn(1, 1, 28, 28), "models/simple_nn.onnx",
                  input_names=['mnist_image'], output_names=['digit_probabilities'],
                  dynamic_axes={'mnist_image': {0: 'batch_size'}, 'digit_probabilities': {0: 'batch_size'}})
```

   The preceding code illustrates additional exports. The state dict approach is what we will deploy; however, you can use the ONNX model to deploy with an ONNX runtime or the TorchScript model for a PyTorch-less serving environment if needed.

   Always ensure to use `model.eval()` mode before saving or exporting for inference.

2. **Apply quantization (optional)**: If we want to reduce model size and possibly improve CPU inference speed, we can quantize the model:

```
import torch.ao.quantization as quantization

model.eval()
model.qconfig = quantization.get_default_qconfig('qnnpack')
# Prepare model for quantization
model_prepared = quantization.prepare(model, inplace=False)
# Calibrate with some sample data
model_prepared(torch.randn(32, 1, 28, 28))
# Convert to quantized model
model_quantized = quantization.convert(model_prepared, inplace=False)
```

   In this snippet, we set up a quantization configuration (**qnnpack** is a backend for quantization suitable for mobile/ARM and x86), prepare the model (which inserts simulation modules for quantization), run some data through for calibration, and then convert it to a quantized version. The resulting **model_quantized** now has 8-bit weights for the linear layers, etc. We could also save this model's state dict (it will have a slightly different structure). In our pipeline, quantization is an optional step. If you encounter issues or if the platform does not support quantized operations, you can skip it. Azure ML can deploy quantized PyTorch models as long as the environment has the right PyTorch version, because quantization still uses PyTorch for inference.

3. **Apply pruning (optional)**: We can prune the model to remove some weights:

```
# Let's say model is an instance of SimpleNN
for name, module in model.named_modules():
    if isinstance(module, torch.nn.Linear):
        prune.l1_unstructured(module, name='weight', amount=0.3) # remove 30% of weights
        prune.remove(module, 'weight')  # finalize pruning (remove the mask)
```

4. The preceding code iterates through modules of the network, and for each linear layer, it applies L1-unstructured pruning, which zeroes out 30% of the smallest magnitude weights. The **prune.remove** call then makes the pruning permanent by removing the prune mask and dropping those connections. This can reduce the number of parameters. After pruning, the model can be saved or evaluated as usual. Keep in mind that PyTorch does not automatically speed up sparse models on the CPU; however, the model size is reduced, and with specialized libraries or hardware, sparse patterns can be effectively exploited. Pruning is illustrated here primarily to demonstrate a step you might take before deployment if model size is a concern.

5. **Verify model performance after optimization**: If you do quantize or prune, always test the model's accuracy on some validation data to ensure the drop in performance (if any) is acceptable. Sometimes, quantization can slightly reduce accuracy; pruning too aggressively can have a similar effect. In our example, since it is an MNIST model with ample capacity, a bit of pruning or 8-bit quantization is unlikely to impact accuracy significantly, but it is a good practice to check.

   After these steps, we should have:

   - **simple_nn_state_dict.pth**: The main model weights file we will deploy.
   - **(Optionally)** simple_nn_traced.pt: TorchScript model, **simple_nn.onnx** (ONNX model), etc., and a quantized version of the state dict.

   Now that the model file is ready, we can proceed to the Azure ML-specific parts of deployment. The next step is to register the model in Azure ML, which is essentially uploading the model to our Azure ML workspace's model registry.

Registering the model in Azure ML

Azure ML provides a *Model Registry*, a central place to store and version your models. Registering a model involves creating a record in the registry, along with metadata (such as a name, version number, description, and tags), and uploading the actual model file(s). Later, when we deploy, we can reference the model by name and version.

Why register the model? It provides version control and traceability. Every time you register a model with the same name, Azure ML will version it (1, 2, 3, ...). You can then choose which version to deploy. The registry also makes the model accessible to other Azure ML workflows (for example, if you want to run batch scoring jobs or evaluate models, etc., they can pull the model from the registry).

Before running the registration code, ensure you have access to an Azure ML Workspace. You would typically set up the Azure ML Python SDK with your credentials or use interactive authentication. For simplicity in our code examples, we assume that you have configured default Azure credentials (for example, via Azure **Command Language Interface** (**CLI**) login or a managed identity if running in Azure). Refer to the book repository for a comprehensive example of every step in this chapter.

Let us examine how to register our model using the Azure ML SDK (v2). First, we connect to the workspace, then use **MLClient** to register the model:

```
from azure.ai.ml import MLClient
from azure.ai.ml.entities import Model
```

```
from azure.identity import DefaultAzureCredential

# Connect to Azure ML workspace
credential = DefaultAzureCredential()
ml_client = MLClient(credential, subscription_id, resource_group, workspace_name)

# Register the model
model = ml_client.models.create_or_update(
    Model(
        name="SimpleNN-MNIST",
        path="models/simple_nn_state_dict.pth",
        type="custom_model",
        description="Simple NN for MNIST digit classification"
    )
)
print(f"Registered model name: {model.name}, version: {model.version}")
```

In this snippet:

- We instantiate an **`MLClient`** with our Azure subscription ID, resource group, and workspace name (you will fill in these details with your own Azure credentials or use a configuration file). The **`DefaultAzureCredential`** is a handy class that attempts multiple authentication methods. In practice, you can also use **`AzureCliCredential()`** if you have already **`logged in`** locally with **`az login`**.
- We then call **`ml_client.models.create_or_update(...)`** with a **`Model`** object. We assign a name to our model (e.g., **`"SimpleNN-MNIST"`**), specify the local path to the model file (**`simple_nn_state_dict.pth`**), and optionally provide a description and type. Azure ML will upload this file to the cloud and register it under the given name.
- The returned **`model`** object includes a `version` attribute. If this is the first time registering **`"SimpleNN-MNIST"`**, it will be version 1. If we register a new model with the same name later, it will be designated as version 2, and so on. The print statement would output nearly look like: *Registered model name: SimpleNN-MNIST, version: 1.*

At this point, our model is now stored in Azure ML's model registry. You can verify this by navigating to the Azure ML Studio UI, selecting **Models**, and locating *SimpleNN-MNIST*. It should display version 1, along with its description and any applicable tags.

The following figure shows the Model List as displayed in Azure ML Studio:

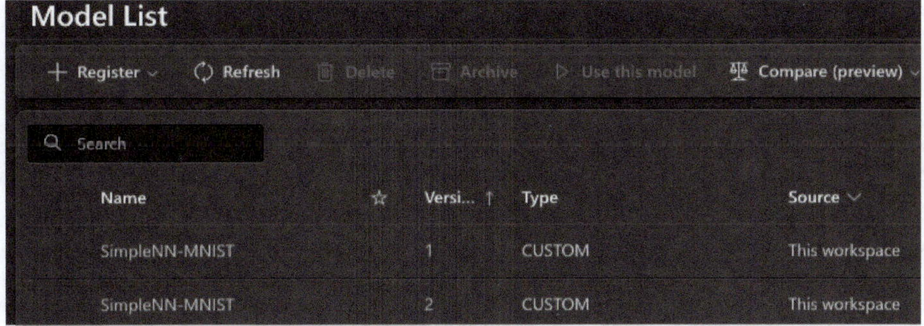

***Figure 20.2:** Azure ML model registry*

In the Azure ML Studio, as shown in the previous figure, you would see the model name and a version number. If you click it, you can see details like when it was registered, by whom, the size of the model file, and the path in Azure blob storage where it is stored. This confirms that our model is ready for deployment.

Creating an Azure ML environment or Docker environment

When deploying a model, it is not just the model itself that needs to be transferred to the server; we also need the *software environment* in which the model will run. This includes the Python version and all the Python packages (and sometimes system libraries) required by our model inference code. In our case, since we are using PyTorch to run the model and possibly other libraries (like NumPy), we must ensure those are installed in the environment on the Azure server.

Azure ML handles environment management through the concept of *environments*, which are versioned recipes for Docker containers. Essentially, you provide a definition (commonly as a Conda environment YAML file, or you can point to a Docker image), and Azure ML will use that to build a Docker image. The Docker image is what will be used to run your deployed service.

For our deployment, we will define a Conda environment YAML (**environment.yml**) that includes all necessary packages. Azure ML will interpret this file, create a Docker container with those packages, and register the environment so it can be reused. PyTorch, torchvision, and other Python packages get updates at least on a monthly basis. Make sure to update your yml file to use the most up-to-date stable versions.

Let us see what our **environment.yml** looks like for this deployment:

```
name: pytorch-cpu-inference
channels:
  - conda-forge
dependencies:
  - python=3.10
  - pip
  - pip:
      # PyTorch and torchvision (CPU version)
      - torch==2.3.0+cpu
      - torchvision==0.18.0+cpu
      - --extra-index-url https://download.pytorch.org/whl/cpu
      # Other dependencies
      - numpy
      - pillow
      - inference-schema[numpy-support]
      - azureml-defaults
```

This environment file specifies a Conda environment named **pytorch-cpu-inference**. We use the **conda-forge** channel (which is a community channel with many packages). Under **dependencies**, we pin Python 3.10 and include pip. Under the **pip:** section, we list the pip packages we need:

- We explicitly install a CPU version of PyTorch (**torch==2.3.0+cpu** along with **torchvision==0.18.0+cpu**). The **+cpu** and extra index URL ensure we get the CPU-only wheels (since in our example, we will assume we are deploying to CPU compute, which is typical for simple deployments unless you provision expensive GPU instances).
- We include **numpy** (for numerical operations, although PyTorch covers a lot; our code may also use NumPy).

- **pillow** might be used if we were doing any image processing (standard in vision tasks).
- **Inference-schema[numpy-support]** is an Azure ML utility that facilitates data serialization. Although not strictly required, it is often included in Azure ML deployments, especially when utilizing certain features or automatic schema generation.
- **azureml-defaults** is a special package that Azure ML suggests including; it brings in the necessary packages for the Azure ML inference runtime (this includes things like Flask or gunicorn servers that host the **score.py** web service inside the container, and Azure ML logging functionalities). Including **azureml-defaults** is essential for an Azure ML deployment to work smoothly.

When we deploy, Azure ML will take this **environment.yml** and do the following:

1. Create a Docker image starting from a base image (if not specified, Azure uses a default or the one provided in the code). In our deployment code, we specify an **image** as shown later, which is a base image with Ubuntu and some shared machine learning libraries.
2. Inside that image, set up a Conda environment and install all the listed packages.
3. Register this environment with a name and version (so we could reuse it for subsequent deployments if desired).

We can also register the environment explicitly via code. For example:

```
from azure.ai.ml.entities import Environment

env = ml_client.environments.create_or_update(
    Environment(
        name="pytorch-mnist-inference",
        description="PyTorch environment for MNIST inference",
        conda_file="environment.yml",
        image="mcr.microsoft.com/azureml/openmpi4.1.0-ubuntu20.04:latest"
    )
)
print(f"Registered environment: {env.name}, version: {env.version}")
```

Here, we assigned a name to the environment (**pytorch-mnist-inference**) and pointed to our **environment.yml file**. We also specified a base Docker image: **mcr.microsoft.com/azureml/openmpi4.1.0-ubuntu20.04:latest**. This is one of Azure ML's curated base images, which already has some common things (OpenMPI, Ubuntu 20.04, etc.). Azure will use that as the starting point and then install the Conda environment on top of it. If we did not specify an image, Azure ML might use a default or build from a minimal image.

After running this, the environment is registered and versioned in Azure ML (just like models, each environment definition can have versions).

Note on ACR: Azure ML automatically uses an Azure Container Registry (associated with your workspace) to store the built Docker images for environments. You usually do not have to interact with ACR directly. Still, it is reassuring to know that when you deploy the model, Azure will either retrieve the existing image for this environment (if it has already been built and cached) or create a new one, and that image will reside in ACR. The endpoint, when it runs, essentially pulls this container image onto the compute that will serve the model.

At this stage, we have:

- A registered model (SimpleNN-MNIST, version 1).
- A registered environment (**pytorch-mnist-inference**, with its own version).

The final piece to prepare before actual deployment is the scoring script, which we cover next.

Writing the scoring script

The scoring script is a Python script that Azure ML will execute inside the deployed container to handle inference requests. Azure ML uses a convention—it looks for two functions in this script—**`init()`** and **`run(input_data)`**. The details are as follows:

- The **`init()`** function is called once when the deployment environment is started. This is where you typically load the model into memory, making it ready to run. It is analogous to a setup phase.
- The `run` function is invoked every time an HTTP request is received. Azure ML will pass the request's **JavaScript Object Notation (JSON)** payload to this function (as a string or dictionary) and expects the function to return the prediction results (usually as a JSON string or Python dict that can be serialized to JSON).

It is important to ensure the **run** function is written to handle the input and output format you intend to use in your API. We also include error handling to return useful messages if something goes wrong (so we can see them in logs or the response).

Let us go through our **`score.py`** scoring script step by step. We will not list the entire file here, but focus on the critical parts:

Initializing and loading the model (in **`init()`**):

```
# score.py
import json
import logging
import os
import torch
import torch.nn as nn

logger = logging.getLogger(__name__)
logging.basicConfig(level=logging.INFO)

# Define the model architecture (should match the training model class)
class SimpleNN(nn.Module):
    def __init__(self, input_size=784, hidden_size=128, num_classes=10):
        super(SimpleNN, self).__init__()
        self.fc1 = nn.Linear(input_size, hidden_size)
        self.fc2 = nn.Linear(hidden_size, num_classes)
    def forward(self, x):
        x = x.view(x.size(0), -1)  # flatten
        x = torch.relu(self.fc1(x))
        x = self.fc2(x)
        return x

model = None  # global model variable

def init():
    """Initialize the model for inference by loading the trained weights."""
    global model
```

```
    try:
        logger.info("Loading model in init()")
        # Determine model path
        model_path = "simple_nn_state_dict.pth"
        if not os.path.exists(model_path):
            # Azure ML puts models in a specific directory when deployed.
            # Look for the model in Azure ML's expected locations:
            for root, dirs, files in os.walk("/var/azureml-app"):
                for file in files:
                    if file == "simple_nn_state_dict.pth":
                        model_path = os.path.join(root, file)
                        break
        # Load the model
        model = SimpleNN()
        state_dict = torch.load(model_path, map_location='cpu')
        model.load_state_dict(state_dict)
        model.eval()
        logger.info("Model loaded successfully")
    except Exception as e:
        logger.error("Error during init: %s", str(e))
        raise
```

Let us understand the code:

- We import the necessary packages (**torch**, **nn**, etc.). Logging is set to INFO level, allowing us to view logs in Azure.
- We redefine the **SimpleNN** class exactly as it was during training. This is crucial since we saved just the state dictionary; we need to reconstruct the model architecture to load those weights. We use the same architecture (784 input -> 128 hidden -> 10 output with a ReLU).
- We declare a global **model** variable. Azure ML will keep the **model** object alive in memory between requests, which is what we want (so that each request does not have to reload the model from disk).
- In **init()**, we find the path to the model file. When you deploy with Azure ML, by default, it places the model file in a directory such as **/var/azureml-app/azureml-models/<ModelName>/<version>/<your file>**. In the preceding code, we first try the current working directory for **simple_nn_state_dict.pth**, but if it is not found, we traverse **/var/azureml-app** to find it. This ensures the script can locate the model file, whether we are running locally (perhaps for testing) or in Azure.
- **We then load the model**: instantiate **SimpleNN()**, use **torch.load(model_path, map_location='cpu')** to load the weights (always map to CPU, since our inference container might not have a GPU), and then **model.load_state_dict(state_dict)**. We **call model.eval()** to set it to evaluation mode (disabling any dropout or batch norm training behavior, though our network does not have those).
- If any exception occurs (file not found, etc.), we log an error and raise an exception, which will cause the endpoint deployment to fail (and we would see the error in the logs). If all goes well, our model is now loaded in memory and ready to serve.

Handling predictions (in **run()**):

```
def run(raw_data):
    """Run inference on the input data."""
    try:
```

```
        data = json.loads(raw_data)
        # Extract input data
        if 'data' in data:
            input_data = data['data']
        else:
            input_data = data  # assume the data is the root if not wrapped
        # Convert to tensor
        input_tensor = torch.tensor(input_data, dtype=torch.float32)
        # If a single image (flattened list of 784),
    reshape to [1, 1, 28, 28]
        if input_tensor.ndim == 1:
            input_tensor = input_tensor.view(1, 1, 28, 28)
        elif input_tensor.ndim == 2:
            # If 2D, maybe already [batch, 784] or [784, batch]
            if input_tensor.shape[0] == 784:
                input_tensor = input_tensor.T  # transpose if needed
            input_tensor = input_tensor.view(-1, 1, 28, 28)
        else:
            # If ndim == 3 or 4, assume it's already [batch, 1, 28, 28]
            pass

        # Run model prediction
        with torch.no_grad():
            outputs = model(input_tensor)
            probabilities = torch.softmax(outputs, dim=1)
            predicted_classes = torch.argmax(probabilities, dim=1)

        # Prepare the response
        predicted_classes = predicted_classes.numpy().tolist()  # convert to list
        probabilities = probabilities.numpy().tolist()
        if len(predicted_classes) == 1:
            result = {
                "predicted_digit": int(predicted_classes[0]),
                "probabilities": probabilities[0],
                "status": "success"
            }
        else:
            # Batch of results
            result = {
                "predicted_digits": predicted_classes,
                "probabilities": probabilities,
                "status": "success"
            }
        return json.dumps(result)
    except Exception as e:
```

```
        error_msg = f"Error during inference: {str(e)}"
        logger.error(error_msg)
        return json.dumps({"error": error_msg, "status": "error"})
```

Key points in the **run** function:

- We receive **raw_data**, which Azure ML will pass as a JSON-formatted string (the body of the HTTP request). We parse it with json. loads.
- We expect the JSON to contain a key **'data'** that holds the input. In our design, the client will send **{"data": [...flattened pixel values...]}**. However, we add a little flexibility: if **'data'** is not present in the JSON, we simply use the JSON itself as the input (this may handle the case where someone sends just a raw list without the **'data'** key).
- We convert the input data to a PyTorch tensor. We ensure it is torch.float32 dtype because our model expects floats.
- **Then we handle shaping**: The model expects a tensor of shape **[batch_size, 1, 28, 28]** for MNIST images (since it is a single-channel 28x28 image, and batch size could be 1 or more). If the input is a single flattened image (784 values), **input_tensor.ndim** will be 1. We then reshape it to **[1, 784]** and subsequently to **[1, 1, 28, 28]**. If the input is a 2D tensor, it may be **[batch, 784]** or **[784, batch]**; we attempt to handle this by reshaping it appropriately. If it is already a 4D or 3D, we assume it is in the correct format. Essentially, we are being cautious about the input format, since users might send a single list or a list of lists, etc.
- Next, we perform the inference **model(input_tensor)** to get outputs (which are logits for each of the 10 classes). We apply **torch.softmax** to turn those logits into probabilities (so that the output is easier to interpret as confidence). Then we use **torch.argmax** to get the index of the highest probability (the predicted digit class for each sample in the batch).
- We convert predictions and probabilities to regular Python lists (via **.numpy().tolist()**) because tensors are not directly JSON serializable.
- We build the result dictionary. If it is a single prediction, we return a dictionary with **"predicted_digit"** and the probabilities array. If it were a batch, we would return lists of predictions. We also include a **"status": "success"** field for clarity (and this could be expanded with additional fields, such as a timestamp or request ID, in a more elaborate setup).
- We use **json.dumps(result)** to return a JSON string. Azure ML will send this back as the body of the HTTP response to the client.
- If any exception occurs (for example, an invalid input format causing a conversion failure), we catch it and return a JSON with an **"error"** message and a **"status" of "error"**. This way, the client could receive some information that something went wrong, and we also log the error.

This scoring script is straightforward yet crucial. A few things to note:

- We included the model class definition inside the script. This is because when Azure runs this script in the container, it does not automatically know what **SimpleNN** is, so we need to define it. Another approach could be to import the model class from a separate module, but that module would need to be packaged with the code. For simplicity, we define it inline.
- The script should be placed alongside the model file when deploying. In our case, since we registered only the model, we will supply this script separately during deployment.
- Azure ML's use of the term **scoring** comes from earlier usage where making a prediction is often referred to as *scoring a data point* (especially in fields like statistics or when dealing with models that output a **"score"**). In our context, scoring is equivalent to making a prediction. So, the *scoring script* is essentially the inference script.

Before deploying, it is a good idea to test this script locally. One way is to simulate what Azure does: call **init()**, then call **run(some_json)**. For example:

```
# Simulate local testing of score.py
if __name__ == "__main__":
    init()
    test_input = json.dumps({"data": [0.0]*784}) # an image of all zeros
    print("Request:", test_input[:50], "...")
    result = run(test_input)
    print("Response:", result)
```

This would load the model and attempt to predict on an all-zero image (which should likely predict class *0* or *1* with some probability). It is a quick smoke test. Of course, for a real test, you would use actual MNIST images.

Now that we have the model registered, the environment defined, and the scoring script written, we are ready for the main event—deploying the model to an Azure ML-managed endpoint.

Deploying to a real-time endpoint on Azure ML

Deployment on Azure ML involves creating two main things: an **endpoint** and a **deployment**. Even though the terminology can be perplexing initially, they are essential to build a thorough understanding:

- An endpoint is the logical web service endpoint; think of it as the front-door URL. An endpoint has a name and can have one or more deployments behind it. For managed online endpoints, the URL will be in the format **https://<service-name>.<region>.inference.ml.azure.com/score** (*Azure will generate this for you*).
- A deployment is a particular set of models, environment, and code that is deployed to the infrastructure and tied to an endpoint. You can have multiple deployments (with different model versions or types) under one endpoint and even split traffic between them (this is useful for blue/green deployments, A/B testing newer models, etc.). Each deployment has a name (commonly, **"blue"** and **"green"** are used as names for primary and secondary implementations, but you can choose any name).

In our scenario, we will create one endpoint (e.g., named **"simplenn-mnist-ep"**) and one deployment under it (we will call it **"blue"**). We will direct 100% of the traffic to this single deployment (since it is the only one). If we later improve the model and want to deploy a new version side by side, we might add a **"green"** deployment and shift some traffic to it. Make sure to check Azure ML Compute documentation, the **instance_type** mentioned in the code below might not be available in all regions or get deprecated.

Let us go understand the deployment process in code:

```
from azure.ai.ml.entities
import ManagedOnlineEndpoint, ManagedOnlineDeployment, CodeConfiguration

# Names for the endpoint and deployment
MODEL_NAME = "SimpleNN-MNIST"
ENDPOINT_NAME = MODEL_NAME + "-ep"  # e.g., "SimpleNN-MNIST-ep"
DEPLOYMENT_NAME = "blue"

# 1. Create a managed online endpoint (if it doesn't exist already)
endpoint = ManagedOnlineEndpoint(
    name=ENDPOINT_NAME,
    auth_mode="key",  # using key-based authentication
```

```
    description=»MNIST digit classification endpoint»
)
endpoint = ml_client.online_endpoints.begin_create_or_update(endpoint).result()
print(f"Endpoint {ENDPOINT_NAME} is at {endpoint.scoring_uri}")

# 2. Create a deployment for the endpoint
deployment = ManagedOnlineDeployment(
    name=DEPLOYMENT_NAME,
    endpoint_name=ENDPOINT_NAME,
    model=model,  # reference to the registered model
    environment=env,  # reference to the registered environment
    code_configuration=CodeConfiguration(code="./", scoring_script="score.py"),
    instance_type=»Standard_DS3_v2»,
    instance_count=1
)
ml_client.online_deployments.begin_create_or_update(deployment).result()
print(f"Deployment {DEPLOYMENT_NAME} created.")

# 3. Set traffic allocation (100% to 'blue')
endpoint.traffic = {DEPLOYMENT_NAME: 100}
endpoint = ml_client.online_endpoints.begin_create_or_update(endpoint).result()
print(f"Traffic set to {DEPLOYMENT_NAME}. Endpoint status: {endpoint.provisioning_state}")
```

Refer to the following list to understand the preceding code:

- We define **`ENDPOINT_NAME`** as the model name plus **`"-ep"`** (just a simple convention to derive an endpoint name). Endpoint names in Azure ML must be unique within the region or workspace and should be generally lowercase.
- We choose **`auth_mode="key",`** which means the endpoint will use API keys for access (Azure will generate a primary and secondary key). The other mode, **`"aml_token"`** uses Azure Active Directory tokens for authentication, which is more secure for integration with Azure services but a bit more complex to use for testing. Using a key is straightforward for demonstration, as it can be included in our request header.
- We create a **`ManagedOnlineEndpoint`** object with the name and description. We call **`ml_client.online_endpoints.begin_create_or_update(endpoint)`** to build it. (The **`.begin_create_or_update`** is asynchronous, hence the **`.result()`** at the end to wait for completion).
- When the endpoint is created, it does not yet have a model deployed. It is like an empty shell with an address. The **`endpoint.scoring_uri`** property gives the URL where it will listen. We print that out (it will not work until a deployment is added, though).
- Next, we configure the **`ManagedOnlineDeployment`**. We give it a name (**`"blue"`**) and associate it with our endpoint by name. We specify which model to deploy—here, the model is the Model object returned from registration (which points to our SimpleNN-MNIST v1). We also specify the environment—the **`env`** object from earlier (pointing to our environment with PyTorch and dependencies).
- **`code_configuration`** allows us to specify the folder where our code (such as **`score.py`** and any other files) resides and which script serves as the entry point. In our case, we assume that **`score.py`** is in the current directory (represented by **`"./"`** in the code path).

- We choose an instance_type, which is the **Virtual Machine** (VM) size for the deployment. Here, **"Standard_DS3_v2"** is a CPU VM with a few cores and ~14 GB of RAM, which is sufficient for our example. Azure ML offers various SKU options, including **graphics processing unit** (**GPU**) options if needed (for example, a GPU instance might be **Standard_NC6** for an NVIDIA K80). Using a CPU instance is more cost-effective and suitable for the MNIST dataset.
- **instance_count=1** means we will have one replica of our deployment. For high availability or scaling, we could set more, but one is fine to start. (Azure ML can also auto-scale based on traffic, but that is beyond our current scope.)
- We call **ml_client.online_deployments.begin_create_or_update(deployment)** to deploy. This step will take several minutes the first time, because Azure ML has to do a lot:
  - It builds the environment's Docker image if it has not already been built.
  - It packages the model files and our code (**score.py**) into a deployment artifact.
  - It spins up a container instance (on the specified compute SKU) running that Docker image.
  - It mounts the model (makes it available in **/var/azureml-app/azureml-models/...**).
  - It starts the Azure ML inference server (which loads **score.py**).
  - It waits for a signal that the service is healthy.
- If everything goes well, the deployment will reach a **Healthy** state. We confirm that the deployment has been created.
- Finally, we update the endpoint's traffic rules to send 100% of traffic to our **"blue"** deployment. (When you have multiple implementations, you can do **endpoint.traffic = {"blue": 80, "green": 20}** for example, to split traffic 80/20). Here is just one deployment, so 100%. We call **create_or_update** on the endpoint again to apply this change.
- We print the endpoint's provisioning state, which should be either **"Succeeded"** or **"Ready"**. If there is an issue, it might display **"Failed"** or a similar message.

During this process, it is good to monitor progress. The **.result()** calls will block until completion, but you can also check Azure ML Studio's Endpoints section. You will see the endpoint being created, and under it, the deployment being created. There are logs that you can view in real-time (events such as pulling an image, starting a container, etc.). Suppose any error occurs (for example, the scoring script contains a bug or the environment fails to build). In that case, Azure ML will eventually mark the deployment as failed, and you can inspect the logs to diagnose the issue. The following figure illustrates what a typical Azure ML endpoint looks like after deployment succeeds:

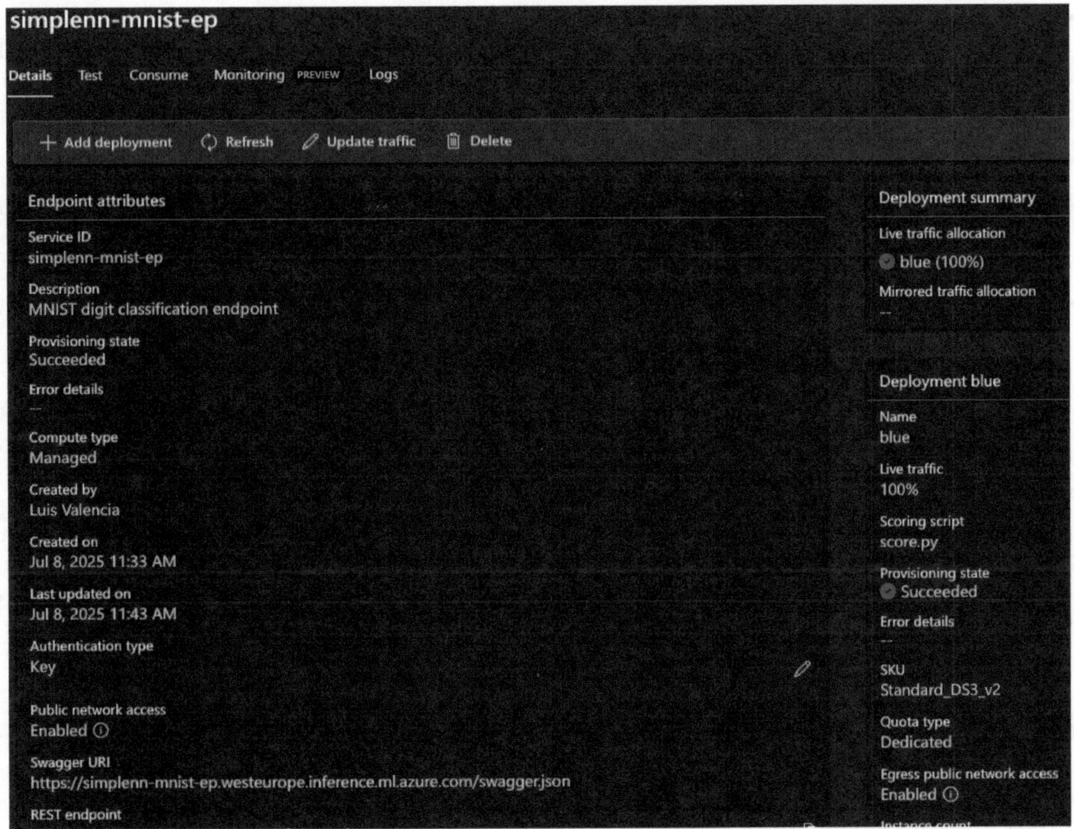

***Figure 20.3**: Azure ML endpoint and deployment*

Figure 20.3 typically shows the endpoint's overview, including a URL (scoring URI) and the two keys (**Test** tab) (primary and secondary keys). Those keys are used for authentication when calling the endpoint (we will use one in a moment). The page also shows if the deployment is healthy.

At this point, if everything is successful, congratulations—your model is now deployed. We have a live endpoint that is ready to accept HTTP requests and run our model to return predictions.

Before we call the endpoint, let us clarify some of the concepts we just exercised in plain language:

- **Managed online endpoint vs. deployment**: An endpoint is like a *door*, and a deployment is like the *person behind the door*. You can have one door (endpoint URL) and swap out who is answering (deployments with different models or versions). This abstraction enables you to maintain the same URL for clients while updating the model or running experiments with a new model (by adding deployments and adjusting traffic).
- **Azure ML environment and ACR**: When we provided the `environment.yml file`, Azure ML essentially created a Docker container image that includes everything needed to run our model (e.g., PyTorch). This image is stored in **Azure Container Registry** (**ACR**). We did not need to handle any Docker commands; Azure did it for us. If you navigate to Azure ML Studio's Environments section, you will see our environment, its version, and possibly a reference to the base image. The container image name in ACR will be auto-generated. For the most part, as a user, you do not need to worry about ACR details; however, it is beneficial to know that images are being built and stored (especially if you need to clean up or reuse them).

- **Scaling and instance type**: We chose a CPU instance with count 1. Azure ML endpoints can be updated later to scale out (increase instances) if you need to handle more requests. You can also scale to zero (which Azure refers to as *deallocate* or *stop endpoint*) to avoid incurring charges when not in use, although the startup time for the next request will be longer.
- **Authentication (auth_mode)**: We used **auth_mode="key"**, meaning the endpoint requires an API key. The keys can be found in the portal or via **ml_client.online_endpoints.get_keys(name)**. A client must provide the key in the header of requests (we will do this next). If we had used token auth mode, clients would need an OAuth Bearer token from Azure AD—more secure for enterprise scenarios, but unnecessary complexity for our example.
- **Provisioning time**: The first deployment can take a few minutes (3-15 minutes), as the image may need to be built. Subsequent updates might be faster if the environment is reused. Azure ML tries to cache and reuse the environment image if nothing has changed in it between deployments.

Now, with the model up and running on Azure's servers, let us see how to use it by sending an inference request.

Testing the deployed model real-time inference

To test our deployed model, we will send an HTTP request to the endpoint's scoring URL. We can do this in many ways: using the Azure ML SDK (**ml_client.online_endpoints.invoke**), using the Azure CLI (az ml online-endpoint invoke ...), or simply using an HTTP library like requests in Python. Using requests is nice because it shows the raw mechanics of how a client would consume the service, and it does not require any Azure-specific tooling on the client side.

First, we need two pieces of information from the deployed endpoint:

- The scoring URL (also called inference URL or endpoint URL). This is the address of the service (it will end in **"/score"** for default settings).
- The authentication key for the endpoint (since we used key auth). Azure ML endpoints have a primary and secondary key. We can use either. Think of them like passwords - you include them in the request header so that Azure knows you are allowed to call the service.

You can get these from Azure ML Studio (on the endpoint page, there is usually a **"Consume"** section that shows the REST endpoint and the keys). You can also get them via code:

```
scoring_uri = endpoint.scoring_uri
keys = ml_client.online_endpoints.get_keys(ENDPOINT_NAME)
primary_key = keys.primary_key
print(scoring_uri, primary_key)
```

Suppose **scoring_uri** is something like:

https://simplenn-mnist-ep.<region>.inference.ml.azure.com/score and **primary_key** is a long string, such as "**abcdefghijklmnopqrstuvwxyz123456**" (just an example).

Now, let us use Python's **requests** library to call the endpoint. We will create a dummy test image (or you could use a real one from the MNIST test set if you have it) and send it as JSON:

```
import requests
import json

# Example: create a dummy test payload of one image (28x28 of all zeros)
test_image = [0.0] * 784  # 784 zeros
payload = {"data": test_image}

```

```
# The header with authentication - use the primary key
provided by Azure ML
headers = {
    "Content-Type": "application/json",
    "Authorization": f"Bearer {primary_key}"
}

response = requests.post(scoring_uri, headers=headers, data=json.dumps(payload))
print(«Status code:», response.status_code)
print("Response:", response.json())
```

In this code:

- We define **`payload`** as a JSON with a **`"data"`** field. The value is a list of 784 floats (all of which are zero in this case). This matches what our **`score.py`** expects (a list of 784 elements).
- We set the **`Content-Type`** to **`application/json`** (since we are sending JSON).
- The **`Authorization`** header is where we include the key. Azure expects the key to be given as a Bearer token in the format **`"Bearer <your-key>"`**. (Even though it is not an OAuth token, Azure ML endpoints accept the key this way.)
- We use **`requests.post`** to send the HTTP POST request to the scoring URI, with the headers and the JSON payload (notice we used **`json.dumps`** to convert the payload to a string and could also use **`json=payload`** parameter of requests, which would do it for us).
- We then print out the status code and the returned JSON.

If everything is working, the status code should be 200, and the response JSON might look something like:

```
{"predicted_digit": 0, "probabilities": [0.99, 0.001, 0.0005, ..., 0.0003], "status": "success"}
```

This indicates the model thinks the image is a **`"0"`** with very high confidence (which would make sense for an all-zero image that looks like a black background—the model might confuse it with the digit 0, which is also mostly blank in the center). If we test with different input data, we should get different predictions.

We can also test sending multiple images in one request by making **`payload = {"data": [image1, image2, ...]}`** where each image is a list of 784 floats. Our scoring script can handle batch inputs and will return a list of predicted digits.

In the following figure, you can see the endpoint logs where a score request was received and a response was sent back, HTTP 200:

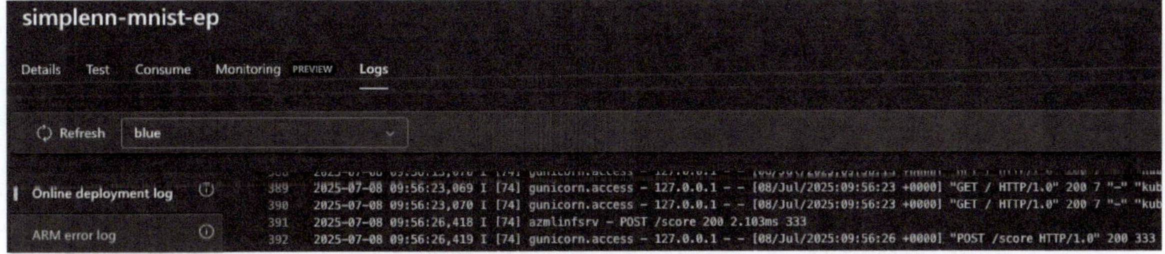

***Figure 20.4:** Azure ML scoring logs*

You have now successfully deployed and invoked a machine learning model as a service.

Let us recap what we have accomplished in this deployment:

- We took a trained PyTorch model (SimpleNN on MNIST) and saved its weights.
- (Optional) We optimized it with quantization and pruning, and then exported it to various formats (this step was not strictly necessary for Azure ML, but it is good practice for production readiness).
- We registered the model in Azure ML, creating a versioned entry in the model registry.
- We created an environment definition to specify all the dependencies the model needs, and Azure ML built a Docker container from that.
- We wrote a scoring script that knows how to initialize the model and handle prediction requests.
- We created a managed online endpoint (with key authentication) and deployed our model+environment+code to it as a live service.
- We then sent a test request to the endpoint and received a prediction, verifying that everything works end-to-end.

Throughout this process, we also touched on essential concepts:

- **The scoring script (entry script)**: It is the piece of code that runs inside the deployed container to do the inference (often referred to as scoring in Azure's terminology).
- **Real-time endpoint**: It is the live API endpoint where your model can be reached; it is managed by the cloud service to be available (and you do not have to manage the underlying server explicitly).
- **Azure's use of Docker environments and Container Registry (ACR)**: The environment definition was converted into a Docker image, which was stored and then used to run our service. This ensures reproducibility (the model runs in the same environment as we defined, avoiding *it works on my machine* problems).
- **Model versioning**: Our model is version 1 in the registry. If we train a new model tomorrow and register it as SimpleNN-MNIST again, that will be version 2. We could deploy version 2 to the same endpoint (perhaps as a **"green"** deployment) and test it out. Azure ML helps keep track of these versions.
- **Pruning and quantization**: These are techniques to compress models. We discussed and showed how they might be applied. In practice, whether you deploy a pruned/quantized model or the original depends on trade-offs between size, speed, and accuracy.
- **Authentication and security**: We saw that keys or tokens can secure Azure endpoints. It is important not to expose an endpoint without auth if it is a sensitive model or if usage needs to be controlled. For our demo, the key is our simple security measure.

Model versioning and updating deployments

Before we conclude, let us discuss how you manage models and deployments going forward. Deploying once is great, but *what happens when you have a new model or need to change something?*

Azure ML's model registry makes it easy to manage multiple versions of a model:

- If you retrain your SimpleNN model on new data or with a better architecture and get, say, a SimpleNN-MNIST v2, you can register it (it will appear as version 2 under the same name).
- You can then deploy version 2. There are a couple of ways: you could create a new deployment under the same endpoint (for example, a **"green"** deployment pointing to model version 2 and using maybe a new environment if needed). Then, you might gradually shift traffic from blue to green. This approach allows testing the latest model in production with maybe a small percentage of real traffic (a technique known as canary deployment).
- Alternatively, if you are confident in the new version, you could update the existing deployment. This may cause a brief downtime while the endpoint is updated (unless you performed a blue/green swap). With managed endpoints, separate deployments and traffic swaps are recommended for high uptime.

- Azure ML also allows you to have staging versus production endpoints, among other advanced features.

Cleaning up: If you no longer need an endpoint, it is important to delete it (to avoid incurring charges for the compute). You can do so with `ml_client.online_endpoints.begin_delete(name)`. Likewise, you can archive or delete old model versions if needed.

In our example, since it serves as a guide, we will not conduct a full version 2 deployment. However, you can imagine the process: register a new model, create a new environment if needed, deploy as green, test, and then switch traffic.

One more thing to mention is monitoring. After deployment, you will want to monitor the health of your model service. Azure ML endpoints provide logs (as we saw), and you can also collect metrics, such as the number of requests and latency, through Azure Application Insights, which can be easily integrated. Those details are beyond our scope here, but in a real project, monitoring is crucial to ensure your model is performing as expected (and to catch any errors or slowdowns).

Conclusion

Deploying a machine learning model is a significant milestone in any project – it is when your work becomes accessible to the world (or to other systems within an organization). In this chapter, we covered the complete journey of taking our MNIST digit classifier (SimpleNN) from a trained model to a hosted, live prediction service on Azure Machine Learning.

We began by discussing the importance of model deployment and how it enables real-time AI applications. We prepared our model for deployment by saving the state dictionary and considering optimizations, such as quantization and pruning, to enhance the model's efficiency. We then stepped into the Azure ML ecosystem: registering the model (to keep track of versions and centrally store it) and defining an environment so that our code runs consistently in the cloud. We wrote a scoring script to handle initialization and inference—essentially embedding our model's prediction logic into a simple API handler.

Using Azure's managed endpoint capabilities, we deployed the model with just a few lines of code, benefiting from Azure ML handling containerization, scaling, and serving infrastructure. Once deployed, we successfully made a REST API call to get a prediction, demonstrating end-to-end functionality. We also examined key concepts, such as how Azure ML uses Docker and container registries behind the scenes, how it distinguishes between endpoints and deployments for flexible version management, and how to secure and interact with the service.

It is worth emphasizing that while our example used Azure ML, many cloud providers offer similar workflows. The specifics may differ (such as different CLI commands, SDK functions, or UI layouts). Still, the core ideas-packaging the model, environment, and inference code, then hosting it behind an API-are universal in machine learning deployment. You could take the same model and deploy it on *AWS SageMaker* or *GCP Vertex AI* by following analogous steps (in fact, as a next step, you should explore how that would be done to broaden your skill set).

By deploying the same model we started building in the earlier chapters, we have come full circle. In *Chapter 9, Building Blocks of Neural Networks in PyTorch*, you built a simple neural network for MNIST; now, in this chapter, that neural network is running live in the cloud, ready to predict digits for anyone who asks. This demonstrates the full lifecycle of a machine learning project, from data and model development to production deployment.

As you deploy models in real scenarios, you will encounter additional considerations - things like data preprocessing in the service, input/output schema standardization, setting up custom domains or authentication for endpoints, monitoring model performance over time (data drift, etc.), and possibly automating the deployment as part of a **continuous integration/continuous deployment** (**CI/CD**) pipeline. The foundation you have learned here will enable you to approach those advanced topics with confidence. Deployment is an ongoing process: models may be updated, improved, rolled back, or scaled according to demand. With the skills from this chapter, you are well-prepared to integrate your machine learning models into real products and services.

In conclusion, deploying a model is both a technical challenge and an empowering step—it is when your machine learning model starts interacting with the real world and users. Congratulations on deploying your first PyTorch model to a cloud service.

Exercises

To solidify your understanding of model deployment, try making a small change and redeploying:

1. **Deploy a new version of the model**: Go back to your training code (from *Chapter 9* or any improved version you have) and train a new model for a few more epochs or with a different configuration (for example, change the number of hidden units or use a different optimizer). Register this new model in Azure ML as a new version (it will automatically increment the version number for the same model name). Then create a second deployment (you can name it "green") under the same endpoint using this new model version. Route a small percentage of traffic to the new deployment (e.g., 10% to "green" and 90% to "blue") and observe the results of calling the endpoint multiple times. Do you get predictions from both versions? This exercise will teach you how to manage multi-version deployments and perform a blue/green deployment scenario.
2. **Test with real data**: Write a small script to take an actual image of a digit (you can use the MNIST test dataset or even draw a digit yourself and load it as a 28x28 image) and send it to your deployed endpoint. Verify that the prediction is correct. This will give you practice in formatting real input data and interpreting the model's output.

By completing these exercises, you will gain experience in updating a deployment and ensuring the endpoint responds correctly to different model versions and inputs. Deploying machine learning models is an iterative process, and these hands-on tweaks will prepare you to maintain and improve deployed models in the future. Happy deploying!

Multiple choice questions

1. **What is the primary purpose of deploying a machine learning model?**
   a. To train the model with more data
   b. To reduce the model's file size
   c. To make the model available as a service that can provide predictions in real time
   d. To visualize the model using TensorBoard
2. **Which of the following are valid formats for exporting a PyTorch model for deployment?**
   a. TorchScript
   b. ONNX
   c. Jupyter Notebook
   d. PyTorch state dictionary
3. **In Azure ML, what does the scoring script (score.py) define?**
   a. How to visualize the model's layers
   b. How to optimize the model using quantization
   c. The functions used to initialize and serve inference requests
   d. The batch size used during training
4. **What is the primary benefit of registering a model in the Azure ML model registry?**
   a. Faster training speed
   b. Allows model versioning and reuse
   c. Visualizes training loss in real-time
   d. Avoids the need for Docker
5. **Which components must be provided to Azure ML in order to deploy a model?**
   a. The dataset used for training
   b. A registered model

c. An environment definition

d. A scoring script

6. **What does pruning do in the context of a trained neural network?**

a. Adds new neurons to increase model accuracy

b. Removes low-importance weights to reduce model size

c. Changes the loss function used during training

d. Converts the model into a cloud-native format

7. **Which of the following are advantages of using Azure ML's managed online endpoints?**

a. Automatic scaling and infrastructure management

b. Real-time inference capability

c. Direct access to the underlying GPU

d. Built-in model training pipelines

8. **What is the role of environment.yml in the deployment process?**

a. It specifies the model's training hyperparameters

b. It defines the dependencies and base image for building the Docker container

c. It manages user authentication

d. It sets the model's learning rate and batch size

9. **What are valid authentication modes when creating an Azure ML endpoint?**

a. Token-based (aml_token)

b. Password-based

c. Key-based

d. Certificate-based

10. **Which function is called once when the scoring service starts in Azure ML?**

a. run()

b. predict()

c. init()

d. main()

Answers

1.	c.
2.	a,b,d.
3.	c.
4.	b.
5.	b,c,d.
6.	b.
7.	a,b.
8.	b.
9.	a,c.
10.	c.

Key terms

- **Model deployment**: The process of making a trained model available for production use, typically as a web service or API.
- **Real-time inference**: A deployment method where predictions are served on demand with minimal latency.
- **Azure ML**: Microsoft's cloud platform for building, training, and deploying machine learning models.
- **Model registry**: A centralized location in Azure ML to store, manage, and version trained models.
- **Scoring script (score.py)**: A script that defines two functions: init() to load the model and run() to handle prediction requests.
- **Managed online endpoint**: A cloud-hosted HTTP endpoint provided by Azure ML to serve real-time predictions.
- **Deployment**: The combination of a model, environment, and scoring code hosted behind an endpoint.
- **Environment (environment.yml)**: A YAML file specifying the dependencies and configuration needed for deployment (used to build a Docker container).
- **Quantization**: A technique to reduce model size and speed up inference by lowering precision (e.g., float32 to int8).
- **Pruning**: The process of removing unimportant weights or neurons from a model to reduce its size or increase efficiency.
- **Docker**: A tool for packaging code and dependencies into containers that can run consistently across different environments.
- **Azure Container Registry (ACR)**: Azure's private registry for storing Docker images used in machine learning deployments.
- **Model versioning**: Keeping track of different iterations of a model (e.g., v1, v2) to enable updates and rollbacks.
- **Authentication modes**: Methods for securing endpoint access, including API key (key) and Azure Active Directory token (aml_token).
- **Blue-green deployment**: A strategy for deploying new model versions by gradually shifting traffic from an old version (blue) to a new one (green).

References

1. *PyTorch Documentation:* **https://pytorch.org/docs/**
2. *Azure Machine Learning Documentation:* **https://learn.microsoft.com/en-us/azure/machine-learning/**
3. *AWS SageMaker Documentation:* **https://docs.aws.amazon.com/sagemaker/**
4. *Google Cloud Vertex AI Documentation:* **https://cloud.google.com/vertex-ai/docs**
5. *Docker Documentation:* **https://docs.docker.com/**
6. *ONNX (Open Neural Network Exchange):* **https://onnx.ai/**
7. *TorchScript Documentation (PyTorch JIT):* **https://pytorch.org/docs/stable/jit.html**
8. *Azure Container Registry (ACR):* **https://learn.microsoft.com/en-us/azure/container-registry/**
9. *REST API Design Guidelines:* **https://restfulapi.net/**
10. *Blue-Green Deployment Strategy Overview:* **https://martinfowler.com/bliki/BlueGreenDeployment.html**
11. *Han, S., Pool, J., Tran, J., & Dally, W. (2015). "Learning both Weights and Connections for Efficient Neural Networks." Advances in Neural Information Processing Systems, 28. Available at:* **https://arxiv.org/abs/1506.02626**
12. *Géron, A. (2022). Hands-On Machine Learning with Scikit-Learn, Keras, and TensorFlow (3rd ed.). O'Reilly Media.*

Index

D

E

F

G

H

I

J

K

L

M

N

O

P

Q

R